IBERIAN AND LATIN AMERICAN STUDIES

Projections of Peronism in Argentine Autobiography, Biography and Fiction

Series Editors
Professor David George (University of Wales, Swansea)
Professor Paul Garner (University of Leeds)

Editorial Board
David Frier (University of Leeds)
Lisa Shaw (University of Liverpool)
Gareth Walters (University of Exeter)
Rob Stone (University of Wales, Swansea)
David Gies (University of Virginia)
Catherine Davies (University of Nottingham)

IBERIAN AND LATIN AMERICAN STUDIES

Projections of Peronism in Argentine Autobiography, Biography and Fiction

LLOYD HUGHES DAVIES

UNIVERSITY OF WALES PRESS
CARDIFF
2007

© Lloyd Hughes Davies, 2007

All rights reserved. No part of this book may be reproduced, stored in a retrieval system, or transmitted, in any form or by any means, electronic, mechanical, photocopying, recording or otherwise, without clearance from the University of Wales Press, 10 Columbus Walk, Brigantine Place, Cardiff, CF10 4UP.
www.wales.ac.uk/press

British Library Cataloguing-in-Publication Data
A catalogue record for this book is available from the British Library.

ISBN 978–0–7083–2014–3

The rights of Lloyd Hughes Davies to be identified as author of this work has been asserted by him in accordance with the Copyright, Designs and Patents Act 1988.

Typeset by Columns Design Ltd, Reading
Printed in Great Britain by Antony Rowe Ltd, Chippenham, Wiltshire

Contents

Series Editors' Foreword — vii

1. Introduction — 1

Part I: Autobiographical Writing — 21

2. La razón de mi vida and Mi mensaje — 23
3. Wounded Bodies and Wounded Writings: The Sexual/Textual Deficiencies of Juan Domingo Perón — 55

Part II: Biographical Writing — 91

4. Telling the Full Story: Joseph Page — 93
5. The Limits of Testimonial Biography: Borroni and Vacca; Sebreli, Taylor — 121
6. Indiscreet Portraitures: Llorca, Navarro, Dujovne Ortiz — 149

Part III: Creative Writing — 175

7. Pale Fire at the Margins of La novela de Perón — 177
8. Portraits of a Lady: Postmodern Readings of Tomás Eloy Martínez's Santa Evita — 203
9. Fictive Shadows of Santa Evita: Posse, Pagano, Frers — 229
10. The Fictive Afterglows of Peronism: Puig, Szichman and Valenzuela — 261
11. Conclusion — 313

Bibliography — 321

Index — 337

Series Editors' Foreword

Over recent decades, the traditional 'languages and literatures' model in Spanish departments in universities in the United Kingdom has been superceded by a contextual, interdisciplinary and 'area studies' approach to the study of the culture, history, society and politics of the Hispanic and Lusophone worlds – categories which extend far beyond the confines of the Iberian Peninsula, not only to Latin America but also to Spanish-speaking and Lusophone Africa.

In response to these dynamic trends in research priorities and curriculum development, this series is designed to present both disciplinary and interdisciplinary research within the general field of Iberian and Latin American Studies, particularly studies which explore all aspects of **Cultural Production** (*inter alia* literature, film, music, dance, sport) in Spanish, Portuguese, Basque, Catalan, Galician and the indigenous languages of Latin America. The series also aims to publish research on the **History and Politics** of Hispanic and Lusophone worlds, both at the level of region and that of the nation-state, as well as on **Cultural Studies** which explore the shifting terrains of gender, sexual, racial and postcolonial identities in those same regions.

Chapter 1

Introduction

Juan and Eva Perón furnish their own peculiar brand of proof (if proof were still required) that the clichéd notion of Latin American reality exceeding the limits of the literary imagination is based on historical fact. Perón's exceptionality derives from his failure to conform to any familiar model of Argentine leader; from his self-contradictory impulses; from his impenetrable psyche; from his ambiguities and equivocations that resist resolution and draw writers as diverse as Joseph Page and Tomás Eloy Martínez into their vortex of shimmering surfaces. Perón's enigma is peculiarly postmodern: while he projects the promise of depth, he provides no more than a frustrating shallowness.

By any standards the historical Perón was a larger-than-life figure. He promised a new Argentina based on social reform and national emancipation. In the end he failed to deliver. Such failure might be seen not only as unexceptional but as the norm in Latin American politics. Peronism, however, is anything but unexceptional and it defies the usual norms. The man and the message resist straightforward definition. David Rock remarks that his 'mix of several authoritarian-populist styles defied easy labels or characterizations'[1] and Miguens comments that Perón's impact on the working class threatened the traditional hegemony of socialism and communism.[2] Perón promoted egalitarianism and elevated the Argentine labour movement to centre stage in national politics. His own formidable political appeal, conjoined with the mythical aura enjoyed by Eva both during her life and (particularly) after her death, gave rise to his messianic status. His early achievements cannot be denied – he increased the share of national wealth received by the workers from 38% in the early 1940s to 46% in 1948 – and his charismatic influence held all kinds of people, including intellectuals, in its mesmerizing power.[3] The debit side of Peronism is equally impressive, however: 'for many social justice had meant imprisonment or exile, and some claimed torture. Peronism was denounced as a "pornocracy" that governed by fraud, indoctrination, false propaganda, and persecution'.[4] The internal divisions and contradictions of this heterogenous movement were to have tragic consequences on Perón's return to Argentina on 23 June 1973, when union thugs and security agents clashed with the left-wing *Montoneros* at Ezeiza airport, resulting in scores, if not hundreds, of deaths.

The elusiveness of Perón and Peronism is reflected in the contradictory reactions he continually aroused. Even before his election as president the public held deeply divided opinions of him; he 'used' and 'abused' power, combining in his own person both legitimacy and illegitimacy. Rock remarks that 'in dealing with the workers, Perón grew increasingly adept at using propaganda, theatricality, display, and charismatic authority'. He also distanced himself, 'behaving as if the state and himself were separate from and suspended above society at large' (p. 285).

Rock's historical portrait of an abstracted and theatrical figure looking down at his creatures from on high, accords with Martínez's fictional portrayal of Perón's God-like mien and influence. Part of the historical Perón's theatricality is his manipulation of language, his mastery of rhetoric and of persuasive clichés. In his dictated memoirs, Perón shows a marked partiality for proverbs.[5] He also used a 'radical language previously unheard in government officials but appreciated by the workers because it was their own'.[6] Indeed, the popular appeal he exercised as a military man who espoused nationalist and social-Christian principles, while rejecting socialism and communism, constituted 'a phenomenon that went against a whole system of reasoning and evaluation, creating an enormous "cognitive dissonance" that needed to be rapidly dispelled'.[7] But the attempts of conventional social scientists and historians to dispel it have proved fruitless: thus Miguens points to the chameleon-like evolution of Gino Germani's inconsistent theories of Peronism (pp. 148, 152–3) and Page notes that Perón 'has bedevilled political observers who have tried to classify him as Fascist, personalist dictator, populist and even leftist'.[8] Commentators such as Mora y Araujo and Smith admit that their understanding remains 'partial and fragmentary'[9] thus approximating to the position of Tomás Eloy Martínez, who declares, in his acknowledgements at the end of *La novela de Perón* (1989), that 'narrar a Perón es un oficio inagotable'.[10] Indeed, Martínez limits himself to assembling the raw materials of his subject matter, refraining from any attempt to make them cohere and signify in the manner of fully rounded narrative.

The figure of Eva is similarly resistant to the traditional historian's urge to rationalize, domesticate and categorize. The historical Eva traces a personal trajectory embracing dissonant identities, ranging from an impoverished childhood further blighted by the stigma of illegitimacy, to the adolescent years consumed by the precarious struggle to become an actress in Buenos Aires, to her much-maligned liaison with Colonel Perón – her aura of scandal seemingly confirmed by her open cohabitation with him – to her triumph as youthful *presidenta* when her excessive though informal power and her flagrant disregard for bourgeois niceties, notably in her dealings with Perón's military colleagues, enhanced rather than diminished her reputation as a dangerous woman. Her final role was inevitably marked by contrast and contradiction, the mental vigour of the fanatical *compañera* coinciding with her extreme physical decline. The historical Eva thus offers a kaleidoscope of often clashing and contradictory images embracing both provincial obscurity and marginality and dazzling iconic status at the centre of the national stage. On the one hand is the powerful and attractive *presidenta* who reinvents the role of first lady and becomes in the process the most powerful woman in the world. On the other is the militant *compañera*, looking even less like a wifely supplement to Perón than she did before, her soft shapeliness now replaced by a severity of demeanour suggesting physical confirmation of her perceived manliness. Eva's final role is the most poignant, if not the most memorable, of all: once waited upon as the powerful arbiter of the state's largesse, she is transformed into a frail figure who smiles weakly as she waits for the inevitable culmination of her terminal illness. Beyond the metamorphosis of the physical, historical Eva lies the mythical Eva, an immortal figure sustained by the excessive encomiums of her devotees and by the equally excessive excoriations of her enemies.

The key to both Perón and Eva lies in their shimmering multiplicities, their repudiation of single, coherent identity, their disquieting lack of essential being, of psychological depth. Both represent in their different ways the principles of instability and elusiveness. Both literalize in this respect the tropes of postmodernism: Perón's theatrical persona offers little substance beneath the surface while Eva's chameleon-like trajectory suggests perpetual motion and play. According to Dujovne Ortiz, 'Perón liked to divert the truth, often multiplying the versions'[11] while Eva was reputed to have said: 'volveré y seré millones'.

The present study will focus on traditional and innovative representations of the Peróns in both the auto/biography and the novel. There are good reasons for conjoining autobiographical and biographical writings despite critical claims highlighting the significant differences between them. Molloy, for example, observes that autobiography relies on memory, biography on documents.[12] For Lejeune, 'identity' is the 'actual starting point for autobiography; resemblance is the unattainable goal of biography'.[13] Other critics point to the proximity between these modes of writing: Spengemann traces the 'movement of autobiography from the biographical to the fictive mode'[14] while Susan Groag Bell and Marilyn Yalom point out that 'autobiography' and 'biography' are linguistically united by their common roots in the Greek word 'bios' (life) and 'graphe' (writing), both being 'hybrid creations of historicity and textuality'. While acknowledging that literary scholars still treat the two differently, Bell and Yalom maintain that the traditional boundaries separating them are not as distinct as may be implied by their definitions:

> biography is generally defined as the story of a person's life written by another and autobiography as the story of one's life written by oneself. Most theoreticians by now agree that biography – reputedly the more objective of the two – is commonly colored by the subjective world of the biographer [...] Autobiography masquerading as biography is one of the central discoveries of this book.[15]

The central tenet of postmodern approaches to autobiography and biography is that while both modes of writing are founded on the factual data of lived existence, the 'bare facts' can only serve as the basis for imaginative recreation which cannot pretend to offer the 'truth' about the person's psyche or the events of her life. If the work of the auto/biographer is largely imaginative then his creative work approximates to that of the novelist. There may be important differences between auto/biographical and novelistic writing as noted by Epstein who describes the 'conventional recognition of the biographical subject'.[16] He distinguishes between the 'trans-discursive' figure of Jay Gatsby whose life is always mock biographical, '"lived" entirely in cultural and literary discourse and read always and only as fiction or criticism' and the extra-discursive figure of Marilyn Monroe: 'enjoying the same opportunities as Jay Gatsby to be portrayed, satirized, analyzed, and typologized in creative and critical discourse, she can also be recognized as an individual human whose existence prior to Mailer's 1973 biography cannot be completely or ultimately reduced to semiosis' (p. 223). Epstein claims, however, that such an apparently commonsensical conclusion is based upon an appeal to a transcendental signified 'that is formally outside discourse but is knowable only in and through discourse'. For Epstein, traditional biography (and we might add, autobiography) takes the unified, sovereign subject as given. But such givenness is underwritten by an act of recognition which is 'always an activity of subjection, violence committed in the guise of interpretation' (p. 224).

Some of the auto/biographies we shall consider are traditional, devoted to a quasi-legalistic process of uncovering the truth about Juan or Eva Perón. Other works, however, adopt an overtly postmodern or New Historical approach, consciously fictionalizing their subject – and so rejecting any notion of a verifiable 'truth' upon which traditional autobiographical and biographical writings are based – or else highlighting the textuality of their writing and the discontinuity of all historical writing. The writer who most conspicuously flaunts the textualism of his work, showing thereby that there can be no direct appeal to the unmediated 'facts' of history, is Tomás Eloy Martínez whose academic knowledge of Peronism, his interviews conducted with Perón in Madrid prior to the latter's return to Argentina in 1973 and his creative reinvention of Peronism give him an unique position in Peronist scholarship. Curiously he embodies both traditional and New Historical approaches, the first in *Las memorias del General* (1996)[17] and the second in *La novela de Perón*. He 'polices' the first text, assuming a kind of guardianship of the truth as he exposes Perón's inconsistencies, subjecting his subject's account to the rigorous criteria of conventional historical investigation. Here he appears to be seduced by the lingering aura of autobiography as the last bulwark of 'reliable' writing immune to the challenge of deconstructive critique. In *La novela de Perón*, by contrast, Martínez celebrates Perón's narrative mode – which privileges multiple versions of events, repudiating a single truth – and acclaims him and Eva as novelists of a kind, just like himself: 'actuaron como actúan los novelistas' (p. 144). Here any notion of an authoritative editor 'correcting' his subject disappears since the emphasis – on textual play rather than fixity – allows Perón to emerge in a starring role with López Rega, his collaborator, acting as his foil. In *Santa Evita* (1995) Martínez acknowledges repeatedly Eva's posthumous presence which exercises a kind of corporeal power over him: 'si no la escribo, voy a asfixiarme'.[18]

The materials of a biography are not life but documents, as Molloy states. No less than any other genre, biography is conditioned by the inherent instability of language. Consciousness of the problematic nature of language and discourse distinguish the postmodern approach: Middlebrook refers to the 'postmodern anxiety about authorship' based on the 'awareness that both author and subject in a biography are hostages to the universes of discourse that inhabit them'.[19] In her 'real' autobiography, *La razón de mi vida*,[20] Eva shows glimpses of such awareness as does Martínez's 'fictional' Perón who is fearful that ownership of his own life story will slip from his grasp as the limitless resonances of language elude his control in *La novela de Perón*. Other writers, however, show little awareness of this aspect of language, being oblivious to their own highly subjective procedures whether they are launching a vituperative tirade against their subject (Mary Main) or offering an extravagant idealization of her (Carmen Llorca). Yet others lay emphasis upon their unimpeachably authentic sources (Borroni and Vacca). In his *Perón: a Biography* (1983) Page is equally assertive and mindful of the quality of his evidence as he seeks to domesticate Perón for a US audience.[21] Dujovne Ortiz, by contrast, shows a capacity to reflect on her own procedures as she distances herself from any pretension to 'truth'.

Postmodern auto/biography approximates to the novel as the validity of the 'law of genre' is called into question. Again Tomás Eloy Martínez is the central figure in this respect. Zuffi describes *Santa Evita* as a 'biografía oral'[22] and the author himself describes the initial project for *Santa Evita* as 'una biografía que pensaba escribir' (*Santa Evita*, p. 64). Hayden White, the leading New Historical theorist, seeks to rationalize the complete removal of what he sees as artificial boundaries between biography and fiction when he states: 'it does not matter whether the world is conceived to be real or only imagined; the manner of making sense of it is the same'.[23] Curiously, however, Tomás Eloy Martínez, whose view of history would appear to coincide in most respects with that of White, seemingly reinstates traditional generic boundaries by his explicit designation of his works as novels: *Santa Evita* is followed by the redundant qualifier, 'novela', while at the conclusion of *El vuelo de la reina* (2002), Martínez notes that 'todos los personajes y lugares de esta novela, aun los que parecían tomados de la realidad, corresponden al orden de la ficción. Leerlos de otro modo violentaría su naturaleza'.[24]

If, as Virginia Woolf claims, the biographer can give us 'much more than another fact to add to our collection. He can give us the creative fact; the fertile fact; the fact that suggests and engenders'[25] then the boundaries between the biography and the novel become blurred. The novels of Tomás Eloy Martínez not only overlap with auto/biography but also with history. In *Tropics of Discourse* White remarks on the extent to which the discourse of the historian and that of the imaginative writer overlap, resemble or correspond with each other: 'there are many histories that could pass for novels, and many novels that could pass for histories, considered in purely formal (or, I should say, formalist) terms. Viewed simply as verbal artefacts, histories and novels are indistinguishable from one another'.[26] Given that historians do not present the past but rather fashion the past into a whole 'whose integrity is – in its re-presentation – a purely discursive one' (p. 125), their activity approximates to that of the novelist since both 'fuse events, whether imaginary or real, into a comprehensible totality capable of serving as the object of a representation in a poetic process' (p. 125). Backscheider makes a related point: 'the best biographers know that they are inventing through their selection and arrangement of materials; they are establishing cause–effect and other relationships and they are determining what was most formative and important for someone else, someone they do not know. They must choose what to include, leave out, emphasize and subordinate [. . .]'.[27] The biographer's selection of materials itself suggests a personal and creative input but the facts not only call for arrangement and classification but also for a kind of invention, for firmness in place of fluidity, for a settled pattern in place of uncertainty. Mailer remarks on 'the abominable magnetism of facts. They always attract polar facts.

Rare is the piece of special evidence in any life that is not quickly contradicted by other witnesses'.[28] The biographer has to chart his own path through the quicksand of competing, often contradictory, versions. Mailer also wonders (in relation to Marilyn Monroe) to what extent a person can be comprehended by the facts of a life. Any consideration of Eva's life would produce similar questions. Indeed the 'facts' of her life show a startling series of parallels with those of Marilyn Monroe's life as described by Mailer. Both were illegitimate, both were tomboys, both lacked formal education, both were 'cultureless' (as Mailer describes Marilyn) – which led to embarrassment for both when questioned about their tastes in music (Marilyn pretended to like Beethoven, Eva claimed an affinity with Chopin). Both were reputed to have had abortions (Mailer describes Marilyn's 'gynaecological insides' as 'unspeakably scarred' (p. 171). Both were sex objects: Marilyn and Eva complained about the passes men made at them. Both were undisciplined and both were particularly poor timekeepers. Aspects of Marilyn, highlighted by Mailer, are uncannily reminiscent of Eva; or rather the images of Eva, disseminated by her biographers, match those features selected by Mailer in his portrait of Marilyn: sexuality – Marilyn 'was a general of sex before she knew anything of sexual war' (p. 43); tenacity – 'she is more and more single-minded about a career, as if not only sanity but life depends on this' (p. 60); appearance – 'she becomes a blonde, her hair was naturally light-brown' (p. 63); physical imperfections – 'her front teeth protrude just a fraction' (p. 71); lack of real talent – 'Marilyn was a dumb and not so unvulgar broad' (p. 67); poverty – Marilyn lived at times on 30 cents per day (p. 68) and was out of work for several months (p. 71); private life – which is 'all but buried' (p. 76); madness – Marilyn lives under the shadow of insanity (p. 22). Marilyn's orphanage years meant that a 'rootless resentment would occupy central positions of power in her psyche' (p. 37). These are the 'facts' of Marilyn's life story: 'the facts live', says Mailer, 'but Marilyn is elusive' (p. 19). Precisely the same facts and the same comment apply to Eva yet she and Marilyn are very different people: that difference must be located beyond the facts; as Mailer notes, 'even if a few of the *facts* of Monroe's life can be verified [. . .] how little is established' (p. 18). The facts sometimes appear to be irretrievably tainted by the conventions by which culture orders the world.

Mailer is reacting against the lingering respect and authority still accorded to traditional biography and hinting at those New Historical principles pioneered by Hayden White which focus on the intersection of literary, non-literary and social texts and illuminate a kind of cross-cultural collage. Traditional autobiographers and biographers are comparable to traditional historians: they do not scrutinize their own practices and appeal – to lesser or greater degrees – to an objective reality seen to be relatively unproblematic. New Historical writers like postmodern auto/biographers are sceptical about whether the truth about what really happened in the past can ever be purely and objectively known. Alice Jardine points out that in contemporary French thought it is not the 'event' that assumes importance as a historical mark, but the epistemological *configurations* surrounding that event, especially with regard to language.[29] New Historical writers criticize all types of authority but especially that of historiographical discourse which, through citations, references and notes sets itself up as knowledge of the other. Writing itself is an instrument of authority for Michel de Certeau: he refers to 'economies of writing' (recordings, transcriptions etc.) which organize and divide social space and institute forms of hierarchy.[30] We shall see how some writers such as Joseph Page reinforce such hierarchies while others, notably Tomás Eloy Martínez, put such economies of writing on display, so undermining their claims to authority. Martínez's work is informed by the driving impulse of New Historicism – the breaking of boundaries between literary texts and those once regarded as extraneous to literature, including autobiography and biography. New Historicism also breaks the boundaries dividing those traditionally central and traditionally secondary texts and in so doing weakens hitherto dominant codes or 'grand narratives', be they sociological, political or cultural. Attention is refocused towards the non-canonical and the hitherto unspoken: Martínez was attracted to Eva not because of her glamour or her power but rather because of her 'márgenes, su oscuridad, lo que había en Evita de indecible' (*Santa Evita*, p. 64). In the words of de Certeau, Martínez represents the writer as prowler who advances towards the frontiers of the great regions that have already been exploited: 'he deviates [*fait un écart*], moving in the direction of sorcery, madness, festival, popular literature [...] all zones of silence'.[31] Martínez shares New Historical tentativeness, its open acknowledgement of its own 'situatedness', its preference for discontinuity and disruption to unity and closure. For him the Truth is fascistic and must be abandoned, but a kind of truth, a 'limping' truth, should be retained.

In dramatizing the inseparability of narrative history and creativity, Martínez undermines the claims and pretensions of 'old' historicism and opts instead for the epistemological modesty and self-consciousness of the new. Old historicism sought (and seeks) to maintain the traditional barriers between history and other spheres of intellectual enterprise be they literature or social sciences such as anthropology and sociology. The central presumption of much narrative history is that coherent and consistent stories can be forged out of the shapeless raw materials of the past. As Holton points out, such narratives are purportedly communicated not constructed and potential difficulties such as the discrepant accounts of 'jarring witnesses', and the problematical status of historical 'truth', are often elided.[32]

Far from indulging in such practices, New Historical writers highlight the faultlines of apparently seamless historical narrative. For Martínez historical truth is multifaceted and elusive and cannot be controlled or circumscribed. What can be achieved is 'un cierto efecto de verdad al yuxtaponer las diversas verdades que hemos ido encontrando, de tal suerte que todas ellas jueguen entre sí, libremente, sus propias ceremonias dialécticas'.[33] Playful juxtaposition is complemented by playful creation: when the documentary record is incomplete, says Perón, López Rega resorts to invention. In *La novela de Perón*, narrative history has more to do with construction and fabrication than with the discovery and communication of past realities. The difference between the respective approaches of Martínez and Page can be illustrated by reference to Barthes' claim that the value of writing lies in pleasure rather than assertion; as Sontag puts it, his plea is for a 'festive (rather than dogmatic or credulous) relation to ideas' and for a language which is sensuous rather than one with pretensions to power.[34]

If historians, like novelists, construct their narrative, then the distinction between historical writing and fiction becomes blurred. Both choose the kind of story they will tell, their 'emplotment' taking the form of romance, tragedy, comedy or satire.[35] It is a subtle blend of the comic, satiric, ironic and carnivalesque which marks Martínez's particular emplotment. As narrated in *La novela de Perón*, the final return of Perón to Argentina accompanied by his third wife Isabel, a former cabaret dancer, and the malign astrologer López Rega (known as 'El Brujo'), aboard an aeroplane named 'Betelgeuse' (the dying star), is a tragicomic affair. While a massacre is orchestrated at Ezeiza airport by 'los halcones de López Rega' (305), Perón's main concern is his memoirs and Isabel's her dogs (314–15). The ageing Perón, about to serve his third presidential term, looks back dismissively at an earlier incumbent, Yrigoyen: 'tener un presidente tan viejo nos envejecía' (201). López Rega is unconcerned that Tomás Eloy Martínez (playing the role of investigative writer in his own plot) may have a photograph implicating Perón in General Uriburu's overthrow of Yrigoyen in 1930: 'le damos un buen susto y se acabó' (168). Perón and his accomplice can, seemingly, manipulate the record at will but, as we have seen, they in their turn are vulnerable to the intervention of others.

History is informed by the general 'situatedness' and subjectivity (suppressive as well as creative) of the writer. New Historicists flaunt their limitations as objective analysts by highlighting the temporal and personal circumstances which condition their writing. As they themselves acknowledge, their fallibility is compounded by their reliance on language which is itself prone to misrepresentation – offering, as Brook Thomas puts it, 'only a trace of what it seeks to represent'.[36] The sermons of Don José Cresto (Isabel's one-time mentor) serve to illustrate – in exaggerated, carnivalesque fashion – the slippage to which all language is prone: 'no decía capellán sino pecallán y no Padre Nuestro que estás en los cielos sino pan y güeso que estás por el suelo' (*La novela de Perón*, p. 25). If truth is largely beyond human comprehension and representation then the distinction between truth and falsehood is undermined. For New Historicists, therefore, there can be no single, authoritative, univocal version of the past but rather a proliferation of different accounts. Traditional distinctions between literature and history are undermined and the unresolved conflicts and contradictions of the literary sphere are reflected in the domain of historical writing. 'History', remarks Foucault, 'becomes 'effective' to the degree that it introduces discontinuity into our very being – as it divides our emotions, dramatises our instincts, multiplies our body and sets it against itself'.[37]

In *La novela de Perón*, history is irrevocably bound to prior textualizations and no 'fact' of the past can escape mediation.[38] For the journalist Emiliano Zamora, the past is no more than a spectacle of shimmering representations: 'es aquí algo irreal, como una pantalla de cine. A cada instante una proeza nueva (y peor) de la realidad lo sustituye. Ni siquiera es olvido' (188). Derrida's famous dictum, 'Il n'y a pas de hors texte'[39] refers to the pervasiveness of textuality: reality is always linguistically encoded. New Historical writers focus on the relentless proliferation and diversity of texts, highlighting their chaotic and discontinuous forms. They often give priority to the unofficial, the marginal, the exotic and anecdotal aspects of the historical record – as Martínez does, for example, in his references to Isabel's dubious associates: Don José Cresto, evangelical director of the 'Escuela Científica Basilio' (25), Joe Herald, 'un artista muy prestigioso del Caribe' (28), and particularly 'El Brujo', José López Rega, who claimed that Perón had led four previous lives (68).

Critics of such New Historical practices point to the dangers of losing traditional human values in a boundless tide of relativism. If the past exists only in texts and if there is no way of deciding between rival textual versions of the past, then one interpretation or account is as valid as any other and even deliberate falsification can be condoned. But despite their aversion to fixed transhistorical notions, New Historicists cling to the concept of a 'limping' truth. History may be constituted as language but the category of the historically real is not excluded as a result. Dorothy Lipstadt argues that there is a certain irreducible element which stands firm against any postmodernist equivocations about 'reality' and 'truth': 'by its very nature the business of interpretation cannot be purely objective. But it is built on a certain body of irrefutable evidence: slavery happened; so did the Black Plague and the Holocaust'.[40] Peronism happened; it touched the lives of millions of Argentines. What is undecidable is how it should be interpreted since it resists rational explanation, as we shall see. Martínez's own position is that although 'los hechos históricos son como son', they alone are insufficient to do justice to the complexity of reality: 'es preciso salir en busca de otros hechos que la enriquezcan'.[41]

One of the best definitions of the (New) Historical novel is that offered by Alexis Márquez Rodríguez:

Lo que le da carácter histórico a una novela es la presencia de personajes y episodios históricos, tratados de un modo tal que sufran un proceso de ficcionamiento. Y no que relate hechos de un tiempo que ya era pasado para el autor.[42]

This definition permits us to describe Martínez's novels, particularly *La novela de Perón* and *Santa Evita*, as New Historical works, a genre inaugurated by Alejo Carpentier's *El reino de este mundo* (1949) and, since 1979, the dominant trend in Latin American fiction.[43] An important feature of this genre is the use of famous historical characters as protagonists. Of all the colourful political figures of twentieth-century Latin America, few can rival Juan Domingo Perón in terms of literary appeal: as already mentioned, his enigmatic personal life, his psychological instability, and complex, sometimes contradictory political instincts, seem on occasion to belong more to the realms of fiction than to history. His life and character serve to destabilize such distinctions even before Martínez brings his New Historical practices to bear on his subject.

There is much overlap between New Historical and postmodernist practice: self-scrutiny; emphasis on textuality;[44] the breaking down of stable concepts and fixed oppositions; the rejection of ahistorical essentialisms and myths of authenticity; the promotion of the marginal[45] and the hybrid[46] and the consequent weakening of centre–periphery models. Both engage in the modern project to 'unravel the illusion that some kind of universal truth exists which can be proven by some so-called universal experience'.[47]

But postmodernism is more detached than New Historicism, more ironic, 'putting inverted commas around what is being said' as Hutcheon remarks.[48] Baudrillard's notion of 'hyperreality' implies that models replace the real;[49] for Gianni Vattimo emancipation is based on oscillation, plurality and ultimately on the erosion of the very 'principle of reality'.[50] Postmodernism rejects 'simple' referentiality which 'cannot recognize that the reality to which it appeals is a traditional ideological construction'.[51] New Historicism ultimately clings to referentiality, rejecting the gay relativity of things which postmodernism sometimes embraces. But in making such distinctions it is well to remember that the

Latin American variety does not fit seamlessly into the postmodernist mainstream, being as Williams points out, 'resolutely historical and inescapably political': imbued, then, with those twin qualities that have shaped the Latin American novelistic tradition.[52] As far as the Latin American writers considered here are concerned (notably Tomás Eloy Martínez, Abel Posse and Luisa Valenzuela), they may be regarded as both New Historical and postmodern (though their postmodernism is peculiarly Latin American). New Historical and postmodern practices are often inconsistent: Thomas points out that the authority of New Historicism – which challenges our knowledge of the past – rests on its faith that knowledge of the past matters for the present.[53] Postmodernism is similarly contradictory: as Calinescu puts it, it is 'self-skeptical yet curious, unbelieving yet searching, benevolent yet ironic'.[54] These writers all keep their distance from what Eagleton calls a disabling rationality 'which can know nothing beyond its own concepts, forbidden from enquiring into the very stuff of passion and perception'.[55] They are keenly aware of the problematic nature of representation, of language and of truth but that awareness is balanced by their Latin American sensitivities, their conviction that the Latin American writer cannot indulge to the same extent as his foreign counterparts in the iconoclastic practice of deconstruction.

While traditional generic categories will be used to structure this critical study, the emphasis throughout will be upon the limitations of the 'law of genre'. The fictional emerges as the dominant component whether the text is nominally autobiography, biography or novel. Part I analyses autobiographical writings: we will consider Eva Perón's *La razón de mi vida* (1951) and *Mi mensaje* (1952); Juan Perón's *Del poder al exilio* (1958) and *Yo, Juan Domingo Perón* (1976); and finally Tomás Eloy Martínez's *Las memorias del general* (1996) which contains autobiographical material. Part II turns to biography and looks at representative texts on Juan and Eva Perón. Biographies of Perón are not as plentiful as those on Eva: this study focuses on the most important: Joseph A. Page, *Perón: a Biography* (1983). Biographies of Eva Perón treated here offer a wide range of perspectives and techniques. The testimonial account of Borroni and Vacca, *Eva Perón: Tomo 1: Testimonios para su historia* (1970) is notable for its truth claims; in *Eva Perón ¿aventurera o militante?* (1966) and *Evita Perón: the Myths of a Woman* (1979), Juan José Sebreli and J. M. Taylor respectively offer approaches to Eva conditioned by the perspectives of sociology and anthropology. The works of Carmen Llorca, Marysa Navarro and Alicia Dujovne Ortiz can be seen as representative of the trajectory of twentieth-century biographical writing: the traditional, unselfconscious and frequently sycophantic approach of Llorca contrasts with the psychoanalytic, playful and postmodern aspects of Dujovne Ortiz.

Part III focuses on the novel, beginning with an analysis of *La novela de Perón* whose creatively postmodern reconstruction of Perón's life stands in stark contrast to Page's traditional approach grounded on the principle of meticulous documentation. The analysis of *Santa Evita* will be followed by a consideration of further fictional representations of Peronism, designated here as the 'fictive shadows' of *Santa Evita*, namely Abel Posse's *La pasión según Eva* (1995); Mabel Pagano's *Eterna* (1982); and Ernesto Frers's *Evita* (1997). This analysis will seek to show how the traditional biographical and 'factual' elements of these texts achieve a less 'truthful' portrait of their subject than does the more playful and experimental *Santa Evita*. The study concludes with a consideration of three further novels which can be described as the 'fictive fallout' of literary Peronism: works not directly concerned with the two main protagonists but displaying, none the less, heavy traces of their presence. Thus Juan and Eva Perón are barely mentioned in Manuel Puig's *Pubis angelical* (1979) but there is explicit discussion of Peronism and one of the characters, Ana, suffers from cancer, an illness that – inevitably in this context – evokes Eva Perón. Puig's text uses the discourse of psychoanalysis to present Peronism as a kind of pathology whose grip on the national psyche seems unshakeable. Peronism and psychoanalysis (which has exerted far more influence on Argentina than on any other Latin American country) are parodied as master narratives whose influence on the political and psychological profiles of the country are excessive. Mario Szichman's *A las 20:25 la señora entró en la inmortalidad* (1981) is concerned with the suicide of an adolescent Jewish girl who stands in ironic contrast to Eva. The text is about identity, genealogy, legitimacy, and the subversion of the 'grand narratives' of the Bible and of Peronism. In typical New Historical fashion, Szichman probes the underside of official history and illumines the marginality of Jewish life in Buenos Aires. The spirit of parody is dominant and the cult of Eva is the main target. Peronism and the perverse are conjoined in

José López Rega, the protagonist of Luisa Valenzuela's *Cola de lagartija* (1983). This text provides a variation on the same theme – the gravitation of the marginal to the centre – since the undistinguished, eccentric and sinister figure of José López Rega (known as 'El Brujo') aspires to supreme political power in Argentina following the death of Perón and becomes pivotal to the history of Peronism. In his 'becoming-woman' he subverts normal gender categories: the metaphorical masculinity of Eva inspires him to undergo his literal metamorphosis in the other direction. Peronism is often viewed by its opponents as a kind of contagion and Perón himself often used medical metaphors of infection and resistance, highlighting, for example, the positive role of antibodies.[56] All three texts project Peronism in the literary sphere and in their textual reincarnations of Eva contribute to the fulfilment of her (probably apocryphal) prediction: 'volveré y seré millones'.

NOTES

[1] David Rock, *Argentina 1516–1987: from Spanish Colonization to the Falklands War and Alfonsín* (London: Taurus, 1987), p. 285.
[2] José Enrique Miguens, 'The presidential elections of 1973 and the end of ideology' in Frederick C. Turner and José Enrique Miguens (eds), *Juan Perón and the Reshaping of Argentina* (Pittsburgh: University of Pittsburgh Press, 1983), pp. 147–50.
[3] Frederick C. Turner, 'The cycle of Peronism' in *Juan Perón and the Reshaping of Argentina*, p. 4.
[4] David Rock, *Argentina 1516–1987*, p. 264.
[5] Juan Domingo Perón, *Yo, Juan Domingo Perón: relato autobiográfico*, ed. Torcuato Luca de Tena, Luis Calvo and Esteban Peicovich (Barcelona: Planeta, 1976), pp. 54–5.
[6] Susan and Peter Calvert, *Argentina: Political and Cultural Instability* (Basingstoke: Macmillan, 1989), p. 127.
[7] José Enrique Miguens, 'The presidential elections of 1973 and the end of ideology' in *Juan Perón and the Reshaping of Argentina*, p. 148.
[8] Joseph A. Page, *Perón: a Biography* (New York: Random House, 1983), p. 6.
[9] Manuel Mora y Araujo and Peter H. Smith, 'Peronism and economic development: the 1973 elections', in *Juan Perón and the Reshaping of Argentina*, pp. 171–87 (p. 171).
[10] Tomás Eloy Martínez, *La novela de Perón* (Madrid: Alianza, 1989), p. 323.
[11] Alicia Dujovne Ortiz, *Eva Perón*, trans. Shawn Fields (New York: St Martin's Griffin, 1997), p. 87.

12 Sylvia Molloy, *At Face Value: Autobiographical Writing in Spanish America* (Cambridge: Cambridge University Press, 1991), p. 143.
13 Philippe Lejeune, 'The Autobiographical Contract' in Tzvetan Todorov (ed.), *French Literary Theory Today: a Reader*, trans. R. Carter (Cambridge: Cambridge University Press; Paris: Editions de la Maison Des Sciences de L'Homme, 1982), pp. 192–222 (p. 213).
14 William C. Spengemann, *The Forms of Autobiography: Episodes in the History of a Literary Genre* (New Haven: Yale University Press, 1980), p. xiv.
15 Susan Groag Bell and Marilyn Yalom, 'Introduction' in Susan Groag Bell and Marilyn Yalom (eds), *Revealing Lives: Autobiography, Biography, and Gender*, Suny Series in Feminist Criticism and Theory (Albany: State University of New York Press, 1990), pp. 1–11 (pp. 2–4).
16 William H. Epstein, '(Post)modern lives: Abducting the biographical subject' in William H. Epstein (ed.), *Contesting the Subject: Essays in the Postmodern Theory and Practice of Biography and Biographical Criticism* (West Lafayette, IN: Perdue University Press, 1991), pp. 217–36 (p. 222).
17 Tomás Eloy Martínez, *Las memorias del General* (Buenos Aires: Planeta, 1996).
18 Tomás Eloy Martínez, *Santa Evita* (Barcelona: Seix Barral, 1997), p. 390.
19 Diane Wood Middlebrook, 'Postmodernism and the biographer' in *Revealing Lives*, pp. 155–65 (pp. 164–5).
20 Eva Perón, *La razón de mi vida* (Buenos Aires: Buro, 1988).
21 Joseph A. Page, *Perón: a Biography* (New York: Random House, 1983).
22 María Griselda Zuffi, 'Atravesando géneros: cuerpo y violencia en Santa Evita', *Romance Languages Annual*, 10 (1998), 869–73.
23 Hayden White, 'The Historical Text as Literary Artifact' in *Tropics of Discourse: Essays in Cultural Criticism* (Baltimore and London: The Johns Hopkins University Press, 1978), pp. 81–100 (p. 98).
24 Tomás Eloy Martínez, *El vuelo de la reina* (Madrid: Alfaguara, 2002). Although the title of Joyce Carol Oates's novel, *Blonde: a Novel*, signals its fictional status as explicitly as does *Santa Evita*, Oates includes a note at the back of the title page reiterating her work's status as fiction: '*Blonde* is a work of fiction [. . .] not [. . .] a biography of Marilyn Monroe'.
25 Virginia Woolf, 'The Art of Biography' in *Collected Essays*, ed. Leonard Woolf, 4 vols (New York: Harcourt, Brace and World, 1967), IV, 221–8 (p. 228).
26 Hayden White, 'The Fictions of Factual Representation' in *Tropics of Discourse*, pp. 121–43 (p. 121).
27 Paula R. Backscheider, *Reflections on Biography* (Oxford: Oxford University Press, 1999), p. 18.
28 Norman Mailer, *Marilyn* (London: Chancellor, 1992), p. 18.
29 Alice A. Jardine, *Gynesis: Configurations of Woman and Modernity* (Ithaca and London: Cornell University Press, 1985), p. 83.

30 See Jeremy Ahearne, *Michel de Certeau: Interpretation and its Other* (Cambridge: Polity Press, 1995), p. 20, pp. 52–3.
31 Michel de Certeau, *The Writing of History*, trans. Tom Conley (New York: Columbia University Press, 1988), p. 79.
32 Robert Holton, *Jarring Witnesses: Modern Fiction and the Representation of History*, Postmodern Theory (Hemel Hempstead: Harvester Wheatsheaf, 1994), pp. 29–32.
33 Tomás Eloy Martínez, 'Ficción e historia en *La novela de Perón*', *Hispamérica* 49 (1988), 41–9 (p. 49).
34 Susan Sontag, 'Writing Itself: On Roland Barthes', in *A Susan Sontag Reader*, introduction by Elizabeth Hardwick (Harmondsworth: Penguin, 1983), pp. 423–46 (p. 432).
35 Hayden White, *Metahistory: the Historical Imagination in Nineteenth-Century Europe* (Baltimore and London: The Johns Hopkins University Press, 1973), p. 29.
36 Brook Thomas, *The New Historicism and Other Old-Fashioned Topics* (Princeton, NJ and Oxford: Princeton University Press, 1991), p. 250.
37 Michel Foucault, 'Nietzsche, Genealogy, History' in *The Foucault Reader* ed. Paul Rabinow (London: Penguin, 1984), pp. 76–100 (p. 88).
38 Taking the postmodern to its logical extreme, Elizabeth Deeds Ermarth reduces reality to text: 'we are always deciphering a text: the Republican convention, the intentions of a friend, Hiroshima, the emergence of mass media, *glasnost*, the behaviour of a relative, the invasion of a country, the painting of Paul Klee – all are texts; all are constructs; all are readable inventions'. See *Postmodernism and the Crisis of Representational Time* (Princeton NJ: Princeton University Press, 1992), p. 23.
39 Jacques Derrida, *De la grammatologie* (Paris: Minuit, 1967), p. 227.
40 Dorothy Lipstadt, *Denying the Holocaust: the Growing Assault on Truth and Memory* (New York: The Free Press, 1993), p. 21.
41 Tomás Eloy Martínez, 'Ficción e historia en *La novela de Perón*', *Hispamérica* 49 (1988), 41–9 (p. 44).
42 Alexis Márquez Rodríguez, 'Raíces de la novela histórica', *Cuadernos Americanos* 28 (1991), 32–49 (p. 40).
43 Seymour Menton, *Latin America's New Historical Novel*, Texas Pan American Series (Austin: University of Texas, 1993), pp. 14, 20.
44 As many commentators have pointed out, New Historical principles are hardly new: Eagleton notes that David Hume in his *A Treatise of Human Nature* (1739/40) comments on the multiple copies by which any particular historical fact is transmitted: 'Before the knowledge of the fact could come to the first historian, it must be convey'd thro' many mouths; and after it is committed to writing, each new copy is a new object, of which the connexion with the foregoing is known only by experience and observation'. Eagleton comments that Hume 'well-grasped, *avant la lettre*, the modern principle of intertextuality and the scepticism with which it is sometimes coupled'. Terry Eagleton, *The Ideology of the Aesthetic* (Oxford: Blackwell, 1990), p. 68, n. 22.
45 Eagleton notes that postmodernism, at its most militant, 'has lent a

voice to the humiliated and reviled, and in doing so has threatened to shake the imperious self-identity of the system to its core'. See *The Illusions of Postmodernism* (Oxford: Blackwell, 1996), p. 24.

46 Nelly Richard points out that Latin American cultural practices are 'deemed to have prefigured the model now approved and legitimized by the term 'postmodernism'. The very heterogeneity of the experiences which have created a Latin American space out of its multiple and hybrid pasts creates, at least on the surface, the very qualities of fragmentation and dispersion associated with the semantic erosion characteristic of the crisis of modernity [. . .]', 'Postmodernism and Periphery' in Thomas Docherty (ed.), *Postmodernism: a Reader* (Hemel Hempstead: Harvester Wheatsheaf, 1993), pp. 463–9 (p. 467). The Latin American relationship to postmodernism is foundational in another sense since the work of the Argentine writer Jorge Luis Borges provided one of its central perspectives through its view of the world as a labyrinth of possibilities, of parallel times, of alternative pasts and futures.

47 Alice A. Jardine, *Configurations of Woman and Modernity*, p. 37.

48 Linda Hutcheon, *The Politics of Postmodernism*, New Accents (London and New York: Routledge, 1989), p. 1.

49 'The real is not only what can be reproduced, but that which is always already reproduced. The hyperreal'. See Jean Baudrillard, 'From *Simulations*', in *Postmodernism: Reader* (London: Arnold, 1992), pp. 186–8 (p. 186).

50 Gianni Vattimo, *The Transparent Society* (Cambridge: Polity, 1992), p. 7.

51 Alice Jardine, 'The demise of experience: Fiction as Stranger than Truth?' in Thomas Docherty (ed.), *Postmodernism: a Reader*, pp. 433–42 (p. 440).

52 Raymond Leslie Williams, *The Postmodern Novel in Latin America: Politics, Culture, and the Crisis of Truth* (New York: St Martins Press, 1995), p. 17.

53 Brook Thomas, *The New Historicism and Other Old-Fashioned Topics*, p. 194.

54 Matei Calinescu, *Five Faces of Modernity: Modernism, Avant-garde, Decadence, Kitsch, Postmodernism* (Durham: Duke University Press, 1987), p. 278.

55 Terry Eagleton, *The Ideology of the Aesthetic*, p. 14.

56 See, for example, Tomás Eloy Martínez, *Las memorias del General*, p. 62.

Part I:

Autobiographical Writing

Chapter 2

La razón de mi vida and *Mi mensaje*

> Born in rural poverty, she acted on the stage and radio, married the president of a rich and powerful country and became the most famous woman in the world. Eva Perón's impassioned devotion to social welfare earned her the love of the common people, while her ambition and vindictiveness made most others hate her. Some considered her a whore; others wanted her canonized. Consequently, it is hard to achieve an objective view of her career.[1]

Clive Foss's introduction to his biography of the Peróns offers a succinct account of the spectacular drama of Eva Perón's life and of her uneven impact upon her fellow Argentines. The reader would reasonably expect such a life to provide the basis for lively reminiscence in Eva's autobiography, *La razón de mi vida*,[2] looking to its pages for some fresh insights into the unknown Eva: her early life in Los Toldos and Junín (both in the province of Buenos Aires); her adolescent years as an actress in 1930s Buenos Aires; and, in particular, her life-defining encounter with Perón in January 1944. On all three counts, however, *La razón* is disappointing since it says little that is new about Eva's life and, moreover, does not attempt to tell a life story in the conventional way. It comprises a series of vignettes whose main focus is the public persona of the political Eva. There is a great deal on Perón and Peronism as the defining influences underpinning both her often strident rhetoric of affirmation and certainty and also her routine and vitriolic attacks on her political opponents. There is much about her impassioned devotion to social welfare and there is emphatic denial of personal ambition. Her extraordinary commitment to the Peronist cause, together with sparing references to her personal sacrifice and suffering, help to explain why her *descamisados* regarded her as a worthy candidate for canonization. But there is nothing of the young and disadvantaged girl from the provinces which might have reinforced her message with a stronger sense of personal immediacy. Neither is there any new information about her life as an actress – although her theatrical self is often evoked indirectly by references to the roles she was performing on the national stage. As actress, Eva played the role of 'dangerous woman', free of familial ties but open to the pleasures and pitfalls of the big city. It is, of course, unsurprising that she should remain reticent about this period of her life which was to give rise to the *leyenda negra* of a promiscuous Eva who would go to any lengths to enhance her theatrical career. More surprising are other omissions, notably her failure to provide any comment on her married life. She merely reiterates her (political) subordination to Perón, exaggerating the sense of humility inspired in her by her perception of his infinitely superior qualities. Her private self, her personal joys and sorrows, the stuff of the traditional biography, remain resolutely suppressed. Her relentless focus on what she sees as the outstanding virtues of Perón and the inestimable benefits of Peronist policies, shuts out her personal experience. In this respect Eva's autobiography can be compared with that of Golda Meir which, as Spacks points out, has 'no self at its center'.[3]

Foss notes that *La razón de mi vida*, published on 15 October 1951, sold 150, 000 copies on the first day and within a month had broken all publishing records in Argentina. But in the same breath he describes *La razón* as 'this vapid ghost-written production, a work of propaganda that revealed virtually nothing about Evita' (p. 67): public acclaim clearly bears little relation to literary quality – or so Foss implies. A closer look reveals, however, that *La razón* is, in fact, a limited but fascinating text, bearing many of the hallmarks of Eva, despite having been ghostwritten by a Spanish journalist, Manuel Penella de Silva. Several commentators have not been deterred from treating *La razón* as a literary text, authored by the spirit if not by the pen of Eva Perón. Thus Foster remarks that 'it matters little, therefore, whether the "real" Eva Perón authored the text published under her name: Eva Perón the author is as much a product of political fiction as Eva Perón the narrator is a product of narrative fiction'.[4] For her part,

Marysa Navarro in *Evita* (1994) quotes liberally from Eva's 'autobiografía', clearly uninhibited by its ghostwritten status. Dujovne Ortiz makes the interesting point that while Evita would have liked a 'neat, embellished, bourgeois style', Penella de Silva adopted instead a 'simple, slightly clumsy, and very sentimental style that reflected Eva's candour and raw intelligence'.[5] She goes on to note that the repetition of certain words 'signal an attempt to express oneself that could only belong to Eva' (p. 254). Their corporeal quality point to her distinctive style: 'she must have transmitted it to her writers who, finding no danger, transcribed it' (p. 254). It is also worth noting Eva's personal reference to her engagement in the act of writing: 'creo que ya he escrito demasiado [...] Aquí veo ahora a mi lado verdaderas pilas de papel fatigado por mi letra grande' (p. 157). While the present study will credit Eva with the authorship of *La razón*, this background of uncertainty is nicely reminiscent of contemporary challenges to authorial 'rights' over the meaning of the text in the light of heightened critical awareness that what the text signifies need not coincide with what the author intended at the time of writing.

Another related angle on authorship emerges from the 'conversion discourse' of *La razón*, deriving from the perception of a pivotal life-changing moment — in Eva's case her momentous meeting with Perón to which she constantly returns, as we shall see. Dorsey's points about conversion discourse have clear relevance to Eva:

> those who describe conversion normally locate the source of personal change outside the self. This is true even of those who employ it in a secular context. Rather than present themselves as 'writing' conversion discourse, they present themselves as being 'written' by it [...]. Those who encode conversion 'create' a self that does not act 'for' the self, but rather for a source (divine or otherwise) whose motives transcend the worldly context at hand. This expectation opens a space for actions and beliefs that go against existing cultural norms.[6]

The reader of *La razón* often forms the impression that this text is not constructed by a calculating author but rather that the author is herself the instrument for the transmission of a message emanating from a higher source: she is being written, in a sense, by Perón who is accorded quasi-divine status ('yo he dejado de existir en mí misma y es él quien vive en mi alma', p. 33); she is also being written by the religious languages of love and hatred which speak more of Eva's possession by her politico-religious passion than of her personal agency: during her last few years, Eva's fanaticism and resolve were driven by her awareness of imminent death: her final role of woman possessed suggests her subordination to a higher power. Sarlo specifically relates the redundant and repetitive qualities of her language to her passion.[7]

It is not unreasonable to assume, however, that Eva chose her own title, *La razón de mi vida*, which indicates that her aim was to fix the meaning and purpose of her life. Rather than being a mere self-portrait, it seeks, as Gusdorf puts it, to reconstruct 'the unity of a life across time'.[8] Eva's emphasis will be squarely on the truth value of her work and the reader will be expected to believe that the 'real' Eva lies behind the text. Had Eva read Philippe Lejeune's work she would have subscribed to his broad definition of autobiography (while baulking at the level of personal disclosure implied by his statement): 'a retrospective prose narrative produced by a real person concerning his own existence, focusing on his individual life, in particular on the development of his personality'.[9] Lejeune's 'autobiographical contract' (between author and reader) establishes an equivalence between the author, narrator, and protagonist, 'the affirmation in the text of this identity, referring in the last resort to the *name* of the author on the cover' (p. 202). Eva would have concurred with this logic since she assumes direct textual communication between author and reader. She would see her work as reflecting her experiences as they were lived, her feelings and emotions transmitted with complete reliability by her writings. She, like Elizabeth Bruss, would see a clear demarcation between autobiography and the novel, based on the truth value inherent in the former.[10] Like Lejeune she would not question the integrity and the authority of the 'I' in her text. Nor do the flaws in the glass of language give her pause to question the mirror-like qualities she takes for granted in her writing – much in the manner of many traditional autobiographers. Eva seeks to report, duplicate and verify the 'truth', oblivious to the objection that the self in autobiography is largely invented and that the past is not to be captured as it really was, however sincere and tenacious the efforts of the writer. A text which presents a single univocal self, presiding over an equally coherent life story is now seen, inevitably, as false and artificial.

Some critics such as Mandel have attempted to impose moral standards on the autobiographer who must not, so they say, falsify the facts in the manner of the creative writer[11]. The problem is that – as Nabokov states in his discussion of Gogol – 'bare facts do not exist in a state of nature, for they are never really quite bare. The recollection of the past is compromised by the fallibility of memory, the imposition of coherence and meaning and the intrusiveness of language'.[12] The past is reconstructed in language and, as Egan states, 'fiction-making is an inevitable human process'; 'fiction [...] ensnares reality from the beginning'.[13] It is, of course, only recently that autobiographers have taken such considerations on board. Writing in 1960, Roy Pascal was probably expressing a majority view in claiming that the best autobiographies 'give that unique truth of life as it is seen from inside'.[14] Recent theory, however, works on the basis of Foucault's dictum that 'nothing in man – not even his body – is sufficiently stable to serve as the basis for self-recognition or for understanding other men'.[15] Such an approach is peculiarly apposite in the case of Eva given her distinct and often radically disjunctive personae ranging from a seemingly apolitical actress,[16] to glamorous *señora*, to militant *compañera*. Yet her political passion could not have found a more appropriate form in which to express itself, since 'autobiography 'seems to stabilize "truth" and a subject who may utter it'. It is driven by an 'authoritarian complex'.[17]

To take *La razón* at face value the reader would need to accept what Elbaz describes as the 'myth of autobiography' which involves two related postulates: 'that the self is inside each one of us and that it is a pre-given structure, a finished product'.[18] Eva's self assumes an aura of stability following her meeting with Perón, which she claims to be the single, decisive event in her life. In *La razón* Eva returns repeatedly to this episode as if she were seeking to consolidate it as the fulcrum of a life previously bereft of meaning and riddled with guilt feelings over past transgressions. In Perón, the representative of God on earth, she saw the light. Through him she finds her way out of the darkness and into the clear sunlight of Truth.

Purity of any kind is in short supply in the field of autobiography. As a narrative arrangement of reality it is difficult to separate from fiction, as we have seen. Some critics have identified a separate current of women's autobiography distinguished by 'diffuse organization'[19] and blanket coverage of the life work (in contrast with the masculine style perceived to be more likely to possess the virtue of summary and concision): 'women chatter, talk incessantly about trivial details, are obsessed with "dailiness"'.[20] A commonplace of women's writing is – allegedly – its unstructured narrative.[21] Here, however, the policing of gender proves to be as ineffectual as the policing of genre: Eva's writing may be desultory and repetitive, its chaotic form contrasting with the clarity of the principles purportedly governing her life. But *La razón* cannot be accused of an excess of 'dailiness' or obsession with inconsequential detail. The problem with her text seems to be that it has nothing to say beyond her exaggerated protestations of loyalty to Perón and vitriolic diatribes directed at political opponents.

While it is prudent to resist, with Nussbaum, 'temptations to read the history of women's autobiographical writing as a separate and self-contained reflection of the essence of woman' (p. 133), it is clearly significant that Eva as author of *La razón* was a trespasser on a male preserve: the tradition of autobiographical writing in Argentina was overwhelmingly male and overwhelmingly elitist. It belonged to the patrician heritage of an Argentina whose history, according to one of Eva's harshest detractors, Victoria Ocampo, consisted exclusively of the 'history of our families'.[22] The autobiographical tradition was a pillar of Argentine high society, encapsulating 'la historia de la élite del poder en la Argentina'.[23] Genealogy is concerned with the purity of origins and protected identities, with the unsullied, and the uncontaminated, with policing the borders between races and classes. But in a frontier society whose history was conditioned by slavery, such borders proved permeable and fluid: 'las genealogías más acendradas sufren, a menudo, la interferencia de vástagos impuros' (p. 121). Some such impurities might have been covered up but the presence of another Argentina, previously invisible, could no longer be suppressed. Adolfo Prieto discusses an autobiographical work, 'La historia que he vivido', written by a member of the now embattled elite, Carlos Ibarguren, and in particular an episode of 1940 which encapsulated the collision of classes. Ibarguren took his sons to a football match, a wholly new experience for them since they had never previously witnessed such a large, jostling crowd. Having stood up to get a better view, Ibarguren felt an orange brush past his head and looked round to identify the aggressor, 'cuando del fondo rumoroso y brillante de la muchedumbre surgió este grito estentóreo "¡Siéntate, degenerado!"' (p. 194). Prieto comments that 'la simple emisión de esa voz significa una ruptura más profunda entre hombre y hombre que la que pueda apoyarse en un estilo de vida diferente' (p. 195).

It is Eva's voice, similarly stentorian and uncompromising (at least from the perspective of Victoria Ocampo and her class) which will prime these same masses in mid century. Prieto's anticipation of the future direction of the Argentine autobiographical tradition is prescient: 'el próximo capítulo de nuestra literatura autobiográfica registrará, sin duda, los pasos de este proceso singular, y nos ilustrará sobre los profundos desgarramientos sufridos en los esquemas de comprensión anteriormente aceptados' (p. 198). But the nature and gender of the individual who would embody the 'protagonista formidable y desconocido' – whose emergence he had anticipated – would have shocked Prieto. The violation of this patrician preserve of male autobiography is perpetrated not only by an *intrusa* of the wrong gender but by one who is, moreover, illiterate and illegitimate, who appropriates the *patria* for the *chusma* and whose voice is all the more searing for emanating from the margins between life and death. Eva as woman represents the 'wound', the mark of woman; she represents a wound in the body politic, exercising excessive power from the seedy *arrabales* at the margins of official government; her writing is a wound in the literary body of the Argentine autobiographical tradition known for its high-flown, erudite and passionless decorum. As the holder of the phallic pen, transmitted from father to son, she becomes the usurper of male prerogatives. She is an 'unnatural' woman who has progressed from a lowly state – perceived as one of debauchery by her enemies – to spheres of activity which would normally be out of bounds to her: politics and writing. She represents, par excellence, the sex out of control.

Yet she seeks to establish a transcendental truth, a truth that can be communicated in writing. Her sensitivity to the injustices she witnesses in the city is linked to her nostalgia for the literal and true: 'solamente una vez he sentido una tristeza igual a la de aquella desilusión; fue cuando supe que los Reyes Magos no pasaban de verdad con sus camellos y con sus regalos' (p. 13).

The most salient feature of *La razón* is its simplicity. The author believes that she possesses the truth – that the truth is in her –

and she seeks to disseminate it forthwith. In this respect Eva's text is not very different from mainstream Spanish American autobiography which, according to Molloy, is restrained in its speculation on the act of remembering: 'memory is given short shrift, its workings barely mentioned, let alone questioned'.[24] The world is seen as eminently manageable rather than as being under the control of blind chance. Eva specifically rejects chance as an influence on her life: 'No. No es el azar lo que me ha traído a este lugar que ocupo, a esta vida que llevo' (p. 10). The irony is, of course, that her own life was shaped by a chance encounter. Her 'día maravilloso' was 'el día en que mi vida coincidió con la vida de Perón' (p. 19).[25] But for Eva life can be explained and understood: its basis is a kind of benign rationality which has been perverted by the festering persistence of social injustice but remains readily recuperable by human agency. Eva's simplicity is evident in her recourse to definition and bald assertion which lends her writing an aura of certitude, if not of conviction. She is the mistress of the slick aphoristic statement appealing to eternal human values while oversimplifying practical realities: 'el amor alarga la mirada de la inteligencia' (p. 41); 'el amor es darse y «darse» es dar la propia vida' (p. 52); 'para un peronista no hay nada mejor que otro peronista' (p. 102); 'la felicidad de una mujer no es su felicidad sino la de otros' (p. 148). But what might be dismissed as empty cliché in other writers, resists such treatment in Eva's case since she did, arguably, lay down her life for her people (in the sense that her undiminished devotion to their cause implied neglect of her own declining health).

Like Perón her style inclines to the pat and proverbial[26] but her statements evoke ambivalent responses, particularly when, as in some instances, they go against the grain of her own generally rigid view of the world: 'cada uno ve las cosas según sea lo que quiere conocer en ellas [. . .] las cosas son del color del cristal con que se miran' (p. 40). Unfortunately, she does not allow such insights to temper her own principles, often conditioned by preconceived and reductive notions: 'ahora sé que los hombres se clasifican en dos grupos' (p. 19). She sees the world in black and white terms: 'los buenos dirigentes [. . .] Los malos dirigentes [. . .]' (p. 74) and frequently adopts extreme positions: '– ¡Nada de la oligarquía puede ser bueno!' (p. 146). Such an attitude smacks of childish petulance and it is, in fact, her child-like immaturity and naivety that informs much of her writing: thus her chastening realization that the poor outnumber the rich not just in her village but in the city too (p. 15). Also child-like is her appeal to a kind of natural spontaneity and harmony to explain her mission: thus her social work stems from 'un entendimiento mutuo y simultáneo entre mi corazón, el de Perón y el alma del pueblo' (p. 82). She offers not the rational review of her life as promised in her title but rather an appeal to sentiment and spirituality as embodied in 'corazón' and 'alma'. She also deviates from reason in her worship of Perón before whom she prostrates herself with ostentatious, Pauline self-denial: 'yo he dejado de existir en mí misma y es él quien vive en mi alma' (p. 33). All the glory is Perón's as Eva's contrapuntal style makes clear: 'él, con la inteligencia; yo, con el corazón [...] él culto y yo sencilla [...] El la figura y yo la sombra' (p. 35); 'donde él daba una lección magistral, yo apenas balbuceo [...]' (p. 60).[27] Foster comments that Eva's self-portrait is as unconsciously parodic as it is paradigmatic of the shibboleths concerning masculine mind versus feminine heart.[28] Eva compounds her error in this respect by associating female submissiveness with authentic womanhood: 'la mujer auténtica, por ser precisamente auténtica, se refugia silenciosa en los hogares del pueblo, donde la humanidad se hace eterna' (p. 152). Here Eva propounds those same patriarchal myths of female virtue which have been instrumental in maintaining female subordination. She is at least consistent in also defending those pillars of the patriarchal order – 'Patria', 'Nación', 'Fe', 'Religión' – which have promoted historically those same social injustices which she deplores (pp. 17–18).

In heralding the authenticity of the silent woman, Eva touches on the quality she is most keen to project in her work: her craving for an impossible authenticity which embraces all that is spontaneous (as opposed to calculated) and all that is inside and intimate rather than outside and foreign: she refers repeatedly to 'lo íntimo de mi corazón' and to her desire to represent Perón's brave new Argentina, 'pero no por fuera como un pintor sino por dentro, tal como yo lo he visto' (p. 83). She believes in an essential self, the kind of self described by Culler as 'something inner and unique [...] an inner core which is variously expressed (or not expressed) in word and deed'.[29] Eva's outlook is marked by binary divisions: 'buenos dirigentes' are opposed to 'malos dirigentes' (p. 74), as we have seen, and 'almas estrechas' to 'almas que todavía creen en la sinceridad' (p. 80).[30] Eva displays an emotional exclusivity which banishes the other in its craving for the Same: the New Testament notion of perfect unity of believers in Christ is mimicked in Eva's dream of blissful oneness with her *descamisados*: 'es nuestro corazón (el de Perón y el mío) que quiere reunir en la nochebuena a todos los corazones descamisados de la Patria, en un abrazo inmenso, fraternal y cariñoso' (p. 110). In this schema the oligarchy plays the role of the damned ('de ese pecado no se redimirán jamás', p. 146). Eva makes a relentless case for her own personal authenticity by the repetition of certain emotive words, notably 'corazón' but also 'franqueza', 'verdad', 'sinceridad', 'lealtad', 'cariño', 'pueblo', 'alma' – all pointing to Eva's commitment to old-fashioned values, to those same eternal verities which Eagleton defends.[31] Truth is associated with depth ('en lo más hondo de mi corazón', p. 14), 'en el fondo de mi alma' (p. 18). The true and the good will last for ever: hence the high frequency of words suggesting permanence, immutability, unchanging essence. Perón has left a permanent mark on her, an 'estampa indeleble' (p. 19). She responds by expressing her love in a permanent way ('permanentemente', p. 26). In giving her love, a woman 'alcanza su eternidad' (p. 34) but enemies too are for ever: 'los «hombres comunes» son los eternos enemigos de toda cosa nueva' (p. 21).

While Eva's writing is devoid of analysis, intellect and 'substance', it is brimful of feeling, emotion and intuition. Her style avoids even the most simple argumentation, preferring to trade in what she sees as self-evident facts rather than in controversial propositions: 'los hombres no sienten ni sufren tanto el amor como nosotras las mujeres. Esto no necesita demostración' (p. 40). On the rare occasions when there is some effort to argue a case the result is comically naive. Thus Eva feels vulnerable to attack for her total personal subordination to Perón but deals with feminist criticism by claiming indifference to it: 'no me interesa sin embargo la crítica . . . Además, reconocer la superioridad de Perón es una cosa distinta. ¡Además . . . me he propuesto escribir la verdad!' (p. 131). This echoes her earlier reaffirmation of Perón's belief that trade union support was crucial to the success of his policies as embodied in 'justicialismo': 'y esto es verdad, primero, porque lo ha dicho el General Perón, y segundo, porque efectivamente es verdad' (p. 62).

The style of *La razón* is flawed in many ways: the frequent use of exclamation marks suggests a child-like desire to ram home a self-evident point: '¡es tan grande la lucha y son tan pocas mis fuerzas!' (p. 111). Eva seeks to lend weight and authority to her discourse by frequent citation from a variety of sources but mainly from Perón (p. 87) and the Gospels: 'nadie ama más que el que da la vida por sus amigos' (p. 111). The text is also characterized by frequent repetition: chance is first mentioned at the outset only to re-emerge later (p. 27). The imagery of the condor (Perón) and the sparrow (Eva) recurs (for example, pp. 8, 86).[32] Eva repeats too the patriarchal notion that the realm of intelligence is masculine, that of feeling, feminine (pp. 35, 142) and returns to her attack on the affluent who dismiss the plight of the poor as melodramatic (pp. 93, 145). Her style sometimes lapses into a turgid spiral of repetitiveness: 'la justicia cumplirá inexorablemente, cueste lo que cueste y caiga quien caiga [...] y cuando digo que la justicia [...]' (p. 93). She rejects 'las mujeres masculinizadas' (p. 36) and 'la masculinización de la mujer' (p. 39) – although she herself spends little time at home and displays a distinct lack of biddable femininity in the traditionally male preserve of politics. Claiming to uphold 'la cultura femenina' (p. 37) she describes man – allegedly too ready to accept the destruction of human life – as the true enemy (p. 38).

Eva's text is not only inconsistent, however, but also not as straightforwardly candid as it initially appears to be. Evita's self-effacement ('una humilde y pequeña mujer', p. 26; 'una sombra de su presencia superior', p. 60) is not total: she has forged her own destiny – she refers to 'el camino que yo elegí' (p. 43) and reasserts her personal agency a few pages later: 'yo elegí ser «Evita»' (p. 45). Her occasional bursts of arrogance are tempered but hardly neutralized by subsequent displays of humility: 'los demás pueden aspirar al derecho de mi amistad [...] Viendo cómo los obreros tratan y aprecian a los demás he aprendido mucho' (p. 67). Elsewhere she refers to her own personal uniqueness: 'como Evita vivo una realidad que tal vez ninguna mujer haya vivido en la historia de la humanidad' (p. 50).[33]

Eva's language, raw and physical, constantly reverting to flesh, blood and sensation, is, as Dujovne Ortiz remarks, peculiarly her own: 'certain words reappear, signalling an attempt to express oneself that could belong only to Eva. It is not a sentimental expression, but a physical expression that is all about sensations, especially painful ones. We recognize in them a corporeal element that only she could express'.[34] Eva's bodily style emerges in various ways, from the relatively innocuous references to the senses: 'para mí lo más importante es que estas cartas huelen a pueblo porque oliendo a pueblo huelen a verdad' (p. 88) to the fevered intensity of commitment to the cause: 'confieso que padezco casi de fiebre permanente de realizar, y que es una fiebre de contagio' (p. 38). The indignation aroused in her by injustice produces a searing, physical effect: 'de cada edad guardo el recuerdo de alguna injusticia que me sublevó desgarrándome íntimamente' (p. 11). Her sense of powerlessness to remedy the situation gives rise to her sensation of asphyxia – 'como si no pudiendo remediar el mal que yo veía, me faltase el aire necesario para respirar' (pp. 12–13). She suffers in the present but the rich will suffer in the future, not financially but physically, through their bodies: 'hasta la última gota de sangre que les queda' (p. 93). Feelings such as anguish and love assume concrete physical presence: Eva refers to 'aquella angustia íntima que me ahogaba' (p. 28); Perón 'ama entrañablemente a su pueblo' (p. 41).

Eva's literary naivety is not total since she shows glimpses of critical awareness, acknowledging that what she says is not new: 'yo, aunque sea un poco de plagio, diré más bien que el mundo actual padece de una gran ausencia: la de la mujer' (p. 141). She acknowledges her own limitations as a writer: 'todo esto me parece que se va convirtiendo en una charla demasiado larga' (p. 95). She is capable of admitting personal weaknesses (p. 15) and occasionally appeals to the reader for reassurance (p. 17). More significantly she is aware of her own rhetorical procedures and sensitive to her opponents' allegations about her. Her situation in this respect reflects the view that identity is composed not only by acts of self-perception but by 'other-perception', that is, by 'our looking at others looking at us [. . .] even if a view of me is rejected it still becomes incorporated in its rejected form as a part of my self-identity [. . .] Thus 'I' becomes a 'me' who is being misperceived by another person. This can become a vital aspect of my view of myself (e.g. "I am a person whom no one really understands")'.[35] Eva is frequently on the defensive, anticipating the criticism of her opponents: 'ni cuando entro en contacto con los más necesitados podrá decir nadie que juego a la dama caritativa [. . .]' (p. 52). She is obsessed with putting the record straight. Her method of refutation is to substitute a positive word for a negative one. But she is aware that such a procedure might be seen as a mere rhetorical device: 'ellos creen que se llega al resentimiento únicamente por el camino del odio [...] Yo he llegado a ese mismo lugar por el camino del amor. Y no es un juego de palabras. No' (p. 108). Eva is desperate to fix language, to stop its play of substitutions ('odio' – 'amor'), to find some sort of anchor to control its meaning. She is interested only in the 'bare facts' which she is keen to remove from the arena of contention and dispute. But as we have seen the facts are never quite bare and the play of language is relentless and interminable. Eva has some inkling of this: 'perdóname estas explicaciones que, sin quererlo, casi han venido a dar con cierto tono de filosofía que no entiendo y no deseo hacer' (p. 27). She is not short of self-awareness as she distances herself from her own previous incarnations: her artistic career was a period of bad faith when she attempted to suppress her real vocation ('intenté evadirme de mí misma', p. 14). She is also aware of the staleness of language, stepping back from her own well-worn phrases of personal consolation to meditate on their limitations: 'algún día todo esto cambiaría [...]. Aunque la frase es común en toda rebeldía, yo me reconfortaba en ella como creyese firmemente en lo que decía' (p. 15). She is also conscious of the possible structural demerits of her own writing: 'este capítulo tal vez desentone en la mitad de estos apuntes destinados a explicar mi misión' (p. 119). The literary allusions found in Eva's writings, notably to the Bible (*La razón*, p. 111; *Mi mensaje*, p. 26),[36] to Plutarch (*La razón*, p. 127; *Mi mensaje*, p. 19) and to Dante (*Mi mensaje*, p. 28) indicate a degree of culture, albeit second-hand, for which she is rarely given credit. The fact that she mistakes Lenin for Marx in *Mi mensaje* ('yo no creo como Lenin que la religión sea el opio de los pueblos', p. 57) suggests that such references were her own rather than the handiwork of her intellectual superiors. However, the intertextual is a minor aspect of Eva's style: the major thrust of her writings relates to the 'real' world rather than to literature. Her longing for literalness (*La razón*, p. 15), her wariness of the limits of language and its inherent playfulness beyond her control, suggest a search for pure origins, a language uncontaminated by double meanings and tropes. Her text is punctuated by references to the infinite and to the absolute which speak of an unfulfilled textual passion.

The diversity of Eva's writing suggests the presence of distinct selves, some of whom are indicated by her stylistic shifts. In *La razón* she mentions in particular her different roles as Eva Perón, the president's wife, 'un papel sencillo y agradable' (p. 46) and as Evita, the militant *compañera*, 'que me resulta un papel difícil' (p. 47). In *Mi mensaje* there emerges yet another Eva, a posthumous Eva who will continue to receive the letters of her *descamisados* (p. 80). The splitting of Eva's self is emphasized by her frequent reference to herself in the third person: 'Evita es vasca, pero es leal' (*La razón*, p. 62); 'también el papel de Evita es a veces amargo' (p. 118). Interestingly, she often showed the same sense of distance in her speeches: at the *cabildo abierto* she asked: '¿Cuándo Evita los ha defraudado?'; and on 27 October 1951 she remarked: 'cuando llegue ese día, entonces Evita se considerará satisfecha [...]'.[37] This splitting gives rise to a sense of the theatricality of Eva's multiple roles in the 'drama de mi pueblo' (*Mi mensaje*, p. 27) – ironic in view of the professional theatricality of Eva's silent past (as actress) and of her fulsome contempt for the empty theatre of the ladies of high society (*La razón*, p. 150). The effect, of course, is to eliminate any notion of a completed self.[38]

Eva emerges as a figure who pays lip service to Peronist ideals (as well as to those pillars of conservative orthodoxy, the 'Patria' and the 'Nación') while subverting them from within. She is a radical force whose words are in tune with the Peronist message ('el hogar es un taller de artista donde cada cuadro es un poco de su alma y de su vida', p. 152) while her personal life style repudiates patriarchal principles: she has no truck with feminism but deals a spectacular blow for the cause by refusing confinement in the 'hogar' and rejecting the traditional role of the president's wife, stamping upon it the mark of the 'dangerous woman', that of the militant *compañera* who subverts the status quo from within. While exceeding her place in the public domain, she underperforms in the private arena of wifely ministrations. As Taylor remarks: 'the Eva Perón of *La razón de mi vida* goes so far as to suggest, if not a sexless marriage, a careful muting of sex, a sacrifice that allowed Eva and Juan better to dedicate themselves to their people'.[39] In her discussion of Emma Goldman, Spacks remarks that 'devotion to the masses mixes badly with devotion to a man, conflicting responsibilities and conflicting desires for gratification proving impossible to reconcile'.[40] Eva's eroticism and her highly-charged libido find satisfaction not in marital relations but rather in collective intercourse with the *pueblo* –

nowhere more dramatically demonstrated than in the exchange of 21 August 1951 when Eva resisted the crowd's insistent demands that she accept the vice presidency.

Eva's relationship with the *pueblo* is carried out entirely in language which often assumes a repetitive quality suggestive of erotic rhythms: they constitute the essence of her passion as conceived by Sarlo.[41] For many commentators Peronism was based on rhetoric, on the relentless repetition of favoured words and phrases which had a powerful incantatory effect. Aizenberg refers to Martínez Estrada's belief that Perón attempted to create a new Argentine reality by creating a new Argentine language: 'it is striking how in his comments on Peronism Martínez Estrada repeatedly invokes language as the instrument with which Perón obtained and maintained dominance, shaping Argentina in his own image'.[42] He used words' magic power to subjugate and pervert his country, and by means of them 'conjured up' the Argentina he wanted. Several historians have also highlighted the importance of Peronist oratory in shaping Argentina. Romero points to the control of the means of communication, indicating that 'radio oratory was a key technique of the government: the virile voice of the president and the throaty voice of Eva Perón had a profound effect on the politically inexperienced masses'.[43] A more recent commentator is no less insistent on the significance of Peronist rhetoric: 'the vocabulary of Peronism was both visionary and believable. The credibility was in part rooted in the immediate, concrete nature of its rhetoric'. It drew its authority 'from its capacity to tell its audience what it wanted to hear'.[44] Those downtrodden masses, previously invisible, were called into existence by a politician who associated them, rather than the oligarchy and the intellectuals, with the nation: the latter could be left to their abstract ruminations about *argentinidad*.

La razón de mi vida belongs to the category identified by Howarth as 'autobiography as oratory',[45] marked in Eva's case by her devotion to Peronist doctrine. Though it is, of course, a written text, it is grafted from Eva's speeches and bears some of the hallmarks of spontaneous, oral delivery rather than the painstaking composition associated with writing. Her text repeats what she had previously spoken – 'no me arrepiento [...]', (p. 157) and the trace of her voice is inscribed in her writing, a peculiarly feminine trait according to Cixous who senses femininity in writing by a privileging of the voice: 'all the feminine texts

that I have read are very close to the voice, are very close to the
flesh of the language, much more than in masculine texts'. The
voice contains the trace of the intensity of the attachment to the
mother: 'to write in the feminine is to put over what is cut off by
the symbolic, the voice of the mother, it is to put over what is most
archaic'.[46] *La razón* represents the voice of the mother (Eva is
'madre de mi pueblo', p. 155) whose bond with her children is
stronger than life itself. But 'no me arrepiento [. . .]' suggests too
that Eva's rhetoric is not confined to an outpouring of maternal
affection: it is also, of course, a rhetoric which attacks the
oligarchy and alternates therefore between words of love and
words that wound, both stemming from her visceral sense of
'indignación frente a la injusticia' (p. 11). In both cases, it is the
rhetoric of passion and excitement charged with physical, bodily
energy rather than a writerly discourse of refined ideas (although
these are not wholly absent, as we shall see). Eva's rhetoric is the
hot, fervent, fanatical language of the emotions gendered as
feminine, rather than the cold language of the mind, gendered as
masculine. Heat and cold, light and dark, often serve for the
simple, metaphorical expression of her binary frame of mind: her
own conversion, for example, is likened to frost and snow melting
in the sun (p. 22).

Eva's world is a knowable world: a world which excludes the
other – whether located inside (the oligarchy) or outside ('la
influencia de ideas remotas muy alejadas de todo lo argentino',
p. 17); a world which is governed by destiny rather than by chance
('no, el azar no gobierna al mundo ni a los hombres', 27); which
finds perfect unity in the holy trinity of 'pueblo', 'patria', Perón
(p. 78). This world is associated with the positive: 'lo auténtico',
'la verdad', 'la sinceridad', words which punctuate Eva's discourse, but fail to achieve the clinching firmness of meaning she
seeks since they contain traces of opposite meanings which are
reinforced rather than suppressed through their repetition. Eva's
affirmative style is designed to convey certainty – 'creo firmemente [. . .] yo creo firmemente que, en verdad [. . .] lo indudable es que [. . .]' (p. 27) – but its effect is the reverse. Just as Eva's
own words are designed to wound ('mis discursos tienen muchas
veces veneno y amargura', p. 93) so she is wounded by the words
of the oligarchy such as 'melodrama' (p. 93) and 'pintoresco'
which she describes as 'la expresión más sórdida y perversa del
egoísmo de los ricos' (p. 84). These words seek to disguise

self-interest and call her life's work into question by purporting to expose and belittle from a superior and detached perspective. She would like to retaliate by converting her words into weapons, making them count not just in the realm of rhetoric but in that of physical action: 'he deseado que mis insultos fuesen cachetadas o latigazos [. . .]' (p. 93). Eva does in fact turn a word into a weapon in the case of 'descamisado'. This word originally belonged to the oligarchy who used it pejoratively of their downtrodden compatriots: 'un pueblo humilde a quien la soberbia de los poderosos llamó descamisado'.[47] Perón reinvented this dismissive word, transforming it into a term of endearment, producing a 'reverse' discourse. Eva followed his lead but her greater emotional intensity and raw energy heightened the figurative violence of this linguistic manoeuvre which skewed the word so that a new meaning is superimposed on the original.[48] Patriarchal language is subverted, resulting in a kind of doubling of profits: the now repressed sense (barbaric and impoverished low life) is retained 'under erasure' but the new sense of class solidarity and pride stands out in relief. Another Peronist word used repeatedly in *La razón* is 'justicialismo': here a less spectacular transformation takes place, the ordinary, rather over-familiar word, 'justicia' being elevated to assume quasi-scientific authority in the new and unfamiliar guise of 'justicialismo', denoting now not a general and abstract concept but a set of practical principles at the core of Peronist doctrine.

Although it is tempting to dismiss *La razón* in terms which might have been favoured by the oligarchy – melodramatic, sentimental, propagandistic – its powerful reformist rhetoric cannot be brushed aside easily: 'la madre de la familia está al margen de todas las previsiones. Es el único trabajador del mundo que no conoce salario, ni garantía de respeto, ni límite de jornadas, ni domingo, ni vacaciones, ni descanso alguno, ni indemnización, por despido, ni huelgas de ninguna clase' (p. 137). The reader can imagine the breathless, declamatory quality of words which belong to speech rather than text, the jarring, insistent tone, the rising indignation, the raw emotion of the voice. But reformism is soon enveloped by conformism and the rush of anger peters out in the flatness of common sense: 'nacimos para constituir hogares. No para la calle' (p. 137). The text ends, however, on a note of renewed excitement and exhilaration with a clarion call for economic independence, 'que nos libere de llegar a ser pobres mujeres sin ningún horizonte, sin ningún derecho y sin ninguna esperanza' (p. 137). Cixous observes that woman proceeds by 'lapse and bounds'[49] – which describes nicely the uneven quality of Eva's prose. What follows in the next section ('Una idea') is a lucid argument about the consequences of failing to provide the housewife with economic independence. Typically, though, Eva feels that she lacks the analytical apparatus to clinch the point and so appeals to the strength of her emotions: 'esto no sé cómo probarlo, pero lo siento como una verdad absoluta' (p. 138).

Eva's remarks about the *Damas de la Beneficencia* recall the well-documented ambiguity of the gift as investigated by several commentators, many of whom highlight its ambivalence: on the one hand it signifies generosity but on the other instills feelings of indebtedness in the recipient: it becomes an obligation that demands reciprocity and once reciprocated, Derrida argues, it has been annulled. Cixous emphasizes, however, that female giving is different, being a disinterested affirmation of generosity without expectation of return: 'for a masculine economy the only return [rapport] worth securing is conceived in terms of revenues and profit, while a feminine economy seeks not to secure profit but to establish rapport/relations'.[50] Cixous points to maternal gifts as ones that escape the logic of appropriation that structures the commodity economy she labels masculine: for Eva the charitable gifts of the high society ladies may not result in a sense of obligation in the recipients but none the less the gift is annulled as gift in Derrida's sense because it is recognized as such, being the product of a staged giving calculated in part to benefit the giver by assuaging her guilt feelings. Eva's giving is disinterested: she frequently insisted that the recipients of her gifts ought not be grateful since they were only receiving what was justly theirs. While the *Damas de la Beneficencia* have an excess of money, some of which could be dispensed to the poor without disadvantage to themselves, Eva's giving is self-sacrificial: it may 'reward' her with feelings of self-justification but she cannot truly enjoy its benefits, since her ultimate gift is her life, consumed in the service of her *descamisados*, a truly maternal gift which expects no return.

Perón emerges not as a man of flesh and blood but as a shadowy, unreal and idealized figure to be admired and emulated from afar. Aware that her portrayal of Perón is remote and unconvincing, excessively deferential in her portrait of an exalted figure who soars condor-like above the ordinary masses confined to solid ground below, she makes some perfunctory efforts to present him as a man of the people: 'aparece ante ellos un amigo, amable y cordial' (p. 37); the *descamisado* 've en él a un padre y a un amigo' (p. 96). She is defensive about her relations with him, insisting that their marriage was based on love rather than on political convenience; but what is claimed as a union of equals turns out to be an alliance based on stark inequality, with the 'superior' qualities stacked on Perón's side: 'él sabiendo bien lo que quería hacer; yo, por sólo presentirlo; él con la inteligencia; yo con el corazón [...]' (p. 35).

Many of the tensions underlying the text relate to Perón. It is clear that Eva has a special interest in women and her message occasionally appears to have a feminist edge. But any glimpses of a radical agenda are repeatedly extinguished by the gaping fault line which undermines her female independence of spirit – her inviolable thraldom to one man and his essentially conservative principles, of which she herself is aware (p. 131). *La razón* was written just prior to the *cabildo abierto* of August 1951. It reflects some of the tensions between Eva and Perón that emerged on that occasion. We have here a text which is marred by the clichéd and proverbial – the influence of Perón's own style – but also one which bears traces of conscious restraint, inhibition and fear. It is in the last section, 'Las mujeres y mi misión' where glimpses of the independent Eva are clearest. She discards, albeit fleetingly, her habitual self-effacement and takes credit for her single-handed organization of the *Partido Peronista Femenino*, a task 'sin ningún precedente en el país' (p. 143). But then she reins herself in as she realizes that she has excluded Perón – a culpable oversight even when she is engaged in her own designated sphere of responsibility: 'todo se compensa con la alegría que tengo cuando, en las fechas nuestras, puedo llegar al Líder con mis mujeres para darle cuenta de nuestros progresos y de nuestras victorias' (p. 144). She is careful that every single one of her works redounds to the glory of Perón – rather than being perceived as a minor though independent sideshow – and that his will is done: thus his desire that Peronist political organizations serve as centres of action and culture are fulfilled in the basic units she organizes (p. 145).

The silences of this text justify a Freudian interpretive strategy: 'what it [the text] does not say, and *how* it does not say it, may be as important as what it articulates'.[51] Eva's concern is not to offend, let alone usurp, the place of Perón the father (he is a figural father in shaping Eva's political development but he is more generally a father figure to Eva being old enough to be her literal father). Eva's fear is that she might threaten Perón's dominance unwittingly, a fear which proved to be well founded: Perón's public irritation at the *cabildo abierto* of August 1951 derived at least in part from his relegation to an unfamiliarly secondary role on the platform. The silences of her text, particularly regarding their domestic relationship, speak of tensions and distance just as its noisy praise of Perón strikes a false note suggesting an overdone attempt to conceal the reality of a situation which is less than ideal. According to Eva the text was written spontaneously – 'todas estas cosas las escribo a medida que brotan de mi corazón' (p. 95) – which is possibly true for the most part. Significantly, however, references to Perón are studied and calculated, consistent in their exaggeration, conscientiously repeated to guard against any hint of independent thought.

It is ironic in the light of Derrida's treatment of the supplement that Eva uses the metaphor of the footnote to emphasize what she claims to be her virtual insignificance in the broad sweep of Peronist history. Grafton comments that while the text persuades, the notes prove – suggesting interdependence, also implied in the slogan 'Perón cumple, Eva dignifica'. Footnotes are curious supplements since they form an indispensable part of modern history.[52] While wanting to emphasize her supplementary status, Eva emerges as a type of 'dangerous supplement' and her choice of the footnote metaphor points, albeit unwittingly, to her indispensable status within the text of Peronism.

It is instructive, in conclusion, to compare and contrast *La razón* with Perón's memoirs as they appear in Perón's autobiography, *Yo, Juan Domingo Perón* and in Tomás Eloy Martínez's *Las memorias del general*. There are some similarities: Perón shares Eva's essentialist views of human nature, compounding them by male prejudice: 'Eva lloró como hacen todas las mujeres'.[53] His discourse is also marked by certainty and self-justification: 'yo no me equivoqué [. . .]' (p. 53). His penchant for the proverbial expression suggests a rigid and predetermined view of the world: 'como dice un refrán árabe [. . .]' (p. 55). He too has a liking for punchy generalization: 'se puede ser humilde de corazón sin serlo de condición' (p. 106); 'el peronismo es lo más heterodoxo que hay: cabe de todo'.[54]

But the differences between Eva's writings and those of Perón are more notable than the similarities. Eva quotes Perón extensively in the eleventh chapter ('Sobre mi elección') of *La razón*, where she reproduces his words verbatim. By contrast, Perón makes relatively few references to Eva in *Yo, Juan Domingo Perón* and deals with her only briefly in the eleventh section of 'Las Memorias del Puerto de Hierro' (*Las memorias del General*, pp. 47–50). Eva's humility and self-effacement contrast with Perón's self-aggrandizement: 'yo ya estoy más allá del bien y del mal' (*Las memorias*, p. 55). Both *La razón* and, more especially *Las memorias*, bear the traces of external manipulation but while Penella de Silva is respectful, preserving the syntax and style which Eva herself might have used, Martínez's mode of editing Perón's memoirs are designed to expose and undermine. While *La razón* lacks an explicit critique of Eva's discourse, Perón's account is consistently undermined by the editor who supplements Perón's text with a series of strategically-referenced 'documents' which expose him as an unreliable narrator, as we shall see. *La razón* is an account which incorporates Eva's contradictions, both her caring tenderness and her ruthless fanaticism, her child-like naivety and her moments of self-awareness, her certitude and faith diversified by her hesitancy and self-doubt. This text may not be written by Eva but its restlessness reflects her personality. Sartre was fond of saying that autobiographers recollect their past passions in order to inter them in 'a calm cemetery'.[55] The style of *La razón* suggests, by contrast, fluidity not fixity, commotion rather than stasis, combative engagement rather than resignation and withdrawal. It is the penultimate word of a dying woman but speaks not of the imminence of death but of the endurance of life.

Eva's last word is *Mi mensaje*, probably written between March and June of 1952 (Eva died on 26 July). This text revisits the major themes of *La razón* but its style is more incendiary and dramatic. It has an interesting life story of its own since it disappeared in 1952 only to re-emerge in 1987 when Fermín Chávez's edition was published. As he points out in his introduction,[56] critics writing prior to 1987 (such as J. M. Taylor and Marysa Navarro) knew of the text's existence but assumed that it was lost. Navarro claims that it had been suppressed deliberately because of its violent attack on the military.[57] In his English edition of *Mi mensaje*, Joseph Page notes that the text finally emerged from the archives of Jorge Garrido who was Argentina's Attorney General during the Perón presidencies. When Perón was removed from office in September 1955, Garrido accumulated as many government documents as he could in the circumstances and converted his garage into a store for them. When he died his family sought to dispose of the material and Eva's text emerged.[58]

Chávez points to several corrections made to the original manuscript, probably by Perón. The most interesting are the suppression of Eva's reference to Léon Bloy (*Mi mensaje*, p. 79) – to whom she refers in *La razón* (p. 123) – and the substitution of 'niños' for 'pibes' (*Mi mensaje*, p. 79), a term which appears in *La razón* (p. 116). These changes have not been made in Chávez's edition where the corrections only relate to spelling errors.

The only part of the text made public in 1952 was the section entitled 'Mi voluntad suprema' (which differs slightly from the version published as part of *Mi mensaje* in 1987). According to Chávez, the main reason for its suppression was not because Eva had become estranged from Perón but because she now identified more strongly than previously with his revolutionary rather than with his conservative persona, 'con un conductor no conservador, sino revolucionario' (p. 9). *Mi mensaje* is an 'extreme' text in another sense since, as Chávez points out, it was written when Eva was hovering between life and death, weighing just 38 kilos but remaining none the less 'espiritualmente poderosa' (p. 10).

The first page of *Mi mensaje* indicates that its main purpose is to supplement *La razón* with a view to rectifying what Eva perceives as the earlier text's deficiencies: 'no alcancé a decir todo lo que siento y lo que pienso [. . .]. He dejado demasiadas entrelíneas que debo llenar'. A further objective of *Mi mensaje* is to counter the anarchic structure of *La razón*, 'aquella mezcla desordenada de sentimientos y de pensamientos' (p. 13). To what extent does *Mi mensaje* fulfil these aims? The first aim is at least partially fulfilled in the sense that *Mi mensaje* foregrounds the dramatic and incendiary Evita who appears only fleetingly in *La razón*, mainly in the third section, 'Las mujeres y mi misión'. The self-deprecating Eva is not absent from *Mi mensaje*: she sees her role as ornamental ('se me ocurre que yo era algo así como un ramo de flores en su casa', p. 20). Elsewhere she implicitly acknowledges her subordinate status as a representative of the people whose problems reach Perón 'por mi voz leal y franca' (p. 45). Moreover, she feels unqualified to offer opinions on the religious question (p. 59). But despite such instances of modesty, it is a confident Eva, exalted to a position of full equality with Perón, who predominates in *Mi mensaje*.

No longer the sparrow of *La razón*, she too soars to the heights – 'tenía que volar con él' p. 18) – claiming for herself a status among women which parallels Perón's among men: '¡la primera mujer del pueblo que no se dejó deslumbrar por el poder ni por la gloria!' (p. 14). Her pivotal role in the movement is made apparent ('estuve en la primera línea del combate', p. 23) and a kind of role reversal emerges as she now becomes Perón's protector and acts as his shield (p. 74) – in contrast with her previously subordinate position as his protégé. Here the reader becomes aware of a different Eva, no longer naive or submissive, no longer burdened by feelings of inferiority. Indeed, it is she who possesses the finer judgement: Perón believes 'la primera palabra de todos los hombres como si fuese su propia palabra limpia y generosa, sincera y honrada' (p. 17). In contrast, her wisdom appears to be infinite: no longer the 'pequeña y humilde mujer' of *La razón*, eternally grateful for her life-defining encounter with Perón, she now proclaims not only her own unique worth as a female pioneer but her possession of infinite knowledge: 'ahora conozco todas las verdades y todas las mentiras del mundo' (pp. 14–15). While the Eva of *La razón* seems ever wary of giving free rein to her political rhetoric lest it offend Perón, here she has no such scruples: the effect is not to reinforce her sense of unity with Perón – one of her main preoccupations in *La razón* – but to highlight her differences from that Perón 'sereno e imperturbable' (p. 39) whom she still admires. Here she makes much of her uncompromising passion, her lack of balance (p. 40) and reasserts her faith in the virtue of fanaticism. Here her voice is distinctly her own, an incendiary, uncompromising voice which would have alarmed Perón. She advocates revolutionary methods, including strikes and sabotage, to defeat the oligarchy: 'Podrán vencernos un día... en la noche o de sorpresa... pero si al día siguiente nos largamos a la calle, o nos negamos a trabajar, o saboteamos todo cuanto ellos quieren mandar... tendrán que resignarse a devolvernos la libertad y la justicia' (p. 51).

Indeed, just as 'corazón' may be seen as the rhetorical centrepiece of *La razón*, so 'fanatismo' is the central point of reference in *Mi mensaje* whose opening section, 'Mi voluntad suprema', owes much of its force to the repetition of 'fanatismo' and 'fuego de mi fanatismo' (pp. 77–8). In launching a powerful broadside against the Church hierarchy Eva's rhetoric bears the hallmark of a sophisticated, anaphoric style, far removed from her previously petulant tone: ' No les reprocho haberlo combatido sordamente a Perón [...] No les reprocho haber sido ingratos con Perón [...] Les reprocho haber abandonado a los pobres [...] Les reprocho haber traicionado a Cristo [...]' (p. 55). This rhetoric is underwritten by a confidence verging on the arrogant since its appeal extends beyond the national frontier: '¡mi auténtica verdad! y espero que alguna vez se imponga sobre tanta mentira ... o por lo menos – aunque no me crean – sirva para algo a los pueblos del mundo en sus luchas por la justicia y por la libertad' (p. 39). Just as Eva's political vision extends to embrace the downtrodden wherever they are, so the targets of her incendiary rhetoric are no longer confined to Argentina's own oligarchy but include capitalist exploitation on a global scale:

> el talón de aquiles del imperialismo son sus intereses... Donde esos intereses del imperialismo se llamen 'petróleo' basta, para vencerlos, con echar una piedra en cada pozo.
>
> Donde se llame cobre o estaño basta con que se rompan las máquinas que los extraen de la tierra ... o que se crucen de brazos los trabajadores explotados ...
>
> ¡No pueden vencernos! (p. 37)

It is no longer a case of mere resistance but of marking, branding, inscribing the enemy, perpetrating a kind of writerly violence on him so that he is immediately recognized for what he is: 'sellarles la frente con el signo infamante de la traición' (p. 54); 'marcarlos a fuego para que nunca se conviertan en dueños de vida ... ' (p. 64). The structure and style of *Mi mensaje* are similar to those of *La razón*: the twenty-nine sections are short and deal with one main theme or pair of themes, some of them reminding the reader that Eva's Manichean mindset and her ideal of a world governed by sameness have scarcely changed ('la grandeza o la felicidad', p. 49; 'una sola clase', p. 83). The style of both texts is clipped and fragmentary, producing emotional vignettes enlivened by the spontaneity of oral speech: Chávez draws attention to the close similarities between the style of *Mi mensaje* and that of Eva's final speeches (p. 10). As in *La razón*, the style inclines towards the pat and proverbial ('la envidia de los sapos nunca pudo tapar el canto de los ruiseñores', p. 24) – suggesting sedimented and stale language on the one hand but also sensual bodily energy, straining for an impossible literalness, on the other. Rather than the language of the skin, it is the language of the viscera, replete with the imagery of bleeding, beating, and burning: Eva's suffering is worthwhile 'si eso sirve para restañar alguna herida [. . .]' (p. 77); 'yo vivo con mi corazón pegado al corazón de mi pueblo y conozco por eso todos sus latidos' (p. 59); certain preachers of religion were completely incapable of communicating 'el ardor de la fe . . . que es fuego ardiente' (p. 61). In addition, however, there are examples of a fluent, metaphoric and formal style that is equally strident: 'se dice defensor de la justicia mientras extiende las garras de su rapiña sobre los bienes de todos los pueblos sometidos a su omnipotencia' (p. 31). Shortly after, Eva refers to her own 'agresividad irónica y mordaz' – a comment which is as apposite to her narrative style as it is to her political fervour – before stepping back into the less self-conscious role of the incendiary Eva whose natural mode of communication is the explosive immediacy of speech: '¡Mentira! ¡Sí! ¡Mil veces mentira !' (p. 33). In *Mi mensaje* (as in *La razón*) Eva shows her linguistic deftness, transforming negative connotations into positive ones: referring to Perón's 'crime' of having sided with the downtrodden against the powerful, she declares: '¡Este es el gran delito de Perón! El gran delito que yo bendigo desde el fondo de mi corazón descamisado' (p. 75).

A notable feature of *Mi mensaje* is that two of the 'vignettes' (25 and 26, pp. 67 and 69) are severely truncated, consisting of three sentences and one sentence respectively, with the result that both pages are mostly blank. This blankness may suggest Eva's awareness that her death is fast approaching, the end of her writing anticipating the end of her life. It may also signify, more specifically, Eva's intuitive awareness of the other side of language, the failure of language to convey feelings which cannot be expressed in words. At this point immediately prior to death, language fails. Eva's writing assumes the invisibility of a colourless flame: there is an emptiness but one inscribed with intensity, suggesting the process of consumption which is raging in Eva's own body, language consuming itself – having reached a point where writing is impossible. Perhaps these sentences that peter out into an engulfing void can be seen as cinders, the remains of a linguistic burning. It is as if the different kinds of burning (the fire of Eva's heart, of her fanaticism, of her speech) all converged here as some kind of mystical contact is made with death (p. 67) and with love (69).

Such intensity can be read by reference to the Derridean concept, developed in *Cinders*, of 'the fire that is still burning at the origin of language'.[59] 'Cinder' refers to that burning within language: 'To hear, to speak, to write, is to feel the heat, to feel the retreat of the fire as a cinder falls, yet again, to ash' (p. 3). Eva literalizes these tropes: as she writes she is consumed by the cancer that burns within; her language is passionate and hot (in contrast with the coldness she hates in the oligarchy). She quotes Christ as bringing fire; her writing is a kind of fire that illuminates those absolute values which she yearns for even as it consumes them: 'the equation of writing with fire [...] brings about the conclusion that the purest site of writing "if there were one", would reside in the ever-present event of consuming words and lying in their ashes'.[60] Her language burns brightly, consumes itself, as she is consumed, falls silent, resonates again. It crumbles and dies but ash remains though the fire retreats; 'por cada golpe me parecía morir y sin embargo por cada golpe me sentía nacer' (p. 24).

Swindells has highlighted the political and subversive aspects of autobiography representing the unofficial voice from below:

> Autobiography has now the potential to be the text of the oppressed and the culturally displaced [...]. In making a claim to a political voice, the auto biographer is often also in the process of contesting, explicitly or implicitly, what the authority of the 'educated' account has to offer.[61]

Eva's writings are marked by a typically postmodern combination of complicity and critique. On the one hand, Eva adopts a fawningly subordinate position vis-à-vis Perón who has changed her life and provides the foundation for her political vision. Her writing style frequently solidifies under pressure from repeated formulae representing passive acceptance of the pat, the proverbial and the commonsensical. On the other hand, Eva's writings are deeply contestatory, evoking postmodern preoccupations concerning authorship, authority and authenticity. She is aware, in her own way, of the prison house of language but resigns herself to the depthless surfaces of her favourite words. She attempts to force language to say more than it can while being wholly aware of its perplexing limits. Eva 'contaminates' the reflexive deliberation of writing with the unselfconscious immediacy of speech. She claims to be a mere footnote in the history of Peronism but plays the role of dangerous supplement, particularly in *Mi mensaje*. She is a self-proclaimed anti-feminist whose role in affairs of state is boldly feminist. In both her texts she writes at the precarious boundary between life and death and the urgent intensity of her words has implications for the origins of language. She is an unstable subject whose inconsistencies and contradictions provide spectacular proof that the 'I' of written discourse can never signify fixity and self-presence. Eva's multiple personae undermine any belief in the 'deep-down sameness of selves'.[62] Joseph Page makes the seemingly sensible remark that in *Mi mensaje* Eva might have wanted to clarify her place in history for the world to know 'what she considered the truth about the "someone" she had become'.[63] But the self is never wholly formed – even at the point of death. Eva was nothing if not the embodiment of postmodernist repudiation of the essentialist self as static and immoveable: she was consistent only in her resistance to the fixity of 'becoming' someone and she could not possibly make any such declaration.

NOTES

[1] Clive Foss, *Juan and Eva Perón*, Sutton Pocket Bibliographies (Stroud: Sutton, 1999), p. xi.
[2] Eva Perón, *La razón de mi vida* (Buenos Aires: Buró, 1998). Later references, which are to this edition, are given in parenthesis in the text and the title is abbreviated to *La razón*.
[3] Patricia Meyer Spacks, 'Selves in hiding', in Estelle C. Jelinek (ed.), *Women's Autobiography: Essays in Criticism* (Bloomington and London: Indiana University Press, 1980), pp. 112–32 (p. 127).
[4] David William Foster, 'Narrative persona in Eva Perón's *La razón de mi vida*' in *Alternate Voices in the Contemporary Latin American Narrative* (Colombia: University of Missouri, 1985), pp. 45–59 (p. 46).
[5] Dujovne Ortiz, *Eva Perón*, p. 251.
[6] Peter A. Dorsey, *Sacred Estrangement: the Rhetoric of Conversion in Modern American Autobiography* (Pennsylvania: Pennsylvania State University Press, 1993), p. 139.
[7] Beatriz Sarlo, *La pasión y la excepción* (Buenos Aires: Siglo XXI, 2003), p. 26.
[8] Georges Gusdorf, 'Conditions and limits of autobiography' in James Olney (ed.), *Autobiography: Essays Theoretical and Critical* (Princeton: Princeton University Press, 1980), pp. 28–48 (p. 37).

9   Philippe Lejeune, 'The Autobiographical Contract', in Tzvetan Todorov (ed.), *French Literary Theory Today: a Reader*, trans. R. Carter (Cambridge: Cambridge University Press and Paris: Editions de la Maison Des Sciences de L'Homme, 1982), pp. 192–222 (p. 193).
10 'The truth value of autobiography is important [...] Whether or not what is reported can be discredited [...] the autobiographer purports to believe in what he asserts'. Elizabeth Bruss, *Autobiographical Acts, The Changing Situation of a Literary Genre* (Baltimore and London: Johns Hopkins University Press, 1976), pp. 10–11.
11 'At every moment of every true autobiography [...] the author's intention is to convey the sense that "this happened to me", and it is this intention that is always carried through in a way which, I believe, makes the result different from fiction'. Barrett J. Mandel, 'Full of Life Now', in *Autobiography: Essays Theoretical and Critical* (Princeton: Princeton University Press, 1980), pp. 49–72 (p. 53).
12 Vladimir Nabokov, *Nikolay Gogol* (London: Weidenfeld and Nicolson, 1973), p. 119.
13 Susanna Egan, *Patterns of Experience in Autobiography* (Chapel Hill and London: University of North Carolina Press, 1984), pp. 5, 14.
14 Roy Pascal, *Design and Truth in Autobiography* (London: Routledge and Kegan Paul, 1960), p. 195.
15 Michel Foucault, 'Nietzsche, genealogy, history' in *The Foucault Reader*, ed. Paul Rabinow (London: Penguin, 1984), pp. 76–100 (p. 87).
16 Sarlo remarks that Eva's feelings of injustice lay dormant prior to her meeting Perón who 'articula en una trama nítida todos estos impulsos vagos. Les da una razón [...]'. *La pasión y la excepción*, p. 27.
17 Leigh Gilmore, *Autobiographics; a Feminist Theory of Women's Self-Representation*, Reading Women Writing (Ithaca and London: Cornell University Press, 1994), pp. xv, 124.
18 Robert Elbaz, *The Changing Nature of the Self: a Critical Study of Autobiographic Discourse* (London and Sydney: Croom Helm, 1988), p. 153.
19 See Lynn Z. Bloom and Orlee Holder, 'Anaïs Nin's *Diary* in context', in *Women's Autobiography: Essays in Criticism* (Ann Arbor, MI: UMI, 2002; Bloomington and London: Indiana University Press, 1980), pp. 206–20 (p. 217).
20 Suzanne Juhasz, 'Towards a theory of form in feminist autobiography: Kate Millett's *Flying* and *Sita*; Maxine Hong Kingston's *The Woman Warrior*' in Estelle C. Jelinek (ed.), *Women's Autobiography*, pp. 221–37 (p. 224).
21 See Felicity A. Nussbaum, *The Autobiographical Subject: Gender and Ideology in Eighteenth-Century England* (Baltimore and London: The Johns Hopkins University Press, 1989), p. 202 and Estelle C. Jelinek, 'Introduction: Women's Autobiography and the Male Tradition' in *Women's Autobiography*, pp. 1–20 (p. 17).
22 Sylvia Molloy, *At Face Value: Autobiographical Writing in Spanish America*, p. 161.

23 Adolfo Prieto, *La literatura autobiográfica argentina* (Buenos Aires: Jorge Alvarez, 1966), p. 21.
24 Molloy, *At Face Value*, p. 140.
25 Roy Pascal refers to Nietzsche's observation that people forget 'how very much chance, mood, caprice once disposed over them when their profession was decided – and how many parts they might have played'. *Design and Truth in Autobiography* (London: Routledge and Kegan Paul, 1960), p. 15.
26 Eva clearly derives her penchant for definition and dictum from Perón whose *Memorias*, as recounted by Tomás Eloy Martínez, are peppered with such remarks as: 'los tres mentirosos más grandes que hay son [. . .] los curas, las mujeres y las estadísticas'; 'liberarse es fácil. Consolidar esa liberación es lo difícil'. Tomás Eloy Martínez, *Las memorias del General* (Buenos Aires: Planeta, 1996), pp. 46, 56. Further references, given in parenthesis in the text, are to this edition. The abbreviation *Las memorias* is used.
27 Eva's self-effacement is balanced by Perón's self-aggrandizement in *Las memorias del General*. He regards Eva as his creation: 'Eva Perón es un producto mío' (p. 47). He is the one to take care of the big things (p. 51) and she, by implication, of supplementary matters.
28 Foster, 'Narrative persona in Eva Perón's *La razón de mi vida*' in *Alternate Voices*, pp. 45–59 (p. 50).
29 Jonathan Culler, *Literary Theory: a Very Short Introduction* (Oxford and New York: Oxford University Press, 1997), p. 110.
30 Foster remarks that 'the patterns of binary opposition in *La razón de mi vida* between corrupt, artificial culture and innocent, spontaneous nature are extensive'. 'Narrative persona in Eva Perón's *La razón de mi vida*' in *Alternate Voices*, p. 52.
31 Terry Eagleton, *The Ideology of the Aesthetic*, p. 415.
32 Brooks refers to Roman Jakobson's two poles of language: 'metonymy could represent the model of traditional *discourse*, of the spaced, articulated phrase; while metaphor appears here as an effort to collapse spaced, articulated language back into a direct, presented meaning: a meaning made visible' (Brooks, 1976, p. 72). Here we might place Eva's repeated reference to Perón as condor to her sparrow: the trope is powerfully communicative, providing immediate visual impact.
33 In her essay 'Is female to male as ground is to figure?', Barbara Johnson refers to Hofstadter's distinction between two kinds of figures: 'cursively drawable' ones and 'recursive' ones: 'a *cursively drawable* figure is one whose ground is merely an accidental by-product of the drawing act [. . .] A *recursive* figure is one whose ground can be seen as a figure in its own right'. *The Feminist Difference: Literature, Psychoanalysis, Race and Gender* (Cambridge, MA: Harvard University Press, 1998), pp. 17–36 (p. 17). In *La razón* Eva's ostensible purpose is to present herself as the insignificant ground (negative space) which is totally subservient to the figure of Perón (positive space). But what we find here is that Eva is moving almost imperceptibly from ground to figure, from footnote (*La razón*, p. 51) to main

text. Her claim to historical uniqueness as a woman is confirmed by Perón who stated that 'no ha habido en la historia del mundo una mujer como ella. Eva representa una figura nueva en la historia', *Yo, Juan Domingo Perón: relato autobiográfico*, ed. Torcuato Luca de Tena, Luis Calvo and Esteban Peicovich (Barcelona: Planeta, 1976), p. 198. Further references, given in parenthesis in the text, are to this edition. The abbreviation *Yo, JDP* is used.

34. Dujovne Ortiz, *Eva Perón*, p. 254.
35. R. D. Laing, H. Phillipson, and A. R. Lee, *Interpersonal Perception: a Theory and a Method of Research* (London: Tavistock; New York: Springer, 1966), p. 5.
36. Eva Perón, *Mi mensaje* (Buenos Aires: Ediciones del Mundo, 1987).
37. Eva Perón, *Discursos completos*, 3 vols (Buenos Aires: Megafón, 1985–7), II (1986), pp. 351, 374.
38. Leah D. Hewitt points out that 'the use of the third person to refer to the narrating subject makes the reader aware that the autobiographical 'I' is in fact like a disguised third-person, a convention that presents itself as coherence, while masking the heterogeneity of the subject'. *Autobiographical Tightropes* (Lincoln and London: University of Nebraska Press, 1990), p. 225, n. 69.
39. J. M. Taylor, *Evita Perón: the Myths of a Woman*, Pavilion Series in Social Anthropology (Oxford: Blackwell, 1979), p. 89.
40. Patricia Meyer Spacks, 'Selves in hiding' in Estelle C. Jelinek (ed.), *Women's Autobiography*, pp. 112–32 (p. 125).
41. Sarlo, *La pasión y la excepción*, p. 26.
42. Edna Aizenberg, 'Kafkaesque trategy and anti-Peronist ideology: Martínez Estrada's stories as socially symbolic acts', in *Latin American Literary Review* 14 (1986), 11–19 (p. 13).
43. José Luis Romero, *A History of Argentine Political Thought*, trans. Thomas F. McGann (Stanford: Stanford University Press, 1968), p. 249.
44. Daniel James, *Resistance and Integration: Peronism and the Argentine Working Class, 1946–1976*, Cambridge Latin American Studies 64 (Cambridge: Cambridge University Press, 1988), pp. 21, 35.
45. William L. Howarth, 'Some principles of autobiography', in James Olney (ed.), *Autobiography: Essays Theoretical and Critical* (Princeton: Princeton University Press 1980), pp. 84–114 (pp. 88–95).
46. Hélène Cixous, 'Le sexe ou la tête?', quoted by Stephen Heath, 'Difference' in *Screen* 19 (1978), 51–112 (p. 83).
47. Eva Perón, *Discursos completos*, 3 vols (Buenos Aires: Megafón, 1985–7), II (1949–52), p. 388.
48. See chapter 4, pp. 98–99 for further discussion of 'descamisado' as a Peronist word.
49. Hélène Cixous, 'Sorties: Out and out: Attacks/ways out/forays', in Alan D. Schrift (ed.), *The Logic of the Gift. Toward an Ethic of Generosity* (London: Routledge, 1997), pp. 148–73 (p. 168).
50. See Alan D. Schrift, 'Introduction: Why gift?' in *The Logic of the Gift*, pp. 1–22 (pp. 10–12).

[51] Terry Eagleton, *Literary Theory: an Introduction* (Oxford: Blackwell, 1983), p. 178.
[52] See Anthony Grafton, *The Footnote: a Curious History* (London: Faber and Faber, 1997), pp. 15, 235.
[53] *Yo, Juan Domingo Perón: relato autobiográfico*, p. 61.
[54] *Las memorias del General*, p. 62.
[55] Sartre's dictum is quoted by Pascal, *Design and Truth in Autobiography*, p. 14.
[56] Fermín Chávez, 'Introducción' in Eva Perón, *Mi mensaje* (Buenos Aires: Ediciones del Mundo, 1987), pp. 5–11.
[57] Marysa Navarro, *Evita* (Buenos Aires: Corregidor, 1981), p. 6.
[58] Joseph Page, 'Introduction', *Evita: In My Own Words*, trans. Laura Dail (Edinburgh: Mainstream, 1997), pp. 7–55 (p. 35).
[59] Ned Lukacher, 'Introduction', Jacques Derrida, *Cinders*, trans. Ned Lukacher (Lincoln and London: University of Nebraska Press, 1991), p. 2.
[60] Hélène Domon, ' "Black fire on white fire": Kabbalah and modernity' in Philip Leonard (ed.), *Trajectories of Mysticism in Theory and Literature*, Cross-Currents in Religion and Culture (London: Macmillan, 2000), pp. 115–32 (p. 128).
[61] Julia Swindells, 'Introduction', Julia Swindells (ed.), *The Uses of Autobiography* (London: Taylor and Francis, 1995), pp. 1–12 (p. 7).
[62] Leigh Gilmore, *Autobiographics*, p. 82.
[63] Joseph Page, 'Introduction', Eva Perón, *In My Own Words*, trans. by Laura Dail (Edinburgh and London: Mainstream, 1996), pp. 7–55 (p. 49).

Chapter 3

Wounded Bodies and Wounded Writings: The Sexual/Textual Deficiencies of Juan Domingo Perón

Perón's autobiographical writings confirm – like Eva's – Prieto's anticipation of the future of the genre in Argentina as reflecting 'los profundos desgarramientos sufridos en los esquemas de comprensión anteriormente aceptadas'.[1] 'Desgarramiento' corresponds to 'tear' or 'wound' which has rich associations, both literal and metaphorical, in the works of both Perón and Eva. The impact of Perón on the Argentine body politic has been seen by his opponents in terms of a pathology,[2] and of a reopening of an earlier psychological wound inflicted by Juan Manuel de Rosas in the nineteenth century. Prieto's description of Rosas's dual image as a 'genio del mal' and a figure 'con estatura de gigante' (p. 69) could be applied to Perón with equal justification. But it is the terms with which Prieto describes Rosas's impact on the country which is of greater interest here: 'el rosismo provoca un trauma en la conciencia colectiva, con repercusiones que se registran fácilmente hasta medio siglo después de extinguido el régimen político dominado por la figura de Rosas' (p. 71). Several commentators have linked Perón to Rosas: Américo Ghioldi declares that 'Rosas [...] está casi rehabilitado por las enormidades y monstruosidades del presente que lo ha superado en rosinadas'.[3] The military officers who overthrew Perón associated him with Rosas.[4] Both were virulently anti-intellectual and both were demonized in literature, with book-length studies devoted to their impact on the body of Argentine literature.[5] The wound opened by Perón bled most profusely in the years following his death: he can be held at least partly responsible for the period of terror inaugurated after the overthrow of Isabel Perón in 1976.[6]

But Perón sustained as well as inflicted wounds. His deepest personal wound related to his mother. Prieto refers to the importance of the mother figure in Sarmiento, the father often being, by contrast, conspicuous by his absence: 'queda la influencia maternal, cuya figura es exaltada en alguna de las páginas más notables de nuestra literatura' (p. 52). Hanway treats the same theme, noting that in Sarmiento's images of the bodily origins of the nation is inscribed 'a maternal politics of nation, a politics through which women are made responsible for society's ills or virtues. Very influential at the time was Rousseau's conception of women's domestic role as the 'chaste guardians of morals'.[7] Perón made a public show of fondness and admiration for his own mother who played a central role in the household: 'veíamos en ella al jefe de la casa, pero también al médico, al consejero, y al amigo de todos los que tenían alguna necesidad';[8] 'Mamita era muy fuerte, muy criolla'.[9] Peronist rhetoric portrayed the mother as both a suffering figure and a source of nourishment: in his speech of 17 October 1945, Perón said: 'esto es pueblo; esto es el pueblo sufriente que representa el dolor de la madre tierra, el que hemos de reivindicar ... quiero en esta oportunidad [...] estrechar a todos contra mi corazón, como lo podría hacer con mi madre'.[10] As James points out, Perón's identification of his own mother with the poor 'establishes a sentimental identity between himself and his audience'.[11] Peronism was itself the 'great nurturing mother' providing power, protection, security and money.[12] The mother was of fundamental importance, both literally and symbolically, and her rich emotive associations were appropriated by Peronist discourse which also made much of the institution of the family sustained by the presence of the mother. Page notes that Perón 'had a very cold attitude towards his mother, with whom he maintained virtually no contact'.[13] His mother, hardly the traditional 'angel of the house' of nineteenth-century culture, was responsible for many of Perón's psychological wounds. She had borne him out of wedlock, as Tomás Eloy Martínez discovered, but far worse, she had inflicted on her son the worst shock of his adolescent years. Returning home from a hunting expedition, the wounded Juan did not find the chaste and protective mother whom he expected, but rather the mother *in flagrante delicto*, fornicating with a labourer twenty years her junior. Martínez portrays her ironically in *La novela de Perón*, keen to 'heal' her son's bleeding arm while claiming that her lover was merely administering a healing massage (p. 80). Perón himself plays the part of 'simulador', covering up and repressing a deep maternal wound but inevitably betraying a wounded psyche. What Perón states about Ché Guevara could equally well apply to him: 'El Ché era un revolucionario, como nosotros. Lo que no estaba con nosotros era la madre. La madre fue la culpable de todo lo que le pasó al pobre' (*Las memorias del General*, p. 53).[14]

While failing to match the raw intensity of Eva's visceral style, Perón's *Del poder al exilio: cómo y quiénes me derrocaron*, resonates with contained emotions that belie the author's reputed lack of feeling. Written in the immediate aftermath of his overthrow in September 1955, Perón's text deals with recent events, the most traumatic of his political career. Perón had been imprisoned briefly in 1945 but after his ten years in power, personal animosities had hardened and in the light of the popularity and influence he still enjoyed among the working classes, some of those who had replaced him in power, notably Admiral Rojas, were calling for his head. Here Perón looks back from the safety of Colón, Panama, at his removal from office and his departure from Argentina aboard a Paraguayan gunboat. His narrative purports to reflect reality in its full immediacy and the style is fluid, often graphic. Perón's famous charm is reflected to some extent in this writing – seductive, smooth, fluent, measured and exuding an aura of perfect reasonableness. He focuses on both the political circumstances which forced him into exile – as indicated in his title – and also (inevitably) on his personal feelings, often described here with a fluency free of sentimentality. Unlike his edited autobiographical writings – *Yo, Juan Domingo Perón* and *Las memorias del General* – considered later, *Del poder al exilio* is not 'policed' by the interventions of other writers keen to highlight omissions and inconsistencies in their subject's account: this text is not undermined from within by the critical perspectives of others. In tracing the origins of auto/biography, Mamigliano points out that it became a precise notion and acquired a specific designation only in the Hellenistic age: it was named 'bios', a word not reserved exclusively for the life of an individual man but also used for the life of a country.[15] In *Del poder*, Perón's personal fate is closely linked with that of his country. This work is different from Perón's other writings because in it he stages the dramas of his diverse selves. He has just crossed an important border, separating almost unchallenged power from relative powerlessness, separating the continual activity of office from the enforced inactivity of life outside the political maelstrom, separating the deferential service of political subordinates from the relative solitude and dependence on others which is the inevitable consequence of exile. Here, the Perón who has been deprived of all power looks back at the Perón who was gaining power; the Perón whose ideas seem to have run their course, at the Perón who was developing his own political ideology; the Perón who depends on the hospitality of lesser countries, at the Perón who was personally identified with his 'Pueblo' and his 'Patria'. There is little danger, therefore, in seeing Perón's autobiography as a straightforward document unified by the 'I' of its author.[16]

The nature of autobiographical writing has been noted by Molloy in her work on Domingo Faustino Sarmiento (1811–88), president of Argentina from 1868 to 1874. She observes that he was not unaware of the pitfalls of autobiographical writing, but chose not to be inhibited by them:

> the intuition that self portrayal, even in the name of truth, may lead to fabulation, and that the need to call attention to oneself may be synonymous with seduction or with authoritarianism, was only that – an intuition [...]. It is to his merit that, perhaps unsurprisingly, he included those fissures which constitute one of the chief attractions of his texts.[17]

The various fissures evident in *Del poder* also constitute its chief attraction; Perón was probably aware of at least some of them. The main fissure is between the political, defensive, devious Perón and the sensitive, intimate and solitary Perón. The ironic and detached Perón contrasts with the pathetic Perón whose sense of isolation is conveyed succinctly, unsentimentally and often with poetic force. Perón, the defensive and self-justifying politician whose selective memory of events dissembles and reconstructs, stands alongside the Perón whose depth of feeling for Eva is evoked by his sensitive description of her last days, where his well-known horror of intimacy is partially overcome. The title, *Del poder al exilio* is significant: it may seem to indicate a chronological structure – tracing his personal trajectory from presidential power and plenitude to personal impotence and exile – but the text, consisting of two parts, begins not with the exercise of power but with its abrupt rupture, 'el golpe de estado que ha derribado a mi gobierno [. . .]' (p. 3), and the second part, which might be expected to focus on exile, in fact moves back in time to the past, in particular to Eva's death. The text begins with political trauma and ends with personal trauma: the violated body of the democratic state (Perón's government was 'elegido con una mayoría de votos aplastante, después de elecciones claras y libres', p. 3) is mirrored by the tortured body of Eva, both bodies wracked by pain and condemned to imminent death. Perón is the victim in both cases, innocent where Eva is concerned but himself bearing some responsibility for the wounding of the national body, notably by attacking the church, one of its vital organs. Ironically, Eva's posthumous power is facilitated by the religious aura she has assumed – her saintliness ('Santa Evita') and her 'immortality' are sustained by doctrines associated with the Church. Rocca and Kohan remark that the representations of Eva are suffused in Christian beliefs: 'el propio paradigma de la inmortalidad y la resurrección nos ha remitido permanentemente a los mitos cristianos'.[18] As Perón himself states, 'el aspecto político de sus actos se unía a un profundo concepto de solidaridad cristiana' (p. 12). While Eva's 'renunciamiento' was seen by her supporters as her final abandonment of material power and personal ambition, Perón's assault on the Church has been interpreted by some historians as an attempt to concentrate all material power in his own hands.[19]

In his self-defence Perón invokes the wounds inflicted on the Argentine body politic: the will of the people had been violated and the coup financed by 'fuerzas que se agitan dentro y fuera de la Argentina' (p. 3). Their main motivation was greed – to expropriate Argentine oil reserves.[20] Perón accepts no personal responsibility for his downfall, attributing it to a combination of anti-Argentine and foreign Masonic elements which had flouted the principles of legitimacy and democracy. They had targeted Perón because he was a towering presence, an iconic figure with superhuman capabilities: Lucero, the Army minister states that 'nosotros podemos cometer imprudencias, usted no' (p. 8).

Perón's disappearance would signal 'una catástrofe moral y material'. Perón reinforces Lucero's emphasis on his personal importance: 'querían terminar conmigo y para eliminar a un hombre, no vacilaron en matar a quinientos' (p. 9). He goes on to refer to himself in the third person, as though the first person lacked the stature needed to encompass his institutional presence, which goes beyond his individual person (just as Eva's mythic status dwarfed her historical persona): 'entonces [. . .] su objetivo final, era suprimir a Perón para eliminarlo de la lucha y tener así la partida ganada' (p. 9). Such use of the third person also implies self-distance, Perón looking at himself from the perspective of an outsider: 'se ha dicho que Perón en cierto momento de su vida decidió atacar la iglesia para destruirla [. . .]. Perón no soñó jamás en combatir a la religión y a la iglesia' (*Del poder al exilio*, p. 25). His split persona indicates that Perón views his political self as an other: he stands back from the political Perón, acknowledging the divide between the historical personage who exercised real power and the present Perón, a much diminished figure who looks back – as a virtual outsider – at his former self, at a distant 'I'. For Perón there is no unity and identity across time: he implicitly repudiates the myth of a single, coherent, stable and essential self and confirms Renza's observation that the 'I' of autobiography is a de facto third-person pronoun: writing's 'law of gravity' dictates that for the autobiographer, writing about his own existence 'ironically entails a denial of this existence *as* his own and thus as a secure referential source for such writing'.[21]

But Perón is also the informal leader, the president who drives himself to work and responds to the greetings of ordinary people: 'me saludaban y yo respondía al saludo' (p. 9). He is the human leader, benevolent even to his enemies, wishing to avoid bloodshed: 'jamás en la vida he deseado mancharme las manos con sangre' (p. 13). He is, of course, plainly hypocritical: having indulged in acts of repression himself (most recently the closure of the Catholic daily, *El pueblo*), as well as having imprisoned political opponents – many of whom, such as the union leader, Cipriano Reyes, had once lent him staunch support – he now assumes the role of statesman whose integrity must not be compromised whatever the degree of provocation: 'dije que toda represión ilegal nos pondría en un mismo nivel con los rebeldes y que entonces, seríamos juzgados con el mismo desprecio' (p. 11). His condemnation of church burning by his own supporters –

actions that inflicted upon his soul 'profundas heridas que el tiempo y cuanto sucedió después no alcanzaron a cicatrizar' (p. 11) – also sounds hollow in the light of his recent assaults on the Church. In an earlier work, *La fuerza es el derecho de las bestias,* published at the end of 1955, he had attributed this destruction to the righteous anger of the 'pueblo enardecido', driven to violence by the abuses of the clergy, whereas in *Del poder* the perpetrators are 'unos grupos de facinerosos' (p. 11). Perón protests his outrage too much: 'fue hecho execrable, un sacrilegio sin nombre que en ninguna oportunidad he dudado en condenar con las palabras más ásperas' (p. 11). The only responsibility he accepts for the uprising is his failure to deal with the rebels with the severity they deserved, thereby encouraging them to persist with their activities. His defence of government policies towards the Church is taken up in chapter five ('Iglesia y Estado') which argues that the government's quarrel was not with Catholicism but with those priests more interested in politics than in their legitimate ministry. He aligns himself with the majority of sensible Argentines: 'lo que el pueblo quiere es que el poder espiritual no interfiera en las cuestiones políticas' (p. 26). He concludes that an episode which had such dire consequences could have been resolved with minimal effort: 'hubiera bastado una nada para revisar nuestras posiciones [. . .]' (p. 31).

The seat of the rebellion was the Navy which sought to enlist the support of the Air Force: 'donde no llegó la persuasión, llegó el dinero, y el dinero se mostró más fuerte que todas las razones' (p. 14). The Navy is different to the Army, being susceptible to foreign influence which diverts it from national duty (p. 14). It is a semi-detached appendage of the body politic, being 'otra cosa', a potentially dangerous supplement. The rebels operated from outside the country, from Uruguay, where they were allowed to carry out 'un insistente y metódico bombardeo radiofónico' (p. 15). The Navy did not share Perón's horror of bloodshed nor did they subordinate, as he did, personal ambition to the national interest (p. 16).

Perón's letter of resignation to Lucero states his intentions plainly: 'hace algunos días [. . .] decidí ceder el Poder. Las circunstancias que son notorias me lo impidieron. Ahora no seguiré consejos de nadie y doy mi decisión, por lo tanto, el carácter de irrevocable' (p. 17). He does not take this decision lightly because no single man is 'capaz de sustituirnos en el mando' (p. 17). He goes on to declare that history will judge him 'y dirá si he tenido razón en comportarme así' (p. 18). He is overcome by nostalgia but eventually signs the letter: 'había concluido uno de los capítulos más importantes de mi vida' (p. 18). He had conducted himself with dignity, remained in control and commanded respect – 'fui el Jefe legítimo del Estado' (p. 19).

Perón claims that his letter was misinterpreted by the military junta – formed to deal with the crisis – which did not consider it 'como un ofrecimiento sino como una verdadera renuncia' (p. 34). His intention, by contrast, had been to facilitate negotiations with the rebels aimed at avoiding bloodshed. The junta initially accepted his explanation but after meeting later to study the text they decided that their original interpretation of it was correct. For Perón, their action was in itself a kind of rebellion, albeit less radical than what Admiral Rojas would have wished – his elimination at all costs (p. 37).

The irony here is that Perón, who had established the Peronization of Argentina largely through his writings and whose 'doctrina peronista' had become the country's holy grail, elevated to the status of 'doctrina nacional', finally finds that the authority of his writing is challenged. The responsibility for this turn of events is largely his own since his letter appears to confirm – unequivocally – his intention to resign: 'decidí ceder el Poder [...] doy mi decisión, por lo tanto, el carácter de irrevocable' (p. 17). But Perón then proceeds to misinterpret his own text, claiming that the offer rather than the fact of his resignation was intended. The generals finally dismissed his clarification, opting for textual rather than authorial evidence with the consequence that what Perón had written prevailed over what he had – purportedly – intended. Perón is already experiencing the uncertainty of exile, where all sense of solidity and anchorage is lost. He finds himself in limbo between the written and the spoken word, unable to impose his will. It is this disjunction between what he had previously written and what he now says which leads to his exile, an exile experienced as an uncertain state of mind even before he leaves the *patria* with which he was once virtually synonymous. His world is turned upside down: Perón's word, which once drew the applause of the masses, is now ignored and Perón, who had previously dispensed favours, is now obliged to request favours of others, ranging from the Paraguayan ambassador (p. 37) to the boy asleep at the wheel of a stationary bus who is asked to help with his broken down car (p. 39). His fall is traumatic, the wound sustained being as deep as it is sudden: in just a few moments Perón loses his authority and status, re-experiencing in the political sphere a trauma akin to that occasioned during his adolescence by his mother's promiscuity. While he is still the acknowledged leader who can impose himself on his subordinates when he meets with the generals to clarify their 'mistake' – 'nos ubicamos alrededor de una mesa grande y tomé de inmediato la palabra' (p. 35) – his loss of status becomes apparent through the less than deferential attitude of the Paraguayan ambassador: 'el Embajador asintió con la cabeza y me cortó la palabra' (p. 38). The abruptness of his changed circumstances has an air of unreality enhanced by the climate: once so generous in providing fine and clear 'Peronist' days, it now seems intent on providing a backdrop to accord with his fall from grace: 'en aquella atmósfera borrosa de lluvia y de niebla todo parecía irreal' (p. 38). Perón himself, once a dominant and charismatic presence, is transformed into an incidental, spectral figure: one of the generals, Manni, 'me miraba como a un fantasma. Parecía que me estuviese viendo ya muerto o que estuviese hablando con mi espectro' (p. 36). This image of the spectral Perón suggests his transitional status: an in-between figure who is neither here nor there. Dispossessed and diminished, Perón's exile begins while he is still physically in the *patria*: 'desde hacía cinco horas, no obstante estar todavía en la Argentina, había comenzado mi exilio' (p. 39). But while the political persona of Perón is diminished, his human capacity for emotion, long displaced by an aura of frigidity and detachment, stirs again in a new Perón who is vulnerable and sensitive. The previously anaesthetized and passionless Perón is flooded with nostalgia: 'esa residencia no era mi casa, pero quedaban entre sus muros muchos recuerdos de años que parecían lejanos y se diría que relegados a la prehistoria' (p. 38). Kaminsky notes that nothing is firm in exile: 'its spatial instability turns out to be only one form of uncertainty'.[22] Perón's uncertainty seems to occupy every corner of his mental space: even his memories have an impossible remoteness (p. 38). His sense of rupture is expressed explicitly when his assistant, Major Máximo Renner, turns down his invitation to join him in exile: 'no insistí. Lo vi descender y alejarse. El rumor del automóvil lo sentí dentro como un desgarrón' (p. 40).

Perón's sense of emptiness aboard the gunboat is profanely filled by false rumours of female visitors: 'dijeron que Perón vivía en un harem [...]. En el exilio me esperaba una vida de maharaja (pp. 42–3). The tripartite structure of Perón's metamorphosis inverts Eva's: while hers traced a line of ascent culminating in an apex of mythical power, his trajectory is one of decline, from power to solitude to target of gossip. The all-powerful Perón, surrounded by faithful devotees, has become the abandoned, friendless Perón whose plight mirrors that of his country, exposed and vulnerable, in limbo between the fall of one regime and the rise of its successor. The Perón who had maintained his youthful mien well into his fifties now finds himself, without warning, at the threshold of old age: 'sobre mis espaldas se habían acumulado de improviso tantos años que temía no poder soportar ese peso' (p. 40).

The second part of *Del poder al exilio* does not move forward in time to Perón's arrival in Uruguay and the recovery of some form of normality. Rather, the narrative ends in irresolution and in-betweenness, in uncertainty and flux. Perón looks for stability not to the future but to what now seems to him to be a prehistoric past, his meeting with Eva, facilitated by natural disaster, the San Juan earthquake (which resonates ironically in the reference to Córdoba as the 'epicentro de la sublevación' p. 33), a time when he stood at a very different threshold: of power rather than of exile. Far from describing her as his personal creation, Perón now acknowledges Eva's crucial contribution to his movement as he recalls 'una mujer joven, de aspecto frágil pero de voz resuelta, de cabellos rubios que dejaba caer sobre su espalda, y de ojos afiebrados' (p. 46). Here Perón demonstrates how autobiography approximates to fiction through the writer's failure of memory, which is decidedly not the faithful replicating mechanism it is often assumed to be by the autobiographer: Eva was still a natural brunette rather than an artificial blonde at that time. His decline and fall is now overshadowed by memories of Perón as Minister of Employment, the rising political star capable of decisive action: 'para socorrer a la población de San Juan movilicé al país entero. Hice participar en colectas a hombres y mujeres [...]' (p. 46). His ambitions went beyond the remedy of one disaster: he looked to provide a new beginning for Argentina, amply supported by his new companion, 'una mujer excepcional', whose ardour matched that of the early Christians (p. 47). Although he underwent a kind of internal exile at the outset of his career, he was able then to count on the dynamism of Eva who 'puso una carga explosiva en el espíritu de la Nación' (p. 48), forcing the government to bring him back to Buenos Aires to address the crowds who had gathered in his support outside the Casa Rosada.

The present contrasts with the glorious past in every respect: the decisive presence of Eva has been removed from the fray (even though she survives as a mythic heroine); the ardent crowds of 1945 fail to stir in 1955; and Perón who was previously enjoined to speak, is now warned not to make any statement. His political reminiscences continue to throw up contrasts with the present: the pomp of Eva's departure to Europe contrasts with the furtive and humiliating circumstances of Perón's forced exit. Whereas once he could divert the Argentine fleet to Italian ports (p. 51), he is now under the control of others aboard a Paraguayan gunboat. The Perón who in 1947 enjoyed favoured status in the Vatican ('un hijo predilecto', p. 52) is seen as an enemy of the Church in 1955.

The deposed Perón finds solace in a triumphant past which includes Eva's death as well as her life. Perón's text offers a brief and moving account of her death, the interval between her European tour and her illness being elided: 'por dos años todavía, Evita vivió feliz, dedicándose enteramente a sus pobres' (p. 52). Perón's style seems matter-of-fact ('los primeros síntomas de la enfermedad se manifestaron hacia fines de 1949', p. 52) but its concentrated terseness conveys effectively the suddenness and irreversibility of Eva's decline: 'Eva se quedaba sin sangre, sin aliento. Estaba blanca y demacrada. Sólo le quedaban nervios y voluntad [. . .] El mal le devoraba sin piedad' (p. 52). The natural world, which now seems to echo the abruptness of Perón's overthrow, had previously lamented the passing of Eva: 'un viento despiadado sacudía los árboles. El cielo tenía el color de un sudario y estaba cargado de lluvia' (p. 54).

Perón now turns to the embalmer, Dr Ara, whose work fascinates him: 'casi podría decirse que el doctor Ara llega a encerrar en el rostro de los muertos aquel último soplo de vida al que ellos tratan desesperadamente de aferrarse' (p. 55). Perón's current plight heightens his sensibilities, giving him a poetic insight into human resistance to death, mirroring his own refusal to accept political death: 'dije hasta luego a la Argentina, no adiós' (p. 45);

'comenzó entonces mi odisea política que duró diez años y de la cual el exilio en Colón es solamente una etapa, no la conclusión' (p. 48).

Perón's attitude to Eva appears to be ambivalent. There is certainly a detached and casual tone to his reminiscences which appear to confirm his reputed coldness and frigidity: 'yo fui tres veces a ver a Evita [...] No sé qué ha sido del cadáver de Evita' (p. 56). His emotions may be suppressed but he highlights the physical sensations produced by these visits: 'delante de la puerta sentí un extraño sudor descenderme de la espalda, el rumor de la llave que giraba en el picaporte llegaba a parecerme un llanto' (p. 56). Ara reassures him as he holds back from touching Eva: 'no tema. Está tan intacta como cuando estaba viva' (p. 56). The barrier between life and death can be overcome: Perón may appear to be a political corpse but resuscitation remains a possibility. Perón finally compares – unfavourably – his own situation with Eva's: she may be dead but at least she is in her own country while he is removed from it (p. 56). Perón was, of course, wrong in his assumption that Eva would remain in her own country since her corpse was to be removed to Italy, but his observation, though inaccurate, lends additional poignance to his own plight. Perón has engaged in a kind of 'writing cure', a term first used by Sturrock in relation to Michel Leiris who turned to the practice of autobiography hoping to find therein a writing cure when the fashionable 'talking cure' failed him. Sturrock observes that Leiris writes 'out of a harrowing sense of insufficiency, of a lack which a certain practice of autobiography can alone make good'.[23] If Perón turned to the practice of autobiography for a similar writing cure then it was to address unfinished business, not just relating to his political project but to his personal life and in particular his relationship with Eva, now (seemingly) given a form of closure through writing. Perón also writes from a positon of powerlessness: autobiography has been seen as the preferred medium of the powerless.[24]

In his book, *Eva Perón: la verdadera historia contada por el médico que preservó su cuerpo*,[25] written between 1956 and 1960, Pedro Ara says nothing about the relationship between Eva and Perón, but refers the reader to Perón's *Del poder al exilio*. The sparse, polished prose of this text gives little away but it does communicate – indirectly – depths of feeling which Perón could not attempt to put into words. While Eva's writing is given to hyperbole and excess, Perón's is sparing and reticent but also suggestive. His spirit is almost broken but his writing appears to display strength and clarity, openness and candour, closure and constraint. It begins with international issues and Perón's fall but it culminates with Eva, diverting attention from the normally egotistical Perón and inverting his customary scale of values by elevating the personal over the political. Perón's imminent exile will open up another wound. As Kaminsky points out, exile has long been associated with a physical wound: 'the first moment of exile, when one is exiled, becomes an exile, is a moment of trauma. The subject's forced break from the homeland is quite literally a physical rupture. The first description in the Hispanic literary tradition of this initial moment of political exile [. . .] tropes exile as a physical injury that recalls classic torture'.[26] Through writing, Perón is able to treat the wound, to reconcile himself with his past and to achieve a kind of desultory tranquillity, the psychological counterpart of Eva's broken handwriting 'irregular, incierta y fatigosa' (p. 56), significantly the last reference in the text.

The fissures of *Del poder al exilio* deserve further investigation because they illuminate critical theory relating to autobiographical writing. In his obsession with self-validation, Perón is implicitly promising the reader to tell the whole truth: his narrative is punctuated with references to the truth, the epithet 'verdadero' being used to unveil the real nature of his opponents: 'se trata de una verdadera traición' (p. 3); 'mis adversarios [. . .] iniciaron una verdadera campaña de escándalo' (p. 22). Philippe Lejeune claims that biography and autobiography are referential texts whose goal is not mere 'vraisemblance' but 'resemblance to the truth. Not the "reality effect" ("l'effet de reel") but the image of reality'.[27] Elbaz indicates that the myth which underlies this position is that '"reality" is a homogenous, consistent and continuous entity which language, the literary text, describes through its pure transparency'.[28] Perón, as might be expected, shares Lejeune's assumptions, being oblivious to the problematical nature of reality and of language. For Perón the truth – readily distinguishable from fiction – springs uncontaminated from his memory to be transcribed perfectly on the printed page. According to his account it is he who is the legitimate ruler, the 'Jefe legítimo del Estado' (p. 19), who was elected democratically with an overwhelming majority (p. 3.). His opponents are illegitimate since they do not represent the will of the majority. Thus legitimacy and illegitimacy are the basis of a Manichean divide whose opposing poles are represented by Perón on the one hand and by his adversaries on the other. Perón respects life and is self-sacrificing: although he could legitimately eliminate enemies of the state, he chooses to exercise restraint rather than justice. His enemies are not constrained by similar scruples (p. 13) and, far from being selfless like Perón, are motivated by the prospect of material gain (p. 14). Perón represents the inside of the country, the *corazón* of the *patria*, whereas the Masons represent foreign interests and the Navy, unlike the Army, is contaminated by its contact with the outside world (p. 14).[29] His regime and his doctrine both speak of permanence ('la doctrina de mi Partido tenía y tiene un carácter permanente', p. 16) while the uprising represents 'sólo un momento, un incidente fortuito' (p. 16): Perón's immediate successor, Eduardo Lonardi, lasted just a month in power (p. 27). Perón stands for calm, his opponents for violence. Whereas Perón is candid, Aramburu is devious, pretending not to have received Perón's telegram about the fate of Eva's corpse (p. 22). Gifts received legitimately in his presidential capacity are paraded by his enemies as the bounty of 'un Perón ladrón' (p. 23). While he is saddened by the plight of his country, his enemies make light of the tragedy by turning it into a theatrical performance. While Admiral Rojas, who would assume the mask of the Argentine General Grant, represents 'la sombra de la mediocridad' (p. 16), Perón by implication, basks in the light of genuine greatness, having no possible need to emulate anyone.

Perón stands for truth and legitimacy; his enemies for falsification and play. But all autobiographers have a mask – as De Man has observed[30] – and Perón creates a mask of candour and self-sacrifice: the self-proclaimed Catholic with his devotional objects, a miniature of the Virgin of Luján and a portrait of Eva, seeks to cover up his recent image as an implacable and aggressive adversary of the Church.

It may not be coincidental that Perón's new mask is disfigured by episodes in which sexuality, in different guises, cannot be suppressed. Part of the explanation lies perhaps in that old maternal wound that refuses to close. The law authorizing divorce and legalizing prostitution is not adequately explained by Perón's appeal to foreign experience (pp. 30–1), particularly since he had previously implied that his own points of reference were internal. More damaging, however, is his cursory reference to his teenage lover whom he dismisses as 'aquella Nélida Rivas', just another of the girls belonging to the 'Unión de Estudiantes Secundarios' who used the grounds of his Olivos residence for their sporting activities (p. 22). He returns to this repressed episode later (pp. 41–2), claiming that the occasions when he indulged his innocent interest in 'los estudiantes y los hijos de obreros [. . .] fueron los más hermosos de mi vida' (p. 42). Apart from the gender slippage which points to duplicity, this declaration seems to cast doubt on the sincerity of his subsequent expressions of perfect spiritual consonance with Eva: 'pensábamos al unísono, con el mismo cerebro, sentíamos con una misma alma' (pp. 48–9). More importantly, it fails to cover up an illegitimate sexual interest on the part of a writer who is claiming a virtual monopoly on legitimacy. Goldar notes that in H. A. Murena's *El coronel de caballería*, a sordid Perón emerges when his mask is removed.[31] Here the reference to Nélida Rivas has a similar effect, marking the point where the mask slips. But to compound the damage to his would-be image as a self-consistent, unified individual, Perón slips into the third person to denote an institutional Perón whom he seems to observe from the outside, almost like a historian seeking to justify the actions of a now dead historical personage: 'Perón no soñó jamás en combatir a la religión y la Iglesia [. . .]' (p. 25).

Perón seeks finality but the self created in language can never be a finished product. His failure to impose the meaning he intended on his own writing can be taken as a metafictional element pointing to the illusory humanist notion of autobiography as a truth-telling exercise based on the transparency of language and the attainability of coherence and authenticity. His experience contradicts the belief that the self controls the effects of language and is the shaping agent of representation and confirms Gilmore's critique of Olney's 'language of presence'.[32] As De Man puts it: 'the interest of autobiography, then, is not that it reveals reliable self-knowledge – it does not – but that it demonstrates in a striking way the impossibility of closure and of totalization [. . .] of all textual systems made up of tropological substitutions'.[33] Perón's tropological substitutions are easy to overlook since he gives a good impression of limiting himself to the 'bare' facts. But his arguments often depend on mere affirmation: thus he responds to his enemies who seek to take advantage of the attacks on Church property carried out, according to Perón by 'algunos grupos de facinerosos' (p. 11): 'fueron ellos los que al informar al Vaticano, evitaron de exprofeso, exponer en su cruda realidad, la verdadera razón de nuestro conflicto' (p. 12). Gilmore refers to the 'metaphorical resonance of *reality*, a metaphor that functions as a trope of truth beyond argument, of identity beyond proof, of what simply is'.[34] In composing this text Perón may have sought a kind of writing cure but its healing properties are illusory: the slipperiness of language denies Perón the fixity he craves (and partly finds in cliché and epigram) since it exceeds his intentions, refusing to be pinned down. Perón's final wound is linguistic: seeking to use and manipulate language to reflect his self-validating purposes, he finds himself caught up in its perpetual motion: ultimately his loss of political control is not cured by his writing but only mirrored by his floundering efforts to staunch its seductive and disarming flow. The tensions and inconsistencies of *Del poder al exilio* illustrate Gilmore's concept of autobiographics that refers to 'those changing elements of the contradictory discourses and practices of truth and identity which represent the subject of autobiography'.[35]

It is not only with the slipperiness of language with which Perón has to contend in *Yo, Juan Domingo Perón: relato autobiográfico* and *Las memorias del General*.[36] Like Eva's writings which bear the imprint of male manipulation, ranging from the minor corrections to *Mi mensaje* carried out by Perón, to Penella de Silva's ghostwriting of *La razón*, these texts, nominally belonging to Perón, are heavily inscribed by the intervention of others. Both are transcriptions of extended tape recordings. Perón's words, occupying sixty cassettes are assembled by three editors in the case of the first work while in the more compact 'Las memorias de Puerto de Hierro' which forms the first part of *Las memorias del General*, Tomás Eloy Martínez employs a range of typographical devices to identify the diverse voices which populate the text. The recordings upon which both texts are based were made while Perón was living in exile in Madrid (1960–73).

In both *Yo, Juan Domingo Perón* and in *Las memorias del General*, Perón emerges in a mainly negative light, largely owing to the interventions of the editors of both works. But few of his 'uncontaminated' memoirs serve to enhance his reputation. It is true that he appears to have a strong sense of justice – instilled in him by his father who was sympathetic to the Indians ('nosotros los llamamos ahora indios ladrones y nos olvidamos que somos nosotros quienes les hemos robado todo a ellos', *Las memorias del General*, p. 26). His sense of natural justice underpins Perón's concept of patriotism which he expresses with a stylistic elaboration reminiscent of Eva's *La razón de mi vida*: 'comencé entonces a concebir el patriotismo no como amor a la tierra de nuestros mayores, ni a sus riquezas, ni a sus ciudades o sus pueblos, sino a nuestros hermanos argentinos, que son los que más merecen y necesitan' (*Las memorias*, pp. 35–6). Perón certainly gives an impression of competence when he discusses economic policy (*Yo, JDP*, pp. 209–10; *Las memorias*, p. 67) and of well-honed man-management skills. His warm tribute to Miguel Miranda, his economics minister – 'era inteligente, capaz y de buena voluntad' (*Las memorias*, p. 45) – is notable because Perón rarely praised anyone (his only public praise for Eva came when she was already dying) but he was fully aware of the limits of Miranda's usefulness which did not extend to the implementation of the second five year plan (*Yo, JDP*, p. 209). Unsurprisingly, the ever-intractable Perón emerges as both a natural leader and manipulator, with an instinct for sound government and also as a shallow and vulnerable figure, displaying signs of poor judgement and eccentricity. Thus his gratitude to Rafael Trujillo, the Dominican dictator, for his hospitality following Perón's overthrow, clearly clouds his judgement as he defends Trujillo's pampered son: 'qué tiene de particular que en esas condiciones privilegiadas el muchacho regale un automóvil a una artista de cinematografía?' (*Yo, JDP*, p. 263). His eccentricity emerges when he describes his fondness for gardening during his long period of exile in Madrid: 'no dejo un día sin visitar cada árbol. Lo converso un poco, ¿sabe?' (*Yo, JDP*, p. 272). Here it may well be that Perón is indulging in self-irony, distancing himself from himself – as he does explicitly in *Del poder al exilio* (see above, p. 71) – just as he distanced himself from most other people.

Perón's avoidance of any artificial construction of a unified self may reflect his general horror of intimacy, both with himself and with others. While he assumes a donjuanesque persona in relating – sparingly – his liaison in Berlin with 'una alemanita lindísima de esas que parecen hechas con huevo y harina' (*Yo, JDP*, p. 101), his normal practice, evident in both interviews and writings, is to avoid such topics: he is reticent not only about his first wife, Potota, but also about Eva. As Martínez remarks in his prologue to *Las memorias*: 'esquivaba cuidadosamente las historias que aludían a su intimidad o a su vida sentimental' (p. 12). This aspect of Perón might point to a longstanding secretiveness about his private and personal relationships (he refused to speak about his mother's marital infidelities) but it might also be related to his candid subordination of sentiment and passion to politics, the sacrifice of personal feelings to total commitment to the collective good: 'en lo económico, la misión fundamental de todo gobierno es dar posibilidad a la gente de que se realice. Para eso hace falta grandeza, olvido de las pasiones' (*Las memorias*, p. 55). Perón's reference here to the suppression of passions is, of course, ironic in the light of his reckless submission to deviant, if not perverted, passions following Eva's death when he formed an improper relationship with the adolescent Nelly Rivas. But apart from its irony, his reference to passions may be seen as an indirect criticism of Eva since she was nothing if not a passionate supporter of Peronism. Perón's explicit privileging of politics over love goes counter to Eva's own insistence on the priority of love in *La razón de mi vida*: 'aquí tal vez sea conveniente que den vuelta la página quienes piensan que entre Perón y yo pudo darse un "matrimonio político" [. . .] Nos casamos porque nos quisimos [. . .]' (p. 34). Perón, by contrast, emphasizes the political aspect of their relationship: 'el romance de nuestra luna de miel fue la política. Y empecé entonces a preparar mis planes de gobierno [. . .]' (*Yo, JDP*, p. 80).[37] Significantly, Eva refers in *La razón* to a glaring omission in Perón's letters: 'busqué con afán en todas sus cartas, una palabra que me dijese su amor' (p. 25). Finding none, Eva seeks to 'cover up' the wound inflicted by Perón's omission by focusing on the word with the highest frequency of use in his letters, 'trabajadores', and converting it into an indirect expression of his love for her (p. 26). None the less Perón's cold, wounding arrogance is most intrusive in his references to her. Although he acknowledges that she represented 'una figura nueva en la historia' (*Yo, JDP*, p. 198), he pointedly claims ownership not only of her ideas ('ella fue una formidable impulsora de ideas que me eran propias' *Yo, JDP*, p. 55) but of her professional identity, designed and packaged by him to undertake a specific task: 'Eva Perón era un producto mío [. . .] La necesitaba en el sector social de mi conducción' (*Las memorias*, p. 47). But Perón fails to acknowledge his debts to Eva: while he drew upon her emotional and human capital while she was alive, so after her death he draws on the financial capital generated by her book, *La razón de mi vida*, which provided a much-needed source of income after his removal from office in September 1955.

Perón clung to a core of idealism in recounting his political past: 'Yo siempre fui un revolucionario, hasta un poco anarquista' (*Yo, JDP*, p. 45). Such apparent candour may endear Perón to some readers despite the dubiousness of the sentiment expressed (during his third presidency, when the notorious José López Rega established his power, Perón repudiated the militant leftist tendencies within his movement that he had previously encouraged). His prescience in 1941 in predicting the German defeat deserves acknowledgement together with his occasionally principled decisions, such as his rejection of help from a representative of the oligarchy (Patrón Costas) when he first entered government: 'es que sabía lo que le pasó a Fausto con el diablo' (*Yo, JDP*, p. 46). But his pragmatism often gives way to plain cynicism. He claims that the political leader could not rely exclusively on 'los buenos' (*Yo, JDP*, p. 43); but the depth of his cynicism seems to call their very existence into question. He does little to conceal his complete absence of faith in human capacity for disinterested action: 'de lo económico proviene lo afectivo, porque la víscera más sensible del hombre es el bolsillo, no el corazón' (*Las memorias*, p. 66). One of the most frequently used words in Evita's speeches and writings was, precisely, 'corazón' which represented, for her, bodily intimacy and passion far removed from self-interested materialism. Indeed, Eva would have been appalled and wounded by the depth of Perón's cynicism as revealed by his belief that 'el hombre es un bicho malo y mentiroso' (*Yo, JDP*, p. 190). Here he is referring to mankind in general but elsewhere his bitterness, sharpened by his removal from office in 1955, is directed at his fellow Argentines as he gloats over their wounds: 'allí está ahora [el pueblo argentino] hambriento, desesperado. Es la suerte que merece' (p. 231). It is possible that Perón later took revenge for this grievance by facilitating the succession of his third wife, Isabel, who was hopelessly unsuited for presidential office, as Perón himself must have been aware. In the light of the tragic events which followed, his advocacy of his own 'revolución humana' (*Yo, JDP*, p. 276) as a universal standard seems ironic: 'será un sistema que dará plena felicidad a todos los hombres, mujeres y niños de nuestro pueblo' (*Yo, JDP*, p. 276). The abuses of the Peronist administrations (1946–55), notably torture and imprisonment, provided a foretaste of what was to happen later on a much larger scale. Perón's threatened violence against the dissident union leader, Luis Gay, ('mire, renuncie ya, porque si no mañana le rompo la cabeza', *Yo, JDP*, p. 188) can be seen as a mild though ominous token of what would become an institutionalized aspect of Argentine life involving a degree of terror which Perón himself could not have imagined: the serious though small-scale wounds which he himself inflicted on the body politic became the grotesque mutilations which disfigured and defaced the country under military rule.

Perón's style is marked by the epigrammatic and proverbial. His mode of argumentation often comprises little more than direct appeal to folk wisdom whose visual imagery and common-sensical force are often surprisingly difficult to counter and resist. Thus to those who objected to his plans to unite and politicize the unions, claiming that it would be a very long process, Perón replied that 'un loro, de maíz en maíz, se comió un maizal' (*Yo, JDP*, p. 44). Here Perón adopts the persona of the ordinary man of the people endowed with an earthy rural wisdom. He characterizes people sharply and succinctly by his use of popular sayings that have immediate and universal impact. Thus Jaime Yankelevich of Radio Belgrano is characterized as a mean and grasping individual: 'si podía le metía a uno la mano en el bolsillo y le robaba los fósforos' (*Yo, JDP*, p. 174). Perón also possesses a large stock of political and other aphorisms which had the virtue of making an immediate, if not lasting, impression: 'el gobierno es para el hombre, y no el hombre para el gobierno' (*Las memorias*, p. 37); 'librarse es fácil. Consolidar esa liberación es lo difícil' (*Las memorias*, p. 56); 'en política del error se vuelve, pero del ridículo no se puede volver' (*Las memorias*, p. 61). Such lapidary statements may have some residual validity despite pointing to an oratorical style predisposed towards cliché, categorization and, occasionally, patriarchal condescension: 'en la mujer hay que despertar las dos fuerzas extraordinarias que son la base de su intuición: la sensibilidad y la imaginación' (*Las memorias*, p. 48). It is unsurprising that such a proclivity towards definition should frequently descend to facile generalization: 'los tres mentirosos más grandes que hay son, como se dice, los curas, las mujeres, y las estadísticas' (*Las memorias*, p. 46). But, even here,

Perón is inconsistent: while his own discourse is peppered with tendentious cliché, he highlights the empty rhetoric of such terms as 'mundo libre' when applied to the United States and demonstrates his capacity for striking and original expression in denouncing Argentina and Brazil as 'dos «democracias» pentagonianas' (*Yo, JDP*, p. 275) and in proclaiming his physical distaste for the American people ('los americanos me producen alergia', *Yo, JDP*, p. 260). He displays his well-known capacity for flouting political protocol, by, for example, colluding with Eva's scandalously insulting behaviour towards government ministers. His speech is equally unbecoming, tainted by an open proclivity towards the disreputable registers of the 'low other': he takes pride in his use of *lunfardo* ('me gusta hablar así: yo me crié en lunfardo',*Yo, JDP*, p. 270) and seeks to resurrect phrases that have fallen into disuse – he applies the rural term for treachery, 'chirinada', to Benjamín Menéndez's abortive coup attempt of 28 September 1951, suggesting thereby that it was an isolated incident, not to be taken seriously. He makes effective use of wordplay to express his contempt for Prince Bernhardt (whom Eva admired): 'ni siquiera me contestó, con lo cual dejó bien sentado que era un príncipe «con-suerte» más que «con sorte»' (*Yo, JDP*, p. 238). Here again he differs from Eva who was wary of linguistic 'slippage' (*La razón*, p. 108) and more sensitive to the negative aspects of cliché (*La razón*, p. 15).

It is ironic that Perón, with his horror of intimacy and his urge to control both his private and public personae, should suffer the indignity of having his autobiography subverted by blatant editorial interference. Perón had not wanted to supplement his memoirs as published in the periodical *Panorama* in April 1970 – upon which he conferred official status as his 'memorias canónicas' (*Las memorias*, p. 12) – but Tomás Eloy Martínez flaunts his violation of Perón's instructions by an equivocal observation reminiscent of Perón himself: 'este libro respeta y al mismo tiempo se subleva contra esa voluntad' (p. 14). Martínez is not the only one to exercise editorial control over Perón's memoirs: in *Las memorias del General*, López Rega plays a key role, blatantly usurping Perón's position and acting as though his own identity and his master's were interchangeable (perhaps attempting to compensate for his failure to infuse Isabel with the spirit of Eva by engaging in a parallel operation involving himself and Perón). Like Martínez, the editorial triumvirate of *Yo, JDP* (Torcuato Luca de Tena, Luis Calvo and Esteban Peicovich) seek to leave their own imprint upon Perón's writings but often adopt a more positive approach: they comment, for example, on what they see as Perón's masterful depiction of Miguel Miranda, referring to 'el enorme interés humano de esta semblanza que con mano maestra traza Perón de uno de sus más importantes colaboradores' (p. 181). They also intervene – superfluously – to clarify Perón's use of the affectionate diminutive, 'Isabelita', to refer to his third wife ('sigue llamando a doña María Estela Martínez con el nombre que utilizaba en Panamá: Isabelita', p. 259). They sometimes adopt a psychobiographical tone (as well as an overelaborate style) to 'explain' Perón's indulgent attitude towards the dictator of the Dominican Republic, Rafael Trujillo: 'y es probablemente esta gratitud la que le mueve, más que a no escatimar, a derrochar elogios a favor de tan discutida figura' (p. 259). Their approach to Perón is often reductive, seeking to fit him into a familiar pattern: according to them he repeats the trajectory of many Latin Americans 'a quienes la lucha política sudamericana empuja en algún momento hacia Europa en busca del dorado, aunque triste final' (p. 269).

Like Martínez they seek to remedy their subject's omissions and half-truths but their procedure is less systematic: thus while they indicate that Perón's mother was Indian, something which Perón in his otherwise meticulously detailed genealogical disquisition fails to mention, they overlook the more significant fact relating to the mother, namely her illicit affair which left a permanent wound on Perón. In fact, many dubious claims made by Perón go unchallenged, for example, his meeting with Mussolini (p. 25), his flimsy self-defence relating to the closure of *La Prensa* (pp. 151–2) and his denial of all personal responsibility in the Bemberg case (pp. 156–7).[38] Neither is Perón's attribution to Eva of a pivotal role in rallying support for him on 17 October 1945 (p. 64) called into question. The editors' obsessive concern with the legitimacy of their sources – 'la autenticidad de estas grabaciones es evidente [. . .]' (p. 11) – is somewhat ironic given their substantial editorial manipulation of their raw materials which would, they claim, have been unintelligible 'sin una previa labor de selección, supresión de repeticiones, ordenación de temas y comprobación de cronologías' (p. 12). They have domesticated Perón's stream of consciousness recollections and suppressed historical errors attributable to failures of memory, clearly compromising the 'authentic' Perón by rendering him all too accessible and comprehensible. Indeed, they are attempting to recuperate a foundational autobiographical discourse, coherent, self-consistent and guaranteed by a single, unified self. They implicity repudiate Roland Barthes's counter-project of 'free-wheeling in language', echoed in the unstructured musings of the Perón who emerges in Tomás Eloy Martínez's *La novela de Perón* as an exemplar of anti-autobiography, with no interest in restoring the 'real' Perón, but rather eschewing mimesis of any kind in favour of a textual freedom configured as an openly aggressive effort to dominate history. In that text, Perón will not be bound to a single version of events but will blow in all directions, 'como el gallo de la veleta' (p. 168). This Perón, who resists López Rega's plea for stable meaning, is reminiscent of Barthes for whom 'the most "meaningful" discourse is discourse which does not allow itself to be "caught", but which "rustles" with different meanings, with a *frisson* or excitation which moves language away from definitive forms, from signs "grimly weighed" by signifieds'.[39] Eakin remarks that Barthes, in displacing 'truth' by 'abolition' as the central dynamic of engagement in self-reference, inflicts a bold stroke (we might prefer 'wound') in the history of a genre 'whose practitioners and critics from Rousseau to Roy Pascal have always accorded the central place to truth, however variously defined'.[40] Perón's equivocations and linguistic incoherencies insult the normal editorial standards of truth, order and clarity. The editors of *Yo, JDP* grasp at the straw of an essential self concealed beneath the quicksand of Perón's intractable mode of being. They assume the role of analysts and historians, not only summarizing the significance of 17 October and Perón's performance but also assuming a condescending attitude towards their subject whom they describe as 'nuestro biografiado' (p. 71), thrusting themselves into the foreground at the expense of the nominal autobiographer of the title. They claim that the tapes do not possess the authority that a written account would – though in Tomás Eloy Martínez's experience the opposite is the case since Perón is able to make changes to the written record but is unable to tamper with the taped recording (Perón had claimed on tape to have saved Ché Guevara but, when questioned about this episode by Martínez, simply crossed out the reference in the text based on the tapes: 'el relato sobrevivió sin embargo en las cintas grabadas, de donde se transcriben ahora textualmente' (*Las memorias*, p. 53, note). Here the usual relationship between the oral and the written is inverted since it is the oral which proves to be the authoritative record and the written less rigid and susceptible to erasure.

The editors of *Yo, JDP* have straitjacketed their subject who has exercised too much freedom for their liking: they come back to this point midway through the text, noting that while Perón's account is marked by freshness and spontaneity, 'adolece de la falta de rigor de quien está improvisando' (p. 111). Thus Perón's freewheeling style of recollection, with major themes displaced by minor ones ('convierte en tema principal el que nació en su memoria como secundario', p. 185) is a source of irritation to their logical minds. Perón's procedure contrasts with that of the traditional autobiographer who typically creates an organizing principle that imposes order on an anarchic set of events. The editors take it upon themselves to create such an order, so violating the independence of their subject (as do, more blatantly and spectacularly, Martínez and López Rega in *Las memorias del general*). They do not feel inhibited about taking certain liberties: despite their obsession with fact they repeat the unsubstantiated rumour about a bad-tempered exchange between Eva and the Spanish ambassador, José María de Areilza (p. 147). They digress from the relevant 'facts' about their subject to offer details of the funeral of the Dominican dictator, Rafael Trujillo, 'un hecho macabre, que creemos inédito' (p. 266). A further irony, given their meticulous eye for order and accuracy, is their failure to transcribe Perón's comments on Eva's illness because the tape contains 'tantos ruidos ajenos a su voz que nos ha sido materialmente imposible reconstruir el texto completo' (p. 195). Disconnected words and phrases follow: '«leucemia; una leucemia bien caracterizada por falta de glóbulos rojos. . . » «era un medico de Córdoba el que la vio. . . »' (p. 196). The failure of the tape means that, here at least, Perón's stream of consciousness style emerges unscathed, resisting all attempts to control and domesticate it. Significantly, editorial control fails at the point where Perón is discussing Eva's diseased body and her proposed surgery which would prove unsuccessful. Here the physical wound coincides with the textual wound; the unsuccessful surgeons correspond to the thwarted editors whose textual operations break down at the point where Perón's 'wounded' speech cannot be healed.

In Martínez's *Las memorias del general*, the 'Documents' which follow the main text serve as a 'dangerous supplement', being both marginal to the main body of Perón's recollections and also, in a sense, central to them since they fill their gaps and expose their lies, 'wounding' their integrity by their systematic, almost surgical incisions in the body of his text. Autobiography is by nature, subjective, partial, personal, at liberty to embellish, conceal, distort, suppress. Tomás Eloy Martínez violates a private text by imposing upon it an external supplement which subverts rather than complements. A subversive Tomás Eloy Martínez is not new; what is remarkable here is the emergence of a Tomás Eloy Martínez who hungers for knowledge, for facts, who seemingly falls for the illusion of the incontrovertible, and who appears to subject Perón to the scrutiny of his judgement. Sometimes the documents correct relatively insignificant detail: recalling his young life in Buenos Aires, Perón identifies a defining moment in his development while living with relatives. His grandmother was very old which allowed him (allegedly) to play the part of head of the family. He exemplifies his precocity by recalling the lead role he played when the family attended ex-President Bartolomé's funeral in early 1906: 'llevé al velorio a toda la familia. Caminamos las dos cuadras que había entre la casa de Mitre y la de mi abuela a paso de entierro: yo iba delante de todos. Detrás venían mi abuela y mis tías y, siguiéndolas, mis primos y López Rega. Nos detuvimos en la capilla ardiente para rendir homenaje al prócer, y yo firmé el libro de visitas' (pp. 27–8). One of Perón's cousins, María Aurelia, offers a radically different account (given to Martínez in 1972): 'los tres juntos, Julio, Juan y yo fuimos al velorio del general Bartolomé Mitre. Y ahí firmamos [. . .] Como estábamos a sólo una cuadra de la casa mortuoria, fuimos solos. Los niños, con la curiosidad de la muerte, van a ver la muerte como si fuera un paseo' (p. 81). Perón's account seeks to identify retrospectively the latent presence of the leader in the ten-year-old boy: he walks at the head of the family on this solemn occasion and himself signs the visitors' book. What Perón perceives as an episode marked by grandeur and formality is much diminished in his cousin's account as is Perón's own role – he is just one of three cousins who go along to a funeral out of childish curiosity.

Other relatively minor points in Perón's narrative are challenged by witnesses: thus the lawyer Luis Ratto contradicts Perón's claim that he studied at the Colegio Internacional Politécnico de Olivos (p. 82) while Perón's self-portrayal as a model soldier who completed – almost effortlessly – challenging and arduous military exercises is given the lie in Documents 10 and 11. One of his last-surviving contemporaries, Lieutenant Colonel Saúl S. Pardo, recalls (in 1972): 'creo que Perón fue uno de los que no pudo llegar. Se quedó sin aliento en la travesía, como tantos otros' (p. 85). Document 11 contains extracts from press cuttings from *La Prensa* and *La Razón*, reporting on the prizes and awards made to the best cadets in Perón's year. Perón's name does not feature.

Other documents make more incisive and 'wounding' revelations. The first points to Perón's illegitimacy, deduced from his parents' marriage certificate, and relates it to his 'ilevantable resentimiento contra la madre' (p. 71). This document indicates that the marriage took place in Buenos Aires, following his birth, and not in Lobos, prior to his birth, as Perón claims (p. 71). Compounding the shame of Perón's illegitimacy is that of his mother's adultery (which we have already mentioned) as revealed in Document 6 (pp. 75–7) consisting of the testimony of Alberto J. Robert, Perón's boyhood friend. According to him, Perón surprised his mother *in flagrante delicto* with a labourer, Marcelino, when he returned home earlier than expected (p. 78). Documents 2 and 3 offer evidence of a lesser shame, but one which Perón was eager to conceal: his impoverished upbringing (p. 73). Shame of a different kind is suggested by Document 15 which transcribes the testimony of María Tizón, sister of Aurelia (known affectionately as 'Potota'), Perón's first wife. Here Perón's virility is called into question since tests taken following his wife's failure to conceive revealed that Potota was fertile (p. 99). Other documents point to Perón's political mendacity. He famously claimed to have met Mussolini during his tour of duty in Italy, a claim refuted by Lieutenant Colonel Augusto Maidana (Document 17, pp. 104–9). This is the most trenchant criticism of Perón: 'si tuviera que definirlo con una sola palabra diría que era un simulador [. . .] Nunca conocí a nadie que supiera manejar los sentimientos como él. Los dibujaban genialmente con su cara. Sabía cómo eran los sentimientos, pero no los tenía' (p. 109). This critique of Perón is particularly wounding (as well as ironic) since it is in precisely these terms that the exiled Perón described his own enemies, claiming that politics was theatre ('todo es teatro') and politicians 'simuladores de un papel que les corresponde en la función'.⁴¹ Maidana offers several examples of Perón's mendacity, such as his false claim that he had not been seasick during the return voyage to Argentina (p. 107) and that he had been present at the war front when in reality 'la única guerra que vio fue desde la embajada argentina [...]' (p. 109). Perón's unprincipled behaviour is also exposed by the widow of Eduardo Lonardi, Perón's predecessor as military attaché at the Argentine embassy in Santiago de Chile (as well as his successor as president following Perón's removal from office in September 1955). Although Perón seems to have been at least partially responsible for Lonardi's expulsion from Chile for an alleged espionage operation that Perón initiated, Perón absolves himself from blame, attributing the unfortunate episode entirely to 'la impericie de un subordinado' (p. 39). Lonardi's widow recounts how she went to plead with Perón at his home in Buenos Aires to help save the career of her husband. Having been privy to the instructions imparted to Lonardi, she is able to contradict Perón's claim that Lonardi had failed to follow them. Her description of Perón's demeanour would seem to lend credence to her account:

> yo ardía de nervios; él estaba impasible [...] Muy suelto de cuerpo, Perón me dijo entonces que las mujeres no debían estar presentes cuando se resuelven cuestiones de Estado, porque siempre lo confunden todo.
>
> Después me dijo que estaba muy ocupado y me cerró la puerta en la cara. (pp. 102–3)

The most wounding of Martínez's exposures, however, relates to allegations that Perón's political opponents were torturados. Perón claims that his government was essentially benign and that police malpractice did not come to his attention until it was too late for him to act (p. 54). But the meticulously documented footnote on the same page offering full details of torture victims, including the subsequent disappearance of one of them, makes a nonsense of his claims.

The documents play a rather paradoxical role in this text: they are not part of the autobiography itself, being supplements to which the reader is directed by means of footnotes. Their purpose is clearly to 'police' the principal text. On the one hand they arrogate to themselves authority based on documented historical evidence: they are the result of painstaking historical research and deserve to be believed. They call into question the claims of the autobiographer, exposing his recollections of the past as partial, selective and often blatantly fictional. They claim to represent 'what really happened' and to judge Perón by the benchmark of truth. They vitiate the freedom of the autobiographer, insinuating themselves into his text to undermine it from the margins. Having shown up the 'wounds' in Perón's writing, they themselves inflict a life-threatening wound on the body of the autobiographical text by violating its privacy and exposing to full view its furtive secrets, half-truths, fictions and blatant lies, all arguably the prerogatives of the autobiographer who has traditionally written his life story free of any fear that it might be undermined by critical detective work. In his prologue, Martínez refers to two chapters included in the text of *Las memorias del General*, 'Días de exilio de Madrid' and 'Ascenso, triunfo, decadencia y derrota de José López Rega'. They both originate in a biography of Perón that Martínez began in 1974 'con la sospecha de que ese género podía derivar en un libro inverosímil' (p. 15). Both chapters are similarly flawed: 'ambos adolecen de una pasión documental quizás excesiva' (p. 15). Another chapter, 'Perón y los nazis' was originally an academic paper: Martínez identifies its weaknesses as follows: 'lo delata el abuso de notas y el afán de probar que cada dato es verdadero' (p. 15). Some of the documents themselves seem to be open to similar criticism since they offer an excess of information. Thus Document 9 contains the (irrelevant) personal and nostalgic recollections of the lawyer, Luis Ratto, who knew Perón while they were both students at the Colegio Politécnico Internacional ('vivía en Floresta y cuando pasaba por ahí lo miraba desde afuera con un poco de nostalgia', p. 82). In Document 20, the account by the Venezuelan journalist, Germán Carías, of the failed attempt on Perón's life when a bomb was placed under his car, includes details of the crane that removed the car and the garage to which it was taken (p. 119).

Here the testimonial Martínez who appeals to the 'facts' stands in strange contrast to the postmodern Martínez of *La novela de Perón* and *Santa Evita* who questions the existence of such 'facts' and focuses rather on their imaginative reconstruction. In *Las memorias del General*, Martínez seems to share the irritation of the editors of *Yo, JDP* with the gaps and contradictions in Perón's account. Perón's own hope was that these partial memoirs, which said little about Eva, should assume canonical status. For a truth-obsessed Martínez, they were clearly unsatisfactory. The irony is that Perón, associated with military rigour and a philosophy of life conditioned by cliché, proverb and bland definition, should stand here for a kind of imaginative self-reinvention whereas Martínez the creative writer, whose usual instinct is to privilege play over fixity seems, in this instance at least, to be seeking to establish a single truth – despite the impossibility of such a task as shown by the conflicting accounts of his witnesses. Thus Martínez determines to check an account that Perón had spent a tour of duty in Tucumán, denied by Perón himself, possibly because he had been posted there for disciplinary reasons. The conflicting versions of events offered to Martínez during his investigation are reminiscent of the widely divergent recollections of the past portrayed by García Márquez in *Crónica de una muerte anunciada*: 'algunos habitantes [de Tucumán] se acordaban de todo [. . .] Otros vecinos, con igual énfasis, negaron que eso había sucedido' (p. 13).

While Martínez criticizes Perón for neglecting episodes which he himself deemed marginal, Martínez himself omits his own questions to Perón which, according to Martínez, structure the account and lend it cohesion. It is Martínez who appears to dictate the univocal values of reason, authority, and logic whereas Perón improvises and digresses. Ironically Martínez's own position is undermined by his paradoxical claim that his work both respects and resists Perón's wishes. On the one hand he is keen to impose order and organization – by placing López Rega's remarks in italics, by seeking to rationalize the composition of his book, emphasizing its veracity and legitimacy; on the other he incurs a kind of illegitimacy in intruding upon the private space of the autobiographer and in subordinating his own imaginative instincts to a new-found documentary zeal. In *Las memorias del General*, Martínez himself fulfils what he imagines to be Perón's worst fear; that others will intervene in his story and modify it: 'ha sufrido pensando que la historia contará a su manera lo que él calló. Que vendrán otros a inventarle una vida [. . .] un hombre sólo es lo que de él se recuerda' (*La novela de Perón*, p. 92).

New Historical writers (among whom Martínez the novelist may be included) focus on the relentless proliferation and diversity of texts, highlighting their chaotic and discontinuous forms. They often give priority to the unofficial, the marginal, the exotic and anecdotal aspects of the historical record, as Martínez does in

La novela de Perón which refers to Isabel's dubious associates, notably José López Rega, who claimed that Perón had led four previous existences (p. 68). But the familiar ludic aspect of Martínez, who elsewhere derides the former president, Bartolomé Mitre, as an 'apasionado coleccionista de documentos',[42] seems to be subordinated here to the opposing values of a different persona, serious, focused and self-justificatory. Having criticized certain chapters of *Las memorias del general* for their obsessive documentation, he goes on in the next sentence to highlight the merits of the work, advancing as strengths qualities previously perceived as weaknesses: 'cada uno de los datos de este libro tiene un documento, una carta, una cinta grabada que avala su veracidad' (p. 15). Martínez plays the part of the traditional historian whose first priority, like that of the editors of *Yo, JDP*, is reliability. His use of a variety of typographical conventions, designed to dispel any possible confusions relating to the identity of the speakers, proclaim the presence of a master narrator policing a customized text. This narrator is far removed from the Martínez of *Santa Evita* who flaunts his lack of control over his subject: 'no sé en qué punto del relato estoy. Creo que en el medio' (p. 391).

Perón's attitude to the historical past not only fictionalizes history but also crosses the border between reason and fantasy: he accepts that López Rega, not yet born at the time, was none the less present at Bartolomé Mitre's funeral in early 1906. As for López Rega himself, he flouts the concept of the self-contained, unified subject by usurping Perón's identity: 'decía "yo" cuando ese yo era el de su jefe' (p. 11). Both López Rega and Martínez 'wound' Perón's text, the former by encroaching upon his sovereign self, the latter by policing his private text, denying him the traditional prerogatives of the autobiographer: the right to be partial, to cover up, to fictionalize and falsify, to reinvent his past. Martínez 'wounds' autobiography as a traditionally authoritarian mode of writing by turning on its head the notion that 'whatever the writer asserts concerning the rightness of his thought is now ungainsayable by others'.[43]

Nussbaum refers to the New Historical argument that rather than 'knowing history directly, as objective intractable fact, we can know it only in textual artefacts [. . .]. While a category of the real exists, our access to it is constrained and held within certain textual and ideological bounds'.[44] The playful, postmodern Martínez, ever conscious that history is only accessible in textual form, seems to be drawn none the less to the category of the 'real' when dealing with the writings of the historical Perón. Martínez may have portrayed him as a quintessentially postmodern figure in *La novela de Perón* but he remains acutely aware that his interventions in Argentine history brought about the torture and disappearance of real people. Martínez is conscious of the danger of New Historical practices losing touch with traditional human values in a 'boundless tide of relativism'.[45] Here the human(ist) Martínez replaces the postmodern Martínez to concur with Eagleton's perspective: 'the discourses of reason, truth, freedom and subjectivity, as we have inherited them, indeed require profound transformation; but it is unlikely that a politics which does not take these traditional topics with full seriousness, will prove resourceful and resilient enough to oppose the arrogance of power'.[46] Martínez's attitude to Perón is clearly ambivalent: it seems that in this text he is more concerned to deflate his arrogance than to celebrate his power as a kind of novelist as he does in *Santa Evita* (p. 144). Certainly the ludic, hesitant, freewheeling novelist seems to give way here to a more authoritarian figure keen to write the last word.

An alternative reading of *Las memorias del General* might focus on the text as metaphor for critical theories of autobiography, particularly those which question any form of authoritative writing and undermine the humanist notion of a single and unified self. Perón's configuration of his own life story is challenged by the competing claims of the Documents. The integrity of his personal individual self is compromised by the usurping action of López Rega. Perhaps this is a kind of postmodern text after all, one in which the author's traditional proprietorial rights over his text are subverted. It may be seen as a kind of meta-autobiography in which traditional assumptions made by the writer, Perón, are subject to an ongoing critique whose ostensible purpose is to 'set the record straight' but which ultimately goes beyond such a banal objective to call into question the philosophical foundations of autobiographical writing itself.

However the text is interpreted, it is clear that it represents writing as competition and conflict; in the case of Perón's writing, as struggle to contend with other adversarial writings and, as Perón puts it in *La novela de Perón*, to 'gobernar a la historia. Cogerla por el culo' (p. 168). Perón might represent the autobiographer as bullfighter. In her discussion of Michel Leiris, Brée remarks: 'that some intimation of the quasi-physical struggle inherent in the act of writing should reveal at least the 'shadow' of the bull's horn – that is, the threat of mutilation, wound, or death – seems to Leiris the guarantee that the writing meshes into a real *hors-texte* [. . .]'.[47] The bull's horns in *Las memorias* are represented by Martínez and his treacherous footnotes which serve not to support the main text, the traditional function of footnotes, but rather to undermine it, and by José López Rega, whose threat is more insidious since he seeks not to expose Perón's mendacity but to assume his identity, ultimately to become Perón.

NOTES

1. Adolfo Prieto, *La literatura autobiográfica argentina* (Buenos Aires: Jorge Alvarez, 1966), p. 10.
2. Mariano Ben Plotkin, *Freud in the Pampas: the Emergence and Development of a Psychoanalytic Culture in Argentina* (Stanford: Stanford University Press, 2001), p. 55. Anti-Peronists frequently drew parallels between Perón and Rosas. See, for example, J. M. Taylor, *Evita Perón: the Myths of a Woman* (Oxford: Blackwell, 1989), p. 31. The most famous anti-Peronist of his day, Jorge Luis Borges, refers to Perón as 'otro Rosas'. See *Prosa completa*, 2 vols (Barcelona: Bruguera, 1980), II, 460.
3. Américo Ghioldi, *El mito de Eva Duarte* (Montevideo: n.p., 1952), p. 22.
4. See Mariano Ben Plotkin, 'La ideología de Perón' in Samuel Amaral and Mariano Ben Plotkin (eds), *Perón: del exilio al poder* (Buenos Aires: Cántaro, 1993), pp. 45–67 (p. 53).
5. *Proyección del rosismo en la literatura argentina: seminario del Instituto de Letras* (Rosario: Universidad Nacional del Litoral, Facultad de filosofía y letras, 1959) and Ernesto Goldar, *El peronismo en la literatura argentina* (Buenos Aires: Freeland, 1971).
6. See William Ratliff, 'Perón y la guerrilla: el arte del engaño mutuo' in Amaral and Plotkin (eds), *Perón: del exilio al poder*, pp. 261–80 (pp. 278–80).
7. Nancy Hanway, *Embodying Argentina: Body, Space and Nation in 19th Century Narrative* (Jefferson, NC: McFarland, 2003), pp. 57–8.
8. *Las memorias del General*, p. 24.
9. Esteban Peicovich, *Hola Perón* (Buenos Aires: Jorge Alvarez, 1965), p. 33.
10. Quoted in Silvio Sigal and Eliseo Verón, *Perón o muerte: los fundamentos discursivos del fenómeno peronista* (Buenos Aires: Legasa, 1986), p. 46.
11. Daniel James, *Resistance and Integration: Peronism and the Argentine Working Class, 1946–1976*, Cambridge Latin American Studies 64 (Cambridge: Cambridge University Press, 1988), p. 23.

12 See Mariano Ben Plotkin, *Freud in the Pampas*, p. 77.
13 'Introduction', *Eva Perón, In My Own Words*, p. 22.
14 His mother was responsible for many of Perón's wounds but not, of course, for all of them. Just prior to his overthrow in June 1955 his supporters indulged in an orgy of church burning: 'en mi alma se abrieron profundas heridas que el tiempo y cuanto sucedió después no alcanzaron a cicatrizar', Juan Domingo Perón, *Del poder al exilio: cómo y quiénes me derrocaron* (Buenos Aires, n.p., 1958), p. 11.
15 Arnaldo Momigliano, *The Development of Greek Biography: Four Lectures* (Cambridge MA: Harvard University Press, 1971), p. 13.
16 Baisnée points to the split in autobiography between narrator and character: 'the person in charge of the discourse, the "I", is talking about another "I", who is like a third person in the story'. See Valérie Baisnée, *Gendered Resistance: the Autobiographies of Simone de Beauvoir, Maya Angelou, Janet Frame and Marguerite Duras* (Amsterdam and Atlanta GA: Rodopi, 1997), p. 6. Perón refers to himself in the third person, as will be seen.
17 Sylvia Molloy, *At Face Value*, p. 199.
18 Paola Cortés Rocca and Martín Kohan, *Imágenes de vida, relatos de muerte. Eva Perón: cuerpo y política*, Estudios culturales (Buenos Aires: Beatriz Viterbo, 1998), p. 97.
19 Robert A. Potash, *The Army and Politics in Argentina, 1945–1962: Perón to Frondizi* (London: Athlone, 1980), p. 174.
20 The agreement announced in early 1955 between the Argentine government and a US company regarding petroleum production in southern Patagonia had united Perón's opponents in their criticism of him.
21 Louis A. Renza, 'The veto of the imagination: a theory of autobiography' in James Olney (ed.), *Autobiography: Essays Theoretical and Critical* (Princeton: Princeton University Press, 1980), pp. 268–95 (p. 279).
22 Amy K. Kaminsky, *After Exile: Writing the Latin American Diaspora* (Minneapolis MN: University of Minnesota Press, 1999), p. 57.
23 John Sturrock, *The Language of Autobiography: Studies in the First Person Singular* (Cambridge and New York: Cambridge University Press, 1993), pp. 262–3.
24 Julia Swindells, 'Introduction', Julia Swindells (ed.) *The Uses of Autobiography* (London: Taylor and Francis, 1995), pp. 1–12 (p. 7).
25 Pedro Ara, *Eva Perón: la verdadera historia contada por el médico que preservó su cuerpo* (Buenos Aires: Sudamericana, 1996), p. 119.
26 Amy K. Kaminsky, *After Exile*, p. 12.
27 Philippe Lejeune, 'The Autobiographical Contract' in Tzvetan Todorov (ed.), *French Literary Theory Today: a Reader*, trans. R. Carter (Cambridge: Cambridge University Press; Paris: Editions de la Maison Des Sciences de L'Homme, 1982), pp. 192–222 (p. 211).
28 Robert Elbaz, *The Changing Nature of the Self: a Critical Study of Autobiographic Discourse* (London and Sydney: Croom Helm, 1988), p. 8. Gilmore points to a similarly unfounded assumption in James

Olney's *Metaphors of Self*: Olney interprets autobiography as a monument to the 'natural' human impulse to order. For him 'autobiography is merely and magnificently the literary reflection of the realized self'. Leigh Gilmore, *Autobiographics: a Feminist Theory of Women's Self-Representation*, Reading Women Writing (Ithaca and London: Cornell University Press, 1994), p. 74.

29 On the surface Perón's claim seems entirely plausible but Sigal points out that Perón always represents the position of outsider in relation to the Argentine people: 'Perón es alguien que viene de afuera. Si ese "exterior" desde el cual llega es, en 1973, el exterior geográfico del exilio, en sus primeros discursos era un exterior abstracto, por decirlo así, *extra-político*: el cuartel'. See Silvia Sigal and Eliseo Verón, *Perón o muerte: los fundamentos discursivos del fenómeno peronista*, p. 29.

30 De Man, 'Autobiography as de-facement' in *The Rhetoric of Romanticism*, pp. 67–81 (p. 76).

31 Ernesto Goldar, *El peronismo en la literatura argentina*, pp. 60–1.

32 Leigh Gilmore, *Autobiographics*, p. 74.

33 De Man, 'Autobiography as de-facement' in *The Rhetoric of Romanticism*, pp. 67–81 (p. 71).

34 Leigh Gilmore, *Autobiographics*, p. 67.

35 Leigh Gilmore, *Autobiographics*, p. 13.

36 *Yo, Juan Domingo Perón: relato autobiográfico*, ed. Torcuato Luca de Tena, Luis Calvo and Esteban Peicovich (Barcelona: Planeta, 1976); Tomás Eloy Martínez, *Las memorias del General* (Buenos Aires: Planeta, 1996). References, given in parenthesis in the text, are to these editions. The following abbreviations are used: *Yo, JDP* and *Las memorias*.

37 Journalists saw the presidential romance as a public spectacle rather than a private and intimate relationship. Thus Philip Hamburger's report for the *New Yorker* (June 1948): 'they are constantly, passionately, nationally, in love. They conduct their affair with the people quite openly [. . .]'. Quoted by Nicholas Fraser and Marysa Navarro, *Evita: the Real Lives of Eva Perón* (London: André Deutsch, 1996), p. 110.

38 Plotkin notes that in 1951 Law 14, 028 'diverted to the Fundación $97 million in fines imposed on the Bemberg Group (an industrialist family, allegedly being punished for their anti-Peronism)'. See Mario Ben Plotkin, *Mañana es San Perón. A Cultural History of Perón's Argentina*, trans. Keith Zahniser (Wilmington DE: Scholarly Resources, 2003), p. 149.

39 Linda Anderson, *Autobiography*, The New Critical Idiom (London: Routledge, 2001), p. 98.

40 Paul John Eakin, *Touching the World: Reference in Autobiography* (Princeton NJ: Princeton University Press, 1992), p. 5.

41 Quoted by Samuel Amaral, 'El avión negro', in *Perón: del exilio al poder*, pp. 69–94 (pp. 89–90).

42 Martínez remarks that Mitre's enthusiastic documentation had the paradoxical effect of introducing into 'el imaginario argentino una

larga desconfianza por la veracidad de lo que aseguran los documentos'. He goes on to invoke Dalmacio Vélez Sársfield, author of the Argentine Civil Code, who maintained that 'al apoyarse tan ciegamente sobre el valor de los documentos, Mitre terminaba condenándose a la parcialidad, porque los documentos han reflejado siempre en la Argentina sólo los intereses de las clases altas y de las minorías ilustradas'. 'Historia y ficción: dos paralelas que se tocan' in *Literaturas del Río de la Plata hoy: de las utopías al desencanto* (Frankfurt: Vervuert; Madrid: Iberoamericana, 1996), pp. 89–100 (p. 93).

[43] John Sturrock, *The Language of Autobiography: Studies in the First Person Singular* (Cambridge and New York: Cambridge University Press, 1993), p. 15.

[44] Felicity A. Nussbaum, *The Autobiographical Subject: Gender and Ideology in Eighteenth-Century England* (Baltimore and London: Johns Hopkins University Press, 1989), p. 11.

[45] Dorothy Lipstadt, *Denying the Holocaust: the Growing Assault on Truth and Memory* (New York: The Free Press, 1993), p. 21.

[46] Terry Eagleton, *The Ideology of the Aesthetic* (Oxford: Blackwell, 1990), p. 415.

[47] Germaine Brée, 'Michel Leiris: Mazemaker' in James Olney (ed.), *Autobiography*, pp. 194–206 (p. 205).

Part II

Biographical Writing

Chapter 4
Telling the Full Story: Joseph Page

Ira Bruce Nadel contends that 'in his need to find a structure, point of view, method of characterization and descriptive technique, the biographer is akin more to the creative writer than the historian'.[1] If Nadel seeks to blur the boundaries between fact and fiction, Hayden White queries hard and fast borders between history and fiction: 'there has been a reluctance to consider historical narratives as what they most manifestly are: verbal fictions, the contents of which are as much *invented as found* and the forms of which have more in common with their counterparts in literature than they have with those in the sciences'.[2]

There are at least two types of biographer and at least two types of historian. On the one hand there is the biographer/historian who believes that he is dealing with facts and views his personal input as essentially recording 'what really happened', his own role in this process rarely acknowledged. On the other there is the biographer/historian who recognizes that his procedures resemble those of a creative writer, who 'emplots' his narrative by choosing from a series of possible frameworks and who recognizes his creative input by drawing attention, self-consciously, to his procedures rather than seeking to cover them up. Epstein notes that 'biographical narratives characterized by virtually dematerialized biographers seldom challenge internal or external generic politics'.[3] In considering the biographies of Juan and Eva Perón we shall note varying degrees of self-consciousness, ranging from the (implicit) view of biography as a branch of history that centres on the 'facts' of the past (Page, Borroni and Vacca), to biography as a kind of fiction (Dujovne Ortiz) that approximates to the imaginative approach and experimental techniques fully engaged by the postmodern novel (*Santa Evita*).

In his preface, Page notes the peculiar difficulties posed by his subject: much of the primary and secondary materials are inaccessible; few available records are reliable; extant writings and taped conversations are riven by contradiction, exaggeration and misstatement; eye witnesses, for a variety of reasons, have proved reticent; and several of the key players have since died.[4] In view of these difficulties, Page might have chosen an 'unorthodox' approach. But the gold standard of biography, for Page as for many traditional biographers, is 'reliability' and despite the difficulties he feels his work passes the conventional tests – thanks mainly to good old-fashioned tenacity in pursuing his research: 'the persistence of seven years' work, good fortune in securing source materials and interviews, hundreds of documents released under the Freedom of Information Act [. . .] the help of many individuals' (pp. ix–x). So, despite the overwhelming odds against achieving traditional biographical wholeness, Page assures the reader that s/he is about to read a full and comprehensive account supported by adequate documentary evidence, the implication being that the fullness of his treatment will compensate for any previous gaps and omissions in the record of Perón's life and work. In other words, Page's perseverance and dedication will triumph over what appears to be a profoundly challenging subject: by dint of close scrutiny and professional analysis, the contradictions, exaggerations and misstatements of his subject will be repaired and rendered whole. Page's view, sharp, rigorous and apparently all-seeing, 'tames' his subject – or at least renders his disturbing shadowiness somewhat less intractable. While Page freely acknowledges that Perón is a difficult subject he would not, presumably, concur with Jack Miles who reminds us how little we know of any person and how subjective that knowledge is: contradiction and dissonance will always expose as illusory any signs of coherence and unity.[5] Page, rather, sees Perón's inconsistencies and contradictions as challenges to be overcome, as surface cracks in a basically solid individual edifice, capable of repair by the biographer's suturing treatment. For Page there is a redeemable core of intelligible matter beneath Perón's uneven, resistant exterior. He shares the implicit belief of the traditional biographer that 'we are an integrated "individual" self, with a coherent persona. Despite considerable psychoanalytic (and indeed empirical) evidence to the contrary, the social expectation [...] is that we are a "knowable" person, a person with a coherent emotional *curriculum vitae*'.[6] Page's opening remarks suggest his uneasiness in the face of ambiguity, contradiction and what Evans describes as absence of definition that 'intrudes into all aspects of biography' (p. 75).

But Page's preface goes on to anticipate a portrait that is full, unified and eminently comprehensible rather than partial, tentative and incoherent. Page's truth-telling programme will seek to dispel all such uncertainty. Yet any coherence will be illusory: biography is 'almost always a discontinuous story which lacks coherence in itself'.[7] As we shall see, Page's approach contrasts with that of Tomás Eloy Martínez's in *La novela de Perón* where Martínez, far from attempting to provide a coherent account, revels in the ambiguities that rupture its sense and meaning.

The 'Literary' Perón

An overview of Perón's multidimensional complexities and of his appeal to the literary imagination will serve to highlight the challenges facing a traditional biographer such as Page. Borges's short story about Perón is entitled, significantly, 'El simulador' and, according to Martínez, Perón's military colleague, Augusto Maidona, described him as 'un simulador' (*Las memorias del General*, p. 109). Hutcheon points out that 'irony', from the Greek *eiron*, meaning 'dissembler', 'pretender', undermines stated meaning by removing the semantic sincerity of 'one signifier: one signified'.[8] Irony repudiates a single truth and points to the problematic nature of language: on the lips of the ironist words do not necessarily mean what they say. Irony denies taken-for-granted certainties by unmasking the world as ambiguity. The ironist cannot be pinned down – s/he is rarely serious, preferring to engage in elusive play. S/he is interested not in intimacy or intercourse but in seduction which, as Baudrillard points out, is a game 'that breaks the referentiality of sex and provides a space, not of desire, but of play and defiance'.[9] Perón may remove his jacket but he keeps his distance from his earthy *descamisados*: resisting physical contact with his people, he envelops them from afar with the seductive force of his voice, his rhetoric and his gestures. Perón is known best not for his political commitment which would imply fixed belief but rather for his pragmatism and flexibility and his capacity for moving from one position to another with the same agility that allows him to say one thing and mean another: he displays, as Halperín Donghi states, 'una orfandad ideológica traducida en un oportunismo que excedía el nivel de la táctica para dominar su entero modo de concebir la acción política'.[10] He would have savoured the irony (for which he himself was largely responsible) of the vice presidency being withheld from Eva while the incompetent Isabel, no match in any political sense for Eva, would aspire not only to the position she was denied but, upon Perón's death, to the presidency itself. This is why Martínez in *Santa Evita* (p. 144) sees Perón as a kind of novelist who makes of his life a fiction, who has scant regard for 'facts' and refuses to be bound to a past that he would rather consign to a Nietzschean forgetfulness. He claims to be above good and evil, to be able to determine his own age ('yo tengo los años que quiero')[11] and to have no successor other than the Argentine people.[12] Perón's mask conceals no depth: even his friends, such as Augusto Maidona, conceded that he had no feelings ('los dibujaba generalmente con su cara. Sabía cómo eran los sentimientos, pero no los tenía')[13] and Goldar notes Marta Lynch's portrayal of a Perón 'sin intimidad, un personaje autosuficiente que deja atónitos a los interlocutores, que no escucha'.[14] Perón plays with people and with ideas, shuffling and discarding both at will, undermining with cold calculation and guile any perceived challengers to his authority. While in exile Perón played the role of detached manipulator, feigning support for opposing sides. Although he deplored the trivialization of politics as theatre, he was himself for a time the most consummate actor on that particular stage. He is drawn to women, or rather, to one particular woman, the most dangerous plaything of all, whom he uses to defy social conventions and propriety (again Perón shows a Nietzschean quality: Nietzsche locates decadence not in deviation from respectable social convention but in conformity to it).[15] He flaunts the adolescent Piraña whom he passes off as his daughter and cohabits with Eva – herself young enough to be his daughter – whose reputation for promiscuity outrages Perón's military colleagues while seemingly enhancing her attractiveness to Perón. Perón, like his political movement, is consistent only in his inconsistencies – and perhaps, too, in his attack on the

Church, the supreme pretender to single unequivocal truth and therefore antithetical to all that Perón stands for. Dionysus was the god of masks or personae and so Perón is a Dionysian as well as a Nietzschean figure who frequently contradicts himself and has no fixed opinions. Ratliff notes that Perón admired both the barricades of May 1968 and De Gaulle; while in exile, he took advantage of extreme and violent support only to renounce it once he achieved power. He had no fear of irrational argument, claiming that Cuba was free of foreign influence despite its patent dependence on the Soviet Union.[16] Perón's ambivalence was also evident in domestic Argentine politics since he failed to repudiate the country's liberal traditions, an ambivalence which 'permea todas las areas del discurso peronista'.[17] Peronism does not conform to modern practice in this respect. Bauman observes that 'the substance of modern politics, of modern intellect, of modern life is the effort to exterminate ambivalence: an effort to define precisely – and to suppress or eliminate anything that could not or would not be precisely defined'.[18] In such an environment Perón stands as a beacon to ambivalence largely because of his refusal to belong, achieving no more than a rhetorical intimacy with the people despite being placed at the heart of the movement by the slogan disseminated by the Peronist paper, *El Descamisado*: 'los tres grandes amores de un peronista son el Pueblo, Perón y la Patria'.[19] Indeed Sigal and Verón claim that Perón's position vis-à-vis the Argentine people was always external: 'Perón es alguien que viene de afuera. Se ese 'exterior' desde el cual llega es, en 1973, el exterior geográfico del exilio, en sus primeros discursos era un exterior abstracto, por decirlo así, extra-político: el cuartel' (p. 29). In addition, Perón is a self-declared man of peace but his peace does not exclude violence: 'cuanto más violentos seamos mayor: al terror no se lo vence sino con otro terror superior'.[20] Perón defies conventional character building blocks, those 'essential traits' beloved of traditional biographers whose portraiture is built on clarity and distinctiveness. Perón is a postmodern figure offering shimmering surfaces but no depths. No amount of biographical research will serve to solidify what will always remain flux, turbulence, ambiguity and contradiction.

In grappling with Perón, historians repeatedly refer to his rhetorical and heretical powers. His rhetorical skills may be seen to complement his depthless surfaces: as Vickers points out, 'rhetoric has been given negative connotations of insincerity, mere display, artifice or ornament without substance'.[21] Rhetoric is persistently viewed as representative of deception and fiction, and is often associated with irony, a technique in which Perón is well versed, as we have seen: 'rhetoric is an art of lying, most readily found in the politician. Irony is a dry, understated, and dissembling manner of speaking [...]. Writing and rhetoric encourage deceptiveness [...]. A flawless eloquence is not to be trusted'.[22] Another important aspect of rhetorical speech is that it has no interlocutor: the audience cannot talk back and the Perón era was described as a 'lengthy monologue' (quoted by Page, p. 3). Daniel James refers to the shimmering immediacy of Perón's rhetoric which showed little concern with the 'intrinsic virtues of Argentineidad'.[23] James also makes much of Perón's heretical power: Peronism aspired to be a viable hegemonic alternative for Argentine capitalism [...]. At the same time, however, Peronism in an important sense defined itself, and was defined by its working-class constituency, as a denial of the dominant elites' power, symbols and values' (p. 39). This vision of Peronism was couched in a language with which the working classes could identify: 'it represented too, a political culture of opposition, or rejection of all that had gone before – politically, socially, and economically; a sense of blasphemy against the norms and self-esteem of the traditional elite' (p. 40). The most notable blasphemy on a linguistic level was Perón's subversion of the meaning of *descamisado*. Page himself notes Perón's sensitivity to language: he deliberately mispronounced the names of people whom he did not like. The name of the general who ousted Perón in September 1955 was changed from Lonardi to 'Leonardi' (Page, p. 35, footnote). Such practice can be fruitfully read by reference to Foucault who describes 'effective' history as the reversal of a relationship of forces, the usurpation of power, the appropriation of a vocabulary turned against those who had once used it [...]'.[24] *Descamisado*, once used as a verbal weapon by the oligarchy to demean Perón's working-class supporters, is now turned against them, serving as a kind of rallying cry for the working classes. Hanway points to the significance of dress as the key to political allegiance.[25] In Perón's Argentina, the worker was immediately recognizable by his 'shirtless' appearance but the connotations of *descamisado* were now inverted, the signifier of contempt emanating from without, transformed into proud self-designation, a verbal icon charged with an infectious sense of solidarity. The rhetorical attachment of the *descamisados* to the figure of Eva Perón (known for her over-dressing) lends the term further ironic resonance. Here is Perón at play, this time with language, exploiting the random connections between signifier and signified in order to subvert conventional meaning and to insinuate into the chinks of a settled though vulnerable ideology the corroding influence of a contagious counter-discourse.

According to Terdiman, the work of counter-discourse is comparable to a linguistic guerrilla struggle.[26] In this struggle Perón, the linguistic guerrilla, not only modifies the ammunition of his opponents but also manufactures his own: thus 'cipayo' and 'vendepatria' were terms of abuse directed by Peronists at opponents who wished to maintain Argentine subservience to the economic interests of foreign countries. James points out that Perón called into existence an Argentina which had previously been invisible and a class of people hitherto mute and unnoticed. He gave voice to an important layer of human experience previously buried. James quotes Sartre to telling effect in summarizing the potential of language in the political arena: 'words wreak havoc when they find a name for what had up till then been lived namelessly'.[27] James presents an oppositional Perón whose enduring legacy will be associated with heretical intervention in hegemonic power structures. It is a complex and problematic intervention which deviates from familiar practice largely because it is subject to the whims of a player who follows no known set of rules, who is inconsistent and self-contradictory, who represents multifarious forces in unresolved competition, who moves seamlessly from one identity to another, rehearsing his multiple parts, refusing to commit himself to any single one of them. It is this Perón whom Page will attempt to master, using the often tried – if rarely proven – procedures of traditional biographical practice.

The 'Factual' Perón

Page's main objective is to 'control' his subject. Driven by the impulse to explain and delimit, he adopts an impersonal and authoritative style, devoid of any acknowledgement of his own input: his personal perspective is erased and his role as biographer dematerialized. There is no reference to his construction of a particular type of narrative within which to accommodate his subject. The implication is that he is merely presenting the facts and that any interpretative activity on his part is determined by those facts. There is therefore no acknowledgement of any type of 'emplotting' in Hayden White's sense ('the way by which a sequence of events fashioned into a story is gradually revealed to be a story of a particular kind').[28] Moreover, the 'biography' of Page's title has none of the ironic connotations of, for example, Virginia Woolf's in *Orlando: a Biography* (1928), a work that undercuts the normal foundations of biography in demonstrable fact, unity of self and chronological time. Page's 'biography' assumes a foundational solidity: his work distances itself from the fictional by mimicking the procedures of historical writing, both in its plethora of footnotes documenting the wide range of sources consulted (among which the works of the historians Richard Potash and Felix Luna are preponderant) and in its standard practice (albeit inconsistently followed) of relegating information of uncertain provenance to the unseemly fringes of gossip and rumour. There are – significantly – few references to literary sources. The most notable is to Borges who is numbered among the 'rabid Evita-haters' for calling her a 'common prostitute' (p. 83, footnote). The implication is that this biographer shares the values and balanced approach of the traditional historian and will have no truck with the fictional 'contamination' of the historical record. His objective is merely to present the facts; to what extent, then, is the organization of the biography governed by the story elements provided by the documentary records rather than by the particular form of narrative chosen by the author from several possible alternatives?

It is worth noting that the opening chapters break with the normal chronology. The book opens in 1944, while the third chapter goes back to the year of Perón's birth, 1895. The reason has obviously to do with narrative technique (a procedure which is unacknowledged by the author though scarcely determined by the facts of the story). Rather than begin at the beginning with the potentially banal details of Perón's early life, Page focuses instead on Perón, as minister of labour, on the threshold of power. The event which will emerge in retrospect as pivotal to Perón's quest for the leadership of the country is the San Juan earthquake of 15 January 1944, a truly remarkable phenomenon, 'the worst natural disaster to hit the country and one of the most devastating ever to occur in the Western Hemisphere' (p. 3). Perón capitalized on the excellent opportunity offered by the devastation to demonstrate his organizational skills, an opportunity which he exploited to the full: 'for Juan Perón, the San Juan earthquake was a godsend, imparting momentum to his rollercoaster ride to immortality' (p. 5). The earthquake provided Perón not only with 'instant national exposure' (p. 3) but facilitated the 'crucial conjunction' with Evita. In Page's narrative, the earthquake assumes metaphorical significance: as an image of natural dislocation it mirrors the couple's groundbreaking political impact on the country. Just as the earthquake was without precedent, so was Perón: 'he has marked Argentina as no one else has [. . .]. In a passionate country he aroused emotions of volcanic intensity in others [. . .]' (pp. 5–6). Page sees man and nature as complementary, both provoking violent rupture in their respective spheres. This image can be positive: in order to cleanse the country of injustice, confusion and instability, a cataclysmic force is required. But it also has destructive connotations and the analogy may suggest that Perón's impact on Argentine history portends disaster rather than renewal. Given the satirical tone of the narrative this latter interpretation prevails.

This first chapter is notable because it throws into clear focus the contrast between the erasure of the persona of the author and the almost obtrusive presence of his techniques: his absence thereby becomes noticeable, even conspicuous, transforming itself into a presence and forcing a reticent author out of the shadows. Here we notice most clearly that facts do not speak for themselves but, rather, that the biographer/historian speaks for them by manipulating them to suit his aesthetic purposes. Like the creative writer, Page disrupts normal chronology in order to highlight an event that is both sensational and pivotal to his narrative – and that makes a memorable opening. Far from merely presenting the facts he is rather re-presenting them, imposing upon them a particular structure, or 'emplotting' them as White would have it.[29] The earthquake speaks of the turbulence of Perón and hints that the final balance of his intervention in Argentine history will be negative. While on the one hand he appears to be a force for good, appealing to the nation for aid for the victims of the earthquake, on the other hand that positive image is tarnished by a quotation from an Argentine magazine, reviewing the episode twenty-five years after the event, describing Perón's speech as 'a lengthy monologue that was to last for a decade'. The image of Perón as benefactor is now coloured by a retrospective judgement that casts him in a negative light as the nascent dictator. The narrator is keen to deflate his subject from the outset and will take full advantage of his omniscient perspective in order to do so. The image of Perón as self-serving and ambitious politician is insinuated by a series of unobtrusive references that have cumulative impact: 'the tragedy of San Juan provided the colonel [. . .] with instant national exposure' (p. 3). His action-packed contribution to the relief effort – 'he met with representatives from private industry [. . .] he utilized his position as secretary to the minister of war to coordinate military assistance [. . .] he set up [. . .] a center for the collection of foodstuffs, clothing and cash [. . .]' – now strike a rather hollow note that is only reinforced by the subsequent reference to him as 'resplendent in his gold-braided white uniform and flashing the infectious smile' (p. 5). This is a portrait of a man who is not what he seems, whose external amiability masks his selfish designs. This is not a biographer who is attempting a value-free representation of the facts, but a biographer whose procedures – in this instance, at least – resemble those of a novelist, whose character portrayal is a creative process dependent on the code of irony. Page thinks he can see beneath Perón's shimmering surfaces and does not appear to like what he thinks he finds there.

Opening the narrative with the earthquake also allows Page to introduce Eva at the outset and to captivate the reader by reference to an incipient romance for which the earthquake can also serve as a metaphor: 'the energy unleashed by this union would change the history of Argentina' (p. 4). Eva's achievement in rising from her impoverished background is enhanced by her patent lack of exceptional qualities: for Page she is 'not beautiful, sexy or particularly talented'. The matter-of-fact quality of this observation masks Page's own subjective judgement: while few commentators would dispute that she was not particularly talented, many would query the claim that Eva lacked beauty and sex appeal. Page's carefully chosen portrait serves his narrative purpose of heightening the fairy-tale aspect of her rise but hardly furthers his subsequent aim of uncovering the 'true' facts of her encounter with Perón, particularly difficult given the 'mythology' which now 'shrouds' it (p. 4). Page is on firmer ground when he describes the couple's mutual attraction, but the opportunity for the imaginative reconstruction of the 'decisive moment' whose 'truth' will not be found in the documentary records is lost and the biographer – as if reminded that he is a mere scribe – descends to a trite and colloquial style: 'the chemistry that drew them together proved powerful stuff' (p. 5).

The final third of the chapter consists of a flash-forward providing a synopsis of Perón's future and US reaction to his political career, ending with a sketch of his contradictory nature and a short paragraph designed to 'domesticate' him for a US audience by identifying the maverick Louisiana governor Huey Long (elected in 1928) as his 'closest North American counterpart' (though, as Page himself admits, there are more differences than similarities between the two). The first chapter of this monumental work is designed, therefore, to arouse the reader's interest in a fascinating story which combines politics and romance; decisive intervention ('he has marked Argentina as no one else has', p. 5) and self-demeaning cowardice (flight in response to the 1955 uprising); hero worship and vilification. It is the preview offered by an omniscient writer who can range at will over the entire span of Perón's life, bringing to bear upon its inscrutability 'the persistence of seven years' work', work which might be seen as a kind of biographer's certificate of qualification, a prerequisite for any serious attempt to master such an intractable subject. Having mentioned his credentials as a researcher in the preface, the biographer subsequently withdraws, absenting himself from his narrative which, by implication, will be perfectly balanced and objective. As we have seen, however, this first chapter displays a range of literary techniques, including metaphor and irony. The reference to Huey Long aims to reassure the North American reader that this Hispanic dictator, Juan Perón, who had been, in his prime, a major political irritant (p. 6) – and had proved to be an irritant, too, to lesser biographers and historians who had failed to grasp the intricacies of his character – will at last be 'fixed' and, deprived of his mythic aura, made the object of a kind of posthumous revenge. Perón's favourite technique will be turned against him and he will be miniaturized in his turn into a mere mortal of wholly manageable proportions.[30]

As if to compensate for the unusual freedoms exercised in the first chapter, Page adopts a densely factual narrative mode in the second, providing an overview of the country's vital statistics[31] and persistently setting Argentina against the benchmark of Europe or North America: Buenos Aires is a kind of Paris, the Boca Juniors football team is the equivalent of the Brooklyn Dodgers. Page emphasizes the importance of getting to grips with the Argentine psyche: the 'collective personality of the Argentines' is an 'essential prerequisite to grasping the Perón phenomenon' (p. 13). The essential traits of the Argentine personality are listed as: 'a predisposition towards authoritarianism, paranoid reaction to foreign criticism, a sense of solitude, sentimentalism, preoccupation with death'. To round off his checklist, Page observes that every Argentine has political opinions and 'an unswerving conviction of their soundness' (p. 14). Page's intention is clear: the disentangling of Perón's roots will lead to a clear understanding of the man himself since man and nation not only reflect each other but are, in essence, one and the same: 'Perón was Argentina and Argentina was Perón' (p. 15). Here the discourse suggests crude journalism, with reductive simplification standing in for serious analysis. The intractable aspects of Perón are diminished through his perfect assimilation to his country, itself thoroughly 'explained' by means of statistics and by a synopsis of the salient characteristics of the Argentine people. Page's approach is essentialist: he sees identity as static and given rather than as something continuously evolving and always in process. Page is reassuring his North American readership that a foreign country, fashioned by alien traditions and by a notoriously elusive president, whose brand of politics has persistently resisted easy categorization, will finally submit to investigation and analysis – although more than 500 pages will be necessary to complete the task. No matter that the national traits identified by Page might have been substituted by others to do with a strongly Europeanized culture (including a strong psychoanalytic tradition)[32] pointing to the country's affinities with – rather than distance from – the metropolis and that some of the traits identified, notably a 'predisposition towards authoritarianism', appear just as applicable not only to the rest of Latin America but also to most of Asia and Africa. If the purpose of the first chapter is to whet the interest of the reader, the purpose of the second is to reassure him/her that all contradictions and discontinuities will be ironed out and the gaps in the record filled by dint of the author's thoroughgoing research effort that will ultimately guarantee a full and coherent story. The references to statistics and documentary evidence contribute to the impression of an author who is in control of his subject. Any lingering notion of a resistant and strange Perón who will not surrender his secrets is now receding and will disappear completely in the course of the next 500 pages.

Since Perón's life was enveloped by rumour, gossip and myth, Page sees his main task as one of separating truth from fiction, fact from hearsay, logical inference from imaginative embellishment. He is driven by the impulse to define, which implies turning Perón into a unified, self-consistent individual who can be made to fit conventional biographical categories. The headings of Page's seven main sections form standard divisions which could be applied with the necessary modifications of detail to any military or political leader: 'The Making of a Leader (1895–1942)'; 'The Colonel (1943–1946)' etc. The life may be unwieldy but this is the first step towards mastery: it is divided up into manageable chronological chunks. Leon Edel warns that a 'chronological biography runs the risk of flattening out a life and giving it the effect of a calendar or a date book' (Edel, 1973, 145). Page may deviate from chronology in the first few chapters but the remainder of the text uses chronology as a structuring principle and makes regular reference to key dates in an effort to domesticate his subject.

Page aims to stabilize a notoriously unstable subject, to glue together his contradictory elements and discontinuities, to foreclose his open-ended series of subject positions. He seeks to offer a portrait of the 'deep-down' Perón, to find the essential figure behind the masks. His purpose is to create a sovereign subject who will find his own voice thanks to the meticulous research work of the biographer. Page will tell the truth and nothing but the truth about his subject and the elements of his life story will be measured against specific criteria of veracity and either upheld or rejected as a result. His procedure is to put on trial the various aspects of Perón's life story, vindicating some, rejecting others.

An indication of Page's legalistic procedures whereby claims and counterclaims about his subject are weighed on the scales of truth and falsehood emerges in Chapter 10 where he dismisses the attempts by various historians to link Juan and Eva Perón to the Nazis: 'the facts upon which the indictment rests contain gaping holes. As so often occurs, the conclusions of Perón's critics have gone far beyond what the evidence warrants. At the same time one may legitimately doubt Perón's total innocence in the matter' (pp. 86–7). This seemingly balanced approach is quite representative of Page's style and serves to reassure the reader: on the one hand this writer will adhere to the facts and will refrain from imaginative excess (unlike many of Perón's critics). On the other hand this writer will also steer clear of dogmatism by presenting an impartial front ('at the same time one may legitimately doubt'). There is a final element of reassurance for the reader: 'as so often occurs'. Patterns will be found not just to undermine rival interpretations but to domesticate a tortuous and potentially intractable reality.

The sifting of facts is a meticulous procedure. The diagnosis of Eva's illness and her reaction to it are problematic areas. Page adopts the role of information ferret who will come as close as humanly possible to the 'truth': 'one possible interpretation is that the first lady could not bring herself to permit the removal of her womb [. . .]. It is also possible that she did really understand how ill she was [. . .]. From the facts presently available [. . .] no evidence has come to light about Perón's role' (pp. 237–8). A similar procedure is employed when Page tackles the question of Perón's disagreement with the Church: a balanced overview of the possibilities leads to the 'safest' conclusion: 'Why did Perón commit himself to a war with the Church? An anti-Peronist explanation [. . .]. The theory falls short of the mark [. . .]. The explanation most commonly offered by Peronists [. . .]. This theory is also weak [. . .]. A final theory, which seems most plausible [. . .] (pp. 298–9).

Often degrees of truth are offered ranging from the full truth, for example regarding the controversial episode at the end of Perón's posting in Chile ('the truth of the matter is more complex as well as somewhat ironic [. . .]', p. 34); to the 'most widely accepted account', though not excluding the 'inevitable derogatory variation', for example, in the case of Evita's departure from Junín (p. 82); to accounts which are included despite being based on mere rumour: 'during production Eva was rumoured to have engaged in a bitter quarrel with Lamarque' (p. 84). Truth, probability and rumour are meticulously labelled and the degree of credence conceded is carefully gauged. But Page's determination to control if not to suppress rumour frequently runs aground as the ebb and flow of shifting generic frames moves decisively away from the historical and 'truthful' towards the fictional and 'unreliable'. Thus, for example, the financial assets of Perón refuse accurate accountability: although his wealth had 'no apparent factual basis [...] the suspicion that he was unable to reach Eva's bank deposits in Switzerland adds to the puzzle. According to one unsubstantiated account [...]. Another rumour holds that [...]. A US consul [...] quoted a "well-informed source" as declaring [...]. There is a strong temptation to conclude [...]' (pp. 371–2). Here Page's conceptual machinery shows signs of strain: unable to produce his finely calibrated list of competing versions measured against the benchmark of solid, documented fact, he is reduced to offering a mere play of possibilities, none of which emerges as more credible than any other and his final reference to 'strong temptation' suggests his awareness of straying from the narrow ground of legitimate investigation. His usual method is to leave no stone unturned in the interests of uncovering the truth: for this reason minibiographies of secondary characters such as the American ambassador Spruille Bradon (p. 111) and of Perón's friend Jorge Antonio (p. 282), are supplied; various versions of secondary issues, such as the appointment of Mario, Perón's brother, to head the municipal zoo (p. 157) are provided; and the claim that José López Rega once worked as a bouncer at 'Happy Land' in Panama City is judiciously dismissed as 'apocryphal' (p. 397). But Page's system ultimately breaks down as the unknown factors accumulate. The disjunction between his methods, which constantly aim for mastery, and his recalcitrant subject matter is highlighted as history merges with fiction and López Rega's excesses, in particular, refuse to be bound by the normal discursive patterns of historical writing. The only way to deal with such elements, which will not be elucidated by documentary evidence or any other investigative tool, is by means of a creative approach since they belong to the uncharted realms of the imagination, speculation, and gossip. Gossip is part and parcel of fiction but it has the capacity to become truth.[33] It exemplifies the permeability of generic boundaries, since biography (according to Justin Kaplan, biographer of Whitman) is now threatening to become 'the highest form of gossip'.[34]

Perón's life does offer some footholds to the traditional biographer: initially unremarkable, his life underwent a turning point which inaugurated the new man endowed with two important qualities, capacity for concentrated work and charismatic appeal, which serve to anchor his character since they 'were to serve him well throughout his entire life' (p. 24). Further qualities designed to fix and arrest his persona are identified: putting and holding together coalitions composed of heterogenous elements would become a *hallmark* of his career (p. 46); he is a coward who *always* shrank from physical danger (p. 49). His deviant sexual behaviour is rationalized by his alleged need for the constant presence of a woman to demonstrate his heterosexuality (p. 293). But Page is exacerbated by Perón's inconsistencies (p. 322), by his failure to explain his ideology (p. 405) and by his underlying indifference (p. 473), qualities which, by contrast, enchant Martínez. He draws some comfort, however, from the claim that 'Perón never stopped being Perón' (p. 443) and finds another mooring-point while attempting to explain Perón's tolerance of López Rega, appealing to those 'patterns of behaviour he had followed all his life' (p. 487). Finally Page attempts to pin down his troublesome subject by proclaiming his uniqueness and domesticating him first through the production of a neat balance sheet listing both his negative and positive qualities and then by acknowledging a 'curious contradiction' located 'at the essence of his nature' (p. 502).

Ultimately Page fails to get to grips with a character who shows such 'cavalier disdain for the truth' (p. 35). Rather than celebrating Perón as the figure who 'looms largest in the Argentine shift from modernity to postmodernity',[35] the often moralistic Page plays the role of *criticón* by exposing Perón's deviousness – undermining, for example, his explanation for his posting to Mendoza (p. 37). He also seeks to suppress Perón's dangerous humour: inspired by her overbite, Perón bestows on his adolescent lover the nickname of 'Piranha' (Page's spelling: the usual version is 'Piraña'). His mischievousness is no cause for celebration for Page who engages in a negative character analysis: the episode, he says, 'evidenced a disregard for convention that pushed beyond indifference into the realm of defiance' (p. 80). He follows up, however, with a rather ineffectual attempt to downplay Perón's deviant sexual interests by noting that prior to his marriage to Eva – older than Piranha but young enough to be his daughter – Perón had planned to marry his sister-in-law who was nearly his own age. Some of Page's rationalizations have the ironically counterproductive effect of diminishing Perón's historical status and emphasizing his potentially fictive qualities. Attempting to explain the assassination of Vandor, who was emerging as a potential rival for the leadership of the movement, Page claims that supporters anticipating the wishes of their leader, rather than acting on his direct orders, may have been responsible. Here Page – unwittingly – moves his narrative in the direction of fiction. His Perón enjoys the same kind of mythic power wielded by García Márquez's Colonel Aureliano Buendía: 'sus órdenes se cumplían antes de ser impartidas, aun antes de que él las concibiera, y siempre llegaban mucho más lejos de donde él se hubiera atrevido a hacerlas llegar'.[36]

Page deplores Perón's tactical contradictions which 'are as natural to him as the twists and turns of his intestines' (p. 220); his amoral approach to politics (p. 223); and, above all, his 'rambling reminiscences, often characterized by outrageous distortions or misstatements of fact' (p. 404). But there are signs that Page is himself contaminated by Perón's discourse: his description of Peronism as a vaccine against communism recalls Perón's favourite medical metaphor of the antibodies needed to neutralize the turncoats and traitors (pp. 394, 411, 466, 490). He concludes with an old saying which Perón himself might have used: 'if Argentines were an orange, Perón would be the juice'. There is clearly no irony here: this phrase, so Page says, contains 'more truth than hyperbole' (p. 502).

How does Page handle Eva? The circumstances of her young life are recounted without embellishment as Page steers a judicious middle course between the 'rabid Evita haters' on the one hand, and those admirers who wanted her to be canonized on the other. It is a stereotyped, or as Norman Mailer would put it, 'factoidal'[37] Eva who emerges, depicted as 'volatile, out of control, uninhibitedly aggressive' (p. 84). She is the 'product of her formative years, unable to shed her culturally disadvantaged past [. . .]. When she spoke extemporaneously, her tone and choice of words were from the heart' (p. 188). Here it seems that it is Eva's vocabulary that has infected Page. Duplicating his procedure vis-à-vis Perón, Page seeks to control Eva by applying labels designed to contain, fix and arrest. Thus she is 'more Peronist than Perón' (p. 198); 'the very qualities that were the *essence* of Evita carried with them a potential for excess that could embarrass her husband' (p. 199). As to be expected, Page's speculations about how Evita might have influenced events had she lived are tentative and minimal: 'it is perfectly conceivable that she might have accepted the conductor's insistence that his quarrel was merely with the 'bad' priests and bishops' (p. 314).

Page controls his narrative making it as accessible and seamless as possible by emphasizing its points of coherence. His main objective is to provide a unified and cohesive account which he achieves to some extent by imposing discernible patterns. The structure, as we have seen, is determined by the familiar template of biographical writing: the beginning ('The Formative Years') leads chronologically to the ending ('The Death of the Caudillo' and 'Aftermath'). Links are forged across the decades – 'instead of Braden or Perón it was now Lanusse or Perón' (p. 449) – and across the centuries: 'Perón did not want to die like Rosas in exile' (p. 460). Re-enactments of the past are highlighted: the newspaper *El Descamisado* equated the resignation of El Tío (Hector Cámpora) with Eva's heroic renunciation (p. 470); there was widespread hope that Isabel would emulate Eva and give up her vice-presidential nomination (p. 474). Neat reciprocations also contribute to a sense of narrative order: 'FORJA (Fuerza de Orientación Radical de la Juventud Argentina) found in Perón the leader for whom it had long been searching [...]. FORJA furnished the colonel with the intellectual element his increasingly heterogenous movement lacked' (p. 57). To facilitate understanding further, decisive moments are clearly identified: 'if any single event was to stamp Argentine history over the next decade it was the nomination of Isabel' (p. 472). Stylistic uniformity together with an aura of objectivity pervades the text: the narrative seems to narrate itself since information merges seamlessly into unobtrusive evaluation: 'Perón made a number of efforts to secure U.S. recognition [...]. It was ironic that the United States pursued an antagonistic policy toward Perón at the very moment he found himself in a power struggle with the ultra-nationalist, pro-Nazi faction led by Perlinger. The exigencies of the situation required him to seek a quiet rapprochement with Washington [...]' (p. 76). Such writing gives the impression that it is merely affirming what, in reality, 'goes without saying': judgements are camouflaged by the smooth flow of the discourse. A similar effect is achieved by the occasional insertion of vignettes of rural and urban life: the images are stereotyped but they provide a sense of familiarity, of an Argentina which is not so complex after all and which arouses curiosity rather than awe: 'on a late Saturday afternoon a rough-hewn gaucho strolls across an intersection.

Cigarette in hand, black boots carefully shined, broad belt studded with silver coins, red neckerchief set off against green-checkered shirt, he is ready for a night on the town. A woman with her hair in curlers rides by him on a bicycle' (p. 19).

The openings and conclusions of chapters follow distinct patterns: the early chapters open with references to significant geographical locations: San Juan (chapter 1); Argentina (2); Buenos Aires province (3); Italy (5) and La Plata (8). Significant dates are also prominent: chapter 15 heightens the significance of 17 October 1945 by recounting the comparatively unremarkable events which occurred in other countries in order to highlight the full momentousness of this date in Argentine history (p. 127); chapter 22 begins with a reference to 1947 as the 'year of the star-shell burst' (p. 188); chapter 26 refers to 1950 as the 'pivotal year' for the government (p. 228); chapter 27 refers to August 1951 as 'one of the great moments in the history of Peronism' (p. 240). The highlighting of significant dates provides a clearly charted temporal map of events, foregrounding pattern and de-emphasizing those less amenable aspects of the story. But Page sometimes deviates from his usual matter-of-fact legalistic style in some of his chapter openings: thus in chapter 30 there is an abrupt transition from the aftermath of Eva's death to the disturbing scene of another death – that of her brother Juan – which was to remain unresolved as either suicide or murder. Page's normal procedure – meticulous assessment of the evidence followed by a suitably judicious conclusion – is put on hold as he stamps his narrative with the stylized opening of a traditional detective story: 'in the bedroom of a fashionable apartment, not far from the building where Perón and Eva once lived, a shirt, jacket and trousers lay neatly folded on a chair near a night table [. . .]. A handwritten note on the night table contained the following message [. . .]' (p. 267). Here we have a welcome glimpse of the more creative Page, his normally hidden presence discernible in the change of style. For a moment the text insinuates its own workings as its continuity is broken, albeit fleetingly. There are a few other examples: chapter 35, dealing with the revolt of 16 June 1955, opens with a detailed description of the Plaza de Mayo, moving to a graphic portrayal of the specific scene on that date, then zooming in for a close-up shot of two men sitting in a bar – thereby creating expectation and suspense in the style of a thriller.

The chapter endings also follow a clear pattern: conclusions of early chapters (3, 4, 6, 16 and 20) generally end on a note of expectation; those of later chapters (21, 23, 25, 26, 28, 37) are distinctly anti-climactic and ominous. Yet other chapters end on a note of reassurance, sometimes achieved through blatant simplification: 'Perón was Argentina and Argentina was Perón' (p. 15), or through an appeal to one of the hallmarks of the 'essential' Perón: 'but the old man was still the master manipulator, and in the end deserved them [left-wing Peronist youth leaders] as much as they deserved him' (p. 489). At the end of chapter 8 Page provides an exquisite insight brimming with reassurance: inconsistent US policies will ultimately prove intelligible by reverting to type: 'a zig that had become a zag was about to zig again' (p. 78). Later chapter endings point more clearly to the technique of an omniscient narrator who teases the reader with clues regarding future developments but is careful to withhold vital information: ' "The first election I won with the men", Perón had declared before the election. "This one I shall win with the women [. . .] and the third I shall win with the children" – an uncannily accurate long-range prophecy that would be fulfilled but in ways that Perón could not have imagined' (p. 254).

Though Page uses novelistic techniques he is careful not to engage in novelistic reconstruction of events. Chapter 9 ('The Emergence of Evita') undoubtedly provides him with an opportunity to do so, to discard, albeit temporarily, the role of the traditional biographer and assume a freer and more imaginative approach. We have already noted Virginia Woolf's observation that the biographer can give us 'much more than another fact to add to our collection. He can give us the creative fact; the fertile fact; the fact that suggests and engenders'.[38] Making a similar point, Lytton Strachey states that 'discretion is not the better part of biography'.[39] Where Perón and sex are concerned, however, Page treads with particular care. He is clearly determined not to underestimate the importance of Eva: 'Perón's liaisons with women provide much more than picturesque footnotes to his public life. They throw light upon aspects of his character that bore upon his capabilities as a leader and statesman' (p. 79). Thus Perón's private life is a legitimate interest for Page only to the extent that it impinges on Perón's political career: it is of little interest for its own sake. Such an interest would inevitably lead to improper speculation and mire the biographer in the quicksand of rumour and gossip: 'an impressive volume of rumor has burgeoned, most of it the work of his political enemies, ascribing to Perón a panoply of sexual aberrations that supposedly provide clues to his behaviour' (p. 77). Page cannot wash his hands entirely of gossip since it forms an intrinsic part of the narrative he is telling but he takes care to provide a source, as he does when referring to the German mistress whom Perón allegedly had during his stay in Italy. Page goes on to observe: 'various deviations ranging from voyeurism to paedophilia have also been ascribed to him' (p. 79). Here the reader might well suspect Page of following a somewhat furtive academic procedure identified by Janet Malcolm. She claims that the voyeurism and 'busybodyism' that 'impel writers and readers of biography alike are obscured by an apparatus of scholarship designed to give the enterprise an appearance of bank-like blandness and solidity'.[40] Again we note a contradiction in Page's procedure: on the one hand he is the reliable narrator who makes few claims that cannot be supported by documentary evidence while on the other he does not refrain from reciting stories which he himself describes as 'suspect': 'Perón himself is said to have asserted that while delayed in Spain in 1940 he spent a number of months in Barcelona, where he met, moved in with and possibly impregnated a Catalán schoolteacher' (p. 80). For Page this is a rare excursion into that dangerous side of biography where the solidity of facts is replaced by the lightness of speculation. The decidedly unromantic terminology and the brevity and haste of the narrative suggest the embarrassment of a biographer who knows that he has strayed into forbidden territory. While Page does not always live up to his own rigorous standards, he would never concur with Spacks's injunction: 'Gossip is gossip – it must be allowed to become truth as often happens'.[41] We can conclude that even a scrupulously factual account of the past cannot always avoid the contamination of gossip. As for Eva herself, Page's strategy is containment: thus when he mentions her letter, dispatched to Perón at the beginning of her European tour, Eva emerges in stereotyped fashion as a village girl made good who fears that her colourful past might yet ruin things: 'in earthy language that was pure Evita, she concluded by urging him not to believe rumors about her childhood in Junín. The letter reflects the state of mind of a girl from the provinces about to plunge bravely into the great unknown, aware of her limitations yet fired by an ambition to be someone'

(p. 192). Page says nothing about the nature of those rumours. His blatantly clichéd description of a girl who conforms to type serves to emasculate Eva, to miniaturize her – just as Perón himself was wont to do, particularly with people whom he perceived to be dangerous.

Page's allusive style is thoroughly eclectic, ranging from well-known jokes, such as that circulating after the mysterious death of Juan Duarte, Eva's brother ('everyone knows he committed suicide but nobody knows who did it', p. 268) to memorable political pronouncements such as Churchill's devastating critique of Perón: 'Perón is the first soldier to burn his flag, and the first Catholic to burn his churches' (p. 310). A taste for the trite and catchy ('The Ten Days that Shook Argentina', p. 114) is matched by fondness for hyperbole: 'youth, glamour, adulation, agony and early death – Evita's lot fed Argentina's lust for sentimentality like nothing else in the country's history' (p. 259). A talent for incisive definition – López Rega is an almost 'organic extension of Perón' (p. 485) whose obsessive desire to bury all Argentine heroes in one place amounts to 'necrophilia transformed into public policy' (p. 486) – is complemented by a discreet brand of ironic humour: 'it was common for military officers to marry into middle class families and settle into stable lives. Perón was no doubt ready to follow the pattern' (p. 25); 'the nickname he [Perón] bestowed upon her [Nelly Rivas, his adolescent lover], Tinolita, was an ultimate show of affection, for it was the name of one of his poodles' (p. 294). Here there are glimpses of the more creative biographer but Page is ever discreet and since the effect of irony is to destabilize, its use is minimized. It is not insignificant that the role of Eva is downgraded: at first she is presented almost incidentally, as an aside following a synopsis of Peron's political manoeuvrings: 'he also entered into an intimate personal relationship [. . .]' (p. 79). Eva is a further threat to the stability of the narrative and Page does not take kindly to her: whereas Perón's illegitimacy is downplayed – 'there is some evidence to suggest that his parents were not married at the time he was born' (p. 19) – Eva's illegitimacy is highlighted by the conspicuous use of legalistic and pejorative expression : 'Juan Duarte's *legal* wife and three *legitimate* children lived in the pampa town of Chivilcoy. Juana Ibarguren, his *concubine*, worked as a servant on the ranch and kept her *brood*, now numbering five, in a house in Los Toldos' (p. 81, my italics). By contrast, Eva's anodyne brand of feminism which, unlike extreme foreign varieties, accepted women's 'traditional responsibilities' (p. 197) meets with Page's tacit approval. Meanwhile, Perón escapes with a perfunctory ticking off (he is 'oversimplifying') for describing Evita as 'a product of mine' (p. 198). Page's conservatism emerges too in the political sphere: although his text occasionally ironizes the inconsistencies of US foreign policy, its perspective is unashamedly American, sometimes stereotypically 'imperialist': Perón was one of several Latin American dictators 'blemishing the free world' (p. 6); Latin America is the North American 'underbelly' (p. 44); Fidel Castro's triumph in January 1959 'destabilized' the Caribbean (p. 368). Such expression is, of course, ideologically charged, but is used by Page as if it were innocently neutral and transparent, connoting nothing beyond its plain meaning. According to White the great classic historians are conscious of the aporia or sense of contradiction residing at the heart of language itself. It is this awareness that 'distinguishes them from their mundane counterparts and followers, who think that language can serve as a perfectly transparent medium of representation and who think that if one can only find the right language for describing events, the meaning of events will *display itself* to consciousness'.[42] White goes on to argue that Darwin's *Origin of Species* 'desires to remain within the ambit of plain fact' and that its author insists that there is a *real* order in nature. *Continuity-in-variation* is seen as the 'rule' and radical discontinuity or variation is an anomaly'. Page's procedure suggests a parallel with Darwin's as summarized by White.

There is no doubt that Page, like so many other traditional biographers, has become blinkered in his quest to uncover and reveal 'the truth'. Foucault points out that the 'very question of truth, the right it appropriates to refute error and oppose itself to appearance, the manner in which it developed [. . .] – does not this form a history, the history of an error we call truth?'[43] Page's pursuit of the truth may be unattainable for many reasons but the most obvious is the nature of his subject: Perón's refusal to be pinned down is uncompromising and spectacular. Owing to his enduring elusiveness, his apparent lack of feelings and emotions, his detachment and indifference, he lends himself ultimately not to discovery but rather to recreation. The 'real' Perón does not exist: his appearance *is* his depth. Page's insistence on 'the truth' does not open new doors to his character: rather it distances Page from the ever-resistant, playful and ironic figure of Perón. Even his rigorous documentation is compromised by the persistent intrusion of gossip and his 'rational' approach sometimes breaks down: he is reluctant, for example, to investigate personal relationships, possibly because supporting evidence is too sparse to form the basis of a 'truthful' account. The consequence can be an insufficiency of significant information on the one hand and an excess of superfluous detail on the other. Thus the Perón-Isabel relationship is covered by a few brief and tentative generalizations: 'there is no evidence that Perón had strong feelings for Isabel [. . .]' (p. 374); 'Perón probably looked upon her as an empty vessel he could fill and manipulate at will' (p. 389). By contrast, Page offers specific details relating to Perón's dogs in his account of Perón's air journey from the Dominican Republic to Spain: 'Perón's two poodles completed the entourage (A third poodle had not survived the Dominican sojourn and lay buried under a tree in the garden of the house where Perón and Isabel had lived)' (p. 369). Surprisingly, no source for these details is given but by now the reader has learned to trust an apparently reliable narrator.

Page's work can be placed alongside Richard Ellman's *James Joyce* and Robert Blake's *Disraeli*, biographies notable, according to Shelston, for their 'monumental organization of the details of their subject's life into a vast total pattern achieved by the detached narrative standpoint'.[44] By contrast, Boswell's *Life of Johnson* is more intimate and open. Boswell had the immeasurable advantage of knowing his subject: he helped – as Edel observes – to '*live* the biography he was ultimately to write', having known a 'palpable Dr Johnson'.[45] Boswell worked from life rather than from the document – an advantage, in the case of Perón, which Tomás Eloy Martínez enjoys over Page. But, despite having had direct contact with Perón, Martínez adopts a conspicuously fictional approach in *La novela de Perón*, a work in which his own presence and activity are highlighted, much like Boswell's in his *Life of Johnson*, where, according to Spacks, 'the interpretive consciousness declares itself integral to the story's import'.[46] That the biographer does not know his/her subject does not, of course, justify self-effacement or the adoption of an unselfconsciously realist approach. In his Freudian study, *Young Man Luther*, Erik Erikson implies that his own writing will not escape the tentacles of ideology despite his keen awareness of them.[47] His work as self-critique is an integral aspect of his biography: 'I said that Luther could not hate his father openly. This statement presumes that he did hate him' (p. 62). Page, by contrast, removes himself from his narrative, as we have seen, presumably in the interests of 'authoritative' and 'objective' writing. Interestingly, in his 'Reconocimientos' at the conclusion of *La novela de Perón*, Martínez acknowledges Joseph Page, 'junto a quien descubrí que narrar a Perón es un oficio inagotable, y que nadie podrá escribir el libro definitivo' (p. 323). The reader might be forgiven for forming the impression that Page – inspired by the unachievable goals of coherence and continuity – has, indeed, attempted to write the definitive work on Perón, whereas Martínez's self-conscious perspective and his use of experimental techniques suggest a greater awareness of the complexity of an elusive subject and (with Virginia Woolf) of the sense that the 'life which is increasingly real to us is the fictitious life'.[48]

NOTES

[1] Ira Bruce Nadel, *Biography: Fiction, Fact and Form* (New York: St Martin's Press, 1984), p. 11.
[2] Hayden White, 'The historical text as literary artifact' in *Tropics of Discourse: Essays in Cultural Criticism* (Baltimore and London: The Johns Hopkins University Press, 1978), pp. 81–100 (p. 82).
[3] William H. Epstein, *Recognizing Biography* (Philadelphia: University of Pennsylvania, 1987), p. 81.
[4] Preface to *Perón: a Biography* (New York: Random House, 1983), pp. ix–x. Future references, given in parenthesis in the text, are to this edition.
[5] See Jack Miles, *God: a Biography* (New York: Knopf, 1995).
[6] Mary Evans, *Missing Persons: the Impossibility of Auto/biography* (London and New York: Routledge, 1999), p. 23.
[7] Norman K. Denzin, *Interpretive Biography* (London: Sage, 1989), p. 61.
[8] Hutcheon, *Irony's Edge*, p. 58.
[9] Jean Baudrillard, *Seduction*, trans. Brian Singer (London: Macmillan, 1979), p. 21
[10] Tulio Halperín Donghi, 'El lugar del peronismo en la tradición política argentina' in Samuel Amaral and Mario Ben Plotkin (eds), *Perón: del exilio al poder* (Buenos Aires: Cántaro, 1993), pp. 15–44 (p. 27).
[11] See Enrique Pavón Pereyra, *Diario Secreto de Perón* (Buenos Aires: Sudamericana/Planeta, 1985), p. 8.
[12] Sigal and Verón, *Perón o muerte*, p. 12
[13] Martínez, *Las memorias del General*, p. 109.

14   Ernesto Goldar, *El peronismo en la literatura argentina*, pp. 59–60.
15   Douglas Smith, 'Introduction' in Friedrich Nietzsche, *On the Genealogy of Morals: a Polemic By Way of Clarification and Supplement to My Last Book, 'Beyond Good and Evil'*, translated with an introduction and notes by Douglas Smith, pp. vii–xxxi (p. xiii).
16   William Ratliff, 'Perón y la guerrilla: el arte del engaño mutuo' in Samuel Amaral and Mario Ben Plotkin (eds), *Perón: del exilio al poder*, pp. 261–80 (p. 267).
17   Mariano Ben Plotkin, *Mañana es San Perón: propaganda, rituales políticos y educación en el régimen peronista (1946–1955)* (Buenos Aires: Ariel Historia Argentina, 1994), p. 196.
18   Zygmunt Bauman, *Modernity and Ambivalence* (Cambridge: Polity, 1991), pp. 7–8.
19   Sigal and Verón, *Perón o muerte*, p. 189.
20   Samuel Amaral, 'El avión negro' in *Perón: del exilio al poder*, pp. 69–94 (p. 77).
21   Brian Vickers, *In Defence of Rhetoric* (Oxford: Clarendon, 1988), p. vii.
22   C. Jan Swearingen, *Rhetoric and Irony: Western Literacy and Western Lies* (New York: Oxford University Press, 1991), p. 5.
23   Daniel James, *Resistance and Integration*, p. 22.
24   'Nietzsche, genealogy, history', *Foucault Reader*, pp. 76–100 (p. 88).
25   Nancy Hanway, *Embodying Argentina*, p. 34.
26   Richard Terdiman, *Discourse/Counter-Discourse. The Theory and Practice of Symbolic Resistance in Nineteenth-Century France* (Ithaca and London: Cornell University Press, 1985), p. 78.
27   Daniel James, *Resistance and Integration*, p. 30.
28   Hayden White, *Metahistory*, p. 7.
29   'Historical emplotment and the problem of truth' in Keith Jenkins (ed.), *Postmodern History Reader* (London and New York: Routledge, 1997), pp. 392–6.
30   'Denying in his heart the existence of another, man or woman, Perón could love only by diminishing and minimizing'. See Alicia Dujovne Ortiz, *Eva Perón*, trans. Shawn Fields (New York: St Martin's Griffin, 1997), p. 62.
31   Page appears undeterred by Perón's attitude to statistics as reflected in one of his favourite aphorisms: 'los tres mentirosos más grandes que hay son, como se dice, los curas, las mujeres y las estadísticas' (*Las memorias del General*, p. 46).
32   See the discussion of Puig's *Pubis angelical* in chapter 10.
33   Spacks, *Gossip*, p. 230.
34   Noted by Rob Wilson, 'Producing American selves: the form of American biography', in *Contesting the Subject*, pp. 167–92 (p. 169).
35   Santiago Colás, *Postmodernity in Latin America: the Argentine Paradigm*, Post-Contemporary Interventions (Durham and London: Duke University Press, 1994), p. 152.
36   Gabriel García Márquez, *Cien años de soledad*, ed. Jacques Joset, Letras Hispánicas (Madrid: Cátedra, 1995), p. 274.
37   Mailer uses this term to designate 'facts' which have no existence before appearing in magazine or newspaper accounts. This concept

recalls Spacks's assertion that gossip can become truth. See Norman Mailer, *Marilyn*, p. 18 and Spacks, *Gossip*, p. 230.

38 Virginia Woolf, 'The art of biography', in *Collected Essays*, ed. Leonard Woolf, 4 vols (New York: Harcourt, Brace and World, 1967), IV, 221–8 (p. 228).

39 Quoted by Alan Shelston, *Biography*, The Critical Idiom, 34 (London: Methuen, 1977), p. 10.

40 Janet Malcolm, 'The silent woman', *The New Yorker*, 69, 23–30 August 1993, p. 86.

41 Spacks, *Gossip*, p. 230.

42 White, 'Fictions of Factual Representation', in *Tropics of Discourse*, pp. 121–34 (130).

43 'Nietzsche, genealogy, history', *Foucault Reader*, pp. 76–100 (pp. 79–80).

44 Shelston, *Biography*, p. 9.

45 Edel, *Literary Biography*, pp. 21, 23.

46 Spacks, *Gossip*, p. 112.

47 Erik H. Erikson, *Young Man Luther. A Study in Psychoanalysis and History* (London: Faber and Faber, 1958), p. 20.

48 Virginia Woolf, 'The new biography' in *The Essays of Virginia Woolf*, ed. Andrew McNeillie, 4 vols (London: Hogarth, 1986–94), IV: 1925–1928, pp. 473–80 (p. 478).

Chapter 5

The Limits of Testimonial Biography: Borroni and Vacca; Sebreli, Taylor

Borroni and Vacca's Tale of the Tape

In an open letter (9 November 1944) to her radio listeners, Eva states rather pretentiously: 'sobre la faz un poco absurda de la novela radial, prefiero la biografía donde está el testimonio de algo que se llamó "mujer" y que amó, sufrió, y vivió, no importa el lugar, ni el tiempo, ni la distancia'.[1] Borroni and Vacca might have taken their cue for their work from this declaration by Eva of her clear preference for the lived intensity of biography over what she sees as the trifling inanities of the radio novel. Barroni and Vacca seem determined to do justice to that intensity by offering a biography sustained throughout by testimonial accounts whose veracity does not depend on human memory or sentiment but rather on the clinical reliability of the tape recording. Clearly their view is that such a narrative method is better qualified than any other to capture accurately the immediate reality of Eva's life.

Despite its clear monologic intentions, however, the account offered by Borroni and Vacca achieves a kind of Bakhtinian dialogism by virtue of its play of diverse voices all purportedly unified in their focus on Eva. They total at least forty with some featuring several times, such as that of Mauricio Rubinstein, a former editor of *Sintonía* (pp. 48, 61, 142). They not only present distinct perspectives on their subject but also offer a variety of narrative styles. Appearing at regular intervals in a text which also comprises traditional biographical narrative supplemented by outline chronological summaries at the end of each chapter, the testimonies are presented without comment and without obvious categorization. They can be classified according to content: the first eight testimonies (pp. 18–29) deal with the substitution of Eva's real birth certificate by a false one which seeks to rewrite her personal history, giving her a new identity. Her surname is now given as 'Duarte' (rather than 'Ibarguren') and her birthplace becomes Junín rather than Los Toldos. The second block of testimonies (pp. 48–51) focuses on Eva's early professional life, while the third (pp. 61–93) deals with Eva's character, her professional career and her early romantic attachments. Subsequent testimonies focus on her role on 17 October (pp. 111–15), her early political activity (pp. 141–7), her European tour (pp. 192–3), her political maturity (pp. 220–7) and her decline and death (pp. 295–325).

In their prologue Borroni and Vacca note that their work will be different from earlier biographies which, they claim, gravitate in varying degrees towards two extreme views – of Eva as saint or Eva as prostitute. Prior to their pioneering efforts, biographies of Eva were, allegedly, little more than 'versiones más o menos politizadas, sociologizantes o psicológicas'. Borroni and Vacca do not propose to contribute yet another ideologically tainted version of Eva but will seek, rather, to 'informar objetivamente acerca de todas las instancias de su vida'. Language, by implication, will serve as a mere instrument of communication, its poetic resources silenced in the interests of objectivity: 'los autores consideraron necesario realizar un relato frío, sin preocuparse obsesivamente por el uso de un lenguaje ameno y novelesco'. Borroni and Vaca resolve not to be distracted by linguistic niceties in their pursuit of what has been described, in the context of *testimonio*, as 'a no-nonsense approach to getting the facts straight [. . .] a kind of discursive manliness'.[2] Their approach denies the widely documented link between biography and fiction and far from acknowledging the construction of story elements whose defining character is determined by the writer, they seek to claim for their account a transparency and objectivity that have eluded previous biographers.

Transparency and objectivity are, of course, unattainable ideals in any sphere of literature including biography. What Borroni and Vacca do provide is a multifaceted portrait of Eva through recourse to a series of diverse testimonies representing the views of people who knew Eva, some superficially, others intimately. These views have the directness and immediacy of oral discourse. Some of the testimonies have been taken from published sources (such as Angel Perelman's, from *Como hicimos el 17 de Octubre*, noted by Borroni and Vacca, p. 112). In some cases the views presented mirror each other so that one testimony serves to confirm the authenticity of another. However, forty or so different perspectives inevitably throw up not only differences but, in some cases, blatant contradictions. One of the notable aspects of Borroni and Vacca's work is its reluctance to resolve differences or even to provide a conciliatory summary of positions: its struggle for objectivity produces a detachment which will not be compromised by arbitration. Rather, the voices speak for themselves, free from overt interference by an author or editor. The failure to suppress differences between accounts gives rise to an often discordant babble of voices, leaving an impression of Eva as elusive and inconsistent, impossible to pin down and resistant to neat interpretation. Marysa Navarro is, unsurprisingly, bemused by such an unorthodox assemblage of materials, describing the work as 'una extraña mezcla de investigación periodística – la mejor publicada hasta la fecha – y de testimonios, de la que surgía una imagen de Evita tan irreal como la que durante tantos años propusieron sus enemigos o sus admiradores'.[3]

Several witnesses concur in their descriptions of Eva's pretty features and political intelligence. Some also highlight her transformation from raw young actress to sophisticated political operator ('de damita joven a ser lo que después fue, hay un abismo. Una total transformación', p. 62). Many witnesses, predictably, offer a wholly positive view of Eva ('Eva Perón fue una mujer maravillosa porque se mantuvo siempre humilde, buena y simple', p. 28); others, equally predictably, if not more so in the case of military personnel, are virulently negative: thus Colonel Gerardo Demetro notes that 'el descaro de esa mujer a veces llegaba a límites inaguantables, por ejemplo, un día en que Eva se puso junto a Perón en el acto de juramento de un ministro, haciendo descansar un brazo sobre el respaldo del sillón presidencial' (p. 114). While the testimony of the trade unionist, Angel Perelman, consists of rapid and racy dialogue (pp. 112–13), other accounts are matter of fact, formal, almost legalistic: thus the testimony of the lawyer, Dario Rodríguez del Pino, who recounts how Eva's sister, Elisa, pressurized his brother, the director of the Office of Births, Marriages and Deaths in Los Toldos, to amend Eva's birth certificate: 'la peticionante insistió y le rogó hiciera ese gran favour que sería bien recompensado' (p. 20). The discourse of General Héctor D'Andrea, who arrested Perón in 1945, is similarly formal and precise: 'su aspecto físico y estado de ánimo eran normales. El diálogo fue escueto y categórico, en nivel de corrección militar' (pp. 113–14). It is immediately preceded by Perelman's but there is no attempt to soften the transition from the perspective and style of the trade unionist to that of the general – a random strength of this seemingly documentary text whose literary resonances elude the truth-telling principles of its authors. Few concessions are made to the reader by way of clarity or order in the organization of the testimonies and unresolved contradictions serve to keep Eva's story, as presented here, incomplete and open ended. Víctor Casaus claims that *testimonio* fails 'cuando ha acumulado información sin lograr una estructura coherente; cuando el autor ha pensado que todo se reduce a apretar el botón de la grabadora [. . .] cuando ha colocado una entrevista detrás de la otra, sin preocuparse por el montaje que eso supone [. . .]'.[4] Borroni and Vacca's work gives the impression of such incoherence, the reader being left to make the necessary connections and highlight the major contradictions without much editorial help; but it can be seen as an unwitting strength rather than a weakness of a biography driven by the naive determination to attain total objectivity. Differences between testimonies abound, ranging from minor discrepancies to important contradictions. Renata Coronado de Nuosi claims that Eva had no boyfriend (p. 28) while the following account, of Julio Otero, documents her relationship with Ricardo Caturla (p. 29). Similarly Mauricio Rubinstein is adamant that the young Eva 'jamás pasó necesidades' (p. 48) while Eduardo del Castillo is equally assertive in his claims that she did indeed go hungry (p. 50). More significant divergences of opinion emerge regarding Eva's character: Rubinstein affirms that Eva 'no amaba la vida nocturna' (p. 48) while Carmelo Santiago's testimony claims that she was 'una chica desenfrenada. Conoció a tantos hombres como el país tiene' (p. 49). While Francisco López, a theatre director, describes her as ambitious and difficult – 'tenía frecuentes peleas y discusiones con todo el mundo' (p. 51) – Pedro Quartucci, a former theatrical colleague of Eva's, characterizes her as 'una muchacha más bien tímida, callada y sumisa. No se metía con nadie y tampoco alternaba con el grupo de actores y actrices de cartel' (p. 64). Discrepancies also inform accounts of what transpired following Eva's death: Atilio Renci, the administrator of the presidential household, declares that 'la familia no se opuso a que la llevaran a la CGT' (p. 324). Florencio Soto's testimony which follows contradicts Renci's: 'Lograr que Eva Perón fuera depositada en la CCT costó bastante: ni Perón ni la madre estaban de acuerdo' (p. 325). Some testimonies flaunt the personal and anecdotal sides of Eva's story, the 'unofficial' hidden Eva to whom very few people had direct access. Confirmation of the self-serving Eva comes from a former stage colleague, Pablo Raccioppi, who discloses that Eva saw the key to success in befriending the powerful: 'después [. . .] el triunfo viene sólo' (p. 90). The harsh, insensitive Eva emerges from the tale of the actress who was roundly refused permission by the future 'Dama de la Esperanza' to report to work later than normal so that she could feed her child ('esto no es un asilo', p. 91). Some anecdotal evidence points to unsuspected aspects of Eva, such as her capacity for irony: Pablo Raccioppi recalls Eva's response in 1950 to the tearful pleas of an actress who had been banned from working in the country: 'con una ironía que jamás le había conocido, Eva Perón le tomó el pelo elegantemente: – Pero qué malos son los oligarcas que no dan trabajo a una actriz de tanta categoría como usted [. . .] – le dijo' (p. 93). But the ironist herself appears in an ironic light when her former maid, Irma Cabrera de Ferrari, claims that Eva, who had cohabited openly with Perón prior to their marriage, was sensitive to gossip about her secretary Isabel Ernst's extramarital relationship with the leading Peronist, Domingo Mercante, and never recibió them together 'porque cuidaba mucho la imagen de ella como esposa del Presidente de la Nación' (p. 146). The fraught subject of Eva's relationship with Perón is treated by Manuel Penella de Silva (ghostwriter of *La razón de mi vida*) who discloses, intriguingly, that Eva did not get on well with Perón: 'Si Eva Perón hubiera vivido unos años más, no me queda ninguna duda, hubiera discrepado políticamente con su esposo' (p. 295). Irma Cabrera de Ferrari reveals other family 'secrets' such as Eva's attitude towards her sister, Elisa: 'a su hermana Elisa no la podía ver' (p. 222). Irma also probes some of Eva's enigmas: while displaying an ambivalent attitude towards the 'oligarca peligroso' Peralta Ramos, editor of *La Razón*, she was openly dismissive of obsequious supporters such as Héctor Cámpora and Raúl Mendé (p. 297). Anecdote confirms the best and the worst in Eva: her political acumen (the trade unionist, José Presta, claims that 'nos dio una solución que nosotros ni remotamente habíamos pensado' (p. 141); her political naivety in suggesting that the firemen should establish their own union (pp. 142–43); and her corruptibility: 'Miguel Molina, regalando un costoso ramo de orquídeas, se compró a Eva y a la Justicia' (p. 88). Anecdotes such as these provide 'privileged' information and indulge the reader by offering 'super-insider' knowledge. The reader is allowed to navigate these diverse testimonies free of intrusive authorial control: they are just there, each contributing something to the portrait of a woman who remains contradictory, inconsistent and incomplete, despite (or, perhaps, because of) the collaboration of so many voices in her portrayal. One of these voices stands out for its 'deconstructive' force: it is the second testimony of Eduardo del Castillo, formerly head of the Information Secretariat. He offers a sharp insight into the workings of the Peronist propaganda machine, pointing out that although 'la imagen que se vendió es que murió a las 20:25', the probability is that she died at 2 p.m. and that six hours were spent creating an appropriate atmosphere for breaking the news: 'era el principio de una nueva era en cuanto a técnicas de acción psicológica' (p. 323). This is an early critique of Peronist manipulative practices and stands outside the trite political discourses of affiliation or opposition. It belongs rather to the master narrative of sociological analysis informed by pseudoacademic objectivity.

The narrative is interrupted not only by these often protracted testimonies but also by numerous citations, several of them lengthy, drawn from a variety of sources, mostly journalistic but also representing dramatic, epistolary, legalistic and medical discourses. But the authors' exhaustive research and collating skills are able neither to fill all the gaps in the story nor to remedy the patent lack of reliable testimony regarding certain episodes such as the circumstances of Eva's departure for Buenos Aires and the precise role of the tango singer, Agustín Magaldi, in her move to the capital. After rehearsing the various versions of events – with the sole purpose, it seems, of exorcising their own frustrations – the authors reach the rather limp conclusion that 'lo único cierto es que viajó el 3 de enero de 1935' (p. 41). Similarly, the exact location of Eva's lodgings in Buenos Aires cannot be determined, but, as if to compensate, the authors produce a surfeit of information regarding Eva's first minor theatrical roles, quoting extensively from reviews published in *La Prensa* and *El Pueblo* which refer only incidentally to Eva. Here the methodology of the authors in the sections of the text narrated by themselves (as opposed to the testimonies and chronological summaries) becomes evident: exhaustive detail is supported by extensive press citations. However, the illusion of infallible knowledge cannot be sustained as further uncertainty emerges: 'aunque no subsisten documentos probatorios, algunos testigos dan cuenta que en diciembre de 1935, Eva Duarte inició su actividad radial [. . .]' (p. 45). The precise circumstances of the assault suffered by Eva while she was rallying support for Perón in October 1945 are difficult to verify (p. 110). Eva's attitude to her own illness is also impossible to determine (p. 243) as is the precise time when her embalmer, Dr Pedro Ara, began his work – although 'los testimonios recogidos por los autores indican que el trabajo efectivo del profesor Ara comenzó antes de la medianoche' (p. 317). If this last statement suggests that the authors' research is finally coming to fruition and that they are at long last getting to grips with their subject, such an impression is dispelled by the climax of their story where any promise of closure evaporates in the title of the last section, 'Las seis versiones'. If the living Eva opened cracks in their authoritative façade, the posthumous Eva destroys any pretensions to authorial control as different versions of the fate of her body proliferate, producing 'un verdadero alud de versiones y testimonios dispares, una verdadera madeja imposible de desentrañar a lo largo de quince años' (p. 341). This final admission calls into question the authors' efforts to achieve an 'objective' narrative and their adoption of a methodology that seems to consist of providing blanket coverage of all the known facts – whether significant or not – on the one hand and of consistently suppressing any creative impulse on the other.

This approach is clearly represented in the introduction to the section entitled 'Ignorando la enfermedad': 'no tiene mayor significación para esta etapa de la vida de Eva Perón una precisa descripción de cada una de sus actividades' (p. 247). The aim is clearly to communicate the whole truth but the downside of this ambitious project is the often mechanical inclusion of secondary and even extraneous matters such as the transcripts of propagandistic radio programmes written by Francisco Muñoz Azpiri in which Eva participated (pp. 74–7), the text of the draft law on the political rights of women (pp. 137–8), and full details of the 'Collar de la Orden del Libertador' (p. 290) awarded to Eva shortly before her death. The effect of such excessive data is contrary to the objectives of the authors. Rather than contributing to a complete portrait of Eva, they contrive instead to divert attention from the message and to highlight the extravagant narratorial methods employed. They constitute congealed textual elements that contribute minimally to the progress of the narrative. Thus while being of marginal interest to the story of Eva, the death notice of Perón's first wife, Potota, reproduced from *La Razón*, immerses the reader in the ornate language and style of obituary and heightens his awareness of obtrusive textuality: 'constituyó una sentida demostración de condolencia el acto de la inhumación de los restos de la señora Aurelia Tizón de Perón [...]' (pp. 55–6).

A contrasting discursive style is found in the next section, 'Eva Duarte en la cartilera', typifying the racy, playful language of the magazine *Antena*, as indicated by the caption beneath a photograph of Eva with the actor, Marcos Zucker: 'Eva Duarte quiere saber por qué Marcos Zucker no se casa y el muchacho la complace diciéndole: "yo permaneceré célibe hasta que llegue el impuesto a la soltería y, aún así, no me casaré hasta que usted se olvide que tiene un abrigo que la convierte en una tigresa"' (pp. 57–8). Similarly the discourse of sentimental love represented by Perón's letter to Eva (pp. 108–9) contrasts with the legalistic discourse of the couple's wedding certificate transcribed shortly after (p. 116). One of the most dramatic story elements of the entire narrative is, of course, that of the *cabildo abierto* of August 1951 when Eva was caught between the vociferous urgings of the crowd to accept the vice presidency on the one hand and Perón's ambiguous posturings on the other. Following their standard practice, the authors refer to a newspaper report (taken from *La Razón*) to set the scene, taking up the narrative themselves at the point when Eva appears on the stage (p. 261). Some sense of the drama of the occasion is given through the transcription of Eva's speech, regularly interrupted by the passionate crowd, who subsequently respond to Perón with perfunctory applause while continuing to clamour for Eva's unequivocal acceptance of the vice presidency. Here the drama is represented directly by the authors rather than by the usual recourse to newspaper reports:

'de todo este diálogo (que los autores reprodujeron de las grabaciones existentes en el Museo de la Palabra del Archivo General de la Nación) los diarios transcribieron sólo los discursos de Perón y Espejo. Los de Eva Perón quedaron reducidos a: "Haré lo que el pueblo quiera"' (p. 264). This disclosure calls into question the authors' overwhelming reliance elsewhere on newspaper reports, exposed here as being partial in their coverage of important events. Indeed Borroni and Vacca cite some patently false reports without comment: *Sintonía*, for example, claims that Eva 'habla tres idiomas – castellano, francés e ingles – admira los libros de grandes autores, se deleita con buena música [. . .]' (p. 81). It emerges later, however, that her companion, Lilian Lagomarisino de Guardo, was obliged to act as Eva's interpreter while they were in France (p. 193). It is not only journalistic mistakes that are overlooked: so is the ironic tone of the *Time* report of Eva's European tour (quoted in its entirety, pp. 180–8). *Time* recounts that Eva described Plutarch as 'un escritor antiguo' (p. 182) and ends with the presentation to Eva of a 1554 edition of *The Divine Comedy*, 'honra de Dante, un autor antiguo' (p. 188), an ironic echo of Eva's earlier reference to Plutarch. But such connections are left for the reader to make.

The authors' obsession with objectivity leads to their inclusion of exhaustive lists and inventories such as the names of Eva's fellow actors (p. 52), of Eva's engagements (p. 134), Eva's speeches by subject (pp. 139–40), the gifts proffered to Eva in Spain (p. 165); the names of writers cited by Peronists and radicals during their debate on political rights for women (pp. 202–3); of the topics covered by *the Escuela Superior del Peronismo*, together with the names of the teachers responsible for the courses (p. 253); and icons used to immortalize Eva (p. 334). Neither do the authors stint on the provision of statistical information (for example regarding the 1946 election results, p. 132) or of technical data (such as those on the proposed monument to Eva, p. 334). The provision of regular chronological summaries of events contributes to the impression of narratorial objectivity and textual control. This is quintessentially realist discourse which, as Hamon notes, is 'ostentatious with knowledge': its 'most extremely typical scene, where the narrative tale coincides most closely with the linguistic task of denomination, is the scene of the *inventory*'.[5]

As we have seen the authors quote from *La Razón* to set the scene for the *cabildo abierto*. The newspaper report notes that it would be impossible to describe every facet of the festive city: 'describir en detalle todas esas expresiones es realmente imposible' (p. 260). This comment might be applied metafictionally to the text of Borroni and Vacca whose attempt to say everything results in saying less: much superfluous information is included such as the name of Potota's funeral director (p. 55) and the *Antena* review of the film *Una novia en apuros* (p. 65) which fails to mention Eva, while techniques such as listing and inventory, associated with exhaustive description, become obtrusive through repeated use. The authors' obsession with objectivity leads them to adhere rigidly to the facts (mainly as established by the newspapers) but the facts cannot in every instance be ascertained ('no existen testimonios confiables [. . .]', p. 41) nor can the gaps in the story be closed: 'un nuevo receso de nueve meses se produjo en la actividad de Eva Duarte durante el año 1943' (p. 67). The authors' faith in the reliability of the testimonial account often appears to be misplaced.

It would seem that Borroni and Vacca's truth-telling programme is designed to counter the age-old conception of biography as a species of fiction making. Felman and Laub observe that 'what necessitates the testimony is always fundamentally, in one way or another, the scandal of an illness, of a metaphysical or literal disease'.[6] So regularly is the term *testimonio* invoked by Borroni and Vacca that it assumes the aura of a talismanic antidote to the disease of fiction. Their method conforms to the conventional 'microscope' model of modern biography which (as Stanley notes) holds that 'biographical truth lies in the amassing of irrefutable verifiable detail [. . .] the facts once assembled speak for themselves, biography merely draws conclusions from them'.[7] The truth-telling programme of Borroni and Vacca is undermined, however, not only by unreliable testimonies and unbridgeable gaps in the record, but also by the non-appearance of the second volume of their work, which was to have buttressed the first with further supporting evidence, much of it photographic (p. 134). It is a curious irony that the biographers' mode of expressing Eva's life becomes the real subject of the biography, despite the total absence in its authors of any self-conscious impulse. Their obtrusive editorial work of collecting, assembling and citing – all designed to ensure reliability – alerts the reader to their over-scrupulous methodology which fails to cover up their blind spots. Their work may be seen as a monument to the failure of realism since it so clearly falls short of the realist ideals to which it aspires. Hamon notes that realism will 'reject reference to the process of articulation, and move instead towards a "transparent" writing dominated only by the transmission of information'.[8] In Borroni and Vacca's work, however, it is impossible to ignore, as Jean Starobinski puts it, 'what is written in favour of what it is written about'.[9] Eva's life is obscured by overelaborate textual procedures such as quotations within quotations, exemplified by George C. Marshall's speech quoted in the *Newsweek* report (pp. 189–90), and the sheer length of quotations which disorientate the reader by blurring the narrative voice. Here Borroni and Vacca's methods produce effects which are diametrically opposed to their intentions, reminiscent in some respects of those achieved by the postmodern novel. Eva remains beyond comprehension as a series of fragmentary images which both complement and contradict each other. Borroni and Vacca's Eva is ultimately a study in division and otherness rather than a 'true' portrait based on impeccably 'objective' standards. They are not guilty of 'recognizing' the subject in Epstein's sense since they themselves do little overt interpretation.[10] Their violence is rather textual: they cut and paste the work of others. Their difficulty, from the point of view of traditional biography, is that they fail to manipulate their materials with sufficient ruthlessness to mould a coherent and recognizable subject. Indeed, Eva remains incomplete, strange, ambiguous, and opaque: their research may be exhaustive but Borroni and Vacca ultimately offer not the crisp and objective portrait of Eva which they initially envisaged but what Navarro describes as an 'unreal' image of her.[11] Despite their aspirations to truth and objectivity, their work only confirms how little can be known of the 'real' Eva and how subjective that limited knowledge is. The unwitting strength of Borroni and Vacca is that they fail to impose a false unity and coherence on Eva's story by, for example, identifying reassuring patterns. Indeed, contradiction and difference refuse to be suppressed. Backscheider remarks that in time, reviewers will look at the biography's structure and style rather than recite the most exciting parts of the subject's life.[12] The structure and organization of Borroni and Vacca's work, particularly the chronological summaries, are designed to promote reliable narrative, a clear sense of what 'really happened'. In fact, however, the effect of such contrived organization is the opposite of what the authors intended: the frequently discordant testimonies undermine the neat and 'neutral' truth-telling purpose of the chronological sections while the incessant authorial recourse to extended citations draws attention to a textual rather than a lived reality. In view of their frequency and length, these citations become almost obscene, running sores on the body of the text: while citations normally play a supporting role in texts, often relegated to footnotes or end notes, here they invade – and often undermine by their sheer preponderance – the main body which they are purportedly designed to support.[13]

Borroni and Vacca's aim is to absent themselves from their narrative, to offer the reader 'objective' data unmediated by them. Such a project is impossible as Ellis points out: 'the claim that the materials of a life are simply being presented to readers so that they can form their own judgements is always more or less disingenuous because presentation must imply both selection and arrangement and the establishment therefore of parameters'.[14] The instincts of Borroni and Vacca are to play down biography as art form; by contrast, Tomás Eloy Martínez's practice is to flaunt its artistry. The results in each case are in some ways similar despite their widely disparate authorial objectives. The techniques of Martínez are open and controlled, producing maximum effect, whereas those of Borroni and Vacca often appear overused and counterproductive since their declared aim of objectivity is not realized. While Martínez flaunts his presence in *Santa Evita*, Borroni and Vacca try to cover up theirs but, despite their efforts, cannot fail to insinuate themselves behind the flawed and obtrusive organization of their text. While Martínez indulges boldly in textual experimentation, the involuntary dialogism of Borroni and Vacca's myriad citations and testimonies undermines their doomed efforts to refine the art of objectivity. While Martínez admits to a kind of erotic submission to his subject, Borroni and Vacca engage in a futile quest to control Eva, to penetrate her truth and to arrest her flight. Martínez prioritizes technique over the communication of message whereas Borroni and Vacca seek – in vain – to subordinate technique to the transmission of clear meaning. Martínez's fragmented text enhances his evocation of a discontinuous and unknowable subject; Borroni and Vacca aim at totalizing narrative but their text is subject to constant interruption and becomes – ironically – a kind of textual adventure which often eludes their control. Martínez admits to losing any sense of clear purpose: 'no sé en qué punto del relato estoy. Creo que en el medio' (*Santa Evita*, p. 391). Borroni and Vacca anticipate the closure of their work by the publication of a second volume; but it is never published.

In a sense *Santa Evita*, with its focus on the posthumous Eva, can be seen as the textual unconscious of *La vida de Eva Perón. Tomo 1: Testimonios para su historia*. In *Santa Evita*, Emilio Kaufman's reference to the biographical practice of presenting a surfeit of inconsequential information while leaving intact important gaps in the story (p. 246) certainly applies to Borroni and Vacca's work (although Kaufman does refer to the pair of journalists as 'los únicos que alguna vez bajaron a su intimidad [de Eva]', p. 245). Martínez, who himself features in *Santa Evita*, disagrees with Kaufman, finding his expectations of biography unrealistic and excessive: '¿De dónde querés que saquen los datos?' (p. 246). Borroni and Vacca's weakness is their blind reliance on their extensive research to close such gaps, their subconscious refusal to acknowledge that some gaps will never be closed. In short, Martínez reveals what Borroni and Vacca attempt to hide: he ironizes the search for coherence to which they are earnestly committed, he exposes as illusion their pretensions to total reliability and he revels in the contradictions which they seek to suppress.

Sebreli and Taylor: the Rationalizing Impulses of Sociology and Anthropology

Here we consider two quasi-biographies of Eva, both written from the perspective of the social sciences but differing substantially in their methodologies. In *Eva Perón: ¿aventurera o militante?* (1966) Juan José Sebreli acknowledges – albeit implicitly – that the phenomenon of Eva Perón exceeds his sociological apparatus. By contrast, J. M. Taylor, in *Evita Perón: the Myths of a Woman* (1979) maintains her faith in the tools of her discipline, making scant allowance for a subject whom she does not, at root, believe to be exceptional.

Juan José Sebreli's is a landmark study, frequently cited by both historians and literary critics. It is the first sociological work to adopt a clearly left-wing perspective: 'el marxismo nos proporcionará el instrumento adecuado'.[15] Sebreli identifies Eva's various personae, ranging from president's wife to militant *compañera*, emphasizing this final incarnation of Eva as the basis of her permanent legacy. D. W. Foster, who has traced the intellectual trajectory of Sebreli, notes that his initial enthusiasm for Evita as a revolutionary figure studied from a Sartrean existential perspective in *Eva Perón: ¿aventurera o militante?* was revised in a later work, *Los deseos imaginarios del peronismo* (1983),[16] which focuses not on Eva's leftist militancy but rather on the fascist underpinnings of Peronism and on Eva's role as an 'integral, if flamboyant, component of its propaganda apparatus'.[17]

Sebreli's main thesis in the later work is that purist denunciations of the betrayal of 'true' Peronism and advocacy of a return to origins are wholly illusory since 'true' Peronism never existed: 'el "verdadero peronismo" fue, pues, un peronismo imaginario que nunca coincidió con la práctica'; 'el mío no era más que un peronismo imaginario, en el que el peronismo real no podía de ningún modo reconocerse'.[18] According to Foster, the mature Sebreli 'definitively liquidates any belief in a positive political meaning for Eva Perón'.[19] Such a categorical conclusion is hardly borne out by the nostalgic tone of Sebreli's preface to *Los deseos imaginarios* which hints at a personal sense of loss: 'para mí Evita era la heroína romántica de folletín, la gran hetaura a quien el destino permitió vengarse de la sociedad que la humillara' (p. 19). Sebreli has clearly modified his previous notion of a revolutionary Eva: 'Eva Perón aceptó conscientemente la pasividad femenina' (p. 99). But his prefatory remarks suggest that his previous personal identities, embracing ideals which subsequently crumbled, are never completely repudiated: '¿En qué medida ya no soy lo que fui y lo que soy ahora deriva de lo que fui ayer? [. . .] Toda una generación, que es la mía, está indisolublemente unida al peronismo para siempre' (p. 17).[20] Sebreli not only admits to his diverse selves but also to his inability to distinguish clearly between them: does the mature 'I' take precedence over the previous 'I's? Sebreli suggests not. Foster, seeking to portray a 'born again' Sebreli, assumes the priority of the present 'I', whereas it is more likely to be the case that the self is in a continuous state of flux, with previous 'I's surviving in creative tension with the present 'I'. Sebreli himself invokes autobiography, often seen as embodying the paradox of continuity in discontinuity.[21] In *Eva Perón: ¿aventurera o militante?* he highlights precisely this aspect of Evita: 'ella arrastró muchos de los lastres de la mujer del pasado, de donde había surgido, a la vez que esbozó en forma rudimentaria, las características de la mujer nueva [. . .]' (p. 102).

Foster is right to point to differences between the Sebreli of *Eva Perón: ¿aventurera o militante?* and the Sebreli of *Los deseos*. The later Sebreli is not only disillusioned with Peronism but is refreshingly less self-confident than his younger counterpart whose pretensions to clinical analysis are reminiscent of Borroni and Vacca's: 'me he propuesto oponer la conciencia histórica a la conciencia mítica, la universalidad objetiva a la subjetividad personal, rescatar el personaje histórico de la heroína mítica' (p. 112). But the subjective and often idealistic opinions of Sebreli (acknowledged as such in retrospect by Sebreli himself) undermine his claims to objectivity: even the insults of Eva's enemies he interprets as a form of involuntary homage, 'el reconocimiento de que el peronismo era efectivamente la redención de todos los pasados, que los valores caducos de una sociedad tradicional habían sido realmente subvertidos'.[22] Tacit approval of Eva's mockery of the suffragettes as typically unmarried, ageing and ugly (Sebreli, 1966, 50) is given short shrift in *Los deseos* where Sebreli highlights Eva's 'prejuicio sexista al hacer de la mujer un objeto sexual y marginar a aquellas que no fueran jóvenes ni bellas' (p. 99).

The Sebreli of the later work would not have made the extravagant claims of *Eva Perón: ¿aventurera o militante?* regarding Eva's literary potential: 'un libro mediocre como *La razón de mi vida* pudo muy bien haber sido *Los Siete Pilares de la Sabiduría* o *La condición humana* si Eva Perón hubiera sabido escribir' (pp. 74–5). A more striking difference between his texts relates to the ideological character of Peronism: according to *Eva Perón* it is not fascist (p. 91) whereas in *Los deseos* Eva is specifically identified with fascism (pp. 76–7).

Important differences of emphasis and even plain contradictions divide these texts. But, contrary to the implications of Foster's argument, the main thrust of the earlier text is hardly invalidated by the greater scepticism of *Los deseos* which does not repudiate, for example, the other-worldly characterization of

Eva's relationship with Perón as based on a mystical union ('se trata de un matrimonio místico donde la devoción no se diferencia demasiado de la erótica', p. 53); the recognition of her achievement in making the workers visible ('comenzaron a sentirse como en su casa, en las fábricas ... en la calle y hasta en la administración pública', p. 70); the acknowledgement of her direct personal help to the *descamisados* (p. 81); and the portrayal of Victoria Ocampo as no more than a paltry rebel 'no contra una clase opresora, sino apenas contra su familia' (p. 27).

In some respects the texts overlap, both emphasizing the fluidity of Eva's public persona which progresses from actress to *señora* to *compañera*. In *Eva Perón*, Sebreli highlights the potential conflict between the last two roles: 'dos estilos de vida antagónicos que asumen la característica de una doble personalidad, una especie de Doctor Jekyll y Míster Hyde morales' (p. 61), an image – reproduced in *Los deseos* (p. 75) – which shows that Sebreli's idealization of Eva in the earlier text is nuanced by unflattering insinuation. Indeed, its conclusion notes the regressive characteristics of the myth of Eva: 'se transforma [...] en un freno ante nuevos procesos del desarrollo histórico, tiende ahora a velar conflictos no resueltos de nuestra sociedad, nos remite a un pasado cristalizado que la evolución incesante de los acontecimientos históricos va dejando atrás [...]' (p. 109). While she does occasionally appear to be larger than history as Foster claims[23] – Sebreli notes her meteoric rise from potential victim to 'la luz enceguedora del poder más grande que jamás haya ejercido ninguna otra mujer en el país y pocas en el mundo entero' (p. 11) – she is more typically portrayed in a balanced and even ironic style, characterized as an actress not just on the stage but also in real life (p. 37). Her limitations as an actress are noted forthrightly in *Los deseos*: 'era una artista sin arte' (p. 74) who found her true métier not on the stage but in the political arena 'donde la mediocre actriz alcanzaba a veces momentos grandiosos' (p. 74).[24] While Sebreli appears on occasion to unveil a feminist Eva in *Eva Perón* – claiming, for example, that she destroys the myth of the 'mujer-objeto' (p. 72) – he also foregrounds the limits of Eva's personal power as well as her negative qualities: 'la astucia de la historia utilizó como instrumento a esa mujer, quien, persiguiendo sus propios y egoístas fines personales, contribuyó sin quererlo a la lucha por la emancipación parcial de la mujer y de la clase obrera de su país' (p. 76). While in *Eva Perón*

Sebreli denies that Peronism was fascist, he does – even here – acknowledge that there are some good reasons to place Eva and Peronism on the side of reaction (p. 105). Indeed, a close reading of this text shows that the occasional hyperbole is more than balanced by even-handed critique and that Foster overstates the 'grandeur' conferred upon Eva by Sebreli's allegedly partial treatment which, according to Foster, 'strains the parameters of history by reaching toward the ahistorically operatic, the Evita who is somehow "larger than history"'.[25] Foster is right however in noting that Sebreli seeks to establish distance between Eva and Peronism: 'el informalismo de Evita es desmitificador, desalienante, contribuye a romper con el supersticioso respeto pequeñoburgués por las jerarquías [...]' (p. 88); 'la auténtica pasión del evitismo estaba irremediablemente condenada a muerte por asfixia bajo el peso de la inercia de esa burocracia' (p. 100). Sebreli celebrates what he describes as the corporeal quality of Eva's speeches (which is lost when they are read): 'aun la teatralidad de sus gestos no chocaba porque era lo que más convenía a la intensidad de su dramatismo' (pp. 66–7). Her theatrical delivery is complemented by the raw force of her language, 'directo, a veces procaz [...] casi un acto de provocación surrealista' (p. 88) and her triumph is all the more stunning for throwing into relief the failure of 'superior' women such as the intellectuals (p. 103).

In taking the flawed, historical Eva as the litmus test for judging quasi-biographical representations such as Sebreli's, Foster overlooks the main reason for Eva's literary magnetism. In 1971 Ernesto Goldar observed that Eva, 'auténtica, desmesurada, obvia casi, se ofrece sin concesiones a la literatura'.[26] This insight is echoed in 1999 by Rita de Grandis who claims that modern critics of both historical and literary backgrounds look beyond the historical Eva: 'a representation of her political and cultural significance is no longer a question of fidelity to ideas or images of her that embrace what she has come to represent'.[27] It is this approach to Eva which Beatriz Sarlo embraces with unabashed exuberance: 'Eva es única. Esto explica la fascinación, el odio, la devoción que la rodearon [...] Eva es única'.[28] Sarlo may be critical of the adulatory fervour and hyperbolic expression fostered by the regime but here the warmth of her appreciation is not far removed from the ardent intimacy of Erminda Duarte's account.[29] Even Eva's writings, frequently dismissed as the sentimental outpourings of an untutored mind, are recuperable for Sarlo since their thematic redundancies and stylistic repetitions are reflective of the one-dimensional obsessiveness of passion (p. 26). Sarlo locates Eva's exceptionality precisely in her lack of those attributes which might seem to be indispensable to stardom, whether political or theatrical, ranging from favoured physical features to good taste and innocence (p. 56). Lack was turned into surplus, 'lo que ella no tenía debía ser descubierto como originalidad, valorado como rasgo diferencial' (p. 56); 'la excepción construida desde lo que falta y no desde lo que se tiene' (p. 231). Her repetitive actions and gestures have the virtue of transcending and renewing themselves, avoiding the tainted aura of the over-familiar by maintaining an effect of the marvellous (p. 81). If her originality was based on lack, her appeal is founded on excess, an excess of giving which left no room for any sense of humiliation on the part of the recipient: it was a 'gasto superfluo y no sólo la seca respuesta a una necesidad' (p. 94). Eva represents a play of lack and excess: her exceptionality depends upon her avoidance of the middle course, her deviation from the norm. This is why she is, in this sense, 'larger than history' as Foster charges and why she exerts a magnetic hold on writers as diverse as Juan José Sebreli and Tomás Eloy Martínez. Ultimately she demands to be treated as a mythical figure, defined by Navarro as a 'representation that gives additional meaning to historical reality, that is to say, a construction that transforms historical reality and goes beyond it'.[30] Foster appears to celebrate the rise of the realist Sebreli of *Los deseos* at the expense of the idealizing Sebreli of *Eva Perón*. But as we have seen, elements of the former survive in the latter: the mature Sebreli appears to look back with regret and a sense of loss rather than with the satisfaction that might be expected to accompany a more refined and mature perspective. The older Sebreli mourns his younger self while remaining partly in thrall to the values of that younger self, from whom he can only try – in vain – to distance himself. The mature sociologist sees the young visionary he once was, and to an extent still is, as contaminated by an unreal, imaginative, mythic view of Eva. He tries – in vain – to struggle free of her spell but, like Martínez, appears to be marked for life.

J. M. Taylor's *Evita Perón: the Myths of a Woman* (1979),[31] written from an anthropological perspective, follows the character templates established by Sebreli in *Eva Perón*. Sebreli's later work, *Los deseos*, confirms one of Taylor's main arguments, that the underlying values of Peronists and non-Peronists were similar but coloured by conflicting perspectives: 'tampoco veía o trataba de ocultarme, que mi visión del peronismo se encontraba muy cerca de la imagen diabólica del antiperonismo de derecha, aunque con distinto signo valorativo' (*Los deseos*, p. 19). By comparison with *Eva Perón: ¿aventurera o militante?*, Taylor's work is more clinically analytical but if Sebreli is naive in his application of Sartrean existential philosophy to frame Eva's left-wing militancy (as argued by Foster, p. 33), Taylor's total faith in the efficacy of her professional approach, 'armed with anthropology's literature on myth and its methods of fieldwork' (p. 1), seems equally naive from our contemporary postmodern perspective.

Taylor notes that claims by middle- and upper-class Peronists that the working classes nurtured the myth of a mystical Eva do not accord with her own findings – that the working class Eva was 'realistic and sometimes revolutionary' (p. 6). She concludes that middle-class propagandists had constructed an image reflecting not working-class culture but rather their own (p. 7). She also finds that the revolutionary Eva 'derives from middle-class values, despite appearances to the contrary' (p. 7). Taylor's objective is to neutralize the intangible aspects of the mythic Eva, as conceived by the literary imagination, by treating her mythic persona as a quantifiable social phenomenon conducive to analysis by the established tools of her discipline. While Sebreli and Sarlo emphasize the exceptional qualities of Eva, Taylor seeks to reduce her difference and otherness by showing that her uniqueness is only apparent. To this end she draws parallels (p. 12) between Eva and other powerful political women: Imelda Marcos of the Philippines and Mrs Bandaranaike of Ceylon (now Sri Lanka). The same effect is sought subsequently by the presentation of the phenomenal aftermath of her death from a reductive historical perspective which purports to show that it was by no means unique: 'the burial of another First Lady, Encarnación Ezcurra de Rosas, slightly more than a century earlier, parallels the homage paid to Eva Perón on a startling number of points [. . .]' (p. 65). Eva's exceptionality is further diminished through the subsumption of her power within a discernible female category of power:

'the ethnographic literature in general', so Taylor claims, supports 'the idea that the qualities thought to characterize the power of Eva Perón are linked both in Argentina and in other cultures with ideas concerning female power in general' (p. 13). The common assumption that women are 'appropriate repositories of a certain kind of spiritual or mystico-religious power' (p. 15) helps to explain the case of Eva whose appeal derives from a realm which is recognized as 'partially or wholly beyond the bounds of its institutions and manipulations: a realm that is uninstitutionalized, uncontrolled, irrational or incomprehensible' (p. 15). The contrasting perceptions of Eva as the Lady of Hope, as the woman of the Black Myth, and as the revolutionary firebrand, all share a similar conception of her power as unofficial and unsullied by that other kind of power exercised within the parameters of 'institutions, laws, and the corrupting constraints of human nature' – the formal power vested in Perón (p. 19).

Taylor's first three chapters provide different kinds of background information: the introduction is theoretical, anticipating the more detailed investigation of woman and power (chapter 1) and of culture and genealogy (chapter 2). Chapter 3, entitled 'The Biography', seems to be an extension of the previous chapter, 'the Backdrop', designed to contribute to the contextual matters outlined in the early chapters prior to the serious investigation inaugurated in chapter 5, 'Preliminary Analysis'. Chapter 3, 'The Biography', has a perfunctory, almost mechanical quality: Eva's illegitimacy, the death of her father, the move to Junín, Eva's departure for Buenos Aires and the beginning of her theatrical career, receive rapid coverage free of any 'unprofessional' speculations. The state of the Buenos Aires theatre is given short shrift as is Eva's meeting with Perón (p. 36). Eva's role in the workers' movement which liberated Perón is left open (p. 38) while her wedding to Perón and his subsequent electoral victory are covered rapidly. While the sphere of personal relations is not ignored, it is clear that Taylor's interest lies elsewhere: 'whether or not Eva had thoughts of making herself independent of her husband or of his particular ideology would be relevant only if she had lived to realize her hopes or if the people had supported her as a figure separate from that of Juan Perón, representing different ideas or goals' (pp. 54–5). From a human point of view, her aspirations to independence from Perón are clearly of great interest irrespective of their failure to materialize; indeed, the acclaim reserved for Eva at the *cabildo abierto* of August 1951 suggests that people were beginning to see her as an independent figure.

Taylor's approach is to suppress wonder even in the face of the most startling events. The narrative of Eva's remarkable posthumous adventures is conducted in a terse and methodical style with total concentration on the known facts: 'after two weeks of removal from one place to another, the embalmed body was placed in the building of the Information Service of the State, where it was hidden in a box labelled "radio equipment" [. . .]. Later versions based on documents of the Army Information Service (Servicio de Informaciones del Ejército: SIE) permit further reconstruction of events' (pp. 69–70). Taylor's only concession to the marvellous aspect of the story is her acknowledgement that the truth about the location of Eva's real body is unknown: 'the odyssey may have ended. But Argentinians ask, where is she really? [. . .]. And the corpse that suddenly reappeared and seemed from a distance to be Eva Perón – that corpse, some Argentinians whisper, may have been a wax doll all along' (p. 71). Chapter 4, 'The Myths: the Lady of Hope and the Woman of the Black Myth', gives the impression that the narrative of events – necessary to set the scene – has been completed and the real business of anthropological investigation can now begin. The chapter is divided into two sections, 'The Lady of Hope' and 'The Woman of the Black Myth'. Taylor illustrates here what Hayden White has designated 'emplotment' whereby the narrator confers meaning on events, articulating them by means of a specific kind of plot.[32] Thus the Lady of Hope emplotment presents Eva in a positive and heroic light: 'on the pampas a delicately beautiful blonde child struggled to overcome the obstacles of humble birth, poverty and isolation' (p. 72). (The erroneous reference to Eva's blondness is a further pointer to narratorial manipulation.) In the section entitled 'The Woman of the Black Myth' (pp. 78–85) the same events are treated in a wholly different way: ' "that woman", "esa mujer", was born in the ill-disguised brothel of her mother' (p. 78). The previous references to Eva's delicate beauty are replaced here by the crushingly negative perspective of Eva's detractors, who see her childhood and adolescence solely as preparatory stages for the infamous trajectory of her adulthood: 'already aggressive and ambitious at fifteen, she linked herself to the troupe of a tango singer whom she had probably seduced, and travelled to Buenos Aires to establish herself as a prostitute' (p. 78). The implication of Taylor's dialogic presentation is that the 'true' story of Eva cannot be known since the 'facts' are buried beneath an accretion of tendentious and often conflicting accounts. Even the most basic facts of Eva's life are subject to diverse forms of reconstruction which produce conflicting meanings: on the one hand, Eva goes to Buenos Aires for the admirable purpose of developing her talent as an actress (p. 72); on the other she goes there for the abominable purpose of practising prostitution (p. 78). Other well-known story elements are subject to similarly opposing interpretations: the tango singer, Agustín Magaldi, allows her to travel with his party to Buenos Aires (p. 72); Eva probably seduces Magaldi (p. 78); in Buenos Aires Eva devotes herself either to displaying her talent (p. 72), or else to unrestrained promiscuity (p. 78); her meeting with Perón is love at first sight (p. 73), or is an exercise by Eva in naked opportunism (p. 78); she is either motivated by a spirit of self-sacrifice (evidenced by her renunciation of the vice-presidency, p. 77) or else she is dominated by her own perverse pleasures which express themselves in the torture of others (p. 82). Significantly, the narrator chooses which story elements to include: her father's funeral and the *cabildo abierto* do not feature in the 'Woman of the Black Myth' because they would arouse sympathy for Eva; conversely, the stark, physical consequences of her illness, paraded vengefully in this version – 'she was rotting while still alive', (p. 82) – are not allowed to cast a shadow over the purity of her sacrifice in the other (p. 77). Taylor pinpoints – from the superior vantage point of the anthropologist – the hallmarks of the myriad narratives that envelop Eva. But she shows little awareness of the limitations of her own anthropological discourse which is itself susceptible to critical analysis despite aspiring to clinical rigour and objectivity. Taylor's earnest focus on meaning makes her vulnerable; Martínez's ludic alternation between tentative narrative and continuous self-exposure removes him from the shackles of authoritative discourse (as we shall see).

In the second section of 'The Woman of the Black Myth', 'Eva the Good', further versions of Eva emerge: she may have been good but was exploited by Perón; or she herself may have been the dominant partner, driving a cowardly Perón towards government and thereafter engaging in a power struggle with him, eventually losing her grip as her health declined. In chapter 5,

'Preliminary Analysis', Taylor seeks to draw general principles from the foregoing discussion: 'in part, Eva's ideology and Juan's strategy can be analysed. But there remains another part of each for which the contradictory and original human beings, Eva and Juan, their personalities and the events each lived, are totally responsible' (p. 133). For once Taylor acknowledges the tangled human factors underlying her story but her main objective, as an anthropologist, is not to grapple with a life but to illustrate a thesis. The thesis is that femininity, mystical or spiritual power and revolutionary leadership all imply marginality vis-à-vis established society and institutionalized authority. The marvellous and phenomenal aspects of Eva are familiarized by the reassuringly schematic character of the myths she generated: a pattern surfaces in the images of the 'Lady of Hope' and the 'Woman of the Black Myth'. Popular acclaim of the first and virulent denunciation of the second have complementary sociological roots: 'the praises of one and the accusations of the other both concern sexuality, femininity, taste and education, and association or mystic rapport with the masses [. . .] From the panegyric of one myth and the contumely of the other emerge the same underlying values' (p. 86). According to the Peronist myth, Eva's sexuality is controlled and her feminine emotions checked by her subordination to her husband. The 'Woman of the Black Myth', by contrast, represents unchecked eroticism and perverse power. Although these myths provide conflicting images of Eva, each categorizes her neatly, either in the positive or in the negative mode. The possibility that Eva is too complex for such schematic assimilation, that she may incorporate certain aspects of both extremes of the common perception, that her fluid being resists such clear categorization, is not properly considered. Having discussed her research in personal terms in the introductory chapter, Taylor promptly shifts in the main body of her work to the impersonal, scientific style that dominates subsequent chapters. Despite the emotive character of her subject, she remains impassive, rarely engaging directly with her, partly because the thrust of much of her argument is that Eva is not really exceptional – though she does concede that 'a woman who becomes as powerful as Eva Perón did, exciting so many lasting and varied myths, is rare' (p. 8). She does, on one occasion, defend Eva against her detractors' jibes based on the perceived inconsistency between Eva's solidarity with the 'shirtless ones' and her own 'very well-adorned self': Taylor notes that similar criticisms were not directed at the extravagant parties held by charitable organizations to benefit the poor (p. 102).

Taylor's analytical method generates sharp contrasts: Eva's style was impulsive, disordered, and emotive; her husband's 'rigorous and scientific' (p. 105). The revolutionary Eva is stereotyped as the woman who broke the rules (p. 128). As an anthropologist, Taylor must seek to 'master' her subject by applying her own particular metanarrative. The problem is that the multifarious Eva cannot adequately be contained within any theoretical framework, as Taylor is partially aware: 'the case of Eva Perón reveals no easily perceptible point at which "reality" ends and myth begins' (p. 9). Taylor's achievement is to have clarified the web of claim and counterclaim deriving from the divergent perspectives on Eva Perón. Here her specialist skills and surgical incisiveness are deployed to effect, probing Peronist and anti-Peronist positions and highlighting their inconsistencies. She never tires of setting one perspective against another, of identifying patterns and structural affinities in opposing myths. The problem is that such clean-cut analysis leaves little room for nuanced judgement nor for much appreciation of Eva's ambivalences that transcend her myths. Taylors' treatment of Eva's *renunciamiento* is a good example: a number of explanations are adduced, ranging from military pressure (p. 59) to Eva's voluntary withdrawal from the vice-presidency motivated by her free-spirited determination to escape the stultifying effects of state bureaucracy (p. 141). But Taylor's treatment of that cauldron of human emotions engulfing Perón as well as Eva is stilted and insipid, limited to a rehearsal of the 'facts' (pp. 60–1). This episode's elusive undercurrents of feeling lend themselves to (partial) literary recreation – demonstrated by Tomás Eloy Martínez in *Santa Evita*, pp. 97–118 – and Taylor's frequent allusions to literary sources (such as Rodolfo Walsh's 'Esa mujer', p. 85) may suggest an intuitive awareness that other perspectives, beyond the anthropological, are needed: as V. S. Naipaul states, truth in the case of Eva tends to disappear 'since it is not relevant to the legend'.[33]

The sociologist, Juan José Sebreli, is not as circumscribed by the traditional limits of his sociological discipline (in both *Eva Perón: ¿aventurera o militante?* and *Los deseos*) as is Taylor by those of anthropology. Whereas Sebreli pays lip service to Marxist ideology, his practical approach shows an awareness of Eva's complexity and even a sense of bafflement reminiscent of Martínez's: 'es creación y creadora a la vez, producto y a la vez productora, reflejo y reflejante, punto de llegada y punto de partida, padece la historia y a la vez la elige' (*Eva Perón*, p. 20). Keen to investigate Eva's human qualities, he breaks out of the normal discourse of sociology and appeals to the alien vision of literary paradox. Noting that Eva was not just a stage actress but also an actress in real life, Sebreli concludes: 'es inútil por eso preguntarse si fingía o estaba representando un personaje; como toda auténtica seductora, sacaba provecho hasta de su sinceridad' (p. 37). He goes on to quote André Gide on the permanence of masks and is aware that the mythical Eva transcends the flawed, historical figure. He is a kind of *bricoleur* who is not driven by any professional instinct to miniaturize or to define. Long before Sarlo, Sebreli had pinpointed Eva's exceptionality (p. 50). By contrast, Taylor diminishes that exceptionality by seeking to contain it within familiar anthropological categories – while failing to suppress her niggling awareness of the limitations of such a procedure. Ultimately both Sebreli and Taylor, in their different ways, confirm Ernesto Goldar's point that where Eva is concerned it is the creative, literary imagination that offers the most promising means of approximating to her: 'Su personalidad destruye el mito de la mujer-objeto y la militancia ratifica la alternativa del sujeto para quien – elegida la acción – la muerte no aniquila y la nada no existe. Auténtica, desmesurada, obvia casi, se ofrece sin concesiones a la literatura'.[34]

NOTES

[1] Quoted by Otelo Borroni and Roberto Vacca, *La vida de Eva Perón. Tomo 1: Testimonios para su historia* (Buenos Aires: Centro Editor de América Latina, 1970), p. 79. Further references, given in parenthesis in the text, are to this edition.
[2] Amy K. Kaminsky, *Reading the Body Politic: Feminist Criticism and Latin American Women Writers* (Minneapolis: University of Minnesota Press, 1993), p. 52.
[3] Marysa Navarro, *Evita* (Buenos Aires: Corregidor, 1981), p. 344.
[4] Quoted by Elzbieta Sklodowska, *Testimonio hispanoamericano: historia, teoría, poética* (New York: Lang, 1992), p. 73.

5   'Philippe Hamon on the major features of realist discourse' in Lilian R. Furst (ed.), *Realism*, Modern Literatures in Perspective (London and New York: Longman, 1992), pp. 166–85 (pp. 172–3).
6   Shoshana Felman and Dori Laub, *Testimony: Crises of Witnessing in Literature, Psychoanalysis and History* (New York and London: Routledge, 1992), pp. 4–5.
7   Liz Stanley, *The Auto/biographical I: the Theory and Practice of Feminist Auto/biography* (Manchester: Manchester University Press, 1992), p. 155.
8   'Philippe Hamon on the major features of realist discourse' in Lilian R. Furst (ed.), *Realism*, p. 175.
9   Quoted by Frank Kermode, *The Genesis of Secrecy: on the Interpretation of Narrative* (London: Harvard University Press, 1979), pp. 118–19.
10 By 'recognizing the subject' Epstein refers to the traditional biographical practice of imposing unity upon a subject and resisting attempts to decentre it. See William Epstein, *Recognizing Biography* (Philadelphia: University of Pennsylvania Press, 1987), p. 82.
11 Navarro, *Evita*, p. 344.
12 Paula R. Backscheider, *Reflections on Biography* (Oxford: Oxford University Press, 1999), p. 235.
13 See chapter 3, pp. 79–86 for a discussion of the comparable role played by the 'Documents' as the 'dangerous supplement' in Tomás Eloy Martínez's *Las memorias del General*.
14 David Ellis, *Literary Lives: Biography and the Search for Understanding* (Edinburgh: Edinburgh University Press, 2000), p. 127.
15 Sebreli, *Eva Perón ¿aventurera o militante?* 4th edn (Buenos Aires: Pleyade, 1990). Page references, given in parenthesis in the text, are to this edition. The title is abbreviated to *Eva Perón*.
16 Sebreli, *Los deseos imaginarios del peronismo* (Buenos Aires: Sudamericana, 1992). Page references, given in parenthesis in the text, are to this edition. The title is abbreviated to *Los deseos*.
17 David William Foster, 'Evita Perón, Juan José Sebreli, and gender' in Foster, *Sexual Textualities: Essays on Queering Latin American Writing* (Austin: University of Texas Press, 1997), pp. 22–38 (p. 36).
18 Sebreli, *Los deseos imaginarios del peronismo*, pp. 14, 20.
19 Foster, 'Evita Perón, Juan José Sebreli, and gender', *Sexual Textualities*, p. 36.
20 Recalling Eva's televised funeral at the Recoleta cemetery, Beatriz Sarlo also acknowledges her own past selves: 'veo a otra mujer (que ya no soy). Quiero entenderla, porque esa que yo era no fue muy diferente de otras y otros'. *La pasión y la excepción* (Buenos Aires: Siglo veintiuno, 2003), p. 11. Sarlo's political trayectoria parallels Sebreli's: 'aunque mi camino político iba a alejarme del peronismo, en ese año 1970 admiré y aprobé lo que se había hecho' (p. 11).
21 See, for example, Francis R. Hart, 'Notes for an anatomy of modern autobiography' in *New Literary History*, 1 (1969–70), 485–511 (p. 492).
22 Sebreli, *Eva Perón ¿aventurera o militante?*, p. 47.

23 Foster, 'Evita Perón, Juan José Sebreli, and gender', *Sexual Textualities*, p. 35.
24 Beatriz Sarlo takes Sebreli's point a stage further, arguing that the reasons for her theatrical failure account, in part, for her political success, based on a kind of displacement or extraneousness: 'sus cualidades, insuficientes en una escena (la artística) se volvían excepcionales en otra escena (la política)', *La pasión y la excepción*, p. 24.
25 Foster, 'Evita Perón, Juan José Sebreli, and gender', *Sexual Textualities*, p. 35.
26 Goldar, *El peronismo en la literatura argentina*, p. 63.
27 'The masses do not think, they feel', *Journal of Latin American and Caribbean Studies*, 24 (1999), 125–32 (p. 131).
28 Sarlo, *La pasión y la excepción*, p. 22.
29 Erminda Duarte, *Mi hermana Evita* (Buenos Aires: Centro de Estudios Eva Perón, 1972).
30 'Wonder woman was Argentine and her real name was Evita', *Canadian Journal of Latin American and Caribbean Studies*, 24 (1999), 133–52 (p. 137).
31 J. M. Taylor, *Evita Perón: The Myths of a Woman* (Oxford: Basil Blackwell, 1979).
32 Hayden White, *Metahistory: the Historical Imagination in Nineteenth-Century Europe* (Baltimore and London: The Johns Hopkins University Press, 1973), p. 7.
33 V. S. Naipaul, 'The return of Eva Perón' in *The Return of Eva Perón with the Killings in Trinidad* (London: Deutsch, 1980), pp. 93–170 (p. 113).
34 Ernesto Goldar, *El peronismo en la literatura argentina* (Buenos Aires: Freeland, 1971), p. 63.

Chapter 6
Indiscreet Portraitures: Llorca, Navarro, Dujovne Ortiz

The purpose of this chapter is to chart the major differences of biographical technique manifested by three recent works on Eva Perón: Carmen Llorca's *Llamadme Evita* (1980); Marysa Navarro's *Evita* (1994); and Alicia Dujovne Ortiz's *Eva Perón: a Biography* (1995). I will seek to show a clear progression from the traditional approach of *Llamadme Evita* to the more self-conscious and experimental stance of Dujovne Ortiz.

Llorca

Stannard has remarked that 'readers who prefer a plain tale, authoritatively told, turn to biography for the security of well-drawn characters, a hero or heroine, and satisfying closure'.[1] Carmen Llorca holds a doctorate in history, and is further qualified to write this biography by her extensive research work carried out in archives and libraries (p. 9).[2] She offers precisely the kind of biography outlined by Stannard: despite the considerable challenges posed by her subject, Llorca's text gives the impression of authorial control over a subject who, far from appearing contradictory and elusive, is presented as very much the opposite – as a knowable heroine with whom, moreover, the biographer seems to have fallen in love. Edel remarks that 'no good biography can be written in total love and admiration

[...]':[3] Llorca's falls squarely into such a category, flawed in precisely the way Edel describes. The pretensions of objectivity expressed both in the blurb ('es la primera vez que la figura de Eva Perón surge contemplada bajo las formas más objetivas [...]') and in the author's opening remarks ('Eva Perón es así, tal cual está en estas páginas, porque es ella misma quien habla y actúa', p. 9) are immediately exposed as groundless by gushing references to Eva as 'este personaje increíble' and 'esta mujer insigne'. At the end of her first chapter Llorca gives the impression that she is to play the part of honest broker by narrating brief anecdotes designed to show distinct facets of Eva's personality: the first recounts her instinctive act of kindness to a member of the oligarchy facing financial ruin. She offers him a valuable ring: 'toma, que me parece que estás en un mal momento'. The second anecdote describes how she was abandoned in the middle of the pampa by a couple of wealthy young men. As they sped away she shouted an ominous threat: '¡Os juro que me vengaré de vosotros!' (p. 21). Llorca appears to have set the scene for a balanced account of Eva's tortuous personality; but the reader will soon find that one side of Eva's character, the one implied by the first anecdote, will be highlighted at the expense of all the others.

Eva is presented as a romantic heroine who prevails against the inhospitable Argentine landscape reminiscent – at least in its overwhelming voraciousness – of that depicted by the Colombian writer José Eustasio Rivera' in *La vorágine* (1924): 'indomable y devoradora que actúa como una losa que oprime las voluntades' (p. 34). Eva's ideals are not extinguished by this hostile environment: 'cree en la belleza, la justicia, los sentimientos. Piensa que estarán en algún lugar de la tierra' (p. 34). Llorca goes on to idealize her subject, often basing her arguments on bald assertion (or on Eva's own unfounded claims). Thus Eva's protestations of innocence – expressed in a letter to Perón as she set out on her European tour – in response to rumours about her past are accepted as the plain truth. Common perceptions of her overweening ambitions are not allowed to compromise her good reputation: 'Eva fue una mujer limpia siempre [...]' (p. 55). Llorca even absolves her (p. 59, footnote 7) of a premarital affair with Emilio Kartulowicz, the editor of *Sintonía*, identified by several other biographers as her first real lover.[4] For Llorca, Eva exercises a total monopoly of the traditional female virtues: she is a 'mujer sincera bella y atractiva por su forma de creer' (p. 62);

more surprisingly, she is described as 'obediente sumisa y respetuosa' when she first came to power (p. 65); she is blessed with 'aquella firmeza de su ánimo, indeclinable, segura de su batalla y del triunfo de la misma' (p. 122); and with stunning natural refinement: 'tenía una desenvoltura y una naturalidad totalmente sorprendente' (p. 166). She appears free of any deficiency since her exemplary character traits are complemented by a fine intelligence, 'una inteligencia y una intuición nada común' (p. 151), and a sense of humour, manifested by her suggestion that her mother should chair the *Junta de Beneficencia*, a function traditionally performed by the President's wife, since Eva herself was deemed too young (p. 165). Given Llorca's evident idealization of her subject it is unsurprising that she frequently resorts to hyperbole: 'es sin lugar a dudas, el matrimonio por razón del Estado, más importante de la historia' (p. 94); Eva is 'la mejor embajadora que pudiera venir de aquellas tierras' (p. 122). She is often elevated to the status of greatness – 'una gran mujer' – but the epithet most frequently used to describe her is the commonplace and insipid 'increíble' (pp. 139, 176, 189, 194, 210). Not only is she compared with Napoleon, Lenin and Mao (p. 96) but she is frequently mythologized: 'ella era el pueblo' (p. 83); 'la historia es ella' (p. 92); she is a kind of goddess (p. 161). The 'facts' are often modified, not in the interests of creative power or 'higher truth', but rather to reinforce an argument and to exalt Eva even higher: when most historians concur that Eva's role in the events of 17 October 1945 was secondary,[5] Llorca sees her as the protagonist who almost single-handedly secured Perón's release: 'se lanzó a la lucha, coordinó la acción de las masas y de los sindicalistas [. . .] y el presidente Farrell no tuvo más remedio que llamar a Perón y hacerle regresar [. . .]' (p. 85).

Llorca's treatment of the *cabildo abierto* (pp. 225–8) is notable not for its portrayal of the dramatic dialogue between Eva and the *descamisados* (superbly recreated by Tomás Eloy Martínez in *Santa Evita*, as we shall see) but for its anti-Perón diatribe which prepares the ground for the subsequent allegation that Eva's illness was manipulated for political purposes by Perón and that she was 'empresarializada' by him (p. 257). In this respect Llorca's perspective anticipates that of Dujovne Ortiz. While it is likely that Perón wanted to curb Eva's power, there were clearly other factors involved in her renunciation of the vice-presidency, not least of course the opposition of the army. The reader cannot but suspect that Llorca's 'emplotment' of this episode is designed to blacken Perón's character in order, at least in part, to throw Eva's virtues into further relief.

Llorca seeks to justify attitudes and actions that at first glance appear dubious if not indefensible. Thus Eva is right to disown her past: 'hace bien en cancelar todo eso y en olvidar que es la hija ilegítima de Juan Duarte, porque ella es el futuro y no tiene nada que ver con ese pasado' (p. 92). Apart from the obvious objection that any individual is inevitably influenced by his/her past, there is the related point in Eva's case that her political appeal is directed at the *descamisados*, people who continued to endure the disadvantages she once experienced. Even from the perspective of traditional biographical practice, Llorca's comments appear one-dimensional and reductive, lacking even a semblance of even-handedness and balance. Llorca exonerates Eva totally, converting her alleged vices into virtues: thus, for example, Eva is admittedly quick to anger but only 'ante la indolencia de los demás' (p. 72); 'no era venganza lo que existía en su comportamiento era [...] una voluntad justiciera que doblegaba las voluntades ajenas a la suya' (p. 74). Rewarding her friends and family may be unpalatable in others, so Llorca implies, but it is wholly natural and logical in Eva: 'enriquece a los amigos que un día le tendieron la mano. Deja hacer a su hermano [...]'(p. 95). She also secured good jobs for her brothers-in-law (p. 100), information which Llorca communicates without comment as though it were the most natural thing in the world for Eva to use her power to further the interests of members of her own family. The background of some of her political confidants may seem inappropriate – Julio Alcaraz was a hairdresser and John Lack an astrologist – but there is absolutely no need for concern: 'no creo que ninguno de ellos tuviera sobre Eva una decidida influencia, sino que eran más bien manejados y utilizados por ella' (p. 100). Manipulation appears justifiable when it is directed at such 'inferior' associates (Eva also possesses 'el arte de fingir ante quienes no le importan', p. 193) or at certain members of government such as Bramuglia – against whom Eva had a longstanding grudge[6] – and Mercante, once acclaimed by Eva for his exemplary loyalty but subsequently discarded as a possible threat to her own political ambitions. Eva's fraught relations with the actress, Libertad Lamarque, is removed from the sphere of petty rivalry and resentment and elevated to the mystical status of an 'odio como ancestral' (p. 69). It is significant that on the rare occasions when Llorca does offer negative information on Eva it is usually consigned to footnotes. Reference to the coincidence of Libertad Lamarque's exile from Argentina with Eva's rise to power – which might reflect negatively on Eva – is relegated to a footnote (p. 70). Llorca claims that it is difficult to imagine Eva as 'cursi' or 'vulgar' (p. 176); an episode that exemplifies these precise features in Eva – her famous exchange with the Spanish ambassador, José María de Areilza, whom she calls 'ese gallego de mierda' – is consigned to a footnote (p. 130). It is one thing, however, to omit or de-emphasize information that would cast Eva in a negative light and quite another to mount a risible defence of her patent weaknesses, as Llorca sometimes does. Thus Eva's poor attendance record at school is put down to her exceptional sensitivity (p. 37) and her lamentable lack of punctuality during her European tour is attributed to the timidity of her entourage (pp. 118, 133).

Llorca's biography, which aims to offer a coherent account of a knowable subject, falls short of its own standards through certain inconsistencies and internal contradictions. On the one hand, Eva's lack of culture is acknowledged: 'la incultura de Eva era evidente y no es ningún misterio el descubrirla' (p. 117). But subsequently, Perón's observations, patently false, that Eva knew English and French, that she read Plutarch and loved music, especially Chopin, are confirmed (albeit rather defensively): 'y esto es perfectamente admisible y no creo que merezca ninguna burla [. . .]' (p. 151). It appears that Eva possessed a modicum of culture after all. Similarly, while Eva is driven by personal ambition to be somebody, 'ser alguien' (pp. 42, 54, 55, 92, 94), she is absolved of all 'egoísmo personal' (p. 166).[7] Some of Llorca's 'arguments' are as ill-founded and tautological as those propounded by Eva in *La razón de mi vida*: thus we read that Eva was right to claim that she was respectable since she was (p. 55); if Perón said that Eva was 'muy superior a todos nosotros' it was 'porque era verdad' (p. 192).

Llorca's unremittingly positive portrait of Eva would suggest that she shares her heroine's strong anti-oligarchic bias. Her feelings are, however, curiously muted on this subject; indeed, she manifests a grudging admiration for the oligarchy that emerges in her anecdote about the Argentine lady taking precedence over the French president while both were awaiting a taxi outside the opera house (p. 12). Llorca's fascination with the upper classes is suggested by her listing of the names found in the social pages of the Jockey Club: 'el más importante apellido es el de Anchorena. Es un nombre que representa algo más que una estirpe, es una dinastía con sus ramas principales y las colaterales' (p. 14). Although Llorca makes it clear that Eva did not belong to that elite circle celebrated by Eugenio d'Ors in his paean to the 'damas de Buenos Aires' – 'después de ellas Eva Perón inicia un nuevo estilo [...] barre ese mundo y da lugar al nacimiento de una nueva era para la Argentina', p. 17 – she notes that Eva was of Basque descent on both sides of her family (p. 16) and seeks to glorify her even further by pointing to the Basques' historical status as great estate owners. Eva's vociferous opposition to the oligarchy seemed absolute but some slight ambivalence may have tempered her feelings, if not her rhetoric: during her middle phase as *señora*, Eva sought to outdo, rather than to repudiate, the traditional extravagances of high society; and her reticence about her humble and illegitimate birth was a lifelong characteristic – which Llorca eagerly seeks to justify (p. 92).

In one of her rare self-conscious moments Llorca declares that 'una personalidad nunca queda definida por una sola versión [...]' (p. 93). Her own version of Eva is, however, wholly one-dimensional, focusing exclusively on the positive features of her subject. She shows no sense of the mythic, iconic Evita as a separate entity from the historical Eva Perón, an admittedly exceptional but also deeply flawed individual. Despite her view that 'en Eva coincidían muchos matices' (p. 231), Llorca's Eva is the woman of the white myth, the saint, the goddess, the immortal heroine; the countervailing myth of Eva as the power-hungry whore is barely acknowledged. Eva once said: 'Perón para mí, que lo he analizado profundamente, es perfecto'.[8] Llorca, who shares her subject's penchant for exaggeration as well as her flawed logic, expresses similarly extravagant sentiments in relation to Eva. One of the most notable features of Llorca's text is its lack of irony: language is used as an unselfconscious device to communicate the 'true' (the 'true' being, as Prendergast emphasizes, 'a property not of the world but of propositions about the world').[9] Llorca, however, shows little linguistic awareness of the problematical aspects of language and endorses rather than challenges her subject's Manichean perspectives.

Navarro

Marysa Navarro's aim in *Evita* is refreshingly different from Llorca's though without being entirely free of the other's idealizing impulse: Navarro aims to 'rescatar a la mujer de carne y hueso',[10] suggesting not only her belief in the possibility of direct access to the real historical figure but also her intention to acknowledge fully her inevitable human weaknesses. Such an opening implies a traditional biographical approach: 'recognizing' rather than 'contesting' the subject, to use William Epstein's terms.[11] One of Navarro's main challenges is to fill perceived gaps in the story of Eva: 'los trabajos de investigación histórica sobre Evita, tanto en la Argentina como en el extranjero, continúan siendo escasas' (p. 11). Moreover, Eva's autobiography is silent on a number of issues, notably her family background. Navarro begins the task of 'recuperating' Eva by comparing her with a more recent first lady, Hillary Clinton, who also exceeded the traditional role performed by the president's wife. Thereafter, Navarro proceeds to fill out the Eva story by, for example, providing exhaustive contextual information on Argentine cinema and theatre of the 1940s (p. 88), the history of women's suffrage (pp. 186–200) and of the *Sociedad de Beneficencia* (pp. 239–43). Such information lends coherence to the account and helps to refine our view of Evita. As an actress, her reputation did not do her justice: although she was not exceptional, she was no worse than the majority of the other stars of her time.

Navarro is particularly adept at steering a middle course where Eva's reputation is concerned and her work serves as a corrective to extreme views on either side. While Eva's social effectiveness has often been overestimated – she was not directly responsible for the extension of suffrage to women which was mainly attributable to Perón's enthusiasm and to the sustained efforts of Argentine feminist groups – so her negative traits have frequently been exaggerated. Navarro points out that she was not the prime instigator of the demise of the *Sociedad de Beneficencia* which her own foundation replaced: reform of such services can be traced back to 1943, prior to Eva's involvement. Here Navarro is effective in correcting exaggerated views of Eva, whether positive or negative. She structures her narrative by identifying key moments or landmarks in Eva's biography: thus Eva's quarrel with her mother, doña Juana, over Eva's determination to go to

Buenos Aires to seek work as an actress, represents 'su primera gran rebeldía' (p. 38); next, Eva's radio broadcasts, devoted to the biographies of famous women, mark a significant transition in Eva's character, since the quiet girl with the sweet smile is now replaced by 'una mujer de mirada más dura, paso firme, que tiene el triunfo en sus manos' (p. 63). The next and most significant landmark in Eva's career, 'la liberación de sí misma y su transformación en una mujer nueva [. . .]' (p. 131) coincides with a new dawn in the history of Argentina: 'los sucesos de octubre marcan un verdadero corte en la historia del país' (p. 112). In this way Navarro charts the high points in Eva's life, rendering coherent a potentially elusive story. She makes much of Eva's almost seamless progression from actress to political orator: 'los libretistas de sus radiotextos son los mismos que preparan sus textos políticos' (p. 82).

Unlike Llorca, Navarro wins the confidence of the traditional reader by her balanced argumentation and carefully nuanced judgements. Thus she refines the view that Eva was responsible for the appointment of Oscar Nicolini as director of Post Office and Telecommunications which precipitated the political crisis of October 1945, pointing out that Nicolini was not an 'oscuro empleado' but was handily placed for the position of *Director General* of *Radiodifusión* (p. 102). Navarro further boosts the reader's confidence by claiming (indirectly) the virtues of clear-sightedness and balanced treatment: 'el detenerse en los aspectos más superficiales del estilo de trabajo de Evita, dejando de lado la obra que realizó en su totalidad y el sentido que le dio constantemente a la ayuda social es tan deshonesto como negar sus rasgos paternalistas o decir que carecen de importancia' (p. 253). Here Navarro implicitly justifies her own procedure, suggesting her own role as 'honest broker' (which Llorca could not claim). Her favoured method is to make a seemingly clear-cut pronouncement which is then qualified: while on the one hand Navarro dismisses Eva's claim that she did not interfere in government as palpably false, on the other hand she carefully circumscribes Eva's real influence: 'los que atribuyen cambios de ministerio y hasta insinúan en ella la existencia de un poder paralelo al de Perón exageran tanto como Evita' (p. 281). Her air of authority is further enhanced by incisive judgements communicated in a memorably punchy style: having lived 'in sin' with Perón for almost two years, Eva drew unrelenting hostility that coloured reaction to her every move. This explains why the shoulder-revealing dress worn by Eva in the presence of Cardinal Coppelli 'fue motivo de escándalo aunque nada tenía de escandaloso' (p. 143). Navarro is particularly sharp in her portrayal of character: thus Quijano is the perfect vice-president (from Perón's perspective) because 'se limitaba a participar de los actos oficiales como si se tratara de un sueño largamente acariciado [...]' (p. 301). In 1947 Eva's star is rising, as is the hostility of her opponents: she displays 'un aire triunfante y desafiante a la vez. Sabe lo que quiere y lo consigue a diario' (p. 159). Navarro also brings to bear her analytical skills on Eva's speeches, uncovering a typical pattern in them. First she identifies three components (the *descamisados*, Evita and Perón) and then goes on to characterize the relationship between them and its essential dynamic: 'el vértice o eje es siempre Evita, lo que varía es el interlocutor y su relación con ella' (p. 352). Not surprisingly, Navarro is fond of this kind of foundational language: she remarks earlier in her narrative that the death of Eva's father may have been 'el eje alrededor del cual se articularía su personalidad con el correr de los años' (p. 23). Navarro appears to be mistress of authoritative explanation, deploying diverse discourses (the exhaustively contextual, the meticulously argumentative, the insightfully descriptive – particularly of character – the memorably terse and forceful) in order to dazzle the reader into accepting her carefully-crafted portrait of Eva. At her best Navarro combines literary artistry and logical rigour to create a seductive image of her subject.

However, in her zeal to fill in the gaps and to say all that she knows about Eva, Navarro becomes obsessive about communicating what Barthes has called 'l'effet du réel'.[12] Barthes points to the role of 'irrelevant detail' in fiction or history as a device for establishing the authenticity of what is reported. It is of course inevitable that some details will remain elusive, such as the exact date of the family's move from Los Toldos to Junín: 'no ha sido possible determiner la fecha exacta de su traslado a esa ciudad' (p. 129). But might the postmodern reader wonder whether a rough date could serve the narrative just as well? Not in Navarro's opinion: accuracy, exactitude and correctness are the guiding principles for a writer determined to maintain her commitment to reliable and unambiguous writing. Thus she compensates for failing to verify some details by providing a stultifying excess of others, relating to: size (the exact dimensions of the railway workshops in Junín, p. 29); quantity (the exact lengths of film received by Mexico and Argentina, p. 76); monetary value (the precise details of donations made to Eva's *Fundación*, (p. 213); voting statistics (p. 225); times and dates (often appearing in quick succession, such as those relating to Eva's approaching death, pp. 313–14);[13] and Eva's embalmment. In the latter case, Navarro quotes extensively from Dr Ara's report: 'su nota indicaba que el cadáver había sido "impregnado de sustancias solidificables" y que podía estar "permanentemente en contacto con el aire, sin más precauciones que las de protegerlo contra los agentes perturbadores mecánicos, químicos o térmicos tanto artificiales como de origin atmosférico"' (p. 323). Further scientific data are reproduced but the narrative does not properly assimilate them since they play no obvious role in its development.

Indeed, the details regarding the preservation of the corpse stand out as a wound in a text founded on coherence and unity (though, ironically, they may have appealed to Navarro because of their own internal coherence and precision, qualities with which she is obsessed). But in a text which seeks to iron out the wrinkles of Eva's story, rather than exploit its conflictual aspects within a context of linguistic play (in the manner of Martínez's *Santa Evita*, as we shall see), such detail serves only to disrupt the narrative flow, creating the impression of an extraneous and redundant interlude rather than of plot reinforcement. The distancing effect which results appears incongruous in the discourse of realism which places serious truth-telling above the claims of ironic play. Navarro's style is also characterized by enumeration: the narrative is broken by exhaustive lists of requests made to Eva by various trade unions (pp. 207–8), of visitors received by Eva (pp. 209–10) and of Eva's own activities (pp. 271–2). Navarro is resorting here to the realist technique of the inventory, following her instinct to say everything about certain aspects of her story partly to compensate for her inability to provide relevant details about others, some of which have been contaminated by the proliferation of alternative versions: thus the two accounts of doña Juana's background are 'diametralmente opuestas' (p. 32). Subscribers to both admit for the most part that they did not know the Duarte family at the time, 'pero insisten en que saben a ciencia cierta que lo que dicen es verdad' (p. 32). Similarly, a single 'true' version of the circumstances of Eva's departure to Buenos Aires ('las versiones al respecto son múltiples', p. 37) and of the altercation between Eva and Libertad Lamarque ('las versiones sobre ésta varían', p. 76) prove elusive. Not only do versions differ but they often contradict one another: Libertad Lamarque claimed that Eva was undisciplined whereas Mario Soffici, who directed two of her films, reported favourably: 'aceptaba con disciplina todas las indicaciones, sin complejos divísticos' (p. 80).

What emerges here is the impossibility of a univocal truth and further confirmation that 'what really happened' cannot be recuperated. Navarro may be aware of this principle but she refuses to accept it, seeking to cover up points of incoherence in her story. A favoured method is to interrogate the relevant sources, classify them by certain criteria of reliability and then decide on what 'really happened'. Such is her approach to the events of October 1945: 'las descripciones de la actuación de Evita en la crisis de octubre son ejemplos interesantes de las percepciones que de ella han tenido los argentinos pero guardan poca relación con lo que sucedió' (p. 121). Having assumed an authoritative posture, Navarro identifies the critics who subscribe to the view that Eva's role was essentially passive. She makes a perfunctory reference to Eva's own observations but then dismisses Eva as an unreliable witness (pp. 123–4). Her investigation of sources ultimately leads to a firm conclusion: 'hasta el momento, el examen de las fuentes no permite otra conclusión: Eva no formó parte del grupo de gente que propulsó la movilización' (p. 125). In fact, Navarro's frequent interrogation of documentary sources leads typically to her identification of two categories of works, one representing truth and the other distorting it: thus Erminda Duarte's version of Eva's departure for Buenos Aires, in *Mi hermana Evita*, is endorsed, albeit with reservations: 'el relato de Erminda tiene sin duda alguna el doble propósito de justificar a su hermana y de reivindicar a su madre. Aún así, y a pesar de no haber sido posible corroborarlo, es probable que en esencia sea el que más se ajuste a la verdad' (p. 37). What is most striking here is that Navarro clings to the concept of truth even when its usual supports in firm evidence are missing. Her usual practice is to dismiss auto/biographies that are not founded on documented 'facts'. If Erminda is Eva's chief apologist and admirer, Mary Main stands at the other extreme, being one of the most avid Evita-haters among her biographers. Navarro dismisses Main's *La mujer del látigo* as a work in which 'los hechos y la documentación brillan por su ausencia y abundan las afirmaciones gratuitas' (p. 90). Eva's *La razón de mi vida* (to which Navarro alludes repeatedly) is 'tendenciosa' (p. 16) and needs to be treated with caution since Eva 'mentía con facilidad y se olvidaba convenientemente de los hechos molestos' (p. 123). Indeed, all post-1955 biographies of Eva should be treated with caution since none is based on vigorous historical research (p. 334). It goes without saying that less academic sources, such as *Antena* and *Radiolandia*, are wholly unreliable since they project false images of Eva (e.g. as a complete sportswoman which she never was, p. 90). Navarro's critique further highlights her belief in discovering 'what really happened' through painstaking research. In this respect her work is straitjacketed – as is that of Joseph Page on Juan Perón – by the constricting norms of traditional biographical reliability.

The relativity of truth and falsehood is acknowledged, at least implicitly, by Navarro when she notes (in relation to the black myth) how rumours, either wholly or partially false, become 'verdades irrefutables para muchos argentinos' (p. 91). Navarro's aim, nonetheless, remains unswerving in its pursuit of truth: her writing is earnest and serious rather than festive and detached (as in Martínez's *Santa Evita*). However, despite her own rigorous approach and painstaking methodology ('el examen imparcial de los hechos revela que [. . .]', p. 186; 'el examen de los hechos no indica que [. . .]', p. 239), the whole truth remains elusive, confirmed by the involuntary tentativeness of Navarro's style marked by the proliferation of such phrases as 'es de suponer que' (p. 22), 'es posible que' (p. 23), 'no sería demasiado aventurado' (p. 25) etc. Ultimately Navarro's persistent search for plausible explanations when a less circumscribed and ludic approach would be in order diminishes her work: instead of exploiting creatively Eva's blatant discourtesies to the Spanish establishment – which defy logical explanation – Navarro offers rather pedestrian reasons for them: 'sus descortesías pueden haber sido resabios de sus tiempos de actriz [. . .] también expresiones de su altivez y asimismo su reacción ante el esplendor puesto a sus pies' (p. 170). Navarro is at her best when she is able to display some semblance of mastery over her subject, when she is able to define and assert, dispel ambiguity and uncertainty, and encapsulate what appears to be a self-evident truth in an authoritative, synoptic style: 'en las condiciones existentes en la Argentina de la década de los cuarenta, todo en ella coadyuvaba a fomenter el maniqueísmo, su origin, su pasado, su temperamento, su ropa, hasta su lenguaje, pero sobre todo sus actos' (p. 365). It is of course difficult, in view of Eva's posthumous existence, to provide her life with a sense of closure but Navarro attempts to do so by means of a rather sentimental conclusion which confers ample meaning on Eva's truncated life: 'aunque sabía que no lo conseguiría, a través de la lucha que emprendió por el pueblo, del amor que le prodigó y que éste le retribuyó con creces, encontró la razón de su vida' (p. 366). Navarro may find a sense of an ending for Eva but it is only superficially satisfying, the neatness of closure striking a false note in relation to a character who resists definition in death as in life.

Dujovne Ortiz

Dujovne Ortiz's *Eva Perón: a Biography* is more experimental than both previous works considered: it manifests a refreshing element of self-consciousness combined with a flippancy of tone and informality of style which contrasts with the proselytizing earnestness of Llorca and the truth-seeking obsessiveness of Navarro. This is not to say that Dujovne Ortiz contests her subject in the radical postmodern style advocated by Epstein since she does ultimately 'abduct' Eva by imposing upon her story the violence of sustained psychoanalytic interpretation (although she does offer many Evas rather than a single unified figure).[14] Dujovne Ortiz makes the telling, if reductive, point that Eva's 'entire life was one of secrets, of forbidden words',[15] a circumstance which, one might assume, authorizes psychoanalytic interpretation, the dominant interpretative strand in Dujovne Ortiz's analysis. Thus while Navarro relates Eva's doll with its broken leg to the family's pecuniary situation (p. 28), Dujovne Ortiz sees an additional meaning: 'Evita tenderly loved the broken creature that, like her, was missing something vital in her life' (p. 14). Indeed, Dujovne Ortiz sees psychoanalytic raw materials everywhere: in the description of the landscape: 'Argentines may complain about not having roots but they forget about the ombu roots where they used to play as if in their mother's womb' (p. 7); in Eva's appearance: 'her tight chignon shows her perfect self-control, indicating that "she held her destiny in her fist"'(p. 41); in jokes: 'which reveal reality and even anticipate it' (p. 181); and in potential rivalries such as that posed by Eva's assistant, Isabel Ernst, the source of Eva's '"narcissistic wound"' (p. 151). Dujovne Ortiz's text is structured by this specific and rather overbearing metanarrative: 'let's return to psychoanalysis in order to examine Eva's "small solution"'(p. 152) – a reference to León Rozichner's claim that one of the essential talents of women leaders is to 'use small means extremely powerfully' (quoted by Dujovne Ortiz, p. 152). It leads her to identify certain overarching patterns which confer some coherence and accessibility on her subject: while on the one hand Eva's psyche is dominated by ambition deriving at least in part from her father's rejection of her – 'at her father's funeral Eva was last in line. She swore to herself that one day she would be first' (p. 13) – on the other hand she 'fits the type of "lost" woman portrayed in the tango' (p. 37). In this latter respect she reflects her country, both Eva and Argentina unified in their instability, their split personality, their gaping divisions often figured as wounds.[16] Most commentators would concur that Argentina still bears the open wound of the conflict between *civilización* and *barbarie*, first identified by Sarmiento in the nineteenth century, whose repercussions penetrate every corner of national life. According to Dujovne Ortiz, Eva offers, on a personal level, a microcosmic reflection of these national divisions, evoking 'whole litanies of opposite terms' (p. 21). The *cabecitas negras* represented a national wound – Argentines were not as white as they thought they were' (p. 50) – but neither was Eva: when Perón was asked whether he called Eva 'mi negrita' he replied that she was blond, possibly from forgetfulness. 'Or', asks Dujovne Ortiz, 'was it a negation born of a social wound that never healed?' (p. 120). The potential consternation caused by the proliferation of national and personal wounds, by the blurred identities of many Argentinas and many Evas, is only assuaged by Dujovne Ortiz's portrayal of them as mirror images of each other. She can only go so far in her celebration of dissonance and division: here a consoling continuity is found between the country as a whole on the one hand and its foremost icon on the other.

Dujovne Ortiz's psychoanalytic approach frequently provides penetrating analysis of human and especially marital relations. Perón's mother is abandoned by a husband who 'vanished in his dream of an endless departure' (p. 68). The flawed psyche of

Perón is clinically exposed: 'denying in his heart the existence of another, man or woman, Perón could love only by diminishing and minimizing' (p. 62). He appeared before the people as dominating father with Eva representing 'the small thing', and certifying Perón's virility (p. 152). Dujovne Ortiz may not be saying anything startlingly new here but her claims have the aura of psychoanalytic authority. More original is her (largely imaginative) probing of the relationship between Perón and Eva, one of the great 'secrets' of Peronism. She claims that Eva loved the image of Perón rather than the flesh and blood Perón – 'the real Perón, the daily Perón, had begun to annoy her' (p. 84). Eva was never more annoyed than at their country retreat of San Vicente: while Perón was 'irresistible' in his riding gear, Eva 'thinking of the poor, who could not wait until Monday, looked at him without seeing him' (p. 257). Dujovne Ortiz provides a clever insight into a relationship allegedly founded on pretence: 'to cheat on her husband with herself was the biggest sin of this Madeleine, who by becoming blond, and by choosing a transfigured image over the real one, had also fooled herself' (p. 85). This is no less stimulating for being speculative: a gap or uncertainty in the 'official' story is (at least partially) filled by an imaginative approach underpinned by the seemingly authoritative discourse of psychoanalysis.

Dujovne Ortiz's portrayal of Perón's 17 October speech suggests the interaction typical of the 'scene' of psychoanalysis, the crowd playing the active role of analyst whose subject is Perón: 'the crowd forced Perón to be himself' (p. 127); 'they tried everything to entice him to speak' (p. 128). Perón finally gives up his terrible secret, his mother fixation (although it is a mother substitute whom he invokes to stand in for his real mother).[17] Another secret of Perón is 'revealed' in Dujovne Ortiz's portrayal of a later public event with even more drama, the *cabildo abierto* of August 1951. It is Perón's jealousy of Eva that leads him to withhold his endorsement of her candidacy for vice-president (pp. 264–7).

Not surprisingly Dujovne Ortiz's psychoanalytic approach sometimes overreaches itself in attempting to explain too much, giving the impression that every trait and every mannerism is potentially significant: Perón's wink of an eye was in fact a tic 'but a revealing one, a nervous joke that was subconsciously imitating his mother' (p. 68). Perón's possible motives in imposing Eva on others were similarly subconscious, but represent the reassuring continuity of an inherited quality whereby Perón exacted 'revenge on level-headed people, on well-wishers, just as his father had done by marrying a mulatto servant' (p. 105). After Perón's resignation from the vice-presidency in 1945 Eva 'felt like his daughter, and she hated food because of doña Juana. For his part, Perón hated mothers' (p. 111). Here Dujovne Ortiz's emplotment of aberrant family relationships becomes intricate and contrived and her psychoanalytic scaffolding, elsewhere robust, shows signs of strain (reminiscent of the excessive detail that obtrudes in Navarro's narrative). The worst case of interpretive 'violence' emerges when Dujovne Ortiz attempts to explain the landmarks of Eva's life in terms of neat psychoanalytic formulae: all triteness about Eva's story vanishes when we consider 'a woman who became a man's light, who willingly transformed herself into his shadow and who, guessing that the light was disturbing him, decided to turn herself off and die' (p. 59).[18]

Unlike Navarro, Dujovne Ortiz does not display excessive respect for the 'facts': while they have their place in her methodology they are not all-important. Thus, for example, she queries the allegations regarding Eva's putative bank accounts as 'perfect constructions erected on a base of unconfirmed reports' (p. 199). Dujovne Ortiz characterizes Marysa Navarro as a biographer 'who likes to stick to the facts' (p. 53), implying thereby that her own priorities are different. Indeed, her refusal to be bound by the known facts emerges in her description of Eva's affair with the editor of *Sintonía*, Emilio Kartulowicz: 'Evita could have introduced herself to Kartulowicz by saying: "If I am here, it is because of you". What she really said is not known [. . .]' (p. 39). Dujovne Ortiz's preparedness to improvise enriches her biography just as Navarro's rigorous adherence to the 'facts' diminishes hers. Dujovne Ortiz does not equate fact with truth: discussing Eva's role in the mobilization of the workers on 17 October 1945, she asks: 'but where is the truth? In life as in dreams, it is often found in feelings'. She goes on to recount the episode of Eva's assault by anti-Peronist students: 'those are the facts. As far as the feelings go, she (Eva) described them in clearly religious terms [. . .]' (p. 125). Facts, and the traditional biographer's virtues such as 'reliability' and 'consistency', are not accorded prime importance: Eva may not have uttered the decisive words 'thank you for existing', but doubts about their authenticity does not prevent

Dujovne Ortiz from exploiting their full psychological potential (p. 61). In this respect at least she would concur with Tomás Eloy Martínez's celebration of the convergence of history and fiction which 'en vez de moverse por esos caminos paralelos que jamás se encuentran, han empezado a entrelazarse y a fertilizarse mutuamente'.[19]

Following her reference to Eva's starring role in a series of Radio Belgrano broadcasts devoted to famous women, Dujovne Ortiz remarks that some biographers, such as Marysa Navarro, 'maintain that we must not draw conclusions from the distinctiveness of these roles. For her and for others, it is more important to isolate each biographical element without taking into consideration the "connections" that link them, the echoes that bounce one off the other' (p. 53). Dujovne Ortiz seems to imply here that for her the bare facts are insufficient, that it is the biographer's right (if not duty) not only to interpret the facts but also to weave them into a creative pattern. This is indeed her own practice as she finds new echoes and associations in Eva's personal history: thus she refers to the claim that the death of Eva's grandmother, Petrona Nuñez, was faked twenty years before it happened and concludes that 'if true an inverse pattern emerges with Eva's survival faked by Ara' (p. 9). Similarly, Dujovne Ortiz notes that when Eva's mother, Juana, was asked to stop sewing, her reply was always: '"I do not have time to stop". These were words that Eva would later repeat, maybe without even realizing their origin' (p. 13). Dujovne Ortiz makes a more telling connection between different reactions to Perón: in October 1945, Perón was booed by his student audience after delivering a speech marred by his failure to remember his words; 'twenty years later, the children of those students would judge Perón's language – which was improved by time, of course – to be immensely sensible. That is how two generations erred; one through hatred, the other through love' (p. 109). Are these cases of contrived coherence or of creative interweaving? Whichever view the reader takes, Dujovne Ortiz shows remarkable sensitivity to previously unnoticed connections between episodes separated, in some cases, by several years. Her practice is novelistic: she enriches her narrative by enhancing its internal patterns and dissonances, moulding the facts in the interests of presenting a story that is both historically true and artistically creative.

The internal coherence of Dujovne Ortiz's account is reinforced by her frequent use of aphorisms. Here she is obviously imitating the style of both Perón and Eva whose speeches and writings were marked by their frequent use of aphorisms. Aphorism can, moreover, be seen as an inherent aspect of Dujovne Ortiz's 'fashionable' psychoanalytic style which colours her maxims: 'those who remain children are the ones whose childhoods are thwarted' (p. 63); 'the criollo condition is a shattered mirror' (p. 67); 'the line between need and love is often blurred' (p. 78); 'everything in life is an echo, a forest of symbols where smells, colors and sounds – but also loves – respond to each other' (p. 39).[20] Marjorie Garber, who considers the question of fashion in the sphere of writing, poses the following question: 'What is the genre, or literary mode, of the fashionable in the realm of morality and style? [...]. It is the aphorism, and its close, sometimes indistinguishable, relatives: the adage, the sentence, and the maxim'.[21] The link between dress and writing is made explicit by Dujovne Ortiz: 'for her ghost written autobiography, Eva wanted a neat, embellished bourgeois style of writing that was identical to her way of dressing and her moralizing taste' (p. 251). She also observes that Eva was frequently overdressed: 'only the gesture mattered, which meant: "I am fashion" [...]. To dress so absurdly was to exert power' (p. 195). Dujovne Ortiz's style of writing, embellished throughout by both the glittering insights of psychoanalytic theory and by a certain aphoristic excess which suggests literary overdressing, offers a writerly image of Eva's own use of fashion – which was mostly to stunning effect though occasionally cheapened by the gaudy and fake – as when her necklace turns out to be made of painted noodles (p. 157). Dujovne Ortiz's use of anecdote may be seen as a further biographical 'fashion accessory'. The anecdote, like the aphorism, is a self-contained unit, complementing the aphorism's timelessness with an often frivolous temporality, and usually possessing its own peculiar powers of illumination, particularly of character. Thus a previously unsuspected trait in Eva's character is revealed by a remark she made in Granada before the recumbent figures of the Catholic kings. Her guide pointed out that Isabel's head was buried deeply in the pillow because it was thought that her brain was heavier than Ferdinand's, perhaps a malicious reference to the inverse relationship between Eva and Perón, the lightness of her mind contrasting with the relative weight of his. Dujovne Ortiz narrates that Eva 'did not hold back from "betraying" him (she who was always so faithful) when she responded with the same malice, "It's still like that"' (p. 178).

A further anecdote serves to illuminate yet another aspect of the unknown Eva: while she displayed a strong sense of fashion in public she was indifferent to her style at home. On one particular 17 October anniversary Eva was, as usual, elegantly dressed for her impending balcony appearance – with the exception of her footwear for she still wore her slippers. Dujovne Ortiz offers a neat explanation that suggests Eva was in some respects in thrall to outward appearance and show: 'the crowd could not see her bottom half, which represented the housewife with swollen feet. Her top half, the one people saw, was Evita' (p. 229). This anecdote offers a fresh insight into Eva's character, showing how its 'litany of opposite terms' (p. 21) – here elegance and casualness – manifests itself even in the sphere of fashion. Again Eva's sartorial impropriety finds its stylistic counterpart in Dujovne Ortiz's writing that often displays a disconcerting flippancy, cocking a snook at biographical convention – just as Eva often did at accepted bourgeois manners. In sharp contrast with Llorca's strange reverence, Dujovne Ortiz's potted version of the Argentine oligarchy is notable for its casual potshots: 'now only the oligarchs – that's what they called those 1,804 happy landowners – lived extravagantly' (p. 17). A similarly dismissive attitude is shown towards the US ambassador, Spruille Bradon: 'in the face of the dangers of Nazism, this ruddy Mr Clean played the part of the Messiah' (p. 106). Neither Eva nor Perón escape Dujovne Ortiz's irony (which illustrates Hutcheon's point that irony always has an edge and sometimes has a sting[22]): she describes Eva's attire while greeting Franco as 'stiff but not without humour [...]. The gallego dictator [...] bowed to kiss her hand. So she too bowed slightly, in a gesture borrowed from the nobility, a gesture she would later repeat before numerous other European personalities, and each time it would be more successful' (p. 172). Eva's lack of culture is also targeted: 'that evening, when she entered La Scala, the second act of *Orpheus* was ending. She was escorted to the royal loge, where she enjoyed the show that much more since it was so short' (p. 186). Dujovne Ortiz also ironizes the hypochondriac Perón whose illnesses she reduces and minimizes (in the same way that Perón himself, according to Dujovne Ortiz (p. 62), reduces and minimizes people to whom he feels close): 'the colonel was often sick with bilious attacks and flus, harmless and useful complaints if, by expressing discomfort in little doses, one is saved from true illness' (p. 63).

The ironic impulse counters the univocal thrust of realist writing by removing 'the security that words only mean what they say'. Hutcheon goes on to observe that 'the power of the unsaid to challenge the said is the defining semantic condition of irony.'[23] Her use of irony distances Dujovne Ortiz from her subject since Eva's political commitment necessitated an unambiguous discourse of engagement. Dujovne Ortiz's ironic irreverence makes no exception of Eva and contrasts with Llorca's sustained obsequiousness (indeed Llorca highlights in this respect the pitfalls of an earnestness unrelieved by any sense of irony or humour). It also cuts across the traditional biographer's paranoid obsession with certitude and points instead to the proliferation of meaning associated with literary discourse. As we have already seen, the etymology of 'irony' links it directly to the idea of the mask, for it derives from the Greek word for dissembler.[24] Irony was, of course, one mask that Eva rarely wore.

Dujovne Ortiz also distinguishes herself from both Llorca and Navarro by the self-consciousness of her narrative, itself often informed by irony. Although she, like them, does not feature in any significant way in her own narrative (she refers in passing to the imprisonment of her father, a communist, at Neuquén from 1943–5, p. 106), she does offer some comments on the art of biography. She implicitly acknowledges the frequent futility of seeking to uncover the facts, of pinpointing what actually happened, given the inevitable accretion of disparate versions. In the process she makes an important point which theorists, if not practising biographers, frequently alludes to: 'a mystery of foggy collective memory' veils the past, forcing the biographer to look inwards as well as outwards: 'by selecting one version over another, each of Evita's biographers and each witness to her life retells his or her own biography' (p. 9). Backschneider makes the same point: 'writing a biography implies self-discovery'.[25] In this way narratorial authority and pretension are deflated and attention diverted from the events narrated to the writerly implications of the way in which they are recounted. Later, in her opening chapter, Dujovne Ortiz returns to the difficulties faced by the biographer confronted by the uncertainties of Eva's life story: 'the slightest detail always seems to be mirrored by its opposite or followed by many facts that are similar but not completely the same [. . .]' (p. 25). She proceeds to review the four main versions of Eva's departure from Junín for Buenos Aires, thereby illustrating some of the practical problems faced by the biographer. The inevitable conclusion is that however painstaking the biographer's procedures s/he will fail to identify a 'correct' or 'factual' version of events and 'what really happened' will remain beyond reach: 'within this succession of possible scenarios there is only mystery' (p. 26). Dujovne Ortiz goes on to evaluate each version: 'the first version, the family's version, tends to present things conventionally [. . .] The fourth enjoys its salacious suggestion' (p. 26). From the four versions outlined, Dujovne Ortiz chooses the third which she 'improves' by having Eva travel by train to Buenos Aires and then seeking out the tango singer, Magaldi, rather than having Magaldi and his wife drive her to the capital. The facts may not be left behind entirely ('one thing is certain: Magaldi met Evita', p. 27) but they are conditioned by the biographer's preferences. The final paragraph of the opening chapter 'stages' Dujovne Ortiz's preferred version, emphasizing her choice of events rather than the events themselves: 'let us then embrace the most convincing scenario. On January 2 1935, at fifteen years of age, Evita left her mother and her sisters and took the train to Buenos Aires. Clutched in her hand was a scrap of paper on which Magaldi had scribbled his address [. . .]' (p. 27). In this respect Dujovne Ortiz belongs to that elite group of biographers, identified by Backschneider, who 'know they are inventing through their selection and arrangement of materials [. . .]. They must choose what to include, leave out, emphasize and subordinate [. . .]'.[26] Dujovne Ortiz also discusses aspects of biographical writing in connection with Eva's movements during Perón's imprisonment in October 1945. After recounting that Eva took refuge one night at the home of her actress friend, Pierina Dealessi, Dujovne Ortiz observes: 'the need for coherence that historians have toward a famous individual allowed us to consider Dealessi's account proof of Evita's weakness. Why not say that Eva was weak in front of Pierina and strong in front of the union workers who were prepared to listen to her? [. . .] And finally, why not say that both the fear and the courage were real?' (p. 117). Although her own narrative is marked by strategies designed to reinforce coherence (the use of psychoanalysis as a metanarrative confers a semblance of cohesion, consistency and authority on her text), Dujovne

Ortiz at least pays lip service to alternative models of biographical writing which would seek to 'contest' rather than 'recognize' the subject which, as Epstein points out, is always an act of subjection, violence committed in the guise of interpretation.[27] Here Dujovne Ortiz gestures tentatively towards contradictions and inconsistencies (in preference to imposing contrived unities): 'a series of different Evitas, innumerable Evitas began to emerge, one after another – frivolous Evita, greedy Evita, manipulative Evita, Evita who dreads blunders, insolent Evita who shows off to hide her fear, sensitive Evita, the protagonist of a beautiful story' (p. 157).

It is evident that Dujovne Ortiz does not share Navarro's respect for the facts, still less Llorca's conception of a sovereign and saintly subject. Indeed she is guilty of a few errors which contravene the known facts: her 'spotlighting' of Evita leads to her suppression of the marginal figure of Potota, Perón's first wife (mentioned on p. 260). Thus Dujovne Ortiz argues that prior to Evita, Perón 'had known women only as prostitutes' (p. 65) – an error compounded by Perón's apparent intimacy with Potota and his grief at her loss – and she refers to Isabelita as Perón's second wife (p. 133). She also attributes that well-known slur on Perón – 'the man who Evita was'– to Cabrera Infante rather than to its real author, Ezequiel Martínez Estrada (p. 159). But for what Dujovne Ortiz lacks in biographical accuracy she more than compensates with novelistic flair. She alludes to a host of writers, both Argentine (Güiraldes, Marechal) and foreign (Kundera, Tolstoy, Dostoievsky) and literature is an important reference point for character portrayal: thus Perón's wonder on realizing that Evita was 'an instrument endowed with a certain look no doubt equalled the wonder that the protagonist from Milan Kundera's *Book of Laughter and Forgetting* felt when his eyes met those of the "woman-object" he was making love to' (p. 59); Perón and Franco have that type of sentimentality which Dostoievsky identified in the old Karamazov (p. 180); and Perón is characterized as the 'autumnal patriarch' (p. 287), recalling García Márquez's *El otoño del patriarca* (1975).[28] This form of postmodern intertextuality equates the 'real' historical world to its 'unreal' fictional counterpart, so blurring the traditional generic divide between the biographical and the novelistic genres. Dujovne Ortiz is a novelist as well as a biographer: her *El árbol de la gitana* (1997) has been described as 'una saga familiar, frondosa y multisecular, cuyo "hilo del sentido" se halla en las manos enigmáticas de la Gitana, más "real" – se dice – en su fuerza mágico-simbólica que la misma narradora'.²⁹ It is unsurprising therefore that she looks beyond the bare facts towards what Virginia Woolf called the creative and fertile fact, 'the fact that suggests and engenders'.³⁰ It might be objected that Dujovne Ortiz's flashes of creativity and self-consciousness are overshadowed by the dominant influence on her narrative of Freudian interpretive strategies – a charge difficult to refute, although such strategies do provide some original insights, as we have seen. If Dujovne Ortiz's biography is inscribed by the master narrative of psychoanalysis to illumine Eva's life, the work of Pedro Ara, Eva's embalmer, draws on the prestige and authority of another medical discourse to present the 'verdadera historia' of his subject's death.³¹ Dujovne Ortiz gestures beyond the limits of psychoanalysis toward a creative, postmodern experimentalism which anticipates Tomás Eloy Martínez's novelistic enterprise. Ara's writing makes sparse use of the professional expertise of his calling, serving to confer from the margins a veneer of authority upon a text that assumes from the outset a blatantly self-conscious character as attention is diverted from the subject towards the writer, Ara himself.

NOTES

[1] Martin Stannard, 'The necrophiliac art?', in Dale Salivak (ed.), *The Literary Biography: Problems and Solutions* (London: Macmillan, 1996), pp. 32–40 (p. 33).
[2] *Llamadme Evita* (Barcelona: Planeta, 1980), p. 9. Further references, given in parenthesis in the text, are to this edition.
[3] Leon Edel, 'Biography and the science of man', in Anthony M. Friedson (ed.), *New Directions in Biography* (Hawaii: University Press of Hawaii, 1981), pp. 1–11 (p. 9).
[4] See, for example, Dujovne Ortiz, *Eva Perón*, p. 39.
[5] Sigal notes the blatant falsification of Eva's role in this respect: 'y poco importa que investigaciones históricas muestren hoy el papel de las organizaciones obreras en el movimiento del 17 de octubre y que otras prueben que Eva Perón se había quedado obedientemente en su casa'. See Silvia Sigal and Eliseo Verón, *Perón o muerte: los fundamentos discursivos del fenómeno peronista* (Buenos Aires: Legasa, 1986), p. 118. Gillespie makes a similar point, noting that the *Montonero* claim crediting Eva with mobilization was 'belied by all historical investigations of the event'. See 'Montoneros: Soldiers of Perón' in Gabriela Nouzeilles and Graciela Montaldo (eds), *Argentina Reader: History, Culture, Politics* (Durham: Duke University Press, 2002), pp. 377–85 (p. 379).

6 When Perón was imprisoned in October 1945 Bramuglia had refused Eva's request to sign a document of *habeas corpus* which would have allowed him to leave Argentina. Bramuglia's motives were not malicious: he regarded Perón's continued involvement in politics as being in the best interests of the country.
7 Curiously Llorca quotes with apparent approval Areilza's depiction of Eva as rather unattractive, lacking sex appeal and consumed by megalomania (p. 168). Llorca seems to be endorsing here an image of Eva very much at odds with the one she herself is projecting.
8 Hugo Gambini, *Historia del peronismo*, 2 vols (Buenos Aires: Planeta, 1999–2001), I, p. 136.
9 Christopher Prendergast, *The Order of Mimesis: Balzac, Stendhal, Nerval, Flaubert* (Cambridge: Cambridge University Press, 1986), p. 68.
10 Marysa Navarro, *Evita* (Buenos Aires: Corregidor, 1981), p. 13. Further references, given in parenthesis in the text, are to this edition.
11 For Epstein 'recognizing' in this context implies conferring a false unity on the subject by means of interpretative violence; 'contesting', by contrast, refers to the acknowledgement of the subject's multiple and elusive selves. It is driven by an impulse to de-centre (rather than unify) and seeks to disrupt any theoretical apparatus or master narrative aimed at the production of a univocal truth. See William H. Epstein, '(Post)modern Lives: Abducting the biographical subject', in William H. Epstein (ed.), *Contesting the Subject: Essays in the Postmodern Theory and Practice of Biography and Biographical Criticism* (West Lafayette IN: Perdue University Press, 1991), pp. 217–36.
12 Roland Barthes, 'L'effet du réel', *Communications*, 11 (1968) 84–9.
13 Leo Bersani states that 'the specified year not only serves the illusion of historical authenticity; it also allows us the luxury of assigning precise beginnings to experience and of thereby making experience more accessible to our appetite for sense-making distinctions and categories'. 'Leo Bersani on realism and the fear of desire', in Lilian R. Furst (ed.), *Realism*, Modern Literatures in Perspective (London and New York: Longman, 1992), pp. 240–60 (p. 241).
14 Discussing Norman Mailer's biography of Marilyn Monroe, Epstein claims that his narrative 'becomes the scene of an abduction, a discursive practice in and through which the biographer can detain and defile his biographical subject'. William H. Epstein, '(Post)modern Lives: Abducting the biographical subject', in William H. Epstein (ed.), *Contesting the Subject: Essays in the Postmodern Theory and Practice of Biography and Biographical Criticism*, pp. 217–36 (p. 218).
15 Alicia Dujovne Ortiz, *Eva Perón*, trans. Shawn Fields (New York: St Martin's Griffin, 1997), p. 9. Subsequent references, given in parenthesis in the text, are to this edition.
16 For Joseph Page, Perón is a microcosm of Argentina: 'for Argentines, understanding Perón is a prerequisite to understanding themselves' (p. 502).
17 In his 17 October speech, the importance to Perón of the mother figure emerges clearly: 'Esto es pueblo; esto es el pueblo sufriente que representa el dolor de la madre tierra, el que hemos de

reivindicar [. . .] quiero en esta oportunidad, como simple ciudadano, mezclado en esa masa sudorosa, estrechar profundamente a todos contra mi corazón, como lo podría hacer con mi madre' (see Sigal and Verón, *Perón o muerte*, p. 46).

18 Dujovne Ortiz's scenario is reminiscent of the suicide (in Berlin, in 1834) of Charlotte Stieglitz – motivated by her desire to liberate her husband's petrified poetic powers. See Elizabeth Bronfen, *Over Her Dead Body: Death, Femininity and the Aesthetic* (Manchester: Manchester University Press, 1992), p. 360.

19 Tomás Eloy Martínez, 'Historia y ficción: dos paralelas que se tocan', p. 99.

20 Dujovne Ortiz also shows remarkable flair for the stunning aphorism outside the sphere of psychoanalysis: 'a certain truth can often slide into the emptiest rhetoric, as if smuggled in' (p. 86).

21 Marjorie Garber, *Quotation Marks* (New York and London: Routledge, 2003), p. 41.

22 Hutcheon, *Irony's Edge*, p. 15.

23 Hutcheon, *Irony's Edge*, pp. 14, 59.

24 Lionel Trilling, *Sincerity and Authenticity* (London: Oxford University Press, 1972), p. 120.

25 Backschneider, *Reflections on Biography*, p. 90.

26 Backschneider, *Reflections on Biography*, p. 18.

27 '(Post)modern lives: Abducting the biographical subject' in *Contesting the Subject*, pp. 217–36 (p. 224).

28 Though Dujovne Ortiz is more experimental and self-conscious than both Llorca and Navarro, there is nothing detached about the vitriol she directs at Juan Perón: it was he who was the 'truly brilliant actor' (p. 259) rather than Eva whose love for the people was genuine, and it was he, Eva's 'imaginary man', devoid of feelings and empty inside ('nothing was bleeding or trembling in him', p. 265), who finally became the outcast (p. 295). Dujovne Ortiz reserves one of the sharpest and most memorable of her many epigrammatic remarks to reduce Perón to what she sees as his true proportions: 'there was a day, long ago, when she had tried to be like him. Now he was incapable of imitating his imitator' (p. 286).

29 María Rosa Loja, 'Pasos nuevos en espacios habituales' in Noé Jitrik (ed.), *Historia crítica de la literatura argentina* (Buenos Aires: Emecé, 1999), xi; Elsa Drucaroff (ed.), *La narración gana la partida* (Buenos Aires: Emecé, 2000), pp. 19–48 (p. 33).

30 'The art of biography', in Virginia Woolf, *Collected Essays*, ed. Leonard Woolf, 4 vols (New York: Harcourt, Brace and World, 1967) IV, 221–8 (p. 228).

31 Pedro Ara, *Eva Perón: la verdadera historia contada por el médico que preservó su cuerpo* (Buenos Aires: Sudamericana, 1996).

Part III

Creative Writing

Chapter 7

Pale Fire at the Margins of *La novela de Perón*

In *Las memorias del General*, Martínez remarks that he had begun work on a biography of Perón in 1974 but was hindered by the suspicion that 'este género podía derivar en un libro inverosímil' (*Las memorias*, p. 15). The implication is that biography is associated with verisimilitude and 'truth', concepts which Martínez's writing practice constantly challenges. Indeed, Martínez approvingly quotes Borges who, typically, conflates truth and fiction, refusing their rigid separation as spurious: 'Somos elécticos, y en esa vacilación del lugar está nuestro lugar, en esa historia fingida está en buena parte, nuestra historia verdadera'.[1] In recent years the link between biography and truth-telling has weakened and there has been an increasing acceptance that, as Nadel points out, the 'best biographies reinvent rather than re-construct'.[2] Taking Barthes's life of Fourier as an example, he describes it as a work consisting (rather like Martínez's) of an 'assemblage of bits of information, knowledge and images' (p. 200). In the composition of any biography, fictive rather than historical content dominates: the past, as it really was, is irrecoverable. Martínez's title, *La novela de Perón*, suggests that novel and biography converge since the imaginary world suggested by 'novela' is balanced by historical 'reality' indicated by 'Perón'. Indeed the text can be seen as a novelized biography (similar to Joyce Carol Oates's 'novel', *Blonde*, about Marilyn Monroe[3]) or, better perhaps, as a counter-biography since it contests what the traditional biography takes for granted: the ultimate recognition of a single self-consistent subject whose unknown or hitherto contradictory aspects are resolved by dint of the biographer's tenacious and single-minded pursuit of the truth. The basic difference between Joseph Page's work, explicitly designated a biography, and Martínez's, which is in effect a hybrid form, lies in their approach to historical writing and their differing views about the accessibility of the past. Page may not deny the truth of fiction but he believes that it should be distinguished from the truth of fact; that the biographer's task should be to find out 'what exactly happened'; and that his standing as a biographer is to be judged by his perceived 'reliability'. Despite having had – as we have already mentioned (p. 116) – the immeasurable advantage of extended face-to-face encounters with Perón during the latter's exile in Madrid, – which might have inclined him towards a more 'factual' approach – Martínez's priorities are very different from those of Page. Rather than seeking to arrest his subject, to offer an official, 'canonical' Perón, Martínez 'contests'[4] his subject, flaunts rather than suppresses his contradictions and constructs his text not on the basis of the 'authoritative' word of Perón but rather on the uncertain foundation of his blatant unreliability, on his inconsistencies, on the fissures of his character which preclude the elaboration of a single and unified self. Martínez thus rejects a 'humanist' view of the individual as a free subject possessed of an irreducible human 'essence'. More spectacularly than any other Latin American writer, Martínez illustrates Richard Holmes's observation that 'biographers base their work on sources which are inherently unreliable. Memory itself is fallible; memoirs are inevitably biased [. . .]'[5]

Martínez does not allow his reader to become, in Kermode's words, 'drugged by the comfort of the conventional'. Whereas Page highlights the points of coherence in his story, Martínez denies the reader his accustomed comfort of 'followability', of ignoring 'what is written in favour of what it is written about'.[6] Apart from its fragmented structure, *La novela de Perón* is notable for its melange of typographical effects that further ensures that language and discourse are foregrounded and problematized rather than subsumed in an unruffled and transparent textual flow. The normal temporal and spatial coordinates that structure Page's biography are immediately called into question by Martínez whose text opens with a reference to Perón's dream about the South Pole: 'cuando despertó, tuvo la sensación de no estar en ningún tiempo. Sabía que era el 20 de junio de 1973, pero eso nada significaba' (p. 11). Later, stepping on to the balcony of his Puerto del Hierro residence in Madrid, Perón moves into a new spatio-temporal reality to re-experience an earlier self, ensconced in Buenos Aires, in power, and in public esteem: 'el General alzaba los brazos y allí entraba, de pronto, el arrullo de la muchedumbre [...] Más allá [...] junto a la casilla donde se apostaban los guardias civiles del general Franco, se abrían las bocas del subterráneo Anglo-Argentino' (p. 13). In fact this other self, 'el Perón del pasado' (p. 12), will increasingly overshadow the present Perón: although the apparent focus of attention is on the elderly figure returning to Buenos Aires to assume his third presidency, this 'empty' Perón, devoid of feelings and shunning human contact, will remain haunted by his own earlier and much younger self, from whom he now feels remote. His past will live a posthumous existence, overwhelming his present. The richness of this past is represented by his perfume that is associated with Eva and with her immortal (though probably apocryphal) phrase, 'Gracias por existir' (p. 15).

In *La novela de Perón* traces of the neatly documented procedures of traditional biography are barely visible as Martínez points to the novel as the genre best placed to capture Latin American reality: 'primero, porque la realidad es ya de por sí novelesca. Y luego, porque la complejidad de esa realidad novelesca exige que la nación sea narrada con instrumentos más flexibles y, por supuesto, más complejos'.[7] Not only does the opening chapter refer to Perón's dream world but it relates the excesses of his secretary, López Rega, who attempts to measure the density of the air in the General's lungs by penetrating it with his thoughts (p. 12). Refusing to accept the relative brevity of his association with Perón (facilitated by Perón's third wife, Isabel), López Rega intrudes into Perón's past, claiming that the 'Altísimos Poderes' entrusted him with the responsibility of caring for Perón and Eva in 1946 (p. 31). López Rega's colourful background as radio singer and policeman and his esoteric interests in the Kabbala and in alchemy confer upon Martínez's plot an otherworldly and mystic quality that can be related to its densely textual structure. As an obsessive and tautological text that proliferates between speech and writing, the Kabbala is reminiscent of *La novela de Perón*, while metaphorical alchemical practices are readily discernible both in López Rega's well-documented effort to infuse Isabel with the spirit of Eva by means of a 'transfusión espiritual'

(p. 121) and on the level of writing: Perón's *Memorias* convert the base metal of his life story – his illegitimate birth, his lifelong mother fixation, the insecurity of his early military career which almost culminated in desertion – into the gold of the heroic young Argentine leader who combines determination to resolve social problems with unwavering confidence in his own destiny. Perón's procedure here is not unremarkable: as Lowenthal observes, we often 'improve' the past by 'exaggerating aspects we find successful, virtuous, or beautiful, celebrating what we take pride in, playing down the ignoble, the ugly, the shameful [. . .] relics of failure are seldom saved and rarely memorialized'.[8]

The novel form is the most appropriate for Martínez's purposes because he is concerned not so much with what happened – in any case, inaccessible – as with representations of what happened, with images of the past, often second hand and clichéd, that expose any notion of immediate perception as wholly illusory. The text is designated a novel but it consists of a corpus of writings which includes most genres and offers a kaleidoscope of images: the shifting images of human identity, the practised images of calligraphy and signature, the moving images of TV and film, the static images of photography. Images of textuality include epigraphs, a footnote (p. 68), a list of acknowledgements and lengthy citations dispersed throughout the text, some from newspapers (with handwritten marginal notes, pp. 202, 243), some from literary figures such as Rodolfo Walsh (p. 202) and Roberto Arlt (p. 208). Documents featuring in the text range from those of central importance, such as Perón's *Memorias* to those of marginal interest, such as the tribute to the former president Eduardo Lonardi, being written by his eldest daughter Marta, and the loose, unpublished notes on Perón's sojourn in Europe which Martínez – who appears in his own text – passes to the journalist Zamora. This incomplete and scrappy document is interesting because it has been burnt in places by cigarette ash (p. 241). 'Corpus' refers not just to a body of writing but also, of course, to the dead human body. Argentines are 'cultivadores de cadáveres' (p. 287); Perón's associate, Captain Trefaletti, is a taxidermist (p. 179) and, most notably, Eva's body is embalmed. Some textual images, notably the photographs, are cadavers of a kind, since they 'embalm' particular moments of the past. Indeed as a kind of (fictional) biography, the text as a whole is a literary cadaver, the biographer's art often compared to that of the embalmer.[9] The most important cadaver of all, however, is that represented by a now dead Perón, the Perón in his prime, whose ashes still smoulder decades after the intense 'burning' of his power from 1946 to 1955, their posthumous glow throwing his present persona into shadow. Significantly, Perón enjoins López Rega to treat the various documents (including a photograph of Eva) from that past with care: 'por fuera se han calcinado en sus cenizas pero por dentro están vivos' (p. 279).

In some respects the past is, indeed, a foreign country, as David Lowenthal's title proclaims. Perón sees his younger self as 'el otro Perón' and the process of writing his past emphasizes its difference from his present. But traces of that past continue to smoulder like red-hot ash radiating its heat into the present. Such imagery has been explored by Derrida in *Cinders*, a text constructed on the metaphorical associations of fire, conflagration, heat; embers, ash, residue. Lukacher points out that 'in the warmth of a cinder one can feel the effects of the fire even if the fire itself remains inaccessible, outside cognition though not without leaving a trace'.[10] Derrida refers to a fire which has consumed access to the origin of language and therefore to the truth of being. In Perón's case, the effects of time consume his earlier selves precluding any return to the intensity of the past. Yet afterglows remain, cinders smoulder in the ashes of the present: 'a cinder is a very fragile entity that falls to dust, that crumbles and disperses. But cinders also name the resilience and intractability of what is most delicate and most vulnerable' (Lukacher, p. 2). Perón's past remains luminous and often painfully hot in the present. The brightest cinder from his past is, of course, Eva, the quintessential Argentine Cinderella, whose body, according to Perón, contained 'más fósforo que carne. El que no sabía tocarlo se quemaba' (p. 270) and whose corpse was embalmed with inflammable substances (p. 49). Her embalmed body, removed from Milan to Madrid, rarefies the atmosphere in Perón's Madrid residence and her palpable presence at Ezeiza airport at the time of Perón's return to Argentina inflames the passions of Peronists of both left and right. The title of Derrida's *Feu la cendre* indicates, by virtue of its double displacement of the two meanings of *feu*, yet a further connection, to mourning: 'fire' but also 'deceased' or 'departed'. In *La novela de Perón* the past has been burnt but traces remain, so that the past is both absent and present. Mourning ends when it has consumed itself but the process leaves the trace of something that cannot be consumed. In Perón's case his mourning for Eva belongs to the distant past but an equally ardent emotion returns to consume him in the present, his repressed jealousy: 'en Eva gastaron toda la lumbre que me debían a mí' (p. 266). Images of fire, ash, cinders, and lava recur in a text which emphasizes the emptiness of Perón whose feelings are warmed now by a feeble resentment. His brother Juan notes that when Perón entered military college 'lo marcaban a fuego, pero con la marca de nadie' (p. 137). But Perón clings to a past which, he thinks, is not consumed; he tells Martínez 'todo se puede recuperar' (p. 240) and sometimes the smouldering remains of the past become palpable: 'oí cómo se agitaba la multitud, encendiendo a la ciudad como un torrente de lava. Sobre mi memoria llovieron las cenizas incandescentes' (p. 240). The life of Diana Bronstein, a former Trotskyist, now a Peronist *montanera* guerrilla, has burnt brightly in the fires of politics and sexuality but it is soon to be extinguished when she becomes the victim of the right-wing Arcángelo Gobbi; her red hair suggests the fire which will consume her: 'Diana estaba ya recostándose sobre los sopores de su lava roja, volviéndose un ovillo dentro de los larguísimos hilos de su lava' (p. 252). Even documents retain their heat long after turning to ash: Perón tells López Rega to treat their plans and maps with care: 'por fuera se han calcinado en sus cenizas pero por dentro están vivos' (p. 279).

Domon notes that the metaphor of fire can be seen as one of the finest figurations of writing. It represents the infinite oscillation between two models of representation, speech and writing, producing their antagonistic inscription. It is a process that 'engages the friction of all terms, creates the possibility of a collision of interpretations [...] writing must be redefined as essentially divisive, decisive, abrasive, erasing, just like fire'. She refers to Serge Bourjea's concept of the 'erotics of writing', the 'pure pleasure of keeping oneself burning in the fire of writing, aligning tautological words, endlessly, between speech and writing [...]'.[11]

In *La novela de Perón* the 'Memorias' have an uneasy relationship with the 'Contramemorias' (the extended biographical extracts from the *Horizonte* issue devoted to Perón which appear in numbered sections beginning in chapter 5, continuing in chapter 8 and concluding in chapter 11, this final extract containing the interview with Perón conducted by Martínez and the poet

César Fernández Moreno). While the 'Memorias' both extinguish details of Perón's life and consume (or plagiarize) other writings, the 'Contramemorias' reduce to cinders the secrets of the 'Memorias', notably the adultery of Perón's mother, as competing interpretations collide. The pleasure of writing is felt by López Rega who transcribes the recorded memoirs with enthusiasm: 'aunque tenía la cara rayada por el desvelo, la corriente de la escritura lo sostenía' (pp. 49–50). López Rega offers more fuel for the fire of writing by providing exact recollections of the funeral of Bartolomé Mitre, (president of Argentina between 1862–8, who died in 1906). López Rega insists that he himself attended that funeral though his claim clashes with Perón's recollection. But it does not really matter: in this process of oral recapitulation and writing, any notion of an absolute is consumed – Perón's own memories collide with each other: 'son dos recuerdos que no pueden juntarse' (p. 51).

Some memories, such as those of the military college, should be allowed to extinguish themselves: 'están bien donde están, en su nido, apagándose' (p. 96). Words lose their original heat once they are uttered and written down: Perón knows that the story he reads has lost its former intensity: 'no es la que lleva todavía dentro de sí, marcándole con fuego el pensamiento' (p. 97). But López Rega's readings often reach fever pitch, his eyes 'rayados por la exaltación, en la penumbra del claustro' (p. 167). Images associated with burning recur throughout the text. An equally important figure is that of swarming and its associated images: flies, buzzing, density. The references to flies suggest textual obsession with memories of the past and, by extension, with death. The text is replete with various kinds of swarms: swarms of flies which fill the General's aeroplane (p. 16) and Martínez's car (p. 238); swarms of people at Ezeiza airport: one of the right-wing Peronists, Lito Cobo, 'ha ido registrando cada zumbido sospechoso en el enjambre' (p. 254); swarms of memories such as those of doña Mercedes: 'recordatorios, polen de margaritas, recortes amarillos: las memorias que ha copiado doña Mercedes llegan a las últimas páginas con la lengua afuera' (p. 218). Similarly the novel itself proliferates, swarms with different kinds of texts, both written and visual, some short and complete (such as the letters of Potota, Perón's first wife), others extensive but fragmented (such as Perón's 'Memorias'). Swarming suggests excitement, proximity to the object of desire, the illusion of imminent fulfilment. Where burning connotes annihilation, swarming indicates intense and focused activity stimulated by heightened awareness of the past and of the truth. But the past is inaccessible and there is no single version of the truth. The swarm moves from object to object never reaching its goal. The fly does not, of course, maintain its perpetual motion, it frequently alights ('se posa') on some surface and is relatively still. So Martínez's text occasionally comes to a standstill, engaging in self-reflexive introspection: like the fly, the text stops to preen itself before taking off again. It becomes self-conscious, 'posing', as it becomes self-absorbed, oblivious to anything other than its own appearance.

La novela de Perón is dominated by a past that is only imperfectly accessible through the often obtrusive mediation of text and image. Even people are 'packaged'; Perón not only feels remote from his other, younger self, but even in his present any pretentions of an 'authentic' self are hidden behind an artificial, theatrical persona which is carefully crafted: 'aquel cuerpo va entrando lentamente en los gestos que ha fabricado para su personaje [. . .]. Resignado, el General camina hacia el jardín. Suspira. Y luego avanza, con la sonrisa de Perón ya puesta' (p. 110). Clearly the 'real' Perón, the persona whom the journalist Zamora is enjoined to reveal by his editor ('¿Quién era el General, Zamora? Descífrelo de una buena vez [. . .]', p. 34) is no more accessible than the past which is similarly constructed and framed: even Perón's cousin, María Tizón, who has no literary pretensions as far as we are aware, sits motionless in her seat, 'puliendo los recuerdos que leerá esa tarde ante la prensa' (p. 178). She refines her memories subjecting them to a process of aestheticization. She is preparing a eulogy of Potota and (significantly) of her skills as a painter. The political world can often be accessed only via the media. In response to Perón's question about what Peronism meant to him, Tomás Eloy Martínez states: 'mi recuerdo es algo que conocí en los cines, que oí por la radio. Nada que haya pertenecido a mi realidad' (p. 240). Similarly Zamora reflects: 'veo la historia por el ojo de la cerradura. La única realidad que conozco es la que aparece por la televisión' (p. 315). The implication here is that immediacy of perception is illusory; reality is invariably 'framed' and is not directly accessible even to the experienced journalist; the density of visual images emerges in Martínez's account of his meeting with Perón, mentioned above. Perón had compared the trade unionist Augusto Vandor (leader of the 'Peronism without Perón' movement) with Simon the Magician (p. 239). Martínez subsequently discovers that Perón's reference to the Gnostic gospels has been mediated by a Jack Palance film (p. 240).

Film and television feature prominently in this text but the dominant image is undoubtedly the photograph to which there are at least fifty references. The camera both renders the moment dead, turning movement and animation into static image, and also allows each moment killed to live again as an image in posthumous space. The posthumous image is, indeed, the quintessential mode of perception of modern culture, thwarting all dreams of immediacy. The ubiquitous presence of the photograph in *La novela de Perón* reinforces the aura of posthumous survival that pervades the text. Photography touches very closely the lives of these characters: Potota's father, for example, owned a photographer's shop (p. 159). Heartbroken by the death of her mother, Potota attempts to console herself with a tear-stained photograph of her. Photographs offer a trace, a remnant of the person who was there (just as smouldering ash is the 'remnant' of fire). The trace is tactile like a footprint.[12] The photograph itself arrests, even embalms, its subject.[13] Though itself lacking animation, it does possess the power to animate the viewer, turning his present into a shadow that gives way to the presence of the past. Thus Cámpora returns to the past through the photographs he sees in the dining room of Perón's Madrid residence; they reanimate those iconic images of Peronism which overshadow the muddied present:

> el General en los balcones de la Casa de Gobierno alzando los brazos hacia la masa remota, el General desfilando sobre el caballo Mancha, Evita engalanada en el teatro Colón. Se ve a sí mismo en dos de las fotos, siempre sonriendo. Todo era más claro en aquel pasado: cada quien deseaba, exactamente, ser lo que era. (pp. 87–8)

The past may be beyond reach but the photographer's art is like the embalmer's, offering such a faithful likeness that false hopes are raised (Perón half expected the embalmed body of Eva to come to life).[14] Julio's photographs are blotched and imperfect but still he feels 'la precisa llama del instante en que fueron tomadas' (p. 38). López Rega shows Perón a photograph of his parents' rustic dwelling: 'el portal, el letrero: «Estancia La Porteña» ¿Puede ver el recuerdo? Todo lo veo, López, como si fuera ahora' (p. 158). An undercurrent of emotion, rare in Perón, is aroused by this image of the past. María Tizón's photographs are 'respiraciones tan vivas del pasado que no parecen fotografías sino fantasmas' (p. 37). Martínez's characters become enveloped in a world of images. Susan Sontag refers to Feuerbach's observation that the contemporary world 'prefers the image to the thing, the copy to the original, the representation to the reality, appearance to being'.[15] Thus Perón, whose exile in Madrid had been energized by the prospect of eventual return to Argentina, finds the hope superior to the reality which he seeks to escape by means of a John Wayne film with its 'polvo de los westerns adonde no podían llegar las humedades de Buenos Aires' (p. 13). Increasingly the 'real' world loses its reality. As Sontag puts it: 'to possess the world in the form of images is, precisely, to re-experience the unreality and remoteness of the real'.[16] Photographic images become a potent means of turning the tables on reality, of turning it into a shadow. Photographs are comforting, as a source of mere distraction for Perón's feckless third wife Isabel (p. 12), but assuming iconic status for fervent Peronists: after Perón's death his 'foto venerada' is bedecked in lace, implying that presence and image converge 'como Nuestro Señor en cada hostia' (p. 320). His television image enchants doña Luisa and her neighbours at the Villa Insuperable. Inspired by radio reports that people in outlying areas were holding wakes and masses for Perón in the belief that his physical presence was embodied in his image, in the same way that Christ is reincarnated in the host, doña Luisa builds an altar out of fruit boxes and places a television on it. The distinction between the real corpse and its representation disappears: 'al llegar frente al televisor, los dolientes se arrodillaron, acariciaban la pantalla, y se marchaban en silencio. Cada tanto, doña Luisa limpiaba la imagen del General con un pañuelito negro y le tocaba el pelo a través del vidrio' (pp. 320–1). As Baudrillard puts it, the seduction of absence (of meaning) by presence (of artifice) is 'the only existing form of immortality', turning even death into a 'brilliant and superficial appearance'.[17] Sontag refers to the 'primitive' belief that an image participated in the reality of the object depicted.[18] This sense of unity contrasts with the contemporary sense of the photographic portrait as pose: Barthes describes how he assumes another persona in front of the lens: 'je me constitue en train de « poser », je me fabrique instantanément un autre corps, je me metamorphose à l'avance en image'.[19] Martínez is all too familiar with a Perón who behaves like Barthes, a posing Perón who is also the only 'real' Perón. When the flesh and blood Perón replaces his image, the effect on Martínez, sated with the icons and images of Perón and Peronism, is disconcerting rather than reassuring: 'era como entrar en una fotografía de ningún tiempo' (p. 236).

Images may be seen as being more 'real' than their 'real' counterparts but even the photograph is not a 'natural' representation: its constructed, artificial quality is emphasized frequently. On the one hand the photograph may be seen as a certificate of presence with the power to incriminate (López Rega warns Perón that Martínez has threatened to publish the photograph demonstrating Perón's complicity in the overthrow of the Liberal president, Irigoyen, showing him riding on the running board of Uriburu's car with a smile of triumph (pp. 167–8). On the other hand the infallibility of the photograph as token of presence is undermined by López Rega's ruse that destroys his 'rival', José Cresto, in Perón's eyes: he modifies the photograph of Marcelino Canosa, the lover of Juana, Perón's mother, in order to make him resemble Cresto. The irony is that Perón is moved to anger not by 'real' evidence but by a falsified representation.

The artifice of visual imagery emerges explicitly in the text when Perón states: ' – Nadie sabrá jamás qué cara tenía la Mona Lisa ni cómo sonreía, porque esa cara y esa sonrisa no corresponden a lo que ella fue sino a lo que pintó Leonardo' (p. 46). Similar self-conscious awareness emerges in the writing of his memoirs. He reflects that exact recall ('memoria') is not paramount, rather 'lo que uno aprovecha de ella: el color con que se la tiñe' (p. 53). More negatively, he wonders whether 'este después desde el cual está narrándose no ha destruido ya para siempre el ayer donde las cosas ocurrieron' (p. 103).[20] Such matters are aired in the often fractious exchanges between Perón and López Rega on the subject of Perón's 'Memorias' which have been transcribed from tape by López Rega. The latter is not content to act as a mere scribe carrying out routine editorial work. Rather, he takes it upon himself not only to impose his own style but also to tamper with the content, omitting and inserting material at will and, most daringly, recreating Perón's past by inventing his own participation in it. This is a classic case of

Derrida's 'dangerous supplement':[21] the secretary, normally subordinate to the writer, supplants rather than serves.

The mechanics of text creation are exposed as Perón seeks to reassert his authority over his 'Memorias'. Ironically his rewriting of the section marked 'Ancestros' by López Rega betrays his caution and creative timidity, the influence perhaps of a lingering respect for the truth which he will soon discard: 'Hasta donde llegan mis noticias [...] Hay quienes dicen que [...] Más bien creo que [...]' (p. 45). His omission of some details – 'para no enredar la claridad del cuento' (p. 45) – suggests that he has his readers' interests in mind though he tells López Rega subsequently that consistent narrative is impossible given his sense of remoteness from his previous self (p. 48) and that he is totally indifferent to the perception of his readers. His own editorial work is an exercise in textual dilution: pruning López Rega's florid style (such excisions are given in parentheses in the text of the 'Memorias') and reducing its specificity: 'el General tacha la última frase y escribe en los márgenes una version más difusa' (p. 52). In military quarters the perception of Perón was as a 'máquina de palabras' (p. 250): it is unsurprising therefore that he is interested in López Rega's choice of words: '¿Con qué palabras había contado aquello?' (p. 92). López Rega's strategic obsequiousness ('¿He interpretado bien lo que usted pidió, mi General [...]?', p. 48) does not dispel Perón's suspicions. López Rega pays lip service to integrity and academic convention, warning Perón not to engage in overt plagiarism (p. 154) and inconsistent narration ('lo que quiero es que elija una sola versión para los hechos. Una sola: la que fuere', p. 168), while in reality having less respect for historical truth than Perón himself.[22] While it is Perón who declares that his aim is to 'gobernar a la historia. Cogerla por el culo' (p. 168), it is his secretary who more spectacularly performs such a feat, arrogating to himself a substantial role in a drama from which he is excluded by the most basic laws of historical logic. Thus López Rega not only carries out biographical research for Perón – tracking down, after much effort, the lines of the poet and critic Leopoldo Lugones, that Perón wants to quote in his 'Memorias' – but also moulds the text by insinuating into it his own techniques ('Y en este punto, interrumpe López, quise poner la máxima, el acabóse. Lo puse a usted en letras de carne y hueso', p. 171) and contriving, as already mentioned, his own active participation in the plot. Such inventiveness, taken to absurd extremes by López Rega, bears out Martínez's scepticism about the reliability of historical documents that reconstruct and reinvent rather than document and record: 'cualquier historia, cualquier dato puede ser fabricado o inventado'.[23] The left-wing Peronist and friend of Diana, Nun Antezana, is alarmed by the 'Contramemorias' published in *Horizonte*, in particular by what he views as the 'erosiones que los cien testigos han ido dejando sobre el cuerpo biográfico del patriarca' (p. 62). López Rega's interventions are more damaging, however, since they seek to remould the Peronist past and to control the writing of the 'Memorias', the authoritative version of the leader himself. López Rega contaminates, retrospectively, the most poignant period in Peronist history, the slow and painful death of Eva: he contrives for himself a central position as advisor to the woman who is defying death by preparing to attend Perón's second presidential inauguration. He is a parasite who forges a history for himself by profaning the most intimate memories of others: 'se posó en aquellos recuerdos como si en verdad estuviera creándolos, preparándolos para suceder' (p. 32).[24]

López Rega's fiction is the most memorable in a text replete with inventions (and omissions) – as highlighted by the numerous discrepancies between the 'Memorias' and the 'Contramemorias'. The most notable relates to Perón's family, particularly his mother, Juana. In the 'Memorias' Juana emerges as an ideal mother: 'ella era una amazona. Y en la cocina, ni hablar: todo lo manejaba con seguridad' (p. 48). In the 'Contramemorias', Juana's Indian ancestry is tainted by incestuous liaisons (pp. 65, 293); she is portrayed as a seductress (p. 66); Juan and his brother are born prior to their parents' marriage; and to cap this rather sordid background, a third child, still-born, is described in grotesque detail: 'en vez de ojos padecía de dos huevos negros sin párpados [. . .]' (p. 69). The most notable disclosure of the 'Contramemorias', however, is the section entitled 'Revelación terrible' (pp. 75–80) narrating the episode which will inflict lifelong psychological damage on Perón: in a variation on Freud's primal scene, the young Perón witnesses his mother engaged in frenetic sexual activity, not with his father, but with a mule driver, Benjamín Gómez. This episode takes place at the family ranch, 'El Porvenir', whose name is ironic given that what Perón saw there would blight his future: when he heads home to Patagonia the following Christmas he is found at the docks calling for his mother. Perón rejects the affection of his aunt, Vicenta – 'nunca voy a dejar que una mujer me ponga la mano encima' (p. 137) – and later adopts a cold and suspicious attitude towards his first wife, Potota (p. 197). His repressed memory of his mother's betrayal returns repeatedly in the form of a dream in which his path to the South Pole is barred: 'cada vez que recomenzaba el sueño, la madre se plantaba en el mismo sitio, con la cabellera destrenzada y un poncho de hombre sobre el batón' (p. 150). The heat of his mother's reckless passion burns Perón's future. He seeks, unsuccessfully, to douse those flames in the ice of the South Pole. According to the 'Contramemorias', his mother's action is the 'historia que le cambió la vida' (p. 76); but the 'Memorias' suppresses it entirely while identifying Leopoldo Lugones's appeal to the military to seize power as the episode which 'marcó mi pensamiento para siempre' (p. 156). Perón substitutes male empowerment for female obstruction and the military for the family arena.

But the claims of the 'Memorias' are systematically undermined. Perón's account of his meeting with Mussolini is notable for its precise detail: 'entré directamente a su despacho. Estaba casi a oscuras. Un quinqué alumbraba de pleno su cabeza imponente, afeitada [. . .]' (p. 228). But a military associate of Perón, Augusto Maidona, claims (in notes passed by Martínez himself to Zamora) that the Perón–Mussolini encounter, like Perón's stories about Berlin and the Masurian Lakes, never took place: 'nada de eso ocurrió, dijo Maidona. Y sin embargo, Perón no mintió al contar esas historias. Eran mentiras, sí, pero las contó tantas veces que terminó creyéndolas'(p. 247). Truth and falsity are largely subjective notions that can be defined only fleetingly, against a background of shifting perspectives rather than by reference to some fixed standard. For Nietzsche there is truth in every falsity and falsity in every truth: 'truths are illusions of which one has forgotten that they *are* illusions'.[25] Martínez's Perón emerges as a Nietzschean figure in his determination to forget history, suppressing some aspects of it while inventing others, such as his claim that Peronists offered vital assistance to Che Guevara, which does not accord with Guevara's own account (p. 236). Perón explicitly refers to the need to forget history, telling López Rega that the experience of military manoeuvres in the heat of December 1913 must be forgotten: 'haremos con todo eso un buen fardo de olvido' (p. 98). Nietzsche saw the power to forget as positive, as a safeguard against predictability. Remembering implies a present orientated towards the past, thus denying new possibilities for the future; forgetting promises a 'free' present. Perón does possess an ability to dream, to clothe his finitude in dream-like intimations of immortality – qualities that Nietzsche advocated. Martínez has himself suggested that history should be treated with a kind of creative licence rather than with excessive respect, subscribing here to Nietzsche's concept of 'Critical' (as opposed to 'Monumental') history.[26] However, where Perón is concerned, his creative forgetting must be set against his obsession with history and his fear of it. He knows that his own story is unsafe and he anticipates the intervention of others: 'ha sufrido pensando que la historia contará a su manera lo que él calló. Que vendrán otros a inventarle una vida [...]' (p. 92).

Perón's fears are confirmed by the interventions of others, including those of Martínez, as noted in chapter 3. Well before becoming a national figure and prior to the death of his first wife Potota, Perón held a diplomatic post in Chile that ended on a sour note with his successor, Eduardo Lonardi (who also succeeded him as president in September 1955), becoming embroiled in espionage activities initiated by Perón. This episode is elided in the 'Memorias' but Perón's alleged deviousness and treachery are documented in the diary account of Mercedes, Lonardi's widow, and made available to the journalist Zamora (pp. 212–18).

Perón sees his 'Memorias' as a canonical text, a kind of Bible for the Peronist Church which will fill a previous gap: 'la cruz que le faltaba a la iglesia peronista' (p. 43). Perón's old energy, diminished by his physical decline and mental fatigue, is renewed by the 'Memorias' which serve as an escape from the present and provide a kind of lifeline to the past: 'abstraído en la lectura, el General ha olvidado que abajo en los jardines de la Quinta, sigue la fiesta' (p. 100). Thus Perón warms his old age at the fire of reading and writing. This is the main source of his pleasure and not his wife, Isabel, who frequently disturbs his 'erotics of writing' and its dramatic intensity: 'y como en el teatro, Isabel espera que se agote el discurso para llamar desde un recodo de la escalera. "¡General, el almuerzo!" [...], (p. 171). Perón wants to impose his own truth: 'la historia se quedará con la verdad que yo estoy contando', p. 47). His truth is a textual representation which both suppresses the past ('Olvídese de los detalles incómodos' says López Rega, p. 47) and supplements it (through its incorporation of López Rega's fictions). But his own text is contaminated by the work of others: dismissing López Rega's objections ('nadie osará mancharme, ni siquiera de plagio', p. 155) he indulges in blatant plagiarism: 'al invocar a Napoleón, le recreaba [. . .] Las ideas de Schlieffen, en cambio, lo seducían a tal punto que, en vez de modificarlas, prefirió olvidar de quién eran' (p. 199). Perón's personal control is also compromised by his sense of remoteness from his own previous self – '¿quién soy aquí, diciendo lo que sigue?' (p. 229) – and memory becomes estranged by its entry into language: 'ya por volverse palabras ha dejado de pertenecerle' (p. 261). He is afraid of history since it might give voice to what he has silenced (p. 92). This is, of course, precisely what happens since his versions are challenged by the 'Contramemorias' and episodes glossed over by him are filled out by others, such as Mercedes Lonardi.

Perón's former military colleague, Augusto Maidona, claims that Perón believes his own lies (p. 247) but here Maidona underestimates him. Perón knows that the past is unstable, elusive and ultimately incomprehensible. His aim (which he suspects to be futile) is to determine the configurations of his own past. It is to this enterprise that he devotes his remaining energy. Elsewhere the detached and frivolous Perón dominates: when he greets Cámpora he is dressed in 'el conjunto más chillón de su vestuario' and his thoughts are elsewhere: 'juegan como escarabajos entre los rulos de las perras' (p. 41). He plays a series of roles, handling his physical self with far greater confidence than he does his textual persona: 'aquel cuerpo va entrando lentamente en los gestos que ha fabricado para su personaje [. . .]. Suspira. Y luego avanza, con la sonrisa de Perón ya puesta' (p. 110). His ability to act the part is well-established since he was an accomplished actor even as a young man: 'no era Perón a secas sino el cadete Perón' (p. 141). There is no 'real' Perón behind these carefully contrived personae: he is empty inside. Perón is a postmodern Nietzschean figure who loves surfaces and is suspicious of depths; he represents shifting modes of being rather than fixed identity: he is no more than an appearance even to himself. It is no coincidence that he chooses Isabel to be his third wife: she sees only the surface of things and is mainly preoccupied with her photo magazines (offering a display of appearances) and her festooned lapdogs.

Any depth to be found in this text lies not in the characters themselves but rather in the past. Certainly the present is subject to the invasive encroachment of the past: Nun at Ezeiza feels 'la liviandad del tiempo yéndose' (p. 311). There are constant reminders of a foreshortening of the present, ranging from the name of Perón's aeroplane, 'Betelgeuse' (the dying star) to Eva's hyperactivity induced by her consciousness of the progressive exhaustion of her remaining time: 'era como si el tiempo, yéndose, la quemara' (p. 277). An active posthumous past invades the present, converting the real into representation. Arcángelo Gobbi senses his present turning into past, anticipating that 'leería alguna vez su nombre en las páginas de ese tiempo' (p. 131) while Perón and López Rega, photographed by the guards at Perón's Madrid residence, are fixed for posterity by a visual image. The seven witnesses assembled by Zamora are described as ghostly relics of the past ('los fantasmas retratados en *Horizonte*, p. 65; 'sus apariencias son fantasmales', p. 289). It is Perón himself who has the sharpest sense of a past that takes the form of a moving image: 'dentro de mí siento el pasado como una película que fuese trastabillando en la máquina proyectadora' (p. 93). His present is dominated by the ghost of his past, a past represented in myriad formats: newsprint, photographs, film, tape and now also in López Rega's transcriptions. His past self has been absorbed by its various representations and is capable of infinite return. He exemplifies Baudrillard's concept of simulation whereby the copy is confused with the original. In Baudrillard's terms, Perón has become 'hyperreal', the real Perón replaced by his representation. William Bogard points out that although simulation may be an artificial miracle, its secret aim is real magic and an enchanted world.[27] Martínez infuses his work with such an aura through, for example, the repetition of significant numbers and iconic phrases. Thus the number seven, which is a mystic or sacred number, features prominently. Zamora assembles *seven* witnesses from Perón's past; in order to transfer the spirit of Eva to Isabel, López Rega needs to utter *seven* words (p. 223); and Arcángelo Gobbi's final mission will be carried out with the participation of *seven* men (p. 306). Three is also a significant number: for example, Eva's magical phrase, 'Gracias por existir', is repeated three times (pp. 15, 274, 295). It is the purportedly marginal figure of López Rega who contributes most centrally to the text's magical and mystical aura and seems to have infected Perón with his own supernatural powers: the car used by Martínez and his friend, the writer César Fernández Moreno, to travel to Madrid to interview Perón, fills with the sound of flies that attack the pair, drawing blood and prompting Fernández Moreno to recite a charm against the evil eye. He puts the incident down to the malign influence of Perón (pp. 238–9). It is significant that López Rega 'se preciaba de dominar la cabala y la alquimia' (p. 30). His belief that Isabel could be infused with the spirit of Eva seems to owe something to Kabbalistic doctrine. Bloom refers to the teachings of Isaac Luria, the main source of the new Kabbala: 'Luria seems to have taught that there were families of souls, united by the root of a common spark. Each person can take up in himself the spark of another soul, of one of the dead, provided that he and the dead share the same root'.[28]

The Kabbala is pertinent to *La novela de Perón* for another reason. Bloom points out that what distinguished the Kabbala from nearly every other variety of mysticism or theosophy was its emphasis upon *interpretation* (p. 33). Interpretation is arguably the main theme in Martínez's text which demonstrates that the past is elusive not only because of the failings of memory but because of the inconsistencies of reality itself, which López Rega calls 'desaciertos de la realidad' (p. 52). In his exchanges with Perón, López Rega is one of the main sources of commentary and interpretation and again plays a central role, here in the text's prominently metafictional character. *La novela de Perón* is a kind of biography but one in which biography and metabiography converge, where the subject, Perón, is 'contested' by the incessant probing of López Rega as well as by the alternative versions of events offered by the 'Contramemorias'. Bloom also points out that 'more audaciously than any developments in recent French criticism, Kabbala is a theory of writing whose God is at once Ein-Sof and ayin, total presence and total absence'.[29] The Kabbala may be seen as a metafictional image of *La novela de Perón* which is also about writing and interpretation and also about the interplay of presence and absence: Eva is absent but always present through the proliferation of her images and the recordings of her voice (while the living Perón is virtually smothered by the incessant accretion of his images).

If Perón himself provides no more than an array of shimmering surfaces devoid of depth what of Peronism, the doctrine that survived him and was, until recently, represented in government? That too is shallow and evanescent according to Sebreli who claims that Peronism consisted only of imperfect copies without an original: 'el "verdadero peronismo" fue, pues, un peronismo imaginario que nunca coincidió con la práctica'.[30]

In *La novela de Perón* meaning wanders like a fly from text to text, alighting only briefly and failing to assume a concrete form. As meaning fails to congeal, the focus of attention turns to the materiality of words and in particular to the extraneous discourses introduced by López Rega (e.g. p. 230). While the emptiness of the rhetoric welcoming Perón home to Buenos Aires: 'AL GRAN ARTIFICE DEL REENCUENTRO NACIONAL [...]' is exposed by the violence that attended his arrival, the materiality of the language used by López Rega is laid bare since meaning is entirely absent:

OGUN CHEQUELÁ UNDÉ

CHEQUELÁ

CHEQUELÁ UNDÉ

OGUM BRAGADA É A (p. 230).

La novela de Perón is about the diminishing returns of language and meaning, the absence of any kind of metanarrative, the ubiquity of image and citation that recycle and re-present, negating any possibility of immediacy and directness of perception.

The text also undermines the traditional humanistic notion of the 'sovereignty of the subject' that is still spectrally present in modern biographical writing as a nostalgia for a lost communal humanism. Pierre Bourdieu claims that the 'history of the individual is never anything other than a certain specification of the collective history of his group or class [...] expressing the difference between trajectories and positions inside or outsidethe class'.[31] This conforms to Sebreli's view of Perón: 'la biografía de Perón lo muestra como un pequeño burgués dilettante, de vida sedentaria y mediocre hasta los cincuenta años, de ideas simples y estereotipadas, y de gustos vulgares, box, cine de cowboys, y pocas lecturas.³² Martínez's portrait dismantles any notion of an outstanding individual and sovereign subject, illustrating in his representation of Perón Zamora's characterization of man as 'el tortuoso y laberíntico impulso que lo induce a dibujar una vida que rara vez se parece a su proyecto de vida' (p. 86). The sovereign subject is further diminished by subjection to chance circumstance: had Perón deserted as a cadet his own biography (as well as twentieth-century Argentine history) would have been different. The concept of individual power is vitiated by the vicissitudes of impersonal historical forces which operate randomly and destabilize univocal meaning: 'confunden las palabras: destino, desatino, Perón, nación' (p. 140). This sense of linguistic fluidity is reflected in the hybrid quality of the text where the fictional contaminates the historical and vice versa. An episode apparently rooted in fiction – López Rega's attempt to infuse Isabel with the spirit of Eva (pp. 233–4) – belongs rather to reality, but even so it could not be incorporated seamlessly into conventional historical discourse because it exudes fictionality despite being true: Martínez himself has described such episodes as 'verdades novelescas que se infiltraban dentro de las verdades históricas'.³³

The fly on the journalist Zamora's car mirror has 'compuestos ojos, de cuatro mil facetas cada uno. La verdad dividida en cuatro mil pedazos' (p. 174).³⁴ This image points to truth as boundless proliferation and multiformity that is ultimately beyond human understanding. Biographical/historical writing cannot remain uncontaminated by fiction. This process of contamination is powerfully dramatized in the text: 'truths' are often omitted while 'lies' are included. Zamora tells Lonardi's widow that the *Horizonte* issue devoted to Perón's life offers only a partial account, omitting all mention of the Perón–Lonardi encounter in Chile in 1938 (p. 205). It is Perón himself who draws attention to the inconsistency in the report of the execution of the former president, Aramburu, who is alleged to have told his executioners to get on with the job: '"Proceda" – habló por última vez Aramburu' (p. 183). Perón objects that a man in Aramburu's situation, with a handkerchief in his mouth, would be unable to speak. But the mistake is left uncorrected: 'ese "Proceda" que no existió quedará para siempre' (p. 183).

Epstein remarks that the problem for the emergent 'rainbow coalition' of oppositional biographers [...] is how to avoid burying *their* subjects alive in the murder file of traditional biographical narrative'.[35] Unlike the traditional biography of Page, Martínez's text contests his subject, presenting him as a loosely-assembled bundle of impulses frequently overshadowed by the marginal figure of López Rega and subordinated to the inexorable play of conflicting discourses. *La novela de Perón* is diametrically opposed to the biographical narrative as monument that, as Epstein states, records, identifies, enshrines and entombs.[36] It is rather a nomadic text which wanders among various discursive contexts and perspectives, foregrounding what the traditional biography effaces: the work of the biographer himself and his encoding procedures. Whereas one of Page's cardinal principles is to minimize dissonance, restricting it to momentary hesitation retrospectively elided within the inexorable search for regularity and order, Martínez revels in discontinuity and contradiction which deprive his text of unity. Page's effacement of himself and his narrative work promotes the aggrandizement of his subject by focusing attention on him alone.[37] In *La novela de Perón* biography alternates with metabiography as the construction of the subject is analysed self-reflexively. López Rega, Zamora, Martínez and Perón himself all engage in the latter's auto/biography, Martínez foregrounding his presence by narrating in the first person and freely acknowledging not only his own limitations but the ultimate impossibility of his task: ' – Ya es tiempo [...] de sacar mis flaquezas a la intemperie [...]. El General es una interminable contradicción de la naturaleza [...]. Creo conocerlo bien y sin embargo llevo más de siete años desconociéndolo' (p. 235). This is the text's deepest wound: the narrator acknowledging his failure as information provider, wholly unable to master his subject.

Martínez himself emerges as a divided entity, an 'other' to himself, as he assumes a textual reality, himself as much produced by the language of the text as producing it. This is, indeed, a text marked by wounds: the literal wound suffered by Perón as a result of his hunting accident; the deeper psychological wound – inflicted by his mother – which was to persist throughout his life; the textual wound inflicted on the 'Memorias' by the 'Contramemorias'; the 'wounds' inflicted on the paper on which the 'Contramemorias' are printed: 'página desgarrada, foto de Evita niña, rota y sucia de barro' (p. 294); the metaphorical wound inflicted by the 'real' but empty Perón on Martínez who had previously been exposed only to representations of the General and his movement: 'yo le estreché las manos. Y me fui de allí como quien se desangra' (p. 240).[38] In short, this text is only marginally about Perón. It is mainly about modes of representation and interpretation, about writing techniques, about the slipperiness of language, and about the impossibility of recovering the past. Page presents a unified subject and a coherent account buttressed by documentary evidence. Martínez, by contrast, takes a postmodern Borgesian approach, more interested in acknowledging and exploring the partial perceptions of man and history than in contriving a 'factual' representation of the past. In Baudrillard's terms, Page is interested in biography as sexed or functional writing, Martínez in writing as seduction, in breaking the referentiality of sex and providing a space of play and defiance centring on the theatrics of writing and reading.[39] The fire at the source of being may be extinguished but, as Derrida claims, traces remain and Martínez's text offers some warmth from the surviving embers.

NOTES

1. 'Mitos, historia, ficción: Idas y vueltas' in Raúl Padilla (ed.), *Visiones cortazarianas: historia, política y literatura hacia el fin del milenio* (Cubierta, México: Luis Vargas, 1996), pp. 109–31 (p. 129).
2. Ira Bruce Nadel, *Biography: Fiction, Fact and Form* (New York: St Martin's Press, 1984), p. 8.
3. *Blonde: a Novel* (London: QPD, 2000)
4. This term is used by William Epstein in William H. Epstein (ed.), *Contesting the Subject: Essays in the Postmodern Theory and Practice of Biography and Biographical Criticism* (West Lafayette IN: Perdue University Press, 1991).
5. Richard Holmes, 'Biography: Inventing the truth', in John Batchelor (ed.), *The Art of Literary Biography* (Oxford: Clarendon, 1995), pp. 15–25 (p. 17).
6. Frank Kermode, *The Genesis of Secrecy: On the Interpretation of Narrative* (London: Harvard University Press, 1979), pp. 117–19. Kermode is quoting W.B. Gallie and Jean Starobinski respectively.
7. Tomás Eloy Martínez, 'Historia y ficción: dos paralelas que se tocan', in *Literatura del Río de la Plata hoy: de las utopías al desencanto* (Frankfurt: Vervuert; Madrid: Iberoamericana, 1996), pp. 89–100 (p. 94).

8 David Lowenthal, *The Past is a Foreign Country* (Cambridge: Cambridge University Press, 1985), p. 332.
9 Martin Stannard describes biography as the 'necrophiliac art'. See Stannard, 'The necrophiliac art?' in Dale Salwak (ed.), *The Literary Biography: Problems and Solutions* (London: Macmillan, 1996), pp. 32–40.
10 'Introduction' to Jacques Derrida, *Cinders*, pp. 1–18 (p. 2).
11 Hélène Domon, 'Black fire on white fire: Kabbalah and modernity' in Philip Leonard (ed.), *Trajectories of Mysticism in Theory and Literature* (London: Macmillan, 2000), pp. 115–32 (pp. 128–9).
12 Margaret Olin, 'Touching photographs: Roland Barthes's "mistaken" identification', *Representations*, 80 (2002), 99–118 (p. 100).
13 Roland Barthes, *La chambre claire: note sur la photographie* (Paris: Éditions de l'Étoile, Gallimard, Le Seuil, 1980), p. 30.
14 'No podía retirar la vista de su pecho porque de un momento a otro esperaba que se levantase y se repitiera el milagro de la vida' (*Del poder al exilio*, p. 55).
15 Susan Sontag, *On Photography* (London: Allen Lane, 1977), p. 153.
16 Sontag, *On Photography*, p. 164.
17 Jean Baudrillard, *Seduction*, trans. Brian Singer (London: Macmillan, 1979), p. 97.
18 Sontag, *On Photography*, p. 155.
19 Barthes, *La chambre claire: note sur la photographie*, p. 25.
20 Perón's sentiment recalls James Olney's reference to the propensity to 'recreate the past in the image of the present that is endemic to every autobiographer who tries to recapture his personal history'. James Olney, 'Some versions of memory/Some versions of bios: The ontology of autobiography', in James Olney (ed.), *Autobiography: Essays Theoretical and Critical* (Princeton NJ: Princeton University Press, 1980), p. 254.
21 See Jacques Derrida, *Of Grammatology*, trans. Gayatri Chakravorty Spivak (Baltimore: Johns Hopkins University Press, 1976), pp. 141–64.
22 Perón's narrative inconsistency, for which he is rebuked by López Rega, is reminiscent of the technique of one of his favourite writers, Plutarch, who showed similar literary propensities – as González Echevarría points out in his discussion of Plutarch's version of the Theseus myth: 'The charm, in fact, of Plutarch's rendition is his juggling of so many different versions in one and the same text, versions that cancel each other and blur or abolish altogether the possibility of a master version'. Roberto González Echevarría, *The Voice of the Masters: Writing and Authority in Latin American Literature*, Latin American Monographs, 64 (Austin: University of Texas Press, 1985), p. 100. The impossibility of attaining a 'master version' of Perón's biography is, of course, one of the main conclusions of *La novela de Perón*.
23 Martínez, 'Historia y ficción: dos paralelas que se tocan', p. 94.
24 The relationship between Perón and López Rega can be compared with that between the Paraguayan dictator, Dr Francia, and his

secretary, Policarpo Patiño, as portrayed by Augusto Roa Bastos in *Yo el Supremo* (1974). Dr Francia, like Perón, realizes that he cannot control language, particularly written language, since it has a life of its own. He accuses Patiño of using 'palabras impropias que no se impregnan de mi pensamiento' (*Yo el supremo*, Buenos Aires: Siglo XXI, 1974, p. 64). González Echevarría observes that in the modern dictator novel 'the figure of the dictator – the one who dictates, whose voice is an authority before writing – is demystified and replaced with that of the secretary, a subordinate who usurps power by being able to supplant truth and knowledge with simulacra' (*Voice of the Masters*, p. 94). Perón was not a dictator – at least not in the tradition of dictatorship analysed by González Echevarría – but the creative liberties assumed at his expense by López Rega are striking none the less.

25   Friedrich Nietzsche, 'On truth and falsity in their ultramoral sense' in *Early Greek Philosophy and Other Essays*, trans. Maximilian A. Mügge (London: T. N. Foulis, 1911), pp. 171–92 (p. 180).
26   Martinez, 'Ficción e historia', p. 44. For an excellent survey of Nietzsche's historical categories and other Nietzschean ideas of relevance to *La novela de Perón*, see White, *Metahistory*, pp. 331–74.
27   'Baudrillard, time and the end' in *Baudrillard: a Critical Reader*, ed. Douglas Kellner (Oxford: Blackwell, 1994), pp. 313–33 (pp. 318–19).
28   Harold Bloom, *Kabbalah and Criticism* (New York: Seabury Press, 1975), p. 44.
29   Bloom, *Kabbalah and Criticism*, pp. 52–3.
30   Sebreli, *Los deseos imaginarios del peronismo*, p. 14.
31   Pierre Bourdieu, *Outline of a Theory of Practice*, trans. Richard Nice, Cambridge Studies in Social Anthropology, 16 (Cambridge: Cambridge University Press, 1977), p. 86.
32   Sebreli, *Los deseos imaginarios del peronismo*, p. 37.
33   Martinez, 'Ficción e historia', p. 48.
34   Donna Haraway attempts – from a feminist perspective – to 'rescue' the faculty of seeing, long associated with male power, suggesting that we learn to see in compound, multiple ways, in 'partial perspectives'. She refers to this process as 'passionate detachment', reminiscent of the eye of a travelling lens. See *Simians, Cyborgs, and Women: the Reinvention of Nature* (London: Free Association Books, 1991), pp. 188–96.
35   Epstein, '(Post)modern Lives: Abducting the biographical subject', in *Contesting the Subject*, pp. 217–36 (p. 229).
36   Epstein, *Recognizing Biography*, p. 29.
37   Page's relationship with Perón has a textual counterpart in Martínez's text: Perón's cousin, Julio, recalls the words of their school monitor, Enriqueta Douce: 'solía decir que vos eras mi vampiro: que yo iba desapareciendo para que vos te agrandaras' (p. 39).
38   The effect which Perón has on Martínez may be compared to the possible reaction of the traditional reader to *La novela de Perón*: having approached the text with expectations of fulfilment and of

acquiring a rounded impression of Perón, s/he may leave disappointed, with an anaemic sense of emptiness at having gained few, if any, new 'facts'.

[39] Baudrillard, *Seduction*, p. 21.

Chapter 8

Portraits of a Lady: Postmodern Readings of Tomás Eloy Martínez's *Santa Evita*[1]

The theatrics of writing that dominate *La novela de Perón* are developed in Martínez's best-selling work, *Santa Evita* (1995) which presents its subject from a postmodern perspective, emphasizing the ultimate elusiveness – both in life and in death – of Eva Perón. Dr Pedro Ara's main objective in writing of Eva was to present the truth of his encounter with her, to narrate 'la verdadera historia', recalling Joseph Page's approach to Perón and Borroni and Vacca's to Eva (as discussed in chapters 4 and 5). All of Eva's biographers treated here share, to varying degrees, this same objective. The only writer who shows any awareness of the problematic aspect of the traditional biographer's truth-telling aims is Dujovne Ortiz, who is, significantly, a novelist as well as a biographer. Martínez highlights the fictional rather than the historical aspect of his work (*Santa Evita* is specifically designated a novel) and foregrounds not his conception of the historical Eva nor the results of historical research into what really happened (despite being eminently qualified to do so as a leading scholar of Peronism) but rather his own inability to master a story that will remain distant and opaque. This situation produces ambivalent feelings in Martínez: on the one hand, a sense of being overwhelmed but also, on the other, a curious elation deriving from contact with an ultimately inexhaustible story whose secrets will remain for ever inviolate. *Santa Evita* focuses on the enigma that was Eva Perón – an enigma not only during her lifetime but also after her death: Martínez's main concern is indeed the uncertain fate of her corpse.

Postmodernism, which has dominated recent cultural debate in Latin America,[2] is associated with the decline of 'master' discourses, such as that of psychoanalysis – informing both the work of Dujovne Ortiz (as we have seen in chapter 6) and of Manuel Puig (considered in chapter 10) – and the problematization (as in *La novela de Perón*) of such concepts as 'truth', 'essence' and 'authenticity' that underpin authoritative writing of the kind often found in traditional biography. Historical discourse has traditionally been judged by the persuasiveness of its argumentation and the effectiveness of its presentation of truth claims.[3] It was generally assumed that painstaking investigation would uncover the facts of history. The historian's imaginative capacity, though not redundant, was largely confined to making the mental leap from the present to the past. Today the historian's (and the biographer's) imagination is increasingly used to reconstruct the past, almost to reinvent it, as New Historical discourse gravitates towards literary creativity. In the case of Eva Perón, such an approach is almost *de rigueur*, since primary sources are scarce[4] and the nature of the subject resists coherent analysis.

The postmodern approach problematizes the traditional values of historical and biographical discourse – rigorous documentation, consistency of argumentation, and firm grasp of chronology. Indeed its diminished sense of temporality has led some commentators to diagnose postmodernism as schizophrenic.[5] Much of the impetus for international as well as Latin American literary postmodernism was provided by the work of the Argentine writer Jorge Luis Borges. His predilection for the marginal and heterodox, together with his freewheeling, citational style, blurs the normal jurisdictions and boundaries between individual authors, eras and texts. His brand of creativity finds its most typical expression in displacement, reconfiguration and recontextualization rather than in creation *ex nihilo*.[6] The main thrust of New Historicism may be found in his short story, 'Pierre Menard, autor del Quijote' which offers the now well-known insight that history 'no es lo que sucedió; es lo que juzgamos que sucedió'.[7] The notion that history is a kind of fiction is not new: Sarmiento's *Facundo o Civilización y Barbarie* (1845), for example, is replete with inexactitudes and creative distortions.[8] But contemporary historicism, as Noé Jitrik points out, stands apart from earlier writing through its recognition of the limits of linguistic representation and its flaunted literariness: 'lo histórico deja de estar al servicio de una causa o de implicar una fundada elección del período para pasar a ser nivel genotextual, oportunidad para una transformación literaria cada vez más exigente y más arriesgada'.[9] The past has to be invented, or at least emplotted in the manner of a literary text, because what really happened remains largely beyond the grasp of the historian or biographer. The fallibility of the historical record and of the historian himself inevitably distances historiography from the unproblematic acceptance of such concepts as 'essence' and 'truth'.

Martínez's *Santa Evita* belongs to that current within post-Boom writing which focuses on historical events of the recent past. The events in this case relate to a historical figure who dominated Argentine politics from 1946 to 1952; but Martínez does not portray the 'official' Eva as depicted in the historical record but rather the 'underside' of her history, in particular her paradoxes and inconsistencies which survive her death. Throughout the novel, history is presented as a kind of literature, being infused with the undecidability and openendedness of fiction. Martínez, in typical New Historical style, persistently focuses on conflicting versions of events (pp. 158, 165, 170) and notes that reliable narration, the prime (and purportedly achievable) objective of the traditional biographer such as Marysa Navarro, lies beyond his power (pp. 253, 311). Memory is fallible ('la memoria es propensa a la traición', p. 313) and the past is elusive ('la gente se le desvanecía el pasado más rápido de lo que tardaba en llegar el presente', p. 233; 'era un pasado que se disolvía apenas el Coronel lo rozaba con los ojos', p. 292). For this reason history seems more unreal than improbable (p. 234). Truth claims regarding the location of Eva's body prove to be untenable (p. 301). As if to counterbalance his largely testimonial approach, based on the accounts of several witnesses, which might suggest that the 'truth' will finally be revealed, Martínez consistently emphasizes, through a series of self-reflexive comments, that there is no single, essential, real Eva to be uncovered, nor is there an authoritative story to be told about her posthumous life: 'nada es nunca una sola historia sino una red que cada persona teje, sin entender el dibujo' (p. 207). Far from seeking to establish the 'facts', Martínez deliberately conflates truth and fiction, commenting for example that Eva's most celebrated (and apocryphal) remark, 'Volveré y seré millones', is true despite being false: 'nunca existió, pero es verdadera' (p. 66). As we have seen Dujovne Ortiz accords similar, if less explicit, recognition to Eva's remark, 'Gracias por existir', more than likely also apocryphal (see above, pp. 164–165).

The inaccessibility of the past is compounded by deliberate human manipulation and falsification of documentary evidence. The Peróns' marriage certificate, seemingly a correct official record, turns out to be more fictional than factual owing to the falsifications perpetrated by both Perón and Eva: 'En el momento más solemne e histórico de sus vidas, los contrayentes [. . .] decidieron burlarse olímpicamente de la historia' (p. 143). Martínez's tone is admiring rather than reproachful because he sees the pair as kindred spirits, prepared to mould reality to their own liking, novelists of a kind, like himself: 'actuaron como actúan los novelistas' (p. 144). Marysa Navarro makes the same point about the falsified marriage certificate but adopts a rather legalistic approach, feeling constrained to separate fact from fiction[10] rather than celebrate the mischief and audacity of the perpetrators, as does Martínez. For him misdemeanours become the stuff of a new kind of history: 'Si la historia es – como parece – otro de los géneros literarios, ¿por qué privarla de la imaginación, el desatino, la indelicadeza, la exageración y la derrota que son la materia prima sin la cual no se concibe la literatura?' (p. 146). Reality cannot be fixed but only reinvented (pp. 85, 97).

This is the only way to approach the phenomenon of Eva who moves elusively through the realms of history, fiction and myth, defying every attempt to pin her down, since her various images proliferate endlessly: 'Evita no se resignaba a ser una y empezaba a regresar en bandadas, por millones [. . .]' (p. 83). Evita personifies both eternity and transience, movement on the one hand and stasis on the other, as conveyed in the image of the butterfly with a black wing moving forwards and a yellow wing flying backwards (p. 65). The historical Eva, who refuses to stand still for Martínez despite his attempts to freeze her image by action replay (p. 192), has been subsumed within another timeless, mythical being who represents the myriad longings and recollections of others: 'le había llovido el polen de los deseos y recuerdos ajenos' (pp. 65–6). Elsewhere the repeated references to the buzzing of bees (pp. 121, 130, 140, 172, 209) suggest both the intensity of collective emotions focusing on the figure of Eva and the babel of endlessly proliferating stories which seek to represent her (p. 85). She is removed from the everyday reality of time and place, occupying rather a sphere which is 'sin tiempo y sin lugar' (p. 11). Martínez focuses here on the mythic Eva, on what she has come to represent beyond her historical reality. The biographies we have considered in chapters 4 to 6 (with some exception made for Dujovne Ortiz) aim to present the most convincing account of the documented Eva – rather than explore the mythic Eva which requires greater imaginative than historical input.

The text attempts the impossible task of unravelling the mysteries of Eva. But the chameleon-like qualities of both the living and the dead Eva resist identification. Martínez upsets and sometimes inverts traditional hierarchies which place the historical above the fictional, the 'real' individual above demeaning stereotypes, the literally verifiable which delimits and circumscribes above the figurative and mythical which proliferate uncontrollably. He deconstructs such fixed notions as 'reality' and 'truth' by focusing on three interrelated topics that conspire to undermine 'sense' and to destabilize identity: death, femininity and writing.[11] Eva represents the principle of femininity that invades the text, precluding any form of 'closure'. Both life and death are defined not by any unifying concept of natural order, far less by reason, but rather in terms of image and spectacle, by the 'already made', by 'staged' activities and emotions, by myriad linguistic formulae repeated endlessly in speech and writing. Reconstruction replaces reality as identity turns into myth, body into text and history into fiction. The 'real' does not exist and the text can be seen as a kind of celebration of its disappearance. This goes well beyond the self-imposed limits of the biographers: even Dujovne Ortiz is often keen to verify, convince and lend coherence to her chosen version of events by showing its superiority over alternatives.

The myth of Eva emerges in the first few lines when her still living body, in brief respite from pain, is swathed in 'una beatitud sin tiempo y sin lugar' (p. 11). Following her death, the historical Eva is enveloped by her mythical counterpart: 'dejó de ser lo que dijo y lo que hizo para ser lo que dicen que dijo y lo que dicen que hizo' (p. 21). Her elusiveness is further represented by her contradictory persona: in many ways she represents a fusion of opposites, both eroticism and spirituality, male drive and female fragility, childlessness and motherhood. Her perfect beauty ('una belleza que hacía olvidar todas las otras felicidades del universo', p. 25) produced obsessive devotion in both Dr Ara, her embalmer, and in Colonel Moori Koenig who was charged with the task of disposing of her body after the fall of Perón. It inspired passionate love in her *descamisados*, in 'los que están fuera de la historia' (p. 34). On the other hand, Evita aroused intense hostility not only in the army and the upper classes but also among the intellectuals – as evidenced by Silvina Ocampo's poem (p. 70).

Eva is both evil and good, representative of both the temptress Eve and the holy Virgin Mary: as the president's wife she is the respectable 'señora' but in her role as feminist and friend of the *descamisados* she is the militant *compañera*.[12] On the one hand she heralds imminent destruction, her body is polluted, her beauty a mask for decay. She suffers from cancer which is not just a death sentence but, according to Sontag, is also 'obscene in the original meaning of that word, ill-omened, abominable, repugnant to the senses'. This is precisely how her enemies see her. Cancer has been described as the 'barbarian within', a metaphor for what is most 'ferociously energetic', an 'insult to the natural order'.[13] The disease of Evita's body becomes the disease of the body politic: the one is invaded by cancer cells, the other by the wild hordes attracted by her. Eva's disease is corporeal, an insult to the senses: 'los argentinos veían en Eva una resurrección obscena de la barbarie [. . .] Mientras pasaba, había que taparse la nariz' (p. 70).

Her unseemly background in illegitimacy and provincial squalor may suggest a 'natural' vocation in prostitution: but by becoming the wife of the president she violates the 'natural' order. For the writer, Ezequiel Martínez Estrada, her fatal sin was to disturb the gender balance by dominating Perón: 'en realidad, él era la mujer y ella el hombre' (p. 184).[14] Her colossal willpower also suggests masculinity[15] while her status as a latter-day Joan of Arc places her alongside one of the most deviant women in history. Her speeches, though devoid of substance, are spellbinding even to a scientific ear (Ara, p. 44). Their often violent imagery and naked passion made Perón's rather pale by comparison. Dujovne Ortiz makes this point forcefully: 'Screams of rage and pain burned her throat. Following her rasping voice, her skin turned red. Perón's veiled voice calmed the crowd. Nothing was bleeding or trembling in him'.[16] Her disease extends to language where her 'dicción indecisa entre el arrabal y la cursilería' (p. 215) is recognized even by the untutored cinema projectionist, Chino Astorga. Her contagious subversiveness infects her followers who have the ability to overturn conventional meanings: 'los descamisados no rechazaron por completo la invectiva, pero dieron vuelta su sentido. Evita era para ellos la yegua madrina, la guía del rebaño' (pp. 22–3). Her embalmed body does not invoke the marvels of science but rather the possibilities of magic (p. 27).

But as well as deviance Eva also embodies her own opposite, the Virgin Mary, who represents redemption and triumph over the sin and decay introduced by Eve; as Sebreli puts it: 'ella es la misma, la diosa madre, y a la vez la mujer demonio, la mandrágora, la manta religiosa'.[17] The circumstances of Eva's death are significant since they are reminiscent of Mary's.[18] Marina Warner points out that there was no knowledge of Mary's grave, no body to venerate, no relics to touch. 'The disappearance of Mary's body [. . .] inspired the most fertile imaginings [. . .] For the symbol of purity could not rot in her grave.'[19] She is placed from the start outside the 'feminine' realm of material time and bodily decay and inside the 'masculine' symbolic realm of eternal unchanged forms. In both her negative and positive incarnations, Evita encroaches on the masculine sphere. Even her subversiveness blurs into its opposite, submission, since her feminine mutability which threatens the male, appears to be neutralized in her immobility as embalmed – cleansed and purified – corpse. The dying Evita who implored her mother to ensure that no one should see her naked body, becomes the defenceless focus of the male gaze (of Dr Ara, and, figuratively, of Martínez himself) and of the sexual fantasies of Moori Koenig and of his subordinate, Arancibia. But even here she cannot be repressed since Arancibia's shooting of his own wife Elena is brought about by the presence of Eva, the mad woman in his attic, a woman who, though dead, 'cada día vive más' (p. 262).

Just as the dying Eva loses her sense of time, so the narrative moves forwards and backwards, as though sequential time belonged to another reality. Evita's body is converted into an aesthetic object by Dr Ara, thereby becoming a symbol of the text itself. Elizabeth Bronfen suggests that the death of a beautiful woman 'marks the mise-en-abyme of a text, the moment of self-reflexivity, where the text seems to comment on itself and its own process of composition and so decomposes itself '.[20] As Evita perpetuates herself through an unending series of images so the text renews itself through its chaotic proliferation of narratives.

'Texte veut dire Tissu [. . .]' comments Roland Barthes, 'nous acceptons maintenant, dans le tissu, l'idée generative que le texte se fait, se travaille a travers un entrelacs perpétuel [. . .]'[21] Martínez, like Barthes, associates physical and textual bodies through the figure of weaving: while Eva 'se tejió a sí misma' (p. 12), the text assumes a similar consistency through its 'tejido de versiones' (p. 165). A further link between the body of Evita and the body of the text emerges in the self-conscious comparison between the art of embalming and that of biography: 'el arte de embalsamador se parece al del biógrafo [. . .]' (p. 157). To reinforce the point, Corominas, the intelligence officer whose testimony is found in the final chapter, 'narró con la prolijidad de un anatomista las desventuras nómadas de la Difunta' (p. 389). Her body becomes a repository of collective memory and her death, though obviously ending one kind of existence, facilitates countless others. The reality of the dead Evita becomes textual: 'fue convirtiéndose en un relato que, antes de terminar, encendía otro' (p. 21).

While the biographers considered earlier (Chapters 4 to 6) figuratively 'embalm' their subject by attempting to 'fix' her (Llorca as saint, Navarro as flawed talent, Dujovne Ortiz as performer of multiple roles), Martínez duplicates the motion and drama of her life through the butterfly manoeuvrings of his text which moves nimbly from citation to citation, from perspective to perspective, representing in its own body some of the drama and excess which characterized Eva herself. There is a 'buzzing' of citations drawn from a wide variety of sources that ignore traditional generic boundaries and whose chaotic interaction suggests the exuberance of their subject. Discourses range from Evita's own notes regarding table etiquette written in a 'letra desaliñada [. . .] que parecía hacer acrobacias sobre los alambres de las rayas horizontales' (p. 290) to the formal and legalistic testimony of Margot written in the third person (pp. 263–72) and the precise inventory of items found in Dr Ara's laboratory (pp. 162–3). The footnotes with their bibliographical (p. 44), contextualizing (p. 91) and translatorial functions (p. 277), suggest a token attempt at textual discipline inevitably overwhelmed by the proliferation of discourses. Here Martínez's procedures contrast sharply with Navarro's whose inventories point to rigorous documentation and the pursuit of ultimate fact, totally devoid of ironic purpose (see Chapter 6).

Writing and desire are closely linked. All the male 'creators' of Evita, including the hairdresser Julio Alcaraz, express their desire in writing: 'escribir tiene que ver con la salud, con el azar, con la felicidad y el sufrimiento, pero sobre todo tiene que ver con el deseo' (p. 85). Moori Koenig has even taken notes on Evita's clitoris (p. 134). Writing and embalming seek, by different means, to prolong life beyond death. Ara's laborious and painstaking task is matched by Martínez's intricate weaving of perspectives and data. His investigations, marked by their obsessive scrutiny of their subject and by their manipulations of the corpus of texts at his disposal, can be seen as the textual equivalent of both the voyeurism of Moori Koenig and the necrophilia of Arancibia whose interest in Eva's corpse was, significantly, stimulated by his reading of a book, Mika Waltari's *Sinhué el egipcio*.[22] Martínez himself is light-heartedly accused of necrophilia by Emilio Kaufman, father of the late Irene with whom Martínez was in love ('¿Vas a ponerte necrofílico?', p. 232). However intense the desire – on the part of Dr Ara, Moori Koenig, Arancibia and Martínez himself – it is eventually frustrated. Evita assumes the character of a limitless text in constant motion, ever-resistant to closure: 'existe sólo en el futuro: ésa es su fijeza' (p. 342). Her spirit seems to infect the text and overwhelm Martínez himself: 'no sé en que punto del relato estoy [. . .] Ahora tengo que escribir otra vez' (p. 391).

Spectacle and performance are portrayed in different guises throughout the text. The historical period itself provides an appropriate backdrop: Perón's regime was in many ways a show, and its centrepiece, Evita, led a public life of spectacle which crowded out her private life so that there was no 'real' Eva behind her public persona. Her death continues the theatre of her life. Various rehearsals take place: during the shady operations surrounding the disposal of Evita's body, Galarza (one of Moori Koenig's subordinates) rehearses the part of the widower, Giorgio de Magistris, since Evita (supposedly the 'real' Evita rather than a wax copy) is to be buried under the name of Giorgio's wife, María Maggi. Fake emotions take the place of real feelings: 'De Magistris repetía la historia con acento dolido, verosímil' (p. 325). This is reminiscent of Evita whose own emotions are artificial, as Chino

Astorga, the cinema projectionist, realizes when he visits the Foundation: 'Evita le sonrió con la misma expresión compasiva que llevaba pegada desde el principio de la tarde' (p. 230). Evita's theatricality in life and in death is matched by the staged self-images projected by Martínez himself which range from casual offhandedness ('¿No he dicho esto antes?', p. 189) to the sorrow occasioned by the death of his mother (p. 76). Far from being effaced, the process of the text's construction, together with its intricate textuality – its range of epigraphs, citations and other discourses – is continually flaunted (as in *La novela de Perón*). The extended 'rehearsal' for the novel includes a discarded version of the text (p. 63) as well as intense authorial wrestling with chaotic raw materials: 'se me escurrían las tramas, las fijezas de los puntos de vista, las leyes del espacio y de los tiempos [. . .]. Tardé meses y meses en amansar el caos' (p. 65). Rehearsal is also implicit in Martínez's reading of his own cinema script to Eva's former hairdresser, Julio Alcaraz. The script is based on the famous *cabildo abierto* called by the Confederación Nacional del Trabajo to discuss Eva's candidature for the vice-presidency in 1951. Julio Alcaraz, who was present at the meeting, plays the role of critic, giving Martínez behind-the-scenes insights into what was really going on.

Martínez even confers a certain drama on the often tedious work of research and verification – 'a fines de 1989 me lancé a la busca de Chino Astorga [. . .]' (p. 231). He deliberately provokes the dramatic reaction of Yolanda (Chino Astorga's daughter) when he announces gratuitously that her 'Pupé' – hidden in her father's cinema – was not a doll but an embalmed body: 'ella era un personaje que ya había dado todo lo que podía a esta historia' (p. 241). He flaunts, often theatrically, the unreliability of his narrative: rather than viewing Eva with the detachment and objectivity required in an impartial observer, he is himself in thrall to Eva, just like his characters (Dr Ara, Moori Koenig, and Yolanda). He achieves a kind of mystical union with her, referring to 'la yo que era Ella' (p. 65) and affirming that 'ella no cesa de existir, de existirme: hace de su existencia una exageración' (p. 204). Llorca's intimacies with an idealized Eva appear vapid by comparison: here Martínez seems to absorb the spirit of Eva, drawing upon her posthumous magnetism, succeeding in infusing himself with her vitality – whereas the warlock, López Rega famously failed in his efforts to rejuvenate the hapless Isabel, Perón's third wife, by transferring to her the latent power of the dead Eva.

Evita's immortality is represented by her images which proliferate endlessly after her death – as anticipated by the apocryphal phrase noted earlier: 'volveré y seré millones' (p. 66). The fate of Evita's body suggests the postmodernist concept of reality replaced by its images or copies.[23] The image, a kind of copy of the original, assumes inordinate power in this text: Evita fell for the image of Perón – 'jamás había visto a Perón salvo en las fotografías de los diarios' (p. 191) – and it is the image of Evita which holds the people in thrall: 'la imagen era tan dominante, tan inolvidable, que el sentido común de las personas terminaba por moverse de lugar' (p. 27). In one important episode which takes place in Chino Astorga's cinema, Evita is herself held in thrall by her own screen image (p. 216) and her 'real' self, caught up in the drama represented on screen, is hardly distinguishable from her theatrical self. The text teems with copies of all kinds: literal reproductions include the paintings which adorn Moori Koenig's desk at the Intelligence Service (p. 119) and that which the Pope gives Eva (p. 219). The text is also replete with imperfect copies: approximate likenesses of other people, echoes of previous scenes or events. Former Argentine President Carlos Saúl Menem and his wife present an inverted image of Perón and Eva (p. 243); Perón's crowds copy those of Mussolini (p. 94); one of Martínez's informants in the final chapter is said to be the image of Juan Duarte, Evita's brother (p. 388). Yolanda's theatre of dolls (p. 236) recalls the CGT office which became Dr Ara's embalming theatre containing Eva's body and its copies. Fire, both literal and figurative, informs Eva's life, copying itself in various guises: her scalding by oil as a child leads to her reincarnation as a delicate beauty (p. 369) while at the end of her life she burns with fever and is burned by bungled radiation therapy (p. 30). Her eyes possess the fire of fanaticism while her tears are of real flames (pp. 29, 118). Even the pampa reproduces itself (p. 56). Supreme among these proliferating replicas are the wax copies of Evita herself (pp. 24, 35, 54). The superior image is the most 'unreal', the one depicting Evita seated in an armchair 'reading' a postcard (p. 54). Her mother fears that she will be unable to distinguish the original from the copies, the genuine Eva from the fake Evas. There is no perceptible difference between the images of Evita and the 'real' Eva whose identity is now dispersed among innumerable representations including statues reminiscent of the Virgin Mary (p. 379).

Significantly the mystery surrounding the copies recalls the elusive qualities of Eva, their fate remaining undecidable and unclarified. We read that Fesquet – one of Moori Koenig's men – recovered the copy buried at Olivos and replaced it with the original (p. 340). The writer Rodolfo Walsh claims that Eva was buried in the garden of the Argentine embassy in Bonn (p. 303) while Martínez himself suggests to the dismissive Aldo Cifuentes (who looked after Moori Koenig in his old age) that perhaps Koenig did, after all, bury the 'real' Eva and not a copy ('sería una confusión muy argentina', p. 364). In her study, *Evita Perón: the Myths of a Woman* (considered in Chapter 5), J. M. Taylor conjectures that the corpse that reappeared 'may have been a wax doll all along',[24] though another commentator, W. A. Harbinson, who refers directly to *Santa Evita*, regards claims of wax copies as dubious.[25] In his chronological review of the era, Sabreli refers to the rumours circulating in 1956 about the fate of the body:

> Circulan varias versiones contradictorias: que está enterrada en un convento franciscano en Roma, en Vasconia, en Chile, en Uruguay, en la isla Martín García, en la estancia La Primavera de los Duarte en Monte, en Campo de Mayo, en Monte Grande, en el panteón de los Duarte en la Recoleta, que fue incinerado, o que fue arrojado al Río de la Plata.[26]

Martínez's last witness, Corominas of the Army Intelligence Service, denies that there were any copies at all and claims that Eva was buried in Milan, a version which accords with 'official' history. Whatever the 'truth' – so elusive as to be virtually meaningless in this text – copy and original have become inextricably confused, enveloped in the same aura of haziness and uncertainty.

Art is a powerful – though partial and imperfect – 'copy' of life which often replaces the 'real': in New Jersey, Evita is a familiar figure but 'la historia que se conoce de ella es la de la ópera, la de Tim Rice' (p. 204). Art elicits violent reaction as though it were 'real': a play by Copi so outraged Peronist fanatics that they burned down the theatre shortly after the premiere; their outrage was expressed in words taken from a tango by Discépulo (p. 200). Reality and its artistic representation become fused as reality is packaged by art. The text increasingly refers not to an 'unmediated' reality but to other artistic representations of it. (Joseph Page notes how Eva's political life was an uncanny extension of her leading role in a film called *La pródiga* in which she played a kind of 'Lady Bountiful', always helping the less fortunate).[27] *Santa Evita* is intricately citational in its reproduction of the accounts of various witnesses – 'cito ahora, casi al pie de la letra [. . .]' (p. 147) – and densely intertextual in its references to the ways in which writers and film directors have interpreted the Evita phenomenon. Martínez's text, itself originally modelled on the opening line of a film (p. 63), is replete with references to other texts: Rodolfo Walsh's 'Esa mujer' (pp. 56, 301), Julio Cortázar's 'El examen' (p. 197), Juan Carlos Onetti's 'Ella' (p. 198), Borges's 'El simulacro' (p. 199) and Martínez's own previous work, *La novela de Perón* (p. 64). Martínez admits that he cannot help but copy Borges's description of reality as a system of forking paths (p. 177). The textual web is tightened by passing references to an aestheticized reality as when Eva's departure for Buenos Aires is described by the singer Mario Pugliese (Cariño) as 'una escena de radioteatro [. . .] el príncipe azul rescataba de su infortunio a la provincianita pobre y poco agraciada' (p. 317).

The relationship between art and life is the subject of disagreement between Martínez and Aldo Cifuentes, one of his witnesses. Cifuentes recounts that Moori Koenig determined the burial sites for the wax copies of Eva by sketching Paracelsus's trident on tracing paper over a map of Greater Buenos Aires. Martínez suggests a literary comparison, Borges's 'La muerte y la brújula', but Cifuentes argues for maintaining the division between life and art. He goes on to relate that one of the appointed burial grounds was a church in Olivos alongside a railway station named Borges. It seems that literary connotation refuses to be suppressed.

Evita, doubly marginalized through her femininity and illegitimacy, dominates the narrative as the source of its myriad texts and the ever-elusive object of its tortuous meanderings. This elusiveness derives from Evita's duality and discontinuity: the embalmed body is both Eva and not Eva, and when Moori Koenig opens the coffin and sees Eva, he is confronted by 'una imagen plana, partida en dos como la luna' (p. 181). She continues to elude the masculine gaze: 'desde que intenté narrar a Evita advertí que, si me acercaba a Ella, me alejaba de mí' (pp. 62–3).[28] Her triumph over Borges is even more spectacular: whereas he sought in his story 'El simulacro' to portray her as a 'muñeca muerta en una caja de cartón' (p. 199), his intention is frustrated since Eva emerges as 'la imagen de Dios mujer, la Dios de todas las mujeres, la Hombre de todos los dioses' (p. 199). Despite his masterful, masculine intellect, adept at producing stories of controlled precision, Borges finds that the woman whom he dismissed as a mere whore exceeds his grasp, her unmanageable excess and inscrutability overwhelming him, just as her excessive love overwhelmed Perón (p. 139). She encapsulates death and femininity, 'the two central enigmas of western discourse' which ultimately refuse any fixed answer or stable truth.[29]

Evita can be seen as a per(s)onification of postmodern ideas and culture. Her public life amounted to a series of staged personalities and performances, while her death generated irrational emotions and boundless myths. She represents the volatile, ever-changing Radical Other, a truth which no one can reach: Moori Koenig's definition, as reported by Cifuentes, comes closest to the mark, though it is not an original statement but rather one that derives from the mystical work of Saint Teresa: 'persona es una luz a la que nadie puede llegar. Mientras menos lo entiendo, más lo creo' (p. 363). In life and in death, Evita incarnates the society of the spectacle, where models replace the real and determine the real. She also embodies a mystical power, being neither truth nor falsity but a paradoxical combination of the two in which such binary opposites are drawn out of opposition.

With the exception of Dujovne Ortiz's, the biographies considered in Chapters 4 to 6 are silent about their own processes of construction; *Santa Evita*, by contrast, is replete with references to its own genesis; and to the limitations of writing. We learn that it was during a conversation between Martínez and Julio Alcaraz that the idea for the novel was born (p. 83); we are given a close insight into Martínez's primarily erotic conception of writing: 'escribir tiene que ver con la salud, con el azar, con la felicidad y el sufrimiento, pero sobre todo tiene que ver con el deseo' (p. 85). But Martínez makes clear that writing, irrespective of the dedication and energy devoted to it, cannot resurrect reality which 'nace de otro modo, se transfigura, se reinventa a sí misma en las novelas' (p. 85). Martínez's sources are unreliable, but inevitably so, since language and reality are problematic and unequal, both contaminated by 'verdades impuras' (p. 143). There follows a disquisition on the subject of sources:

> para los historiadores y los biógrafos, las fuentes siempre son un dolor de cabeza. No se bastan a sí mismas. Si una fuente dudosa quiere tener derecho a la letra de molde, debe ser confirmada por otra y ésta a su vez por una tercera. La cadena es a menudo infinita, a menudo inútil, porque la suma de fuentes puede también ser un engaño. (p. 143).

Later Martínez narrates how he is made aware that Cifuentes's testimony is probably flawed but none the less he is reluctant to dismiss his account: '¿Por qué la historia tiene que ser un relato hecho por personas sensatas y no un desvarío de perdedores como el Coronel y Cifuentes?' (p. 146). Here Martínez calls into question what the biographers take for granted: the primacy of reliable, closely documented sources. The sustained self-conscious musings of *Santa Evita* incorporate the dramatization of the divide between traditional biographical writing which prioritizes the 'facts' and the postmodern biography/historical novel (such as *Santa Evita*) which blurs the once hard and fast distinctions between fact and fiction.[30] Martínez's conversation with Emilio Kaufman – the father of his former girlfriend, Irene, who had since died – is reproduced in *Santa Evita*: biographical approaches to Evita, including Borroni and Vacca's work, are discussed. Kaufman offers two criticisms of standard biographical practice relating to Eva: the failure to realize that Eva's life is inseparably linked to her death; and the scrupulous recital of redundant information (such as the list of novels Eva presented on the radio), a meaningless routine compounded by the inability to 'llenar algunos vacíos elementales' (p. 245). Both points are valid: Eva's posthumous life is largely ignored by biographers who (like Marysa Navarro) offer a surfeit of secondary data by way of compensation for their failure to improvise creatively when gaps in the historical record leave them with little other choice. The postmodern Martínez undermines the foundations of traditional biographical writing through his application of novelistic techniques to the sphere of historical narration. His later conversation with the intelligence chief, Colonel Tulio Ricardo Corominas, again highlights the distance between the traditional approach of biographers such as Llorca and Navarro and the imaginative bias of writers such as Martínez, who remarks that in the novel 'lo que es verdad es también mentira'. Corominas's rejoinder encapsulates the guiding principle of many traditional biographers: 'lo único que vale son los hechos' (p. 389). Moori Koenig's reflections while in Germany are also significant in this respect: 'la ventaja de la libertad era que podía convertir las mentiras en verdades y contar verdades en las que todo parecía mentira' (p. 360).

Corominas's view is undermined devastatingly, albeit implicitly, by Martínez's portrayal of the August 1951 *cabildo abierto*. The biographies analysed in Part II base their accounts of this event on the known facts. Llorca's brief account does justice to the political impact of the occasion but not to its intense drama ('la resonancia de la candidatura propuesta fue extraordinaria dentro y fuera del país', *Llamadme Evita*, p. 228). Navarro communicates a sense of the passion and volatility of the occasion by quoting key elements of the extraordinary dialogue between Eva and the crowd: 'en vano trató de explicar, razonar, ganar tiempo, la multitud la interrumpía para decir ¡Hoy! ¡Ahora!' (*Evita*, p. 285). Dujovne Ortiz provides the most poignant account, focusing on the raw physical power of Eva:

> Evita spoke extending her hands, palms facing up. But the nervous tension, the trembling of her hands, demonstrated that there was nothing soothing about it. Was it an imploring or a menacing gesture? Screams of rage and pain burned her throat. Following her rasping voice, her skin turned red [...]. All Argentina witnessed the nervousness that reigned on that stage [...] and heard the battle of the voices. (*Eva Perón*, pp. 264–6)

The approach of each writer is clearly different but their basic objective is similar: to resurrect reality through writing. Dujovne Ortiz tries to probe directly the maelstrom of sensation and emotion that gripped Eva, but she can offer only a pale afterglow of Eva's fire: her effort to reproduce that scene is overshadowed by the limitations of her language, its straining for effect, and its failure to pin down an ever-elusive Eva. For Martínez, of course, language cannot reproduce reality (p. 97). His own approach is to emphasize the mediated, aestheticized quality of his representations. His main source is Eva's former hairdresser and confidant Julio Alcaraz, but Martínez's emphasis is not on his own proximity to Eva but rather the reverse, his distance from the source, implicit in the act of transcription. The problems analysed by Martínez are reminiscent of the issues raised by testimonial literature: '¿Alcaraz habla, yo hablo, alguien escucha, o hablamos todos a la vez, jugamos al libre juego de leer escribiendo?' (p. 86). Alcaraz's 'testimony', reconstructed by Martínez, follows in italic script – which serves as a constant reminder to the reader of its textual status. The mediated character of Martínez's account is reinforced by Alcaraz's reference to the *Clarín* report of events (photographically reproduced in the text): 'en los diarios verá usted más claro el reflejo de lo que pasaba' (p. 93). Alcaraz appears to offer direct insights into Eva's dilemma, prior to the *cabildo abierto*, based on her private disclosures to him regarding her feelings of abandonment and sense of uncertainty about whether to accept the vice-presidential nomination in view of Perón's failure to provide clear guidance. But the reliability of Alcaraz's italicized recollections are immediately questioned: 'tal relato es, por definición, infiel. La realidad, como ya dije, no se puede contar ni repetir. Lo único que se puede hacer con la realidad es inventarla de nuevo' (p. 97). Moreover, the documents and tape recordings of the episode only misrepresent Eva: 'Eva nunca era Evita' (p. 98). Martínez opts for creative reconstruction in the form of a cinema script, which he reads to Alcaraz, emphasizing its mediated, artistic quality: 'haga de cuenta que se apagan las luces. Que hay un telón abriéndose' (p. 98).

The immediacy of the *cabildo abierto* cannot be reconstructed in writing which inevitably distorts; its intensity can be evoked not by seeking to reflect directly the original event by means of a realistic depiction but rather by 'staging' a hybrid reconstruction in which the basic facts are enriched by heightened artistic effects, including a shot from an Orson Welles film (p. 106) and stage directions for 'un montaje erótico, más bien venéreo. Tal vez se logre algún efecto de realidad' (p. 111). The paradoxical implication is twofold: first, that the real can only be recuperated by means of artifice, artifice that can sometimes appear to be more real than the original which inspired its construction (one of Dr Ara's wax copies of Eva looks so much like her that not even her own mother doña Juana, 'hubiera sido capaz de parirla', p. 54); and second, that although the script is largely fictional – the conspicuous stage directions highlighting its artifice – it is also closer to the 'truth' of the original than any realistic version of the event could be. Martínez's treatment of this episode also heightens its creative status by foregrounding the process of artistic creation. It is a script which is dynamic and still open to creative modification in response to any stimulus provided by Alcaraz. Rather than engaging in the arid and ultimately futile task of tracing each contour of an 'embalmed' history, Martínez offers a 'live' episode, still in a fluid state of creative tension and with latent resonances awaiting adequate artistic expression.

The main focus of *Santa Evita* may be the subject's posthumous existence, but of almost equal importance is the mechanics of textual creation and the emphasis on the limitations of writing (themes ignored by traditional biographical writing: Llorca and Navarro remain oblivious to such issues; Dujovne Ortiz's approach is enriched by a degree of self-consciousness). Martínez also diverges from mainstream biography by privileging death over life: Jürgen Schlaeger observes that biography 'pits the abundance of past life against the present monotony of death. Life in biography is luxuriant, death is sterile'.[31] *Santa Evita* provides spectacular proof of the contrary. Traditional biography may concentrate on life – which, in theory at least, is knowable. Death, like femininity, appeals not to biographical research but to the literary imagination and it takes a novelistic biography like *Santa Evita* to explore the darknesses of Eva's posthumous existence.

Martínez's focus on death may be associated with his heightened awareness of artistic representation and his refusal of the notion that reality may be reflected directly through language. Death ruptures the symbolic order: it is inexpressible and inscrutable; culture sustains itself by substituting disruptive instances of the real (such as death and femininity) by representations.[32] The work of Dr Ara in preserving Eva's body is metaphorically duplicated by Martínez who preserves her history by means of a kind of textual surgery. While the natural processes of corruption are interrupted by Dr Ara who converts her real body into an artistic monument, Martínez energizes the historical Eva with the rejuvenating potency of his imaginative infusions. Significantly, his description of the mythical Eva 'borrows' the language of Dr Ara: while the latter notes, with some trepidation, the enormous distance separating '*lo que dijo* y lo que *dicen que dijo*'[33] Martínez observes of Eva: 'dejó de ser lo que dijo y lo que hizo para ser lo que dicen que dijo y lo que dicen que hizo' (*Santa Evita*, p. 21). Martínez realizes that Eva's posthumous power will overshadow the influence she exercised in life, that in a sense, Eva's death will inaugurate a new and limitless life. As her mother doña Juana remarks, 'en vida siempre había estado echándole tierra a su fuego, para no hacerle sombra al marido. Muerta, se iba a convertir en un incendio' (p. 47). She is transformed by 'el polen de los deseos y recuerdos ajenos. Transfigurada en mito, Evita era millones' (pp. 65–6). How is this fantastic proliferation represented in the text? It is through the images of bees, of buzzing and of pollen which recur, suggesting perpetual motion and renewal, all of them figuring a posthumous Eva who assumes countless different guises in the imagination of the people, proliferating on a lesser scale too in the minds of those male 'creators' who have laid claim to her: Juan Perón, Julio Alcaraz, Colonel Moori Koenig, Dr Pedro Ara and Tomás Eloy Martínez himself.

Biographies of Eva tend to be ephemeral. They will continue to proliferate interminably but with few exceptions they will be subsumed within the repetition of the same. By creating a distinct and technically innovative work of literature straddling the old divide between biography and novel, described by Alberto Manguel as 'the most powerful work of fiction to come from Latin America since *One Hundred Years of Solitude*',[34] Martínez's contribution to the immortalization of the spirit of Eva parallels on a literary plane the scientific achievements of Dr Ara which rendered her body incorruptible. Unlike the biographies of Llorca, Navarro and Dujovne Ortiz, *Santa Evita* explores the distant recesses of language, perspective and structure to approach the further limits of representation. It focuses not so much on the known historical circumstances as on the potentially infinite meanderings of the other Eva, known only indirectly and partially through a network of images (butterflies, bees) which contain the trace of Eva's presence, sensed with various degrees of intensity, ranging from tantalizing proximity to impossible distance. Thus Captain Milton Galarza (one of Colonel Moori Koenig's subordinates) 'oía fluir la voz entre las torres de la carga o al otro lado del casco, en el mar. Pero cuando regresaba al camarote se repetía que la voz sólo podía estar dentro de él, en alguna hondura del sur que desconocía' (p. 334). Galarza's sense of frustration is echoed by Martínez himself whose narrative fails to achieve any sense of closure: 'no sé en qué punto del relato estoy' (p. 391). He knows, however, that despite its limitations, its inability to resurrect the past, writing still offers the best hope of approximating to Eva and of assuaging his personal frustrations: 'si no la escribo, voy a asfixiarme' (p. 390). Writing is closely associated with death; but while its embalming effect may seem to produce only a kind of flat immobility and stasis, these same qualities are in fact susceptible to rejuvenation: Walter Ong refers to writing's 'potential for being resurrected into limitless living contexts by a potentially infinite number of living readers'.[35] Eva's posthumous existence is assured by her proliferating images: her body is a kind of text which, like *Santa Evita* itself, will be read in a host of different ways. Despite their fixity, both body and text lack finality: indeed they repudiate any sense of an ending. Both represent the principles of instability which neutralize the conventional tokens of permanence: names and dates provide universally recognized signs of identity but in Eva's case her names proliferate ('Yegua, Potranca, Bicha, Cucaracha, Friné, Estercita, Milonguista, Butterfly', p. 131) and important dates such as her date of birth are changed (p. 135). It is in death, however, that she most spectacularly breaks norms and exceeds limits: for Colonel Moori Koenig, Perón 'era el culpable de que su cuerpo anduviera nómade por el mundo, codiciado, insepulto, sin identidad ni nombre' p. 341). The spirit of Eva contaminates the text: normal chronology is subverted with her death treated at the text's beginning and her life at its conclusion. Ermarth notes that the linear convention of time belongs to what Kristeva calls 'the symbolic disposition of language, that is, the disposition to state, qualify and conclude rather than the disposition to play, multiply and diversify'.[36] Stability in *Santa Evita* is undermined by the proliferation of discourses and perspectives which produce sustained textual commotion. As Colonel Moori Koenig reflects, 'Evita' derives from 'evitar', meaning 'estorbar, impedir, hacer que no ocurra cierta cosa que iba a ocurrir' (p. 131), a definition which gives rise to Koenig's comic resolve: 'evitaría la palabra evita' (p. 131). The text of *Santa Evita* is based on this principle: once a point of resolution appears to be within reach, it is immediately subverted by an abrupt reconfiguration of perspective, as the insuperable limitations of writing, repressed by the often feverish reconstruction of the past, return to focus, through, for example, self-conscious references to the first drafts of the text (p. 63) and the unreliable nature of the sources (pp. 253, 311); and through the constant shifts in narrative perspective, a technique itself discussed in the text when Martínez refers to his conviction that any attempt by him to narrate doña Juana's story in the third person would vitiate her account: 'pocas veces he combatido tanto contra el ser de un texto que se quería narrar en feminino mientras yo, cruelmente, le retorcía la naturaleza' p. 366). It is fitting that Martínez's text, dealing with death, should be imbued with the feminine principle which symbolically disrupts the traditionally male values of consistency, continuity and coherence. *Santa Evita* is a stuttering text straddling the borders of the representable and the unrepresentable, refusing to alight on either side. It is mesmerized by the radical otherness of a subject whose constant motion precludes clear and sustained narrative focus.

The main objective of Llorca, Navarro and ultimately of even Dujovne Ortiz is to present a convincing portrait of Eva, to define, structure and finally master her, with recourse to varying degrees of interpretive 'violence' ranging from the naive idealism of Llorca to the self-conscious detachment of Dujovne Ortiz. Even the latter's approach is tightly chronological and while she acknowledges her subject's multiple personae, her chapter titles ('Illegitimate', 'The Actress', ' The Lover' etc.) stamp on each of Eva's identities an arresting and reductive label.[37] None of these biographers is consistently aware that reality reinvents itself in art (*Santa Evita*, p. 85). Martínez continually emphasizes the aestheticized images of Eva, ranging from the image of the living Eva constructed by her hairdresser Julio Alcaraz to that of the posthumous Eva, fashioned by her embalmer Dr Ara, both men claiming proprietorial rights over their 'creations': 'Eva fue un producto mío' says Alcaraz (p. 83), anticipating Perón's famous remark, while Ara boasts, 'soy [...] su hacedor' (p. 157). It is significant that Martínez's text derives its origins from a conversation with Alcaraz (p. 83) who is repeatedly associated with the art of replication and with mirroring (pp. 80–1). While the traditional biographer's aim, if not achievement, is the presentation of a faithful copy of the real Eva, Martínez is content to offer proliferating copies represented in the text by a network of proliferating images, notably of bees; thus when Colonel Moori Koenig visits doña Juana, 'el chisporroteo de la claraboya se volvió tenaz y monótono. Un largo huso de abejas hilaba su rutina sobre los vidrios' (p. 130). Dällenbach notes that 'the emblematic metaphor of the text as "fabric" reactivates the etymology of the "text" [...] text and textiles both being interwoven – hence the frequent use of terms like "web", "embroidering", and "weaving" to describe the novelist's work – both constituting a *texture* [...]'.[38] Martínez's description of the weaving action of the bees obscuring the glass of the skylight produces a metafictional image pointing to the obfuscation of the narrative by self-conscious reference to the weaving (or self-conscious interference of the 'buzzing') of its construction.[39] Bees seem to be identical to one another, their constant motion and sound suggesting the proliferation of workers swarming around the queen, signalling Eva's presence. As already mentioned, Martínez uses a network of interconnected images relating to bees and compares himself to a beekeeper (p. 132). Following the overthrow of Perón in September 1955, Dr Ara handed over Eva's shroud to the poor people who had gathered at the port. They dismantle their shelters and put them aboard the boats: 'eran muchos y se repartían el trabajo sin estorbarse, como en una colmena' (p. 170). In Martínez's screenplay version of the *cabildo abierto* the roar of the *descamisados* is described as a buzzing: 'zumban los ¡ahora! [...]' (p. 111). Eva's coffin is placed in Colonel Moori Koenig's office, under a Grundig hi-fi 'cuyo color era también de miel clara' (p. 278). Here is the aestheticized Eva in her purest incarnation – at the centre of a symbolic network that pervades the text and suggests the stinging, soothing Eva in perpetual motion both ubiquitous and evanescent. Whereas the biographers considered in Part II attempt in vain to resurrect the historical Eva, Martínez's main focus is on her mythical counterpart and her potentially infinite resonances which will continue to echo independently of the 'facts'. The objective of the traditional biographer may be to 'exterminate ambivalence';[40] Martínez's contrary instincts are to celebrate it.

NOTES

1. Tomás Eloy Martínez, *Santa Evita* (Barcelona: Seix Barral, 1995). Page references, given in parenthesis in the text, are to this edition. An earlier version of this chapter was published in *MLR* 95 (2000), 415–23.
2. See Carlos J. Alonso, 'The mourning after: García Márquez, Fuentes and the meaning of postmodernity in Spanish America', *Modern Language Notes*, 109 (1994), 252–67 (p. 253).
3. This is interestingly discussed by Raymond L. Williams, *The Postmodern Novel in Latin America: Politics, Culture and the Crisis of Truth* (Basingstoke and London: Macmillan, 1995), p. 1.

4   See Joseph A. Page's introduction to *Evita: In My Own Words*, trans. Laura Dail (Edinburgh and London: Mainstream, 1997), pp. 7–55 (p. 9).
5   See, for instance, Fredric Jameson, 'Postmodernism and consumer society' in Hal Foster (ed.), *The Anti-Aesthetic: Essays on Postmodern Culture* (Seattle WA: Bay Press, 1983), pp. 111–25.
6   For a useful discussion, see Françoise Collin, 'The Third Tiger; or, from Blanchot to Borges' in Edra Aizenberg (ed.),*Borges and His Successors: the Borgesian Impact on Literature and the Arts* (Colombia and London: University of Missouri Press, 1990), pp. 80–95 (p. 89).
7   Borges, *Ficciones* (Buenos Aires: Emecé, 1956), pp. 45–57 (p. 55).
8   William H. Katra analyses Sarmiento's treatment of history in 'Reading *Facundo* as historical novel' in Daniel Balderston (ed.), *The Historical Novel in Latin America: a Symposium*, (Gaithersburg MD: Ediciones Hispamérica, 1986), pp. 31–46 (p. 35).
9   Noé Jitrik, 'De la historia a la escritura: predominios, disimetrías, acuerdos en la novela histórica latinoamericana', in *The Historical Novel in Latin America: a Symposium*, pp. 13–29 (p. 27).
10 Navarro, *Evita*, pp. 20–21.
11 Elizabeth Bronfen identifies femininity as destabilizing principle: 'Every theory of culture is ordered around the hierarchical opposition between masculinity and femininity [. . .]. Woman is constructed as the place of mystery, of not knowing, Freud's "dark continent", as the site of silence but also of the horrifying void that "castrates" the living man's sense of wholeness and stability'. *Over Her Dead Body: Death, Femininity and the Aesthetic* (Manchester: Manchester University Press, 1992), p. 205.
12 On this dualism in Eva, see Juan José Sebreli, *Eva Perón ¿aventurera o militante?* (Buenos Aires: Pleyade, 1990), especially p. 58. See also Martínez's *El sueño argentino* (Buenos Aires: Planeta, 1999).
13 Susan Sontag, *Illness as Metaphor and Aids and its Metaphors* (London: Penguin, 1991), pp. 9, 63, 69.
14 This theme is treated from a psychoanalytical perspective in Manuel Puig's *Pubis angelical* (discussed in chapter 10).
15 Pedro Ara, her embalmer, refers to the almost superhuman endurance displayed by Evita during her dramatic 17 October speech: 'debo considerar lo que vi como un caso de inexplicable resistencia biológica y anímica; de colosal victoria de la voluntad sobre la débil naturaleza corpórea'. See *Eva Perón: la verdadera historia contada por el médico que preservó su cuerpo* (Buenos Aires: Sudamericana, 1996), p. 46.
16 Dujovne Ortiz, *Eva Perón*, p. 265
17 Sebreli, *Eva Perón ¿aventurera o militante?*, p. 107.
18 Two wax copies of Evita are buried under the names of María M. de Magaldi (p. 172) and María M. de Maestro (p. 173) while the purportedly 'real' body is buried in Milan under the name of María Maggi de Magistris (p. 329).
19 Marina Warner, *Alone of All Her Sex: the Myth and the Cult of the Virgin Mary* (London: Weidenfeld and Nicolson, 1976), p. 82.

[20] Bronfen, *Over Her Dead Body*, p. 71.
[21] Barthes, *Le plaisir du texte* (Paris: Seuil, 1973), pp. 100–1
[22] Mika Waltari (1908–79) was a Finnish writer noted for his historical novels, of which *Sinuhe, the Egyptian* (1945) was the best known.
[23] Julio Ortega, 'Postmodernism in Latin America', in Theo d'Haen and Hans Bertens (eds), *Postmodern Fiction in Europe and the Americas*, Postmodern Studies, 1 (Amsterdam: Rodopi, 1988), pp. 193–208 (p. 195).
[24] J. M. Taylor, *Evita Perón: the Myths of a Woman* (Oxford: Blackwell, 1979), p. 71.
[25] W. A. Harbinson, *Evita: Saint or Sinner?* (London: Boxtree, 1996), p. 134.
[26] Juan José Sebreli, *Eva Perón ¿aventurera o militante?*, p. 150.
[27] Page, 'Introduction' to *Eva Perón, In My Own Words*, pp. 7–55 (pp. 16–17).
[28] Llorca, Navarro and Dujovne Ortiz all work against the grain of this sentiment, believing – with varying degrees of conviction – that biographical application and skill will ensure proximity to the historical figure of Eva. Backscheider quotes Richard Westfall who had spent a lifetime studying Isaac Newton, and whose views mirror those of Martínez who has spent a lifetime studying the Peróns: 'the more I have studied him, the more Newton has receded from me'. See Paula R. Backscheider, *Reflections on Biography* (Oxford: Oxford University Press, 1999), p. 51.
[29] Bronfen, *Over Her Dead Body*, p. 255.
[30] Maria Griselda Zuffi describes *Santa Evita* as a 'biografía oral'. 'Atravesando géneros: cuerpo y violencia en *Santa Evita*' in *Romance Languages Annual*, 10 (1998), 869–73. Significantly, Martínez's original intention was to write a biography entitled *La perdida* (p. 64).
[31] Jürgen Schlaeger, 'Biography: Cult as culture' in John Batchelor (ed.), *The Art of Literary Biography* (Oxford: Clarendon, 1995), pp. 57–71 (p. 68).
[32] See Bronfen, *Over Her Dead Body*, p. 249.
[33] Ara, *Eva Perón: la verdadera historia*, p. 225.
[34] Alberto Manguel, review of *Santa Evita*, *The Independent*, 11 January 1997, p. 6.
[35] Walter Ong, *Orality and Literacy: the Technologizing of the Word*, New Accents (London and New York: Methuen, 1982), p. 81.
[36] Elizabeth Deeds Ermarth, 'The crisis of realism in postmodern time' in George Levine (ed.), *Realism and Representation: Essays on the Problem of Realism in Relation to Science, Literature and Culture* (Madison WI: University of Wisconsin Press, 1993), pp. 214–24 (p. 220).
[37] Dujovne Ortiz's procedure in this respect conforms to realist practice as described by Gillian Beer: she notes that the twin goals of realism are 'cohering and observing at once. The "other" that realism serves is assumed as prior, already *there*: out there, in there. If necessary to be made there'. 'Wave theory and the rise of literary modernism' in George Levine (ed.), *Realism and Representation*, pp. 193–213 (p. 194).

Martínez, by contrast, implies that any attempt to label Eva would be a futile and potentially endless task.

[38] Lucien Dällenbach, *The Mirror in the Text*, trans. Jeremy Whiteley with Emma Hughes (Cambridge: Polity, 1989), p. 96.

[39] Pagano's contrary instinct is to emphasize narrative clarity. See chapter 9 (pp. 247–48).

[40] Zygmunt Bauman, *Modernity and Ambivalence* (Cambridge: Polity, 1991), p. 7.

Chapter 9

Fictive Shadows of *Santa Evita*: Posse, Pagano, Frers

This chapter will consider three novelized biographies of Eva Perón and compare and contrast them with *Santa Evita*. The three are Abel Posse's *La pasión según Eva* (1995), Mabel Pagano's *Eterna* (1982) and Ernesto Frers's *Evita: la fascinante historia de Eva Perón* (1997).[1] The first parallel between them emerges in their prefaces that seek to clarify their hybrid genealogy. In his 'nota', Posse indicates that his work is primarily a novel although it contains elements of biography, testimony and documentary (p. 9). Pagano describes her work as a 'biografía novelada' (p. 7) while Frers, in his 'nota al lector', states baldly that 'este libro es una novela, una obra de ficción' (p. 7) subsuming those biographical elements – as prominent in his text as they are in the other two texts considered – within the category of fiction. All three writers indicate, albeit implicity, their New Historical credentials: 'fact' is not separated from 'fiction' but rather what passes as reality merges seamlessly with the imaginative. While Pagano observes that 'la verdad absoluta no existe' (*Eterna*, p. 7), Posse and Frers make positive claims for the non-factual: Posse (through his character, Padre Hernán Benítez) suggests that a book which is false or mistaken can be useful for interpreting the truth (*La pasión según Eva*, p. 129) while Frers notes that fiction 'es también una de las maneras de describir la realidad' (*Evita*, p. 7). This approach coincides with that of Martínez for whom 'la ficción histórica y la historia a secas se sitúan en el mismo nivel de verisimilitud'.[2]

Posse

Like many notable writers of his generation, Abel Posse has suffered from critical obsession with the literary giants, such as Borges and García Márquez, which has resulted in the neglect of what David William Foster has termed 'the other vast literary riches of Latin America'.[3] Born in Córdoba (Argentina) in 1936, a near contemporary of his better-known compatriots Manuel Puig (1932–90) and Tomás Eloy Martínez (1934–), Posse has something of the citational, episodic style of Puig and something of the New Historical approach of Martínez. Posse treats the historical figure of Eva Perón within a fictional context, as does Martínez in *Santa Evita*, though Posse concentrates on the last nine months of Eva's life, whereas Martínez's emphasis is on the fate of her corpse. But both writers examine those well-known aspects of her life that have become the stuff of both literary and historical analysis: her illegitimate provincial origins, her relationship with Perón and her political militancy. In keeping with typical New Historical practice Posse focuses in his other novels on historical characters – such as the *conquistadores*, Lope de Aguirre and Alvar Nuñez Cabeza de Vaca,[4] who, like Eva, defy historical consensus owing to their controversial or enigmatic qualities.

The story of Eva Perón lends itself to imaginative reworking partly because of its unresolved mysteries and contradictions. The texts of Posse and (as we have seen) Martínez can be described as New Historical and belong therefore to the predominant narrative mode current in Latin America.[5] Offering a vision of the past based on a combination of historical 'facts', testimonial accounts and fictional recreations, these texts repudiate any form of authoritative discourse. Their authors, who generally distrust historians, focus not on what supposedly happened but on differing, often contradictory, versions of what happened, thus contrasting sharply with the authors of the modernist period (1882–1915) who were concerned with the 'more or less faithful recreation, albeit artistically embellished, of the historical setting'.[6] By contrast with the latter, Posse describes himself as 'un coordinador de las versiones y peripecias que fueron delineando el mito' (p. 9). His text does not offer any objective assessment of the Evita myth which such an authorial role might imply but is remarkable rather for both its often carnivalesque portrait of Eva and for its poignant recreation of the last nine months of her life

– largely through her first person perspective which comprises almost half the text. Posse, the postmodernist, combines benevolence, irony and pathos in his portrait of Eva.[7] The contradictory diversity of her life and character is matched in his account by her extraordinary linguistic range which includes the clichéd and the poetic, the contritely confessional and the passionately militant.

Posse's portrait has much in common with the complex, elusive and ultimately unknowable Eva already familiar to readers of *Santa Evita*: she refuses to conform to the usual categories, being for example, more male than female both in physical appearance and in character. She rails against monetary orthodoxy, military prejudice and macho power. She is a dangerous woman, untainted by domesticity, committed to her own brand of revolutionary politics, openly scornful of male privilege. The trajectory of her life is replete with irony and paradox: the product of an unmarried couple's 'crepúsculo de amor' (p. 53) she aspires to the height of political power, arousing the most passionate feelings of love and hatred among her own people. While occupying a position at the very centre of society, she remains committed to the marginalized and excluded, 'las mujeres, los desamparados, los enfermos, los distintos' (p. 297). She scorns the oligarchy and devotes her boundless political energy to the cause of her beloved *descamisados*. Posse's text is very much in the mould of *Santa Evita* in its presentation of Eva as both saint (pp. 72, 297) and monster (p. 272), loving (p. 99) and vengeful (p. 252). She is a primitive life force who accepts 'la magia de la vida' (p. 51) but is driven by intimations of her 'destino colosal' (p. 137). She seems protected from physical disaster – the oil which burns her face has the long term effect of enhancing her appearance rather than disfiguring it (p. 66) – and also from the allure of materially advantageous liaisons which would have condemned her to a life of obscure normality, to 'una dulce eternidad, en Junín' (p. 90).

In emphasizing Eva's last nine months – when the imminence of death overshadows the remains of her life – Posse approximates to Martínez's focus on Eva's posthumous existence. To some extent Posse's characterization conforms to the postmodern fragmentation of what Eagleton terms the 'unified subject of bourgeois humanism'.[8] However, the originality of his vision can be linked, in part at least, to its stark contradictions which stand out in unfamiliar relief. Extremes merge in Posse's melodramatic

Eva: unconditional love for Perón, passionate hatred for the traitor Menéndez.[9] On the one hand she is in thrall to Perón and to popular culture (pp. 80–2) that once provided her with a lifeline, a means of escaping nothingness (p. 83). On the other hand she fails to follow the norms propounded by popular culture since she displays a strong feminist zeal. Her hostility towards men whom she manipulates ('los usó', p. 142) – despite their power as 'los dueños de la vida, del dinero, de las mujeres, de los autos' (p. 121) – is complemented by her commitment to social change, which places the militant and subversive Eva at the very centre ('corazón viviente') of Peronism (p. 330). But her seemingly dominant fanaticism and passion (pp. 276, 285) are balanced by colder sentiments, for she looks back at her life from a perspective of ironic distance: 'le parece que todo es agradable e infinitamente cómico' (p. 107).

In some respects Posse highlights Eva's dissonance and obsessiveness. Far from seeking to reconcile her contradictions in the interests of artistic control and unity (as most of her biographers have attempted to do), Posse deliberately heightens them by recourse to melodramatic and carnivalesque techniques both associated, in their different ways, with passion and excess: melodrama gives free play to polarized emotions, carnival to the free expression of often base instincts. Masiellos's description of melodrama in late nineteenth-century culture suggests an overlap with carnival: 'It plays with appearances and deceptions, it juxtaposes the superficiality of the visible world with the realm of feelings [. . .] melodrama links the crisis of modernity with the irrecuperable nature of desire and provokes an inquiry into the very limits of representation'.[10] Melodrama is prominent in the episodes describing Eva's meeting with Perón which appear to be written, at least in part, in the language of popular romance, enveloped here in an aura of gentle irony. Eva's passion contributes to the melodramatic mood which informs key elements of the story. Here Posse is offering his own variation on the theme of Eva's life as an extension of her theatrical and cinematic performances. It was the time when Eva became a woman, as if nature herself were contributing to the drama of the moment: 'era como si estuviese arrancando de su cuerpo toda la hembridad que pudiese darle [. . .]. Era como si por fin se hubiese desplegado la mujer que esperaba en ella' (pp. 169–70). The culmination of her physical beauty coincides with her meeting with Perón to provide the perfect setting for romance and the defining moment of her life. She goes on to play the part of the 'strong' woman who knows what she wants and gets it: 'ella quiso a Perón y lo tuvo desde la primera escaramuza' (p. 165). Eva's first person account heightens the aura of romance through its recourse to exaggeration: 'Sí, Silvana, hay un hombre que llamaremos sol' (p. 166). Her discovery of Perón's sublime qualities coincides with the rise of her own fanaticism: 'hay que saltar hacia lo superior fuera de todo lo cotidiano y mediocre' (p. 167). Her passionate social commitment overwhelms Perón who finds himself 'desnudo e indefenso ante las fuerzas que él había lanzado' (p. 188). But Eva's social conscience does not stand in the way of shameless extravagance. Her Dior dress is described – in the typically hyperbolic discourse of melodrama – as 'el más bello y espectacular que se vio en Buenos Aires' (p. 193). Covering up the illegitimate girl from the provinces, the dress represents an inversion of the 'natural' social order but Buenos Aires ('la abierta Babilonia', p. 173) forms an eminently suitable backdrop for ostentation, however outrageous: 'Buenos Aires era una fiesta para los que podían' (p. 116). It is indeed the perfect setting for the carnivalesque figures of Eva and Juan Perón. Their first meeting is facilitated by the volatile carnival atmosphere of 'el ir y venir del interminable festival' (p. 163) that allows Eva to cross into territory normally beyond limits and to take the place of another actress, Libertad Lamarque, at Perón's side (pp. 163–4). Eva leaves the theatre of the stage to enter the theatre of politics, to become immersed in the 'fiesta del poder' (p. 296). Sarlo sees Eva's relatively unremarkable theatrical career as a springboard for her dazzling political trajectory: 'el secreto de Eva es un desplazamiento. Su excepcionalidad es un efecto del fuera de lugar [. . .] sus cualidades, insuficientes en una escena (la artística), se volvían excepcionales en otra escena (la política)'.[11]

In some respects Perón proves to be a worthy partner. Certainly Eva's defiant, subversive character strikes a chord with Perón whose self-discipline and military rigour do not prevent him from playing games with 'los hipócritas del poder mundial' (p. 202) nor from indulging in carnivalesque laughter ('Perón reía' p. 162) which mocks propriety and accepted social standards. He variously passes off his adolescent lover, Piraña, as his niece, his daughter and his goddaughter. He can laugh too at Eva's excesses even when her uncontrolled rage is directed against military officers: far from being outraged when she flings a plate of hot chicken at Avalos, 'el comandante más importante del Ejército' (p. 74), Perón reacts with raucous laughter: 'se rió a carcajadas mientras entregaba la toalla al comandante' (p. 75). Juan Duarte, Eva's brother, is a playboy who assumes various disguises in the carnival (p. 85). But it is Eva herself who is the supreme player, who flaunts her ignorance of both social norms (p. 251) and the political arts: 'Eva trasgrede, desconoce, todos los códicos y trucos de la política moderna' (p. 298). Her relationship with the people is physical, untramelled by the usual distance and reserve: 'es un acto como sexual, y allí nace la verdadera democracia, como algo biológico y no la democracia de los doctores . . .' (p. 40). She has complete faith in her natural energy and intuition and makes no secret of her disdain for culture and learning: 'de música y de pintura entiendo tanto como de chino' (p. 284); 'no puedo dejar de pensar que la educación y las buenas maneras castran' (p. 302).

Eva subverts conventional hierarchies; the 'low' is 'high': 'El Royal, de ínfima categoría, le resultaba *royal*' (p. 132), and the 'high' is 'low': the opera is an 'insoportable barbaridad' (p. 256). Before achieving fame she turns her chastity belt against its normal purpose, using it 'no para defenderme, sino para intentar agredir un poco' (p. 123). After her marriage to Perón, she inverts normal gender roles by herself assuming the dominant role, traditionally male. Here her behaviour parallels that of her country, as viewed from the perspective of the United States: 'pasaba que el que debía bajar la cabeza estaba atacando insensatamente' (p. 207).

During her Spanish tour Eva suggests that the Escorial, 'centro de la grandeza de España, núcleo del Imperio y tumba de todos los reyes' (p. 275) be used to accommodate needy children. Far from being awestruck by the 'Caudillo por gracia de Dios' (p. 273) she is rather bemused by his resemblance to the 'pollero de Junín' (p. 272). Even the Almighty – 'un Dios de segunda, un chambón' – is not spared her ridicule. Nothing appears to escape her carnivalesque view, not even death – 'La muerte vuelve como un juergista [. . .]' (p. 305) – and from beyond the grave she casts her ironic gaze at events subsequent to her own departure from the world: 'tampoco Aramburu podría saber que sería torturado y asesinado por una banda de degenerados políticos [. . .], Juegos del Palacio, que comandan Dios o el Demonio, como en una eterna y aburrida partida' (p. 204). Eva's reference to Aramburu's assassins as a band of political degenerates is ironic since the *Montoneros*, who idolized the revolutionary Eva, were taking revenge for the kidnapping of her body. Posse's evocation here of Eva's posthumous world-weariness contradicts the *Montonero* belief that 'si Evita viviera, sería montonera'. The spirit of Eva cannot be bound within any formula, least of all a slogan, nor can she be appropriated by anyone – not even by those who kill in her name.[12] The passion of the living Eva – which erupted on her deathbed as she negotiated arms purchases to defend the regime against future coup attempts – contrasts here with the ironic detachment of the posthumous Eva. Posse appears to confirm (while Martínez in *Santa Evita* refutes) Schlaeger's dictum that 'life in biography is luxuriant, death is sterile'.[13]

Eva's language also suggests carnivalesque diversity in its startling conjunction of colloquial 'low' language and poetic 'high' language. She describes the history of Argentina, the most 'civilized' and Europeanized of all Latin American countries, as a 'historia de braguetas' (p. 115). She uses a crude phrase – now part of Evitista lore – to refer to the Spanish ambassador as 'ese gallego de mierda' (p. 254). She demeans the normal sobriety of the confessional by the frivolous consumerism of her language: 'Padre ¿por qué no me da un pase permanente, como los del tren, con disculpas para varios meses?' (p. 196). She even disrupts the connotative power of words: 'descamisado', a term of scorn and distance on the lips of the oligarchy, becomes a sign of affection and intimacy on hers.[14] She uses the polite form 'usted' not as a term of respect but as a sign of condemnation (p. 252). She resorts to the language of the street to berate her brother Juan, indifferent to the presence of Artajo, 'el refinado y multicondecorado franquista ultracatólico' (p. 276). But her disruptive colloquial style is complemented by some instances of 'high' poetic usage: thus she describes summer rain as 'lluvia de monedas blandas' (p. 30) and her arms as 'mis brazos exánimes como dos cuellos de cisne' (p. 114). She refers to Perón staying away from her because of her 'estallidos de furia como los aguaciles de campo que saben intuir la tormenta de verano' (p. 114). The poetic cadences of simile contrast with the jarring notes of paradox: '¡Hay que enseñarles que defiendan su pobre amor con mucho odio' (p. 21). Eva also uses a citational style, making reference to such diverse texts as tango verse (p. 122), *Martín Fierro* (p. 215), and the New Testament (p. 316).

The structure of the novel itself suggests carnivalesque play, being a melange of diverse textual discourses which cut across traditional generic boundaries, providing a further destabilizing element. Fictional accounts are diversified by the historical, while formal, literary and poetic registers are complemented by the informal, the colloquial and the clichéd. The text may offer the appearance of a well-rounded investigation but its 135 sections hang rather loosely together and ultimately fail to uncover the 'secret' of Eva's disappearance from public view in 1943 and her subsequent return to the public stage as champion of the oppressed. The only clue we have is that she underwent a momentous personal experience: 'el secreto de Eva fue de tal naturaleza como para hacerle perder y ganar el Paraíso a la vez' (p. 270). The priest claims that 'la verdad final sobre Eva habrá que buscarla en los archivos secretos del Vaticano' (p. 297). The main effect of all this is to reinforce Eva's undecidable quality.[15]

Abrupt transitions between narrative perspectives and temporal frames accentuate the structural fragmentation of the text; its unnumbered units reflect Eva's own sense of life as shattered, and in pieces ('jirones de mi salud', p. 113; 'jirones de mi vida', p. 235). The style is notable for its repeated use of three dots or ellipsis marks, which re-emphasize, on a microtextual level, the limits of language and the incompleteness of the narrative. Discussing the French writer Louis-Ferdinand Céline's famous 'three dots' or points of suspension, Julia Kristeva claims that they 'assert themselves as external tokens of a staccato rhythm, of syntactical and logical ellipsis'; it is as if 'the main information that these descriptions contain were hushed up'.[16] In the case of *La pasión según Eva*, Eva stops short at the unsayable extremes of enunciation. The reader is made aware of meaning and sense in suspension, particularly where Eva's feelings are concerned. Only the tip of her limitless despair (p. 232) and the tip of her limitless suffering (p. 257) can be communicated in language: the greater parts of both remain beyond its reach. The disengaged carnivalesque Eva contrasts with the passionate Eva whose mind is consumed by political fervour and whose body is consumed by the fever of disease. Her passion – her relentless determination to achieve social justice (p. 129) – becomes paramount in her life ('Eva cayó en su pasión, no la traicionó con el buen sentido ni la conveniencia', p. 152). Eva the fiery militant, annoyed that the traitor Menéndez has not been shot (p. 112), becomes aware of her distance from Perón. The passionate Eva sees virtue in revolutionary violence (p. 236). Her incomplete work (originally entitled *Mi último mensaje*) is described as a 'texto furibundo' and chapters of the book – to survive in much reduced form as *Mi voluntad suprema* – are notable for their inflammatory titles: 'el Cristo que trajo fuego' and 'Nuestro divino comunismo' (p. 130).

The most striking aspect of Posse's Eva derives, however, from his peculiar treatment of one of her most familiar aspects, her sensual nature and her heightened physicality. Posse focuses, for example, on her sense of smell (pp. 28, 64, 85–6) and her liking for perfume (pp. 253, 324, 331, 335). Her voice too is important: 'ninguna es capaz de recitar como vos' (p. 87). He somewhat idealizes her early life in order to accentuate the contrast with her ultimate fate. The force and poignancy of the text derive largely from his technique of interspersing third person testimonial accounts with the first person perspective of the dying Eva who frequently looks back with longing to the vitality of her youth. Posse portrays a girl who enjoys close affinity with the natural world – 'una chica rampante: siempre trepada en los árboles' (p. 65) – where she often remains beyond the reach of others. As a young woman she revels in the joys of nature, 'pero ¡qué alegría la de la mañana!' (p. 119). Her first theatrical success leaves her brimming with physical confidence: 'me había puesto los tacos altos y osé creerme irresistible' (p. 127). Posse makes Eva's politics part of her physicality: Perón, before his own death, recalls 'aquellos ojos brillantes y sus manos nerviosas bebiendo el conocimiento político' (p. 188). Her body was once a potent weapon (p. 147) despite being – even in health – delicate and fragile, just as her sexless body, 'un poco neutro' (p. 12), out of harmony with the ideal female figure of the time ('demasiado fino el cuerpo, y las caderas, para el gusto de la época', p. 141) and lacking the 'poder de convocatoria del de las llamadas actrices sexys' (p. 185), was still capable of arousing deep visceral and sexual attraction in her people (p. 40). If the body is, as Rosi Braidotti suggests, an 'interface, a threshold, a field of intersection of material and symbolic forces'[17] then Eva's body in pain becomes the suffering of Argentina; she and her country suffer from the same malady: 'Argentina y yo tenemos un mismo cáncer' (p. 73). Eva falls prey to what Susan Sontag calls the 'barbarian within', her physical suffering suggesting the metaphorical illnesses of her country, prey to the oligarchic forces represented by Menéndez. In both cases natural justice is being perverted. Evita is taken away before her time while the development of the Argentine body politic is thwarted by the forces of reaction. Following her operation performed by Finocchietto, people congratulate her 'como después de un parto feliz' (p. 260). The nine month period of Evita's death suggests a kind of 'demonic pregnancy'[18] which has turned Eva's own 'energía demoníaca' (p. 212) against her.

The poignancy of Posse's portrait derives in part then from this painful contrast – often filtered through Eva's own consciousness – between her past vigour and present sickness. Ironically Eva, who once seemed to exert complete control over her body, even calling it into existence ('se me antojó tenerlo de una buena vez y lo tuve. Lo parí', p. 123) but who, as a 'ser impoluto' also felt 'ajena a mi propio cuerpo' (p. 142), becomes the prisoner of a body which is rapidly degenerating. Her tragedy is all the greater because of the grotesque contrast between the boundless physical glow and energy she previously possessed (and which once showed up the 'catolicismo anticorporal' of Franco's wife, p. 272) and her present situation of helpless immobility which fills her with nostalgia for her previous self ('¡Qué fuerte eras Eva, qué inconscientemente fuerte!', p. 50). Posse's text portrays the corporeal, dying Eva with peculiar force: it probes the limits of that singular physicality which Eva exuded throughout her life and which permeated her speeches and even her writing.[19]

Eva's passionate desire to eliminate social injustice was fundamentally a physical urge, as she herself acknowledges in her autobiography: 'nunca pude pensar, desde entonces, en esa injusticia sin indignarme, y pensar en ella me produjo siempre una rara sensación de asfixia, como si no pudiendo remediar el mal que yo veía me faltase el aire necesario para respirar'.[20] It is the pain of this intensely physical Eva which Posse highlights. Her identity is bound to her diseased body that only shortly before was healthy and energetic. Eva's healthy body connoted desire – 'era el cuerpo para el deseo, para el temblor del deseo' (p. 14) – whereas her actual body represents decay since it is being eaten from the inside (p. 319). Posse presents Eva's femininity as originating in a kind of forced physical birth: 'era como si estuviese arrancando de su cuerpo toda la hembridad que pudiese darle'

(p. 169). Her death is also marked by a physical violence emanating from inside her body and it is a physical disintegration that she suffers: 'aunque deje en el camino jirones de vida' (p. 235). The first page of the text focuses on the concrete circumstances which attend the process of dying: the solitude ('no queda nadie'), the medicines which replace the perfumes and the carnivalesque oxygen tubes, like 'dos palurdos provincianos invitados a una fiesta médica de punta en blanco' (p. 11) which precede the priest. Thereafter her pain becomes an almost palpable presence conveyed by the image of fire (pp. 15, 30) and the repeated references to her 'alfilerazos' (pp. 36, 39) defined as 'las punzadas del mal' (p. 36). Her suffering is described in terms of a dead weight which no amount of rest can remove: 'los brazos y las piernas como rellenos de plomo, llenos de cansancio puro' (p. 257). Her mind is tortured by her heightened awareness of time ever diminishing and of life closing down. She sees her old healthy self as other – 'creo que te estoy viendo' (p. 51) – and seeks to isolate her present diminished self by separating it from her identity as Eva and consigning it to her 'illegitimate' other – 'ese bicho angurriento que quiere renacer del pasado de no ser y me quiere poseer y devorar' (p. 259). Eva's experience corresponds to the human reaction to pain described in a different context by Elaine Scarry: 'even though it occurs within oneself, it is at once identified as "not oneself", "not me", as something so alien that it must right now be gotten rid of'.[21] Even her will, as colossal as her destiny, is incapable of prevailing against such invasion. As she is consumed from the inside, her body becomes grotesque for what ought to be inside and hidden becomes outside and exposed: 'pero me miro de frente, por donde estaba el busto, y busco algo que me alarmó el otro día [. . .]: que se me ve la blancura del hueso del esternón' (p. 259). Her hope that 'habíamos extirpado a la otra' (p. 261) proves groundless: 'la Ibarguren existe' (p. 309) and lives as a kind of parasite inside her. Eva's body is grotesque since it is no longer an organic whole: the disintegrating body signals descent into meaninglessness since the body no longer serves as a point of self-reference.[22]

'Debe de oírme hablar. Debe de oír en la noche los quejidos que lanzo dormida ante las punzadas de su maldad' (p. 309). She is being eaten by 'la Ibarguren' at the rate of a kilo per month (p. 311). The abject horror of Eva's suffering emerges in her discovery that cancer cells derive their name from their crab-like form: 'en algunos casos, cuando el cangrejo se dispone a comer hueso, se provee, según la enciclopedia, de verdaderas mandíbulas. El horrorizado paciente puede escuchar en la noche ese casi imperceptible roer de rata devorando alguno de sus huesos' (p. 310). She has fifty days left to live, her lips have disappeared, and she has lost her voice but she attends Perón's second presidential inauguration. Too weak to stand up in the car unaided, she is strapped to the vehicle to ensure that she remains upright, her 'corseted' body deprived of its freedom and independence if not entirely of its demonic energy. Her physical union with the crowd, which once had sexual undercurrents, remains just as strong, but is now overshadowed by their collective feline presentiment of her imminent death. She herself experiences a kind of 'becoming-cat' at the point of death, craving to be 'sola y quieta en un rincón oscuro para morir' (p. 332). Posse uses vivid animal imagery to heighten the sense of the natural world turned upside down: Eva, once a graceful cat-like creature, is being eaten by evil cells that attack like rats (p. 109). Her once sharp feline eyes are reduced to immobility: 'era como un ojo de pájaro, inmóvil y atento, pero como de cristal' (p. 307). Her death is ongoing ('ésta es mi muerte, el trámite de mi famosa muerte', p. 333) and assumes a kind of obscenity since it is turned into a public spectacle: the privacy she craves is denied her for she cannot escape 'la impudicia de esta muerte tan llorada' (p. 336). The felt experience of physical pain produces, according to Scarry, 'an almost obscene conflation of private and public [. . .]. Artistic objectifications of pain often concentrate on this combination of isolation and exposure'.[23] Eva's experience highlights this paradoxical situation since the intensity of her private suffering cannot be communicated to a world which is receding from her, although its fascination with her increases with her approaching death.

That the process of dying should occupy nine months is no coincidence. According to Margaret Miles 'the most concentrated sense of the grotesque' is specifically associated with woman because of her connections with sex and birth seen as 'quintessentially grotesque'. The pregnant body was especially significant in this respect: in Christian art, hell was often represented as a womb, a 'lurid and rotting uterus'. Eva is grotesque on account of her femininity, her metaphorical pregnancy (her gestation will culminate in death rather than life) and her disease represented by her rotting uterus.[24] She is a notable representative of the monstruous feminine: Carmen Franco, daughter of the Spanish dictator, spied on Eva 'como a un monstruo' (p. 272). Her monstrosity is as multifaceted as her character: on the literal plane she represents the suppressed other, the 'supuesta barbarie de Facundo' (p. 225). She finds a mirror image in the people – 'aquel monstruo múltiple' (p. 43) – with whom she maintains a relationship of obscene carnality marked by a 'pacto de sangre', a 'democracia en carne viva' (pp. 40–1). She is dangerous since she is volatile (p. 13) and frequently loses self-control, as when a communist delegation insults Perón (pp. 204–5). She cannot control her voice (p. 113) which once had a cutting edge suggesting the power to castrate: 'Renzi intenta una frase entusiasta al verla levantada. Eva lo corta con su voz seca [. . .]' (p. 18).

Eva is also a figure of abjection. For Kristeva abjection is 'what does not respect borders, positions, rules', that which 'disturbs identity, system, order'.[25] As Creed affirms, the abject is placed on the side of the feminine, in opposition to the paternal symbolic which is governed by rules and laws. To enter the symbolic order the subject 'must reject or repress all forms of behaviour, speech and modes of being regarded as unacceptable, improper or unclean'.[26] It is significant that Perón represents military order, Eva feminine disorder: 'Cuando Eva se fue a vivir con Perón todavía apretaba el dentífrico de arriba y dejaba las horquillas olvidadas o pegoteadas en la jabonera. Perón soportó esas cosas y muchas más de las que suelen corresponder a la ancestral e irritante torpeza femenina' (p. 185). Perón never rebels against the 'superego' of the army (p. 163). Eva, on the other hand, is part of that 'conglomerado de huérfanos a la búsqueda del padre' to which Perón refers with disdain (p. 163).[27] She incarnates the abject since the territories she inhabits are borderlands: she is born in Los Toldos, 'pueblo de la frontera' (p. 56), the final issue of an illicit union on the verge of dissolution. Living 'al borde de la vida' (p. 216) she seems to be preoccupied with rites of passage, the end of childhood and the beginning of adolescence recollected at another frontier, that separating life and death. It is her position on the border which allows her to be both vilified as whore and adored as saint. Her paradoxical status ('paradójicamente, protagonista y marginal', p. 37) itself repudiates reason and logic, paradox being – as Watzlawick argues – the point at which 'the seemingly all-embracing divison of reality into pairs of opposites [. . .] breaks down and reveals itself as inadequate'.[28] Eva's border position implies impurity and defilement. Her diseased body will soon be a corpse, the final stage of abjection, the most sickening of wastes, a 'border that has encroached upon everything. It is no longer I who expel. "I" is expelled'.[29]

Posse's treatment of time is informed by permeable borders. The most important event in Eva's life is her meeting with Perón, her prior existence being termed 'aquel ««antes de Perón»»' (p. 179). During this stage of her life, time is not significant: she is immersed in youthful living, which is carefree and seemingly timeless. Perón represents the intrusion of the symbolic order which is a temporal order. Ricoeur points out that while all fictional narratives are 'tales of time', few are tales about time 'in as much as in them it is the very experience of time that is at stake'.[30]

Eva's experience of time is an intrinsic part of her suffering. Within the nine month period of her death she endures the extremes of 'subjective' time – both the slow time of pain and fast clock time, for her a countdown to death. Sometimes Eva's internal time collides with 'cosmic' time: 'Ahora quedan sólo 272 días. Aunque el tiempo quedó detenido estos días de recordación, de revivencia, de nostalgia. Pero ahora se trata de días. ¡Nada más que 272 días!' (p. 229). Bakhtin notes that just as 'time thickens [. . .] takes on flesh, becomes visible' so space 'becomes charged and responsive'.[31] During Eva's final public appearance, space and time converge: 'Callao, como un río elegante' (p. 324), 'Córdoba, el otro ancho río que sube desde las dársenas' (p. 325). Buenos Aires itself becomes charged with memories of beginnings: Francia Square reminds Eva of her arrival in the city as an adolescent. The city is also charged with intimations of the future as the crowds sense her approaching death with sorrow while the houses of the aristocracy exude an air of eager anticipation. Temporal boundaries become blurred as Eva's perspective embraces the past and the future (p. 327). The body of the dying Eva returns to its origins – 'es como un retroceso a la infancia [. . .] el cuerpo busca la línea de la adolescencia' (pp. 12–13). Her embalmment will spare her the ultimate abjection of her father's corpse (p. 34), preserving her indefinitely at the border between life and death.

The epilogue reveals that even death does not bring an end to her suffering: following its embalming, her body is kidnapped, abused and denied a resting place until reunited with Perón in 1972 (p. 346). By concentrating on the physical reality of Eva's suffering, Posse is able to transcend the sentimentalism which otherwise might have enveloped his story. Eva fails to beat her physical enemy which merges in her mind with her political enemy: 'el cáncer de la oligarquía en armas' (p. 312). But her failure is magnificent and serves to illustrate anew the eternal truth of those clichéd homages to the power of the human spirit and its capacity to prevail against overriding odds. Writing as 'objective' historian, Sebreli interprets Eva's presence at Perón's second presidential inauguration as 'una imagen de coraje físico poco común'.[32] Posse the artist conveys the full poignancy of the occasion through the first-person narrative of Eva whose decline is marked by the loss of her most potent political weapon, her voice, which had in a sense constituted her entire being: 'soy sólo mi voz. Políticamente, digo . . .' (p. 145). Her voice was indispensable to Eva as radio actress and later as politician when it became the principal conductor of her personal appeal and power. Her physical frailty is compensated by her voice: Perón describes her as a 'joven de aspecto frágil, pero de voz resuelta [. . .] estaba subyugado por el valor de su voz' (p. 164). Eva hones this natural asset to maximum effect: 'adquirió una técnica expresiva, que sería su principal arma política' (p. 190). Her voice is the source of her power and appeal. Its natural inclination is towards the monologic – 'Eva seguía monologando sobre la política casi con furia' (p. 131) – but it resonates dialogically in the presence of the people, resuscitating that collective voice which had lain silent for centuries, as Eva herself remarks (p. 62). When Eva is nominated for the vice-presidency she enters into an 'insólito diálogo' with the crowd: her voice, normally powerful and dominant, is quelled by the voice of the crowd which finds 'una voz única, precisa, misteriosamente exacta para hacer llegar su voluntad' (p. 42). Demoted from his usual lead role, Perón forces Eva to meet that clear collective voice with non-committal equivocations: 'Decí que sí, sin decir sí' (p. 43). Her strength and passion, represented by the clarity and force of her voice, are contaminated by the interference of his insidious whispering. The loss of her voice marks her final defeat: 'hoy no tengo voz [. . .]. Y yo sin voz, francamente . . .' (p. 322).[33]

Secrecy complements passion as a further key to Eva's life since it marks the passage from one identity to another: the actress has to hide the shame of her illegitimate birth; the president's wife has to cover up the actress. The third Eva, the militant 'compañera', devoted to direct political action and at odds with what she perceives as Perón's fatalism and passivity, has to cover up her previous role as subservient wife – as well as the identity of the German general involved in Eva's plan to provide Peronists with weapons with which to defend themselves ('el general no se puede nombrar', p. 29). Eva's penultimate identity as corpse will be 'covered up' by her embalmer, Dr Ara, who transforms the disease-ridden body into an aesthetic object removed from the ravages of time. Her greatest secret (her 'supuesto secreto supremo', p. 180) will never be disclosed: 'escapará a la búsqueda de los historiadores' (p. 182). The epilogue is set in eternal time: 'Ahora tengo una eternidad para mi sonrisa' (p. 346). Here Eva assumes her final identity as immortal other. She is not concerned, however, with the 'high' eternal, as one might expect, but rather with the 'low' temporal as she reviews the nomadic trajectory of her own corpse. Her final reference to the link between her grandfather Diógenes and Perón – they used the same tobacco – suggests the cyclical structure of eternal mythic time.

Bronfen notes that death and femininity are the two most consistent enigmas and tropes in Western culture.[34] Evita represents both: she is a supreme representative of the enigma of woman, a contradictory figure who defies comprehension: her lack ('tenía muy poco cuerpo', p. 136) is at odds with her sexual appeal. She is deeply suspicious of men but finds fulfilment in apparent submission to one man – but then shows that she is more than a mere receptacle for Perón's ideas (p. 188) by initiating Peronist resistance. She embodies the familiar clichés of femininity: she suffers from hysteria (p. 212), she is a monster (p. 272), she is a fanatic (p. 316). Her life can only find expression in paradox: 'la irracional razón de mi vida' (p. 124). But beyond the shimmering surfaces of Posse's Eva lies another paradox: this insubstantial and elusive figure finally leaves a lasting impression upon the reader – of lightness, frivolity and play on the one hand but also of human pain and the intricate relations between human blindness and insight on the other.

Posse gives Eva the last word: her final utterance comes from beyond the grave. She bows out in the guise of immortal other whose spirit has survived death. A final crossing is suggested at the textual level: we move from a narrative that had given the appearance at least of historical veracity – through its appeal to multiple witnesses – to a supplement removed from the real and swathed in the aura of the supernatural.

Posse's treatment of the dying Eva is both poignant and shocking: the portrayal of youthful vigour extinguished by terminal illness is disturbing despite the occasional lapse into sentimentality ('¡Qué fuerte eras Eva, qué inconscientemente fuerte!', p. 50). In some respects Posse's portrait of a complex and elusive Eva is comparable to Martínez's, as we have seen, but there are also important differences between them. What is striking about Posse's portrayal of the dying Eva is his enhanced omniscience: she is the subject of curiosity and he is engaged in the familiar male project of knowing. Bronfen notes that death and femininity 'are used to represent that which is inexpressible, inscrutable, unmanageable, horrible [...] they *must* not be solved, must be left open, undecided, indeterminate, marking a limit a system sets itself'.[35] Posse's impulse is to uncover and reveal: the testimonies he presents are marked by their complementarity (rather than by their dissonance): they echo each other (and often Eva's own words) by highlighting the landmarks of her story: 'el encuentro decisivo de Perón y Eva fue realmente en aquel caluroso 22 de enero en el Luna Park [...]' (p. 160); 'a mí me parece bien que se destaque el encuentro en el Luna Park. Fue decisivo, para ella más que para él' (p. 168); 'Yo le puedo decir que en aquel enero de 1944, cuando conoció a Perón, estaba en su apogeo' (p. 170); 'me sentí en mi apogeo' (p. 193). Posse's loosely structured account is buttressed by geographical mooring points such as the fulsome portrait of Buenos Aires as 'la séptima potencia económico-financiero del mundo' (p. 117). The *nota del editor* that appears as a footnote, giving details of the arms obtained by Eva and of their ultimate destiny (p. 151), serves a traditional documentary rather than a parodic purpose, i.e. to provide additional information in support of the point made in the main text. In this respect, Posse's procedure contrasts with that of Martínez who consistently flaunts the unreliability of his sources. Hutcheon remarks that although the 'validity of the entire concept of objective and unproblematic documentation in the writing of history has been called into question, even today paratextuality remains the central mode of textually certifying historical events, and the footnote is still the main textual form by which this believability is procured'.[36]

Posse emphasizes the dissonant aspects of Eva and the principle of dissonance extends to his own narrative with its range of heterogenous discourses. But beyond these postmodern features, Posse is keen to preserve at least a semblance of narratorial authority and in this instance his conservative mode of writing distances itself from postmodern indeterminacy: his invocation of testimonial witnesses serves the traditional purpose of verification, rather than of calling into question the concept of ultimate truth: 'lo que contó Marcos Zucker es exacto, yo y todos quienes la tratamos en esa época podemos asegurárselo' (p. 139). Such assurances often precede 'hotspots' of turgid factuality in the narrative, reinforcing the impression of realist intentions: 'al principio pagaba el espacio de los Muebles Camba, después se retiraron y es cuando quedó debiéndole esos setenta pesos a Zuker. Un apoyo importante y permanente fue el de la firma Guereño, con el Jabón Radical, cuya publicidad ella realizó' (p. 140). Far from being a problematic concept, truth is almost taken for granted – as when Eva is said to assume her 'verdadera personalidad' when she met Perón (p. 143). Apart from the references of one of the military officers who overthrew Perón in 1955 (pp. 226–7) to Eva's 'cortas capacidades' (p. 228) and to the Peróns as 'dos resentidos' (p. 229), as well as the priest's description of the pair as 'dos reyes en alpargatas' (p. 245), Posse's testimonial accounts are remarkable for their homogeneity and positive, often idealizing perspective: 'La Fundación fue el gran instrumento operativo de Eva y concentró todo el espíritu de acción social del justicialismo' (p. 294). The main thrust of the narrative is to describe and define knowledge rather than to linger – as Martínez does – at its limits. The opening episode is significant in communicating an image of furtive male control since the 'aromáticos mejunjes de la belleza femenina' have been replaced by the (male) appurtenances of medicine: 'con el sigilio con que el libertino desliza en la casa un par de prostitutas' (p. 11). Eva, herself regarded as a prostitute by her enemies, becomes the object of relentless male scrutiny which probes not only her suffering but the memories stirred by the antibiotics and the tranquilizers she has taken (p. 104). While Martínez's narrative displays the textual 'wounds' of imperfect knowledge and inadequate language, Posse's testimonial accounts flaunt their authority and acknowledge no limits in their probing of life at the edge of death. Here Posse falls short of one critical accolade which dubs him the 'apostle of postmodern thought'.[37]

For María José Punte *La pasión según Eva* can be compared on equal terms with *Santa Evita*. But her claim that Posse's text is 'un intento de llegar a una verdad más profunda ante la insuficiencia de la Historia'[38] would hardly apply to Martínez's work which is conspicuous in its lack of such pretensions. Both writers, according to Punte, 'presentan el material de manera similar' (p. 125) by juxtaposing conflicting testimonies and surveying films and photographs of their subject. Both present an Eva who is fraught with contradictions. They also focus on the representations of Eva, the Eva of opera and film, directed at a younger generation who did not know Eva: 'estas reflexiones surgen al finalizar ambas novelas, porque en las dos subyace la misma pasión' (p. 127). Punte fails to account for the important differences between these texts: Posse's Eva may be fraught with contradictions but the testimonial accounts provide beacons of reliability and reassurance, elements conspicuously missing in *Santa Evita*. Moreover Posse, unlike Martínez, does not highlight – and relativize – the range of sources, written as well as oral, that provide imperfect traces of the past: legal documents, newspaper reports, artistic representations. Neither does Posse explore, as Martínez does, the mechanics of writing and representation. He is not concerned with the problematic aspects of recollecting and recording the past nor with the (un)reliablility of his sources – indeed he emphasizes their veracity.

Pagano

In some respects Posse's *La pasión según Eva* has more in common with two much lesser works, Mabel Pagano's *Eterna* and Ernesto Frers's *Evita*. Each of these texts consists of a series of short, unnumbered episodes written from different viewpoints but all dominated by the perspective of Eva herself. It is the vision and technique of *Eterna* which contrast most sharply with *Santa Evita*'s postmodern features. Pagano declares in her introduction that having overcome her initial hesitation, she decided to follow Eva's example in writing her book, 'dándole a las circunstancias el impulso de mis sentimientos' (p. 7). In this same introduction she uses the image of glass to convey her conception of truth which, so she believes, took the form at the beginning of time of 'una inmensa bola de cristal' (p. 7) but subsequently shattered into a multitude of fragments. Significantly the one book-length critical work devoted to Pagano's *Eterna* is entitled *Eva Perón en el cristal de la escritura* and its author, Mirta Corpas Vargas, emphasizes the unblemished limpidity of the text: 'como a través de un cristal, la escritura de Mabel Pagano deja ver el concepto detrás de la materialidad del objeto'.[39]

Images of clarity and understanding – often associated with the removal of a veil – pervade Pagano's 'biografía novelada'. Recalling the death of her father, Eva remarks: 'fue como si alguien descorriera un velo delante de mis ojos' (p. 17). Eva subsequently uses the same image to describe the effect upon her of Perón's clarification of his concept of the 'third position': 'me pareció como si un telón se hubiera descorrido delante de mis ojos' (p. 50). She uses similar imagery to express a surge of clarity: 'es como si una potente luz estuviera iluminando la vida que he dejado atrás' (p. 43). Perón himself is clearly an important source of illumination – not in this instance a god who moves in the shade but rather one who consigns everything other than himself to it: 'lo demás no tenía importancia, porque la luz de él lo taparía todo' (p. 95). Pagano's emphasis on clarity and understanding recalls, by contrast, Martínez's attraction to the 'espacios inexplicados' of history (p. 390) since it posits perfect understanding and univocal truth: 'toda esa gente [. . .] ya formaban de hecho lo que reflejaba la única verdad: el Partido Peronista' (p. 123).

Pagano seeks to eliminate all trace of discord and dissonance in the ranks of Peronism: 'los pañuelos agitados hacia ella, se alzaban en las manos. Y su nombre surgía de todas las bocas' (p. 15); '¿cómo no integrarme a esa comunión increíble y perfecta con miles y miles de personas?' (p. 21). Collective harmony is complemented by equally unproblematical marital intimacy, as emerges in Eva's reminiscences: 'me contabas todo y repetías siempre que yo era la única persona a la que confiabas totalmente' (p. 179). Just as *patria* and *pueblo* are for ever inseparable (p. 209) so Perón and Eva are eternally united (p. 268). Perón has no reason to mourn since 'ella tenía ya otra existencia asegurada' (p. 252), the last flame of her life sparking the fire of her immortality: 'Eva aferró la última chispa de vida que le quedaba y encendió la hoguera de su eternidad' (p. 281).

This is, indeed, a text that admits of no flaws in Eva and few in Perón. Though Perón's neglect of her is sometimes suggested (when he returns so late that Eva is already asleep, p. 201), it is his positive influence that predominates. It was he who changed Eva's life (pp. 44, 113) and although she claims on one occasion that 'yo elegí ser Evita' (p. 43) she subsequently acknowledges Perón's quasi-divine influence on her life: 'soy tu obra, Juan' (p. 166). Pagano eliminates all notions of a cold and frigid Perón who kept his distance from his dying wife: 'la abrazó y la besó con fuerza, abandonándose al llanto que había estado ahogándolo desde el momento de llegar' (p. 270). Eva's notorious complexity and elusiveness are covered up by a reductive, idealizing process that diminishes rather than elevates. Even as an adolescent Eva is politically aware (p. 23) and her absences from school can be attributed to her extreme sensitivity and her preference for reading at home (Llorca's equally tenacious attempts to whitewash the young miscreant come to mind). The familiar image of Eva as a headstrong young actress with little respect for her elders and noted for her indiscipline, particularly her lack of punctuality, is unrecognizable in Pagano's portrait of Eva: 'era la primera en llegar a los ensayos y aceptaba sin discutir todas las indicaciones que le hacían sobre el escenario' (p. 27). Her marriage, overshadowed according to Martínez by the wholesale falsification of the fundamental 'facts' relating to names and dates, is characterized by Pagano as 'un acto fundamental' (p. 94), the logical sequel to Eva's meeting with Perón, seen by Eva as the defining moment of her life. Much of the credit for the achievement of female suffrage is attributed to Eva (pp. 114, 121, 154); and some of the negative aspects of her European tour, for example her disappointment at receiving a mere rosary from the pope (p. 137) and her hostile reception in Switzerland (p. 147) are simply overlooked. Pagano offers glimpses of the revolutionary Eva and her appeal to those rebels who burst on to the national scene 'poniendo una cara a la otra realidad del país, a ésa que a partir de entonces ya no sería posible soslayar' (p. 90); of the raw Eva who confronts the striking railway workers: 'largué puteadas a medio mundo' (pp. 232–3); of the unforgiving and vengeful Eva ('hay cosas que no pueden perdonarse y yo soy de rencores largos', p. 102); of the inconstant Eva who repeatedly acknowledges her affection for the loyal Mercante ('me tranquiliza saber que Mercante, que es un hombre leal, está de cerca de vos [. . .]',

p. 128) only to turn rather abruptly against him because of his
long-standing and perfectly legitimate ambition to succeed Perón
(p. 237). But Pagano's text is remarkable not for its probing of
conflict or contradiction but rather for its idealizing, non-ironic
discourse which purportedly reflects an unproblematic world in
which the presidential couple represent beacons of peace and
security. Eva's declaration of faith in the family and total confidence
in woman (p. 153), despite her own lack of normal family
life and her ambivalence towards feminist ideas, is apparently free
of any ironic edge. Pagano's text is studiously unambivalent in its
celebration of power, authority and stability: it refuses play and is
largely devoid of levity. A rare example of humour – at the
expense of Perón's antagonist, the US ambassador Spruille Bradon,
who after a stormy meeting with Perón, left his hat behind in
his haste to depart – is soon stifled by a rather too earnest Eva: 'yo
también me reí mucho con el episodio, pero como siempre fui
consecuente con mis ideas [. . .]' (p. 56). Given Pagano's lack of
narrative self-consciousness, it is unsurprising that the relatively
few citations in her text do not generate ironic distance (as do
citations in *Santa Evita*) but form an almost seamless continuity
with the main text because there is no obvious 'warping' of the
citation by its context. Thus Delia Parodi's extravagant eulogy of
Perón synchronizes perfectly with the tone of the narrative:

> mientras las palabras de la diputada resonaban en el cuarto, una
> mano de Evita se apoyó suavemente sobre el pecho de él.
>
> 'Si pudiéramos elegir algo de Perón como destinatorio especial de
> nuestro homenaje, elegiríamos su corazón porque el corazón de
> los hombres se mide por el amor y el de él tiene una medida
> incomparable, ya que ha sabido reunir en una sola cita
> extraordinaria, el amor de Evita y el amor de su pueblo'.
> (p. 24)

Similarly, Perón's letter to Eva following his imprisonment consists
of clichéd and sentimental language but the context contrives
to exclude any ironic undercutting: the language of the
letter is of a piece with the language of Eva whose perspective
dominates the narrative:

> subí conteniendo la respiración. Era una carta del Coronel.
>
> 'Mi tesoro adorado: sólo cuando nos alejamos de las personas
> queridas podemos medir el cariño. Desde el día en que te dejé allí,

con el dolor más grande que puedas imaginar, no he conseguido tranquilizar mi triste corazón [...]'. Tendida en la cama, lloré hasta agotarme. (p. 79)

Such extravagant and unctuous sentimentality is unrelieved by any countervailing mode of narrative. Pagano's text is grounded on a single discourse – that of idealization and sentimentality – and makes no attempt to step outside it. She may not be interested in linguistic play or in the 'staging' of diverse discourses in the manner of *Santa Evita*, but her language does not remain invisible as a mere tool of communication, because its saccharine excess inevitably obtrudes. Muecke sees the 'habit of irony' as a 'corrosive and paralyzing disease of the spirit' but points also to 'dangers in earnestness, in not having a sense of irony'.[40] He does not specify the danger that he has in mind but it relates to the slipperiness of language itself which excludes univocal and stable meaning. It is the text's 'unsaid' which challenges its 'said' and it is what Green identifies as structural irony that insinuates itself into Pagano's work to challenge and undermine it: structural irony 'involves an external comparison between a detail of a work and another work altogether – by the same author or another author.[41] Pagano's idealization of one woman, Eva, together with her idealization of the love experience itself, are reminiscent of the central features of courtly literature; but Pagano is writing not in the context of medieval romance but rather of contemporary postmodernism, and to many postmodernists irony is, according to Kathleen Higgins, 'the only legitimate stance of discourse'.[42] Though she clings to a seemingly innocent and pure discourse, whose reflective qualities are purportedly as flawless as those of a clear glass, the postmodern context of her writing, peculiarly sensitive to the pervasiveness of ideology, exposes the innocence as naivety and the extravagant protestations of love as clichéd sentimentalism. While Martínez alternates between 'packaged' images of Eva and flaunts his own artifice, Pagano attempts to reflect directly the uniqueness of a self-consistent subject while seeking to conceal her own artistic procedures.

Having committed herself to one specific discourse, Pagano cannot break out of its turgid and formulaic patterns. Her earnestness has produced an image of Eva that undermines itself from within through repetition, redundancy and overstatement. Having fixed her gaze on what she saw as the semi-divine aspect of

Eva, she succeeds only in burying her heroine beneath the stale accretions of cliché and sentimentality. Corpas Vargas makes the extraordinary claim that 'la disposición textual de la totalidad de la novela de Mabel Pagano permite que la escritura se convierta en un escenario de la palabra'.[43] Language does achieve prominence in *Eterna* but not as in *Santa Evita* through its distanced, carnivalesque diversity, but rather because of its univocal flatness, its unreflecting exaggeration of a single aspect of Eva and its dependence on the clichés of romantic discourse. Even the title, *Eterna*, with its biblical and lapidary qualities, connotes pretensions to absolute truth whereas Martínez's title, *Santa Evita*, resonates with ambivalence. Corpas Vargas further claims that 'el personaje de ficción creado por Mabel Pagano es el que capta con mayor precisión, la innata complejidad de la Evita de la Historia' (p. 68). The reverse is true: Pagano's one-dimensional and idealized Eva is ironized by the dissonant and elusive Evas constructed by the ever-proliferating historical and artistic representations of her.

Frers

Ernesto Frers is a journalist whose literary output appears to have attracted even less critical attention than Mabel Pagano's. In some respects he is reminiscent of Posse: they coincide in their portrayal of a volatile Eva whose communion with the crowd is sexual (Posse, p. 40; Frers, p. 122). Both recycle the myths of Eva: her vengeful treatment of Lamarque (Posse, p. 196; Frers, p. 59), her supreme power (Posse, p. 266; Frers, p. 130) and her unabashed militancy (Posse, p. 154; Frers, p. 185). In some respects his work recalls Pagano's impulse to uncover a truth which is ultimately transparent and univocal. His prologue reveals a secret, that Eva's body is buried in Milan. His opening is about uncovering, bringing to light, verifying: 'Quiten la tapa [...] Debemos cerciorarnos' (p. 12). The wooden casing of Eva's coffin is removed to reveal another coffin: 'el segundo ataúd tenía en su parte superior una ventana de cristal, que permitía ver el rostro intacto del cadaver. Si quiere comprobar, señor [...]' (p. 12). In the lamp light the captain 'reconoció los rasgos conspicuos [...] la línea inconfundible de la boca. Es ella – musitó [...]', (p. 12). The imagery foregrounded in the prologue prefigures Frers's narrative approach, characterized by the impulse to dispel uncertainty and to confer clear meaning. He is a purveyor of facts rather than a presenter of multiple versions; he seeks to fix a stable identity rather than to explore a dynamic and elusive self; he is more comfortable with carefully calibrated linearity than with chronological dislocation. Unity and harmony prevail over dissonance and contradiction.

The first section begins with a childhood episode: Eva's brother, Juan, makes a gift of three silkworms to Eva. This is an invented version of events but is presented as factual, having little to offer beyond its literal reference. While his objective in this instance is clearly not to present 'what really happened', the effect achieved is similar: silkworms are merely silkworms just as the flies which later confront Eva when she visits the slum are merely flies: they do not project the symbolic resonance which insects (flies, butterflies, bees) have in Martínez's fictions. Frers's chronological account continues with the family's move to Junín and then Eva's departure for Buenos Aires. The precise role played by Agustín Magaldi in Eva's abandonment of uneventful provincial life for the dangerous uncertainties of Buenos Aires has been a source of conflict among historians and biographers but such muddle will not spoil the continuity of Frers's narrative which finds firm anchorage in the sociological facts of 1935 Buenos Aires (pp. 29–30) while avoiding obvious areas of contention, in this instance the circumstances of Eva's arrival there.

Frers avoids the blatant idealizations of Pagano (the views of anti-Peronists are represented, pp. 162–3) but none the less, the negative aspects of Eva's visit to Europe and the imprisonment of union leader Cipriano Reyes receive only perfunctory mention, whereas the positive impact of Peronist policies is emphasized: 'en menos de un año de gobierno, Perón había llevado adelante con firmeza sus promesas electorales' (p. 140). Frers's emphatic omniscience dominates his portrait of Eva: in contrast with Martínez who despairs of narratorial mastery, Frers seems to know how Eva's mind works and can explain, for example, her feelings of unease as her childhood ambitions to be an actress are realized (p. 48). Matter-of-fact statements point to the realist thrust of a narrative which purports to reflect reality just as it was: 'aquella mañana, antes de mediodía, el coronel estaba en su despacho, sopesando la situación [. . .]' (p. 65). Repeated references to time provide the underpinnings of coherence and chronological order: 'a mediados de 1944' (p. 72); 'el 6 de agosto de 1945' (p. 81). The geographical setting is described in realist detail: las dos calles más elegantes de Buenos Aires – Florida y Santa Fe – nacen en un ángulo casi recto en la hermosa y aristocrática plaza San Martín' (p. 94). As Philippe Hamon points out: 'historical and geographical proper names [...] function somewhat like quotations in scholarly discourse: they guarantee mooring points' and also couple the text to a validated extra-text [...]'.[44]

The 'reality-effect' of Frers's text is in fact further buttressed by citations from a variety of newspapers including the *New York Herald Tribune* and *New York Times*: these serve as sources of authority (rather than as representations of distinct discursive formations contributing to the play of language as in *Santa Evita*). One of the main features of Frers's text is its excessive urge to clarify which leads to repetition and redundancy as in the description of the significance of 17 October (pp. 114 and 184). Sometimes his style displays archaic or florid qualities that complement his staid and one-dimensional narrative procedure: 'en los albores de la década de los cuarenta [...]' (p. 40); 'diez mil muertos, doce mil heridos, e incalculables pérdidas materiales eran el saldo de aquella revulsión nocturna de la Tierra' (p. 55). His style often assumes a distendida elasticity to cope with his obsessive urge to communicate more and more information: 'aquel hombre maduro, atractivo, que actuaba con seguridad natural y estaba lleno de ambiciosos planes para el futuro, era la combinación ideal de amante, padre y maestro que la muchacha de Los Toldos había esperado desde siempre' (p. 64). It is no coincidence that character portraits have a distinctly visual, film-like quality suggesting the scrutiny of the all-seeing narratorial gaze: 'El general Farrell apoyó las delgadas y oscuras manos en el borde de la mesa de caoba [...] En el otro extremo de la mesa, la adusta figura del general Avalos, inmóvil, parecía un busto de mármol sombrío que alguien había dejado allí por error' (p. 104). As Brooks remarks, 'to know in realism is to see and to represent is to describe [...]'.[45] Frers's Eva is more complex and aggressive than Pagano's idealized and anodyne portrait: she is the driving force behind Perón ('¡Qué fin ni qué carajo! Bramó –. ¡Esto es recién el principio', p. 100) and emerges as a familiar stereotype: coarse ('¡se pueden meter su Sociedad de Beneficencia en el culo!' p. 134); pushy and authoritative (she treats Renzi and Aloé as subordinates, p. 137); flippant and disrespectful (her remarks to Franco about her ability to draw a crowd, p. 146). She is revered by the people for her 'olímpico desprecio y su belleza' (p. 122) and for her ability to convert a term of abuse – 'grasa' – into its opposite, charged with affection and solidarity. Unlike Martínez, Frers domesticates Eva by identifying clear-cut personality changes: 'no era la misma Eva [. . .]' (p. 153); 'ya nada quedaba de la muchacha Silvestre de Los Toldos ni de la dama enjoyada de los banquetes europeos' (p. 157). Frers's Eva, unlike Pagano's, may be multidimensional but her dimensions are clearly demarcated and her dynamic and volatile elements consequently diminished. This account is based on the traditional narrative virtues of clarity, chronology and coherence. A connecting thread in the shape of Gervasio Toloso, provides additional reinforcement as we follow his life story from the loss of his first wife in the San Juan earthquake (pp. 54–5, 77) to his recollection of that event ten years later when it merges with his awareness of another death, the public and momentous death of Eva herself (p. 196). A neat conclusion for a tightly structured account is provided in the epilogue that refers both to Eva's funeral and to Perón's overthrow in 1955. Frers, like Pagano, presents an account antithetical to that of Martínez, offering development and progress, the illusion of objectivity enhanced by the suppression of Frers's own authorial input. The flatness of the tone and blandness of the discourse are relieved by some occasionally lively dialogues that can generate situational irony: thus Yankelovich's conversations with Eva, first against the backdrop of Perón's fall from power, then subsequent to his 'restoration' and marriage to Eva, are cases in point: in the first scenario he breaks to Eva the news of Perón's downfall with some panache: 'no corre más, *kaputt*, está liquidado. – Don Jaime remarcó sus palabras con un expansivo gesto, pasándose el dedo por la garganta' (p. 85). The circumstances of their next conversation are very different and it is a chastened Yankelovich who addresses a vengeful Eva. His chagrin grows when Eva shows him her wedding certificate: 'a medida que leía el documento, la cara de don Jaime se iba desmoronando por partes [. . .]' (p. 119). Here, for once, Frers is not so much interested in explaining what really happened as in converting his raw data into a 'creative' fact and exploiting the human and comic potential of his story. But such episodes mark the infrequent high points of Frers's ludic capabilities. His narrative ends with Gervasio Tolosa's recollection of that famous phrase attributed to Eva but probably apocryphal: '¡Algún día volveré, y seré millones' (p. 196). As we have seen, this statement – whether true or false, or perhaps because it is both true and false – points to the emergence of a new and immortal Eva whose posthumous power and influence outstrip those of the historical Eva. But Frers's narrative is rooted in the 'real' world of geographical space and historical time and cannot respond to the mythical possibilities of such an extravagant statement – which it rejects as 'una desesperada profecía' (p. 196). His narrative remains at a safe distance from the danger zones of a story that encompasses both death and femininity; it ultimately demonstrates the total inadequacy of realism to a Latin American reality that elevates the mythical and the irrational above the factual and the reasonable.

Conclusion

To conclude we might compare and contrast Martínez's treatment of the August 1951 *cabildo abierto* with those of Posse, Pagano and Frers (following the same methodology used in distinguishing Martínez's creative approach from the factually circumscribed accounts of Llorca, Navarro and Dujovne Ortiz). As we have seen, Martínez's version (elaborated in consultation with Julio Alcaraz) is based on the principle that reality can only be reflected indirectly through art: indeed, his account focuses not on what 'really' happened, but rather on the techniques (including the incorporation of a foreign film image, p. 106) most appropriate to the production of an artistic representation which might create an atmosphere analogous to the original historical event. To appreciate his distinctive approach we might juxtapose his stage directions – 'sugiero un montaje erótico, más bien venéreo. Tal vez así se logra algún efecto de la realidad' (p. 111) – with Posse's more direct style which seeks to express a sense of the transcendental but fails to lift Eva's speech above the level of the clichéd and pedestrian: '– yo sentí se lo confieso que estaba pasando algo raro y excepcional. ¡Me alzaban hacia lo Grande!' (p. 40). His Eva has an erotic vision of the proceedings but struggles to express her thoughts to her confessor, Hernán Benítez: 'usted estaba presente. Usted sabe de qué hablo. Es un acto como sexual y allí nace la verdadera democracia, como algo biológico, y no la democracia de los doctores [...]' (Posse, p. 40). This speech appeals to the concepts of cognition: 'presente', 'sabe', 'verdadera', but breaks off in uncertainty as language fails to resurrect the past. Martínez, by contrast, does not draw on the denotative power of words but rather on their evocative and ludic possibilities, on their 'festín loco' (p. 111), on their buzzing sounds – 'zumban los ¡ahora! nada detiene su frenesí, su lanza, su eco de fuego' (p. 111). While Martínez relies on the resonance of such images, Posse's testimonial perspectives on the *cabildo abierto* appeal to such notions as presence, objectivity, assertion, logic: 'si usted considera objetivamente las cosas' (p. 36); 'se lo afirmo' (p. 38); 'pero para terminar' (p. 38); 'pero la verdad es que' (p. 41).

Pagano's coverage of the episode is brief, balanced, and devoid of tension (significantly Perón and Eva receive roughly equal applause from the crowd). The famous dialogue between Eva and the people is recalled by Eva prior to her renunciation but she is unable to express adequately the emotions generated by that occasion: 'cosas así, solamente pueden ser sentidas, porque no hay palabras para hacerles justicia' (p. 239). Eva is reluctant to probe dark areas of her own mind, 'esos lugares donde mis presentimientos entran, pero no mi razón' (p. 239) and seeks to dispel tension by claiming that her decision to renounce the vice-presidency was completely free: 'dirán que los militares presionaron, que hay divisiones internas, que el General me obligó y vaya a saber cuántas cosas más. No me importa' (p. 239). Pagano's Eva renounces the vice presidency on health grounds alone. Her emplotment of this famous episode seeks to eliminate ambivalence, to resolve ambiguity and to neutralize dissonance. She presents one single perspective, thereby holding to the promise of her introduction to abide by 'las exigencias de la armonía y el equilibrio del relato' (p. 8).

Frers's treatment of the episode focuses on Perón as the main source of tension both in the calculated coldness he displays towards Espejo ('se encontró con las pupilas duras, impasible y el rostro absolutamente neutro del « conductor »' p. 172) and also in his equally calculated distance from Eva ('ella miró hacia Perón. El general desvió la vista hacia el ministro del Interior', p. 175). But Frers's direct evocation of the scene also falls flat, confirming what Pagano's Eva says about the limitations of mere words (Pagano, p. 239): 'el reclamo ensordecedor, persistente, infatigable, retumbaba en el aire [...] Ella ondeaba sobre la multitud, flameaba sobre la ciudad, sostenida por la fiebre y las voces encendidas de centenaries de miles de «grasitas»' (p. 175). Here the accumulation of epithets suggests a laborious straining for effect. Martínez demonstrates that the only way to do justice to such an emotionally charged episode is to confer upon it the status of art. His overt artifice approximates closer to the force of reality than does the mimetic approach of Frers who ultimately resolves tension by focusing, like Pagano, on Eva's deteriorating health (Frers, pp. 177–8).

In discussing the orientalist text, Said states that 'in any instance of at least written language, there is no such thing as a delivered presence, but a *re-presence*, or a representation'.[46] Martínez would agree with Said; the other writers are caught up in the illusory quest of a 'delivered presence'. Indeed, Posse, Pagano and Frers share the principal objective of mastering their subject and aim to offer reliable insights into Eva's character. They are not so much concerned with exploring her proliferating images – textual, filmic, theatrical – as with penetrating her surface and exposing her 'secrets'. Martínez rejects such 'interpretive violence' and, far from displaying any sense of mastering his subject, flaunts his bewilderment in the face of her impenetrable qualities.

NOTES

1 Abel Posse, *La pasión según Eva* (Buenos Aires: Planeta, 1995); Mabel Pagano, *Eterna* (Buenos Aires: Nuevo Sol, 1982); Ernesto Frers, *Evita: la fascinante historia de Eva Perón* (Barcelona: Martínez Roca, 1997). References, given in parenthesis in the text, are to these editions. *Evita: la fascinante historia de Eva Perón* is abbreviated to *Evita*.
2 Martínez, 'Historia y ficción: dos paralelas que se tocan', in *Literaturas del Río de la Plata hoy*, pp. 89–100 (pp. 95–6).
3 David William Foster, *Alternate Voices in the Contemporary Latin American Narrative* (Columbia: University of Missouri Press, 1985), p. xvi.
4 See Abel Posse, *Daimón* (Buenos Aires: Emecé, 1989) and *El largo atardecer del caminante* (Buenos Aires: Emecé, 1992).
5 On this subject, see for instance Seymour Menton, *Latin America's New Historical Novel* (Austin: University of Texas, 1993), p. 26.
6 See Menton, *Latin America's New Historical Novel*, p. 19.
7 David H. Bost describes him as an 'apostle of postmodernist thought'. See 'Reassessing the past: Abel Posse and the New Historical novel', in *La Chispa '95: Selected Proceedings, New Orleans: Louisiana Conference on Hispanic Languages and Literatures* (New Orleans: Tulane University, 1995), pp. 39–47 (p. 41).

Fictive Shadows of Santa Evita: Posse, Pagano, Frers 259

8 Terry Eagleton, 'Capitalism, modernism and postmodernism', *New Left Review*, 152 (1985), 60–73 (p. 71).
9 Benjamín Menéndez led an unsuccessful military revolt against Perón in September 1951.
10 'Melodrama, sex and nation in Latin America's fin de siglo', in D. W. Foster and Daniel Altamiranda (eds), *Theoretical Debates in Spanish American Literature* (New York and London: Garland, 1997), pp. 181–90 (p. 183).
11 Sarlo, *La pasión y la excepción*, p. 24.
12 Beatriz Sarlo takes a contrasting view of the *Montoneros*: 'no sólo la afrenta al cadáver de Eva Perón fue lavada; los Montoneros también quedan unidos a esa figura, la de Evita revolucionaria cuya imagen consolidan en sus carteles y consignas: Si Evita viviera, sería montonera', *La pasión y la excepción*, p. 200.
13 Jürgen Schlaeger, 'Biography: Cult as culture' in John Batchelor (ed.), *The Art of Literary Biography*, pp. 57–71 (p. 68).
14 For fuller discussion of such linguistic subversion see chapter 4, pp. 98–9.
15 See Matías Barchino, 'La novela biográfica como reconstrucción histórica y como construcción mítica: el caso de Eva Duarte en *La pasión según Eva* de Abel Posse,' in José Romera Castillo (ed.), *La novela histórica a finales del siglo XX* (Madrid: Visor, 1996), pp. 149–57 (pp. 154–5).
16 Julia Kristeva, *Powers of Horror. An Essay on Abjection*, trans. Leon Roudiez (New York: Columbia University Press, 1982), pp. 198–9.
17 Rosi Braidotti, *Patterns of Dissonance: a Study of Woman in Contemporary Philosophy*, trans. Elizabeth Gould (Cambridge: Polity Press, 1991), p. 219.
18 Susan Sontag, *Illness as Metaphor and Aids and its Metaphors* (London: Penguin, 1991), pp. 63; 14.
19 Marysa Navarro points out that Eva's autobiography, *La razón de mi vida*, ghostwritten by the Spanish journalist Manuel Penella de Silva, contains sentences and even whole paragraphs which she also used in her speeches. Both speeches and writing share the same emotive style and sensuous, corporeal appeal. See Navarro, *Evita* (Buenos Aires: Planeta, 1994) p. 340.
20 Eva Perón, *La razón de mi vida* (Buenos Aires: Buró, 1998), pp. 12–13.
21 Elaine Scarry, *The Body in Pain: the Making and the Unmaking of the World* (New York and Oxford: Oxford University Press, 1985), p. 52.
22 See Alton Kim Robertson, *The Grotesque Interface: Deformity, Debasement, Dissolution*, Theory and Criticism of Culture and Literature, 6 (Frankfurt: Vervuert, 1996), p. 119.
23 Scarry, *The Body in Pain*, p. 53.
24 Margaret R. Miles, *Carnal Knowing: Female Nakedness and Religious Meaning in the Christian West* (Boston: Beacon Press, 1989), p. 147.
25 Kristeva, *Powers of Horror*, p. 4.
26 Barbara Creed, *The Monstrous-Feminine: Film Feminism,Psychoanalysis* (London and New York: Routledge, 1993), p. 37.

27 See chapter 10 for discussion of Puig's psychoanalytical treatment of Peronism.
28 Paul Watzlawick, *The Language of Change* (New York: 1978), pp. 99–100.
29 Kristeva, *Powers of Horror*, pp. 3–4.
30 Paul Ricouer, *Time and Narrative*, trans. Kathleen McLaughlin and David Pellauer, 3 vols (Chicago and London: Univerity of Chicago Press, 1985), II, p. 101.
31 Mikhail Bakhtin, *The Dialogic Imagination*, ed. Michael Holquist, trans. Caryl Emerson and Michael Holquist (Austin: University of Texas Press, 1981), pp. 66–7.
32 Sebreli, *Eva Perón ¿aventurera o militante?*, p. 74.
33 For a lucid and comprehensive account of the significance of Eva's voice, see María José Punte, 'Una mujer en busca de autor: la figura de Eva Perón en dos narradores argentinos', *Iberoromania*, 46 (1997), 101–27 (113–16).
34 Bronfen, *Over Her Dead Body*, p. 11.
35 Bronfen, *Over Her Dead Body*, p. 255.
36 Hutcheon, *The Politics of Postmodernism*, p. 84.
37 See David H. Bost, 'Reassessing the past: Abel Posse and the New Historical novel', in *La Chispa '95: Selected Proceedings. New Orleans: Louisiana Conference on Hispanic Languages and Literatures* (New Orleans: Tulane University, 1995), pp. 39–47 (p. 41).
38 María José Punte, 'Una mujer en busca de autor', *Iberoromania* 46 (1997), 101–27 (110).
39 Mirta Corpas Vargas, *Eva Perón en el cristal de la escritura. Mabel Pagano, personaje literario y postrauma*, Currents in Comparative Romance Languages and Literatures, 88 (New York: Peter Lang, 2000), p. 85.
40 D. C. Muecke, *The Compass of Irony* (London: Methuen, 1969), pp. 243, 245.
41 Dennis Howard Green, *Irony in the Medieval Romance* (Cambridge: Cambridge University Press, 1979), p. 357.
42 Kathleen Higgins, 'Nietzsche and postmodern subjectivity' in Clayton Koelb (ed.), *Nietzsche as Postmodernist: Essays Pro and Contra* (Albany NY: State University of New York Press, 1990), pp. 189–215 (p. 199).
43 Mirta Corpas Vargas, *Eva Perón el el cristal de la escritura*, p. 32.
44 Hamon, 'Philippe Hamon on the Major Features of Realist Discourse' in Lilian Furst (ed.), *Realism* (London and New York: Longman, 1992), pp. 166–85 (pp. 167–8).
45 Peter Brooks, *Body Work: Objects of Desire in Modern Narrative* (Cambridge MA: Harvard University Press, 1993), p. 96. Examples of Brooks's point are frequent in Frers's *Evita*: 'El general Farrell apoyó las delgadas y oscuras manos en el borde de la mesa de caoba. Extendió sus largos brazos [. . .] En el otro extremo de la mesa, la adusta figura del general Avalos, inmóvil, parecía un busto de mármol sombrío que alguien había dejado allí por error' (p. 104).
46 Edward W. Said, *Orientalism: Western Conceptions of the Orient* (London: Penguin, 1978), p. 21.

Chaper 10

The Fictive Afterglows of Peronism: Puig, Szichman and Valenzuela

While the works considered in this chapter bear heavy traces of Peronist influences, they do not appear – at least at first glance – to project Peronism as their central theme. In Puig's *Pubis angelical*, Peronism may, on occasion, form the explicit topic of conversation between Ana and Pozzi but it does not seem to dominate elsewhere. In Mario Szichman's *A las 20:25 la señora entró en la inmortalidad* (1981) the funeral of Eva is barely mentioned directly but its disruptive effects determine the action of the plot and generate ironic contrasts. The focus of Luisa Valenzuela's *Cola de lagartija* (1983) is not on Juan, Eva or Isabel Perón but rather on the perverse figure of 'El Brujo', José López Rega, who has wormed his way to power despite his dubious reputation and complete lack of political experience – courtesy of Isabel who assumed the presidency upon her husband's death in July 1974. Thus, while all three works escape the explicit brand of Peronism, they are, none the less, contaminated by heavy Peronist associations.

Manuel Puig

In view of its references to such figures as Jacques Lacan and Melanie Klein,[1] *Pubis angelical* (1979) invites – unambiguously – a psychoanalytical reading of Peronism. As is by now well known following the pioneering work of Mariano Plotkin, psychoanalysis has exercised a pervasive influence in Argentina, making an impact on the intellectual class as early as the 1930s: Freud's *Complete Works* appeared in Spanish translation in 1922 and contained a foreword by José Ortega y Gasset who promoted psychoanalysis in his journal *Revista de Occidente*, which carried reviews of Freud's new and recently translated works.[2] The subsequent growth of psychoanalytic practice in the country was spectacular: 'By 1985, Argentina, with a population of only thirty million, was second only to the United States in the number of practicing Freudian analysts affiliated with the International Psychoanalytic Association (IPA), most of them concentrated in the city of Buenos Aires'.[3]

Given this background, Puig's interest in psychoanalysis is hardly surprising;[4] neither is it surprising that he should use the conceptual apparatus of psychoanalysis to analyse Peronism which has been seen as a pathology, as 'an evil parenthesis in the history of the country'.[5] But the parenthesis has not closed: Auyero investigates how residual elements of Peronism 'are embedded in networks, embodied in performances, and actualized and (re)processed in concrete practices'. He seeks to show, in the words of Pierre Bourdieu, how the 'dead seize the living'.[6] The Peronist legacy survives partly because it remains unresolved and unassimilated in the national psyche: Goldar mentions that it is 'una historia que irrita porque no se entiende',[7] a sentiment echoed by Tulio Halperin for whom Peronism remains part of 'Argentina's unmastered past'.[8]

It is for this reason that Peronism attracts the terminology of psychoanalysis: Williamson, for example, refers to its 'hybrid, not to say schizoid character' and to its 'almost hypnotic power over the urban masses'; Eva, he says, is object of the 'hysterical devotion' of the *descamisados*.[9] It was, therefore, far more than a political movement since it impinged on the psyche of a generation; as Sebreli puts it: 'es una parte de nuestro destino: está ahí, ineludible, y tenemos que develar su enigma para saber lo que somos'.[10] Psychoanalysis was a milestone in the history of medical science; Peronism had an equally dramatic impact on Argentine political history. The effect of Peronism on society was as far-reaching in its own way as the effect of psychoanalysis on the understanding of human sexuality: Sarlo notes that 'el mundo que antes de conocer a Perón parecía injusto pero inexplicable se organiza en oposiciones comprensibles'.[11] Plotkin makes a similar claim for psychoanalysis which, he says, provides 'interpretive tools for understanding and giving order to the elements of an otherwise chaotic reality'.[12] Perón was as much of a conquistador as Freud: he was also the father who represented the law. As Perilli remarks in her discussion of Osvaldo Soriano's *No habrá más penas ni olvido*: 'es un freno en vez de ser un móvil: nadie se independiza de él, nadie lo cuestiona. Es una especie de padre al que nadie puede superar y muchos aprovechan'.[13] Plotkin notes that 'governments represent parents. Societies, like individuals, have an id, a superego and an ego. Peronism operated as a social superego [...]'.[14] The psychoanalyst, Dr Arnaldo Rascovsky, sees Peronism in the same way: 'when Peronism crumbled, the superego disappeared, and there was no substitute for it. This circumstance condemns us to a structural anarchy [...]'.[15] If Perón represents the father, the law and the superego, Eva represents the return of the repressed, the barbaric past of Argentina breaking through the country's veneer of stability, culture and civilization.

In *Pubis angelical*, Puig emphasizes the contradictions and ambiguities of Peronism and, in particular, its role as Argentina's unmastered – and perhaps unmasterable – past. As a kind of national unconscious it resists intellectual recuperation, reminiscent in this respect of the impact of the Lacanian unconscious on conscious and concrete discourse that it fragments with lacunae, distortions, negations and disavowals.

The text is set during the brief presidency of María Estela Martínez (known as Isabel) who succeeded Perón as president on his death in July 1974 and remained in power until March 1976. One of Puig's main characters is the left-wing Peronist Pozzi, who is hopelessly enmeshed in the tentacles of political and pathological Peronism. Linked to Peronism and reflecting its instability is the fragmentation of fixed and gendered identity: while Peronism – at least in theory – destabilizes the traditional distinctions between left and right in the political arena, so in the domain of human sexuality, the main focus of psychoanalysis, the normal parameters are destabilized as gendered identity is rendered more complex.

Puig ostensibly presents three separate female protagonists – though it may well be that he is presenting aspects of a single individual. Some critics, such as Bacarisse, see the story of Ana as the 'principal text' to which the other two are subordinated: the Actress (known also as the 'Ama') and W218 emanate from Ana's subconscious – whether from thought, dream or delirium is considered unimportant.[16] Whether these are separate characters or aspects of a single character, they are clearly reminiscent, often in rather obvious ways, of Eva Perón. Thus Ama's sense of being imprisoned and her dream of the doctor and the scalpel recall the dying Eva's state of mind as evoked by biographers and novelists. The reference to Ama's former career as an actress is clearly significant and particularly so the need to cover up her past – which recalls Eva's own attempts to efface her own past career as an actress on becoming the wife of the president. Eva's lifelong espousal of different roles (and also, perhaps, the efforts of the most powerful figure in Isabel's government, 'el Brujo', José López Rega, to infuse Isabel with the spirit of Eva) is evoked by the servant's reference to Ama's theatrical role as a woman reincarnated in another (p. 13). The falsification of Ama's birth certificate provides a further link to Eva.

Ana, an Argentine living in exile in Mexico, not only suffers from cancer but feels – as Eva purportedly did – that she is being kept in the dark about her illness and medication (pp. 17–18). Her feeling that her tumour may have originated in her pent-up rage also recalls Eva. Like Eva, she entertains illusory notions about a superior man. She idealized her ex-husband, Fito (p. 30), failing to see him as he really was. Fito is clearly reminiscent of Perón: according to Ana, he has no feelings (p. 27). The left-wing Peronist, Pozzi – with whom the hospitalized Ana revives, albeit fleetingly, an old affair – also recalls Perón through his attempts to use Ana for his own political purposes: Perón was widely believed to have taken advantage of Eva's illness to bolster his own political position.[17] Pozzi's political observations echo those of 'real' commentators: his reference to an Indian woman screaming her disgust at Perón's overthrow (p. 115) recalls Ernesto Sábato's acknowledgement of Perón's popular appeal: 'aquella noche de setiembre de 1955, mientras los doctores, hacendados y escritores festejábamos ruidosamente en la sala la caída del tirano, en un rincón de la antecocina vi como las dos indias que allí trabajaban tenían los ojos empapados de lágrimas'.[18] Similarly, Ana's remark that Pozzi imagined Peronism as he pleased would be echoed in

Juan José Sebreli's acknowledgement of his own 'peronismo imaginario en el que el peronismo real no podía de ningún modo reconocerse'.[19]

Puig's third female character, W218, also recalls Eva: she too dreams of forming a partnership with a 'superior' man, a partnership to which she would contribute her pleasant personality and much-celebrated beauty (p. 158), so evoking Eva's role as bridge between the government and the people (as well as the Peronist slogan, 'Perón cumple, Eva dignifica'). W218's trust in her lover's capacity to thwart all evil (p. 214) is reminiscent of both Eva's total faith in Perón and her simplistic, black and white vision of the world. Moreover, W218's work – albeit involuntary – with contagious patients (p. 251) reminds the reader of Eva's obliviousness to the risks inherent in her own contact with the diseased members of her *descamisados*.

What is clear from the above is that Puig's text offers not only explicit discussion of political Peronism – mainly through the discussions between Ana and Pozzi – but also offers a drama whose hidden key is provided by reference to the main players of Peronism. The political is traversed by the psychoanalytical: even Perón's major achievement – bringing to visibility a previously invisible Argentina – has psychoanalytical connotations. Peronism is complex, ambivalent and contradictory: as part of the Argentine national psyche it offers itself as a kind of pathology for psychoanalytical interpretation. But Puig does not privilege the psychoanalytic over the political: for him both are master narratives fit for deflation through parody.

Hutcheon describes parody's 'target' text as another work of art or, more generally, 'another form of coded discourse'.[20] Parody is readily recognizable in *Pubis angelical* in the repetition and exaggeration of such discourses, its title already indicating an affinity with those of sexuality and psychoanalysis. The character designated W218, who belongs to the futuristic science fiction story, assumes the name of Dora during her work as a sex therapist, thereby recalling the subject of Freud's well-known case history.[21] Ana, who is a cancer patient living in the 'real' world, recalls both Anna O. – the hysteric treated by Freud's Viennese colleague Josef Breuer – and Freud's daughter. The dialogues between Ana and both her friend Beatriz and also her former lover, Pozzi, suggest the 'scene' of analysis, with Ana as patient lying in bed, and her visitors, in their different ways, probing her mental condition (the parallels with vistors to Eva's deathbed are obvious). Lacan's ideas, notably his concept of the unconscious as structured like a language, are discussed by Pozzi and Ana (pp. 170–1). Puig himself might be compared with Lacan since both are 'plagiarists' in the sense that they appropriate the work of other writers: Puig's distinctive style is predicated on the stealing of the styles and words of others while Lacan deliberately immersed himself in the inexhaustible discourse of others.[22] We might add that Perón, at least as portrayed by Tomás Eloy Martínez in *La novela de Perón,* was himself a blatant plagiarist: 'nadie osará mancharme, ni siquiera de plagio. A mi pobre país no le queda otra cosa que Perón' (p. 155).

Freudian psychoanalysis is largely male-orientated, a master discourse aimed at power and domination through coherent storytelling.[23] Pozzi masterfully penetrates Ana's 'hidden' problem: 'Lo que estás es con rabia por algo, contra vos misma, y no sabés cómo desquitarte, como un chico' (p. 149). This is precisely how Perón might have sought to pacify a turbulent Evita – he could love only by diminishing and minimizing.[24] But Ana's response – reminiscent of Eva's typical insubordination – subverts the normal order and propriety of the psychoanalytic situation, whereby the patient believes in the analyst's mastery and her own non-mastery, by denying Pozzi any superiority over her: 'Así que somos los dos iguales, unos ilusos y unos irresponsables' (p. 149) and even turns the tables on him by assuming the role of 'analyst' herself (although she sees his problem as deriving from his nationality rather than from any specifically psychological source): 'Te gusta estar por encima. Te gusta tener razón y que los otros no' (p. 173).

Psychoanalysis is an archaeological process of uncovering hidden thoughts and plumbing depths, both literal and metaphorical, and is frequently described in terms that emphasize the limitless encroachments into everyday life made by the psychoanalytic sphere. Ama's husband refers to the 'último sótano del inconsciente' (p. 42) of his wife while W218 reveals to her lover, LKJS, 'subsuelos insospechados de la realidad nacional' (p. 201). By the time it emerges that the patients at W218's hospital have forgotten that 'estaban en el fondo de un sótano polar' (p. 263), the reader has been conditioned by a novelistic world replete with psychoanalytic connotation. To ensure that even the least competent reader is aware of his purpose, Puig resorts to facile symbolism accompanied by an insistence on gender difference all of which contrasts, of course, with the 'depth' normally associated with psychoanalysis: thus the description of the winter garden which forms part of the Ama's prison: 'Armazón de hierro, fuerza de macho. Cobertura de cristal, ¿sometimiento de hembra?' (p. 64). The commonplaces of psychoanalysis emerge in Ama's dream – easily interpreted by her husband – on the opening page, and in the intensity of father–daughter and mother–son relationships (Fito and his daughter – 'vive pendiente de la hija', p. 28; the professor who worshipped his dead mother, p. 48).

Puig's work exemplifies the Freudian principle that human problems are fundamentally sexual, that man's truth is a sexual secret to be found at the heart of the subject's most forgotten and private inner discourse.[25] Ana tells Beatriz that she has a secret, 'hay una cosa que no puedo decir' (p. 50), which turns out to be sexual, a loss of pleasure from lovemaking with Fito and later with Pozzi (pp. 56–7).[26] Later she maintains a coolness towards Pozzi despite her desire for a new relationship: 'Estaba bloqueada' (p. 88). Even her illness has sexual roots, deriving from her repression of her real feelings for Fito: 'Yo creo que ese tumor me vino de acumular rabia' (p. 29).

Peronism is, of course, replete with sexual secrets, notably the nature of Eva's relationship with Perón, Eva's premarital liaisons and their possible consequences, Perón's illegitimacy and his mother's infidelity.

This stubborn emphasis on the sexual clearly points to a parodic treatment of psychoanalytic discourse, but again, lest there be any doubt, Puig makes his intentions explicit through reference to the pat and formulaic applications of psychoanalyis: thus Ana's reference to 'mi psicología de bolsillo' (p. 52) in relation to Pozzi, concluding that his shabby appearance points to priority being given to the more important aspects of his life. In the story of Ama, her lover perceives her separation from her daughter as indicative of flawed motherhood, a kind of female lack, to be cured by his (male) Hollywood psychoanalyst. Irony is also evident in the extension of the psychoanalytic from the personal to the collective plane to embrace national characteristics – Ana, generalizing about Argentines, says that 'ocultan porque son reprimidos' (p. 146) – and politics. The will to power represented by politics is even more blatant than that of psychoanalysis: Pozzi remarks that 'política es igual a fuerza' (p. 120). Despite the superior tone he adopts in his discussion with Ana, his own comments appear to be somewhat banal, but more significantly, he eventually dies whereas the apolitical Ana survives.

Puig focuses on Peronism as a movement which resists explanation and which even the politically sophisticated Peronist Pozzi cannot fully understand: he refers to its 'gran ensalada ideológica que no se terminaba de entender' (p. 119), reminiscent of Dujovne Ortiz's remark that Peronism is a 'hodgepodge that allows all sorts of interpretations. Indeed, it favours them'.[27] The erstwhile guardian of rationality and logic now wishes to retreat from them, 'No hagamos todo tan racional, tampoco', p. 123). Here the Freudian association of the male with order and reason and the female with excess and irrationality is partially reversed in these portrayals of Pozzi and of Peronism (representing 'lo diabólico masculino' for Corbatta).[28] In view of such heavy Freudian inscription, where the political is subordinated to the psychoanalytical discourse – itself heavily parodied – it appears safe to assume that 'Peronism' transcends its proper political limits to represent the Other of the Argentine nation, her chaotic Unconscious.[29]

The frequent references to the parapsychological parody the oversimplification of Freudian notions current in much psychological discourse: the Actress or Ama, looking in a mirror which promptly falls and smashes to smithereens, attributes the mishap to the intervention of the dead (p. 70). The juxtaposition of a central Freudian symbol, the mirror (taken up by Lacan in the 'mirror stage' which is discussed by Pozzi and Ana, p. 170) and 'primitive' superstitious beliefs, demeans, by association, the practice of psychoanalysis, while in the putative future world of W218, psychoanalysis has regressed dramatically, since her personality assessment will be based on astrological studies 'scientifically' supported, however, by saliva and hair analysis (pp. 189–90). Even here there is a clear echo in Peronism, provided by the excesses of 'el Brujo', José López Rega, who published a 740-page book entitled *Astrología esotérica*.[30] The computer consulted by W218 may be suggesting a more sinister side of psychoanalysis, as a 'skeleton' key providing ready-made interpretations for a multiplicity of cases. W218, who is specifically linked to Dora,[31] may be compared with Cixous's Dora who, as she appears in *Portrait de*

Dora, refuses the idea of the interchangeability of all women;[32] similarly W218 increasingly refuses the 'advice' offered by the machine in response to her 'consultations' (e.g. 'Con rabia oprimió el botón correspondiente al borrado ...', p. 189).

Other more subtle ways in which the psychoanalytic discourse is introduced indicate its stranglehold on the text. Thus the British agent who denounces the Actress to her husband, strives to 'hilvanar fragmentos inconexos de información' (p. 62), a statement with political significance (Ana's attempts to make sense of Peronism), psychoanalytical resonance – suggesting the analyst's task – and literary connotation, pointing to the activity of the reader of a [post]modernist text such as Puig's.[33] Given this background, the episode of the Actress's jewel box, the key of which is lost but the box turns out to be unlocked (p. 69), may be interpreted as ironizing the practice of psychoanalysis using the latter's own symbolic discourse.

LKJS's act of betrayal is similarly couched in rigorously scientific terminology: while W218 is asleep, he takes 'un estuche que contenía dos pequeñas planchas de vidrio de las utilizadas en análisis microscópico.... Muy suavemente introdujo el dedo índice de la mano derecha en el sexo de ella, en busca de secreción vaginal' (p. 189). Puig's use of the cold and precise discourse of medical science for the narration of LKJS's violation of what at least began as a union of lovers seems deliberately to parallel Pozzi's violation of indeterminate Lacanian thought by his advocacy of 'una terminología rigurosa' (p. 171) while Pozzi's glaring lack of the Lacanian virtue of knowing how to listen and how to intervene, how to say the right thing at the right moment reinforces the irony.[34] Pozzi tells Ana that he had informed his wife of their affair (p. 173) and, more seriously, discloses to Ana that her illness was thought to be terminal (pp. 222–3). (Perón is believed to have communicated such information to Eva while his other alleged misdemeanours, such as flirting with college girls while Eva was still alive,[35] make Pozzi's pale by comparison). Though rather at odds with Lacanian ideals, Pozzi's impassive 'scientific' superiority recalls Freud's own determination not to allow his 'scientific' methods to be contaminated by 'inconsequential' female discourse: he strove to maintain the masculine rigour of his analyses.[36] Freudian obsession with figurative language, where everything means, symbolically rather than literally,[37] seems deliberately to echo the W218 story, in the banning of prepolar artistic expression because it is not figurative (p. 201). The implication is that psychoanalysis is an apparatus of exclusivity and domination imposing its own meaning: Freud, unlike Lacan, believed in the healing capacity of coherent storytelling. Puig parodies not just the analyst but the reader seeking narrative closure, whose interpretative drive is equally voracious: Beatriz is hungry for Ana's 'plot' ('No te interrumpas más que quiero saberlo todo', p. 50). Several male 'plots' are thwarted – Ama's husband who plans to suffocate his wife (p. 62); Theo, who plans to arrange the disappearance of Ama (p. 79); Pozzi, who wants Ana to lure Alejandro to Mexico so that he can be kidnapped; and LKJS who plans to sacrifice W218 (pp. 238–9). It may not be too far-fetched to suggest that the denouement of Perón's own political 'plot' – his triumphant return to Argentina and the consolidation of his political legacy – was itself undone by the violence that right- and left-wing Peronists unleashed against each other at the massive reception to mark Perón's homecoming on 20 June 1973 and subsequently by his wife Isabel's disastrous presidency that provoked military intervention and a regime of institutionalized terror. Puig's 'plot'[38] leaves the reader dissatisfied as far as narrative closure is concerned: instead of unveiling an answer he leaves us with an unknown. The story of W218 resists appropriation, recalling Dora's which resisted Freud's will to mastery and coherence: Dora 'refuses to tell further, breaking off before the end'.[39] One might add that the story of Peronism also remains inconclusive and open-ended, resistant to rational analysis and unreceptive to the attentions of many sophisticated readers. Puig would clearly vindicate the tentative artistry of Martínez against the interpretive decisiveness of writers such as Llorca and Navarro who aim at narrative closure.

Puig maintains an unrelenting and parodic emphasis on feminist and gender issues; sexual difference and sameness are foregrounded in irresolute play. Difference is conspicuously emphasized in the reference to the Actress's 'guardaespaldas... del género masculino' (p. 47). Ana's internalizing of essentialist notions of sexual difference – the woman occupying the position of impulsive and uncontrolled Other to the reasonable and equanimous male (e.g. p. 93) – indicates how women (including Eva Perón as is evident in *La razón de mi vida*) can

themselves share fully in misogynist patriarchal attitudes. Like
Eva, both Ana and and W218 search for the superior male despite
sensing his alien qualities: Ana writes, 'Yo nunca los voy a com-
prender, para mí son seres de otro planeta' (p. 227). Puig gives a
more sinister inflection to Lacan's stress on the impossibility of
communication between the sexes in LKJS's obsessive fear that
women with mind-reading capabilities would constitute 'un peli-
gro para este planeta de hombres, mi planeta. Por eso hay que
eliminarla, o por lo menos tenerla bajo control, un control de
hombres' (p. 238).[40] In *La razón de mi vida*, Eva partially justifies
such fears in her call for the prioritizing of a 'cultura femenina'
and her claim that 'el mundo actual padece de una gran ausencia:
la de la mujer'.[41] As for Perón, he was terrified of perceptive
women: Tomás Eloy Martínez indicates that he was attracted to
Isabelita because 'tenía la virtud de ver sólo la superficie de las
personas. Al General le habían aterrado siempre las mujeres que
iban más lejos, abriéndose camino entre sus no sentimientos'.[42]
The emphatically comic idea of woman as man's natural enemy
seems to be a parodic exaggeration of the fears expressed by such
feminist thinkers as Kate Millett who sees the world in terms of
the ruling (male) sex seeking to maintain and extend its power
over the subordinate (female) sex.[43]

A related aspect of Puig's treatment of the gender issue is his
portrayal of the male as plenitude and the female as lack –
another, by now, commonplace Lacanian premise ('Le sexe
féminin a un caractère d'absence, de vide, de trou, qui fait qu'il se
trouve être moins désirable que le sexe masculin dans ce qu'il a
de provocant...').[44] Ana reflects on Pozzi: 'Es buen mocísimo, es
simpático, es inteligente, es sensible, siempre tiene tema de
conversación, es sexy, tiene buen corazón ¿qué le falta entonces?
Nada. Entonces no hay duda que es mi culpa, que yo no puedo
sentir nada por nadie. Pero no ¡no es cierto tampoco!' (p. 87).
Again conforming to a stereotype of the female as a contradictory
and incomprehensible being, Ana is both ignorant and knowl-
edgeable: ignorant of the 'male' and 'scientific' spheres of
psychoanalysis and politics, but at home in the 'female' and
'creative' ambience of opera (p. 168). Conversely, Pozzi is ignorant of the latter, but – ironically – authoritative on the former:
'yo vengo y te expongo todo el asunto' (p. 40). Again the links
with Eva and Perón are clear: Eva was, of course, familiar with the
world of the stage; Perón was the political master: Perón 'se

presentaba siempre como el gran mago para todas las soluciones'.[45] Ana's self-contradictory style points to woman as 'dark continent', as other than herself: she refers to her excessive desire for Fito, to the need to 'sacarme de encima esa fiebre, bajarla hasta un grado razonable' (p. 30). The Actress is similarly given to excess, which is only curbed by her husband: 'El esposo detuvo el desborde histérico con una sabia caricia' (p. 41). W218 reflects playfully on her own excessive behaviour (stabbing LKJS), the narrative resorting here to the 'stock-in-trade' of feminist discourse: '¿quién descifraría el enigma? vaya jeroglífico el de éste mi corazón de mujer' (p. 251). Eva, like Ana, viewed herself as embodying a lack or deficiency to be filled by Perón and the terminology associated with all three women is strongly evocative of Eva: 'fiebre' (Ana), 'desborde histérico' (Ama), 'corazón de mujer' (W218). Here Puig portrays woman as socially conditioned: Ana rejects Beatriz's feminism – as Eva rejected feminism – and places her hopes in the emergence of a superior male, as did Eva; but Puig also portrays woman as subversive of social norms: Ana 'fails' as a mother and is accused of destroying her home by her own mother (p. 33); Eva is only a figurative mother and her social activities and late hours finally remove all semblance of a normal home life. Ana turns what appears to be her deathbed into a lovers' bed (pp. 177–8); Eva turns her deathbed into a 'hotbed' of Peronist resistance by using it as a base for negotiating the purchase of arms.[46] Ana is both open and shut (Pozzi tells her that the surgeons 'abrieron y volvieron a cerrar', p. 221); an exile, out of her proper place, she occupies – like Eva – borderlands, margins, 'in-between' territory, the gap between life and death (she suffers from cancer, the disease seemingly beyond solution, marked by unregulated growth), between submission and rebellion, between the reality of pain and the fantasy of escape ('¿No se puede fantasear un poco, acaso?', p. 172), between stereotyped notions of gender and the creative possibilities of writing, between undergoing 'inscription' by her surgeons and herself effecting 'inscription' via her writing, between insight ('Te gusta estar por encima', p. 173) and blindness (her search for her 'hombre superior'). She remains elusive, resistant to Pozzi's attempts to control her ('Pero estamos hablando de algo serio. Y con vos no se puede', p. 172), remaining beyond Pozzi's reach ('él nunca me había terminado de convencer', p. 87) just as

Eva remained beyond Perón's – as underlined by her uncompromising rhetoric in *Mi mensaje*). Ana's multiple identity is made explicit in the text: 'me estoy desdoblando?' (p. 24). The related theme of the double emerges in the Actress's story: her husband employed a (wo)man Thea/Theo to impersonate her, apparently for security reasons. It is again Eva's lifelong 'impersonations' and their diverse gender inflections that come to mind.[47]

Puig focuses on yet another site of gender conflict when he considers the ambiguities and implications of language. Language, like the notion of male superiority, may give the impression of naturalness, but is, of course, a conventional and arbitrary system, offering no more than an illusion of being transparent and referential. For Lacan, submission to language – which is 'phallocentric' – implies submission to phallic authority. Ana's laborious writing and her sense of confusion as she struggles to express her meaning relate to woman's exile from the symbolic order: 'Estoy loca, escribir cosas sin sentido' (p. 88); 'Bueno, mejor empiezo de nuevo' (pp. 93–4). Eva herself begins again in *Mi mensaje* because she failed – so she claims – to convey her meaning in *La razón de mi vida*: 'tengo que escribir otra vez . . . '[48] It is significant that in *Pubis angelical* language is discussed by *women*, who focus on its shifting and volatile nature, its slippage of meaning and connotation – thus the discussion between Ana and Beatriz of 'cenar' and 'comer' (p. 52) and Ana's recourse to terms she would not normally use: 'En la Argentina habría dicho otra cosa' (p. 25). There is an example in the W218 story of language's inherent capacity to deceive: LKJS mentions to W218 an oak tree which could be seen from his house. Searching for him, W218 realizes that he was referring not to a real tree but merely to a representation of one. It is surely not coincidental that Saussure's model for the arbitrary nature of the linguistic sign is a tree.[49] Eva too was conscious of the slippage of language which exceeded her intentions: 'Perdónenseme estas explicaciones que, sin quererlo, casi han venido a dar con cierto tono de filosofía que no entiendo y no deseo hacer'. She is also wary of word play that also points to language escaping her control.[50]

Another aspect of linguistic fluidity is evident in the use of proper names (Ana/Ama, Theo/Thea) where a variant letter represents difference of identity or gender. In the case of Theo/Thea, the unveiled Thea turns out to be the male Theo. Language is anchored by the symbolic phallus that acts as its controlling centre; it is a male order in which female identity is constructed negatively as 'other'. But there remains a play between the two, sexual difference becoming blurred; after leaving Ama, Theo reverts to being Thea, the implication being that sexuality is not natural but socially constructed, since this character's sexual identity then alternates between male and female: 'Abruptamente Thea, olvidando que debía afinar la voz, lo interrumpió diciendo que tenía mucho que hacer... El travestido optó por hacerse presente unos instantes... Los ancianos lo recibieron con jovialidad... Thea devoró una tajada de torta y se excusó' (pp. 70–1). Forgetting herself, forgetting to play the subordinate role of the traditional female, was a constant preoccupation of Eva Perón as she increasingly overshadowed her husband in the male political arena. Her final incarnation as 'compañera militante' assumes a hard masculine edge that effaces the female softness of her previous incarnations (just as the aggressive manly discourse of *Mi mensaje* supercedes the often exaggerated female subordination of *La razón de mi vida*). Tomás Eloy Martínez quotes the Argentine essayist Ezequiel Martínez Estrada's comment on the active masculine role played by Eva: 'Todo lo que le faltaba a Perón o lo que poseía en grado rudimentario para llevar a cabo la conquista del país de arriba abajo, lo consumó ella o se lo hizo consumar a él. [...]. En realidad, él era la mujer y ella el hombre'.[51] Marysa Navarro echoes these sentiments:

> A pesar de su apariencia femenina, Evita es en verdad un hombre [...]. Los rasgos de su personalidad son mucho más masculinos que los de Perón [...].
>
> Para [Luis] Franco: 'Había sin duda en el carácter peroniano un elemento de molicie femenina'. En contraposición con él, Evita es fuerte y Perón extraordinariamente débil. 'En los diálogos entre ambos', señala Lombille, 'priva siempre la voluntad de la mujer sobre la parsimonia y la blandura del hombre, que oculta su inferioridad bajo una capa de bonhomía y pillería'.[52]

Lacan regarded Freud's stress on the precariousness of human subjectivity as one of the most significant insights of psychoanalysis; bisexuality was seen as a sign of that precariousness since it holds together in one single subject two different directions, two different emphases. Blurring of difference is based on disguise in the case of Theo/Thea; elsewhere physical difference between the sexes is called into question: thus a guest of Ama's husband 'era moreno, delgado, de facciones casi femeninas por lo delicadas, pero la voz ronca y la casi rudeza de los gestos terminaban definiéndolo como viril' (p. 44). Eva's final incarnation represents gender instability: the skeletal, exhausted figure needing support from Perón suggests 'female' weakness but the hoarse power of her voice as well as her dramatic gestures suggest 'male' strength. Foster comments that while critics have examined the relationship between Eva and Argentine popular culture, 'no one has yet connected her with issues like gay sensibility, sexual dissidence or masculine subjectivity'.[53] If *Pubis angelical* is read as a text based on the Freudian principle that everything is a representation of something else then Puig's portrayal of unstable gender identity can be related to Eva and so goes some way towards filling the critical lack identified by Foster.

Several critics have interpreted this novel as an endorsement of bisexuality and the instances of diminished sexual difference and the inversion of gender stereotypes would support this view.[54] However, as Heath points out, though bisexuality may represent rejection of the fixed social order, it can return constantly as a confirmation of that order, 'a strategy in which differences, varieties of existence and experience, are neutralized into the given systems of identity, the two halves – masculine and feminine – adding up to the same old *one*'.[55] Heath urges refusal of the concepts of masculine/feminine. This leads us to the enigmatic conclusion of the novel and the figure of the sexless angel. Does this episode conform to the generally parodic tone of the text, evident as we have seen, in the reiterated commonplaces of psychoanalytic discourse and in the tripartite structure where the repetitions and variations offer an analogy of the psychoanalytic process and its interpretative drive?

On one level it may be seen as further parody of the Freudian idea of woman in need of man to make up her lack. Freud was intolerant of bonds between women and suspicious of knowledge circulating among them. The figure of the angel presents a double lack, the lack of a lack since its 'pubis angelical' has no possible need for the male. The angel may represent the otherness, the strangeness of woman, which is suggested by linguistic slippage in the French *l'étrange* (the uncanny) and *l'être-ange* (the angelic).[56] While Ana (like Eva) represents (diseased) body and

Pozzi (like Perón) represents (ordered) mind, the angel combines the manifestations of otherness, the divine, the feminine and death giving to the feminine what it 'lacks' – spirituality.[57]

The angel may also represent bisexuality, but not in the sense of a straightforward combination of the masculine and feminine but rather a kind of neutralization of both, where traces of the male (the angelic and the divine) merge with the female, now 'under erasure'. The fusion of other polarities is also suggested: human/inhuman, ephemeral/eternal (even the angel is prefigured in the text by the Actress: 'Tripulantes y pasajeros la veían pasar y la creían una aparición con su negligée vaporoso al viento', p. 79), real/unreal, original/copy, sexed/unsexed.[58] Puig's angel may also be associated with the female principle (Kristeva's 'she-truth')[59] which lies beyond binary divisions and which interrogates the sources of our knowledge: 'The space "outside of" the conscious subject has always connoted the feminine in the history of Western thought – and any movement into alterity is a movement into that female space; any attempt to give a place to that alterity within discourse involves a putting into discourse of "woman"'[60] Eva's call for a new space for 'la cultura femenina' in *La razón de mi vida* may be linked to Puig's image of the 'pubis angelical' that points to the unrepresentable, to what lies beyond our present conceptual apparatus and repudiates the male drive to represent and to know all. According to the story told by W218's fellow patient, the angel puts an end to carnage and war, which suggests yet another of its shifting identities: metaphor for the beyond of binary logic which makes language a battleground for signifying supremacy. From being a sex/art object, woman (as angel) becomes an object of language, a linguistic category. The angel image is ethereal and indeterminate, a kind of coming into being which may indicate the possibility of emergence from metaphysical 'sickness' in the philosophical sphere. But it finally remains out of reach, in an uncontrollable excess of meaning which carries it (and the novel) beyond the scope of rigorous interpretation, whether Freudian or other. Indeed, the image of the 'pubis angelical' may also be related to Deleuze and Guattari's unFreudian concept of the 'Body without Organs' that disrupts the gendered organization of the body. The Body without Organs is opposed to the perception of the subject as 'organism' that represents the 'organs organized'. Deleuze and Gauttari describe the Body without Organs as 'nonstratified, unformed, intense matter, the matrix of intensity, intensity = 0, but there is nothing negative about that zero, there are no negative or opposite intensities'.[61] Jardine notes that Deleuze and Gauttari's *lignes de fuite* ('escape lines' or 'vanishing lines') are 'the "way" toward thinking a new body and a new spatiality – a body and spatiality that are, among other things, *lisse*, smooth and sleek [. . .]'.[62] The rupture of conventional bodily hierarchy results in the 'low' (and shameful) being raised to the level of the 'high' (and holy). The angel evokes the image of Eva as 'Santa Evita'. Her embalmment desexualizes Eva and substitutes the 'pubis angelical' for the locus of disease, so transforming the highly sexualized Eve into the virginal Mary who yet retains her erotic intensity, as Martínez emphasizes in *Santa Evita*. Bronfen remarks that 'the absence produced by the bodily decay is filled with the embalmed body and the "nothing" of the female genitals is supplanted by an untouchable idealised feminine body'.[63] The 'pubis angelical' may also represent a further in-between space, being neither of this world ('angelical') nor entirely absent from it ('pubis'). It can be seen, therefore, as a metaphor for the dismantling of rigid conceptual categories. It is an image that combines the divine and the sexual and suggests Freud's enlarged understanding of the nature of sexuality as a metaphor embracing all major human meanings.

Puig effectively parodies the discourses of psychoanalysis and (to a lesser extent) of feminism in *Pubis angelical*. His playfulness emerges in the repetition of commonplace concepts that make up these 'master' narratives. The figure of the angel is itself a commonplace of postmodernism.[64] But here lies another undecidable aspect of Puig's text: clichés do not preclude seriousness and serious purpose probably underlies their orchestration.[65] Where play ends and seriousness begins is difficult to determine; but to attempt to do so would be to fall into the binary logic which *Pubis angelical* seeks to transcend.

Though Puig trifles with the conventions and mocks the excesses of psychoanalytic and feminist discourses, he does not repudiate them: as Hutcheon states: 'even in mocking parody reinforces; in formal terms it inscribes the mocked conventions onto itself, thereby guaranteeing their continued existence'.[66] In this sense Puig both upholds and transgresses the 'Law' of psychoanalysis that inscribes his work and flaunts its power over him even as he baulks at its influence. Here his relationship to psychoanalysis parallels to some extent that of his character, Pozzi, to Peronism. Pozzi remains in the power of Peronism while claiming to be in the process of modifying it from within (p. 124). In its failure to disclose key information (such as the relationship between the three female characters and the significance of the 'pubis angelical') Puig's text is, in a sense, a tribute to Peronism as unmasterable past, as a pathology that still refuses to give up its secret, retaining its hold on the Argentine national psyche and continuing to divide it. Pozzi's aim is to domesticate Peronism from a left-wing perspective; though close to the *Montoneros*, he condemns their inaugural act, the kidnapping and murder of ex-President Aramburu (p. 122). But for many Peronists this murder occupies a proud – rather than shameful – place in the mythology of the movement. From their perspective, Aramburu paid the price not just for the executions he oversaw in 1956 but – more crucially – for his assault on the unreconstructed and mythical aspect of Peronism, for attempting to modify 'el carácter inasimilable, salvaje, revolucionario, sagrado, del movimiento peronista'.[67] There are several unobtrusive references in the text to 'otra cosa': to saying something else (p. 42); to being caught up in something else (p. 52); to showing something else (p. 186). Peronism emerges explicitly in this text at the level of political discussion, usually between Pozzi and Ana; but Peronism also infects the rest of the text where it is, if anything, more powerfully present for being unnamed: as Pozzi tells Ana, 'lo más importante fue lo que no te dije' (p. 175).

Mario Szichman

Szichman's *A las 20:25 la señora entró en la inmortalidad* is a book about the Perón era, specifically about the aftermath of Eva Perón's death – though neither Juan Perón nor Eva are mentioned by name in the text. Szichman is above all a parodist whose main targets are biblical precept (each chapter is allocated – as a kind of epigraph – a book from the Bible such as 'genesis' or 'revelations' that stands in ironic counterpoint to the following narrative) and Peronist mythology, particularly as embodied in the figure of Eva Perón. He deals with a variety of themes, ranging from the socio-political (the treatment of Jews in Argentina) to the philosophical (the stoppage of normal time, the relationship between the sacred and the profane) but the predominant tone or register is parodic, reminiscent in this respect of Puig: no exception is made for any subject, however grave, tragic or horrific it may be.

The novel focuses on the consequences of Eva's death for a Jewish family anxious to bury Rifque, the illegitimate seventeen year old daughter of Dora, whose suicide coincides with Eva's death which officially took place at 8.25 p.m. on 27 July 1952. The problem is that she cannot be buried because the government, seemingly anxious to monopolize death together with the official procedures which death normally sets in train, has proscribed the issue of death certificates until further notice. It is as if the enormity of the death of one woman, who enjoyed almost divine status among her admirers, must now monopolize the country's grief. Lesser deaths must be erased to allow the nation to focus exclusively on the one death that renders all others insignificant.

A las 20:25 la señora entró en la inmortalidad can be described as a postmodern text for a number of reasons. It offers an ironic reworking of the past and undermines the grand narratives of the Bible and of Peronism. Its cast of Jewish characters reinforce its postmodern pedigree: as Bauman observes: 'Forced into the state of homelessness by assimilatory pressures of modernity (and thus discovering the contingency and ambivalence of being) the Jews were the first to sample the taste of postmodern existence'.[68] The Pechofs stand outside Eva's underprivileged constituency and remain strangers in Peronist Argentina which was, at best, ambivalent towards Nazism – as Tomás Eloy Martínez points out: 'es indudable que, por su formación en la Escuela Superior de Guerra y por su concepción autoritaria de la política, Perón simpatizó con la causa del Eje y cultivó "una aparente parcialidad"'.[69] Szichman uses an impure, hybrid language – Castilian inf(l)ected by Yiddish – which poses to the uninitiated reader a serious challenge, one compounded by the anarchic and fragmentary structure of the text where no regard is shown for chronological order. Its unifying thematic thread, however, is the marginal behind-the-scenes plight of a Jewish immigrant family, obliged to keep a corpse in the bathtub until the conclusion of Eva Perón's funeral. Thus we move to the underside of a normally dominant 'official' history whose customary unity and coherence are undermined by the narrative focus here – not on the collective grief centring on the death of the Argentine first lady, but on the indignity suffered by a non-Argentine family as a result of excessive national mourning. In Martínez's *La novela de Perón*, the protagonist's mode of representation is arbitrarily authoritarian – to force the story to serve his narrative objectives: '– Gobernar a la historia. Cogerla por el culo' (p. 168). Szichman follows this dictum more literally than does Perón since he turns the normal order upside down, forcing the dominant and public figure of Eva Perón to the sidelines and thrusting to the centre the private plight of an insignificant immigrant family. Time is a significant factor in the text since its progress is halted for the duration – all clocks in the capital stop at 8.25, the official time of the lady's death. This abnormal situation also contributes to a postmodern sense of loss of stability by reflecting closely Jameson's diagnosis of postmodernism as 'schizophrenic', meaning that it is characterized by a collapsed sense of temporality.[70]

The spirit of parody infuses the text and the cult of Eva is the main target. Her death and its aftermath are most starkly parodied in the suicide of Rifque, but this novel is a kind of 'morisgrafía' (to borrow a term coined by Julio Ortega)[71] containing multiple deaths – of Itzik, Gladys and the doctor, for example – and all assume parodic resonance. Although Eva Perón is not mentioned by name, there are several allusions to her in the text: 'el velorio de la señora convirtió a Buenos Aires en una ciudad de desarrollo detenida [...]'.[72] When Jaime (uncle of Rifque, his sister Dora's illegitimate daughter) seeks out the doctor who is attending Eva's wake at Salaberry Hospital, he passes thousands of mourners carrying torches: 'la luna, amarilla, redonda, casi a ras de tierra, mostraba el perfil de la señora' (p. 243). Later, while travelling by bus, Jaime 'confirmó la coherencia de los funerales al ver impreso en cada respaldo el perfil venerado' (pp. 243–4). He has an altercation with a woman who resents his criticism of the political situation in the country. Provoked by her racial comments, he jostles her, whereupon she threatens to report him: 'yo a vos te denuncio – insistió la mujer –. Volveré y seré millones' (p. 245). She is yet a further reminder of the ubiquitous presence of Eva. But however elevated Eva may be in death, her early life has much in common with Jaime's Jewish past when country walks were not through golf links but broken fields bereft of trees against which to lean. The comparison of the Pechof family's memories to an animated drawing illustrating the spread of cancer (p. 94) confirms the connection. Moreover, following the death of the doctor, Jaime wakes up to find that the house is flooded (p. 275), a reference to the heavy and persistent rain at the time of Eva's death.

Eva is most closely associated with Rifque, the illegitimate daughter of Dora who works as a prostitute and finds herself having to support her brothers, Jaime and Itzik, when they fall foul of the law. While stories about Eva continue to proliferate, overwhelming any remaining boundaries between 'fact' and 'fiction', virtually nothing is known of Rifque except that she has committed suicide and her corpse has been placed in the bathtub until it can be buried. While there can be no doubt about her link with Eva – made explicit by Jaime who says that the lady looks like his niece (p. 253) – it is equally clear that Rifque's life and death stand in ironic counterpoint to Eva's. In many respects Eva herself remained marginalized throughout her life: even when Perón was in power she enjoyed no official position and was rebuffed when she aspired to the vice-presidency. But in comparison with Rifque, she embodies centrality itself since it is her public death and its aftermath that deprive Rifque of prompt burial as required by Jewish law. Both Eva and Rifque are illegitimate but whereas Eva clings to life in defiance of disease until she finally succumbs at the age of 33, Rifque is a healthy young woman who takes her own life while being only half Eva's age. The one inspires outpourings of grief in people she does not know personally; the other appears to be unloved even by her own family, her death merely compounding their already considerable burdens. Eva's body is suspended from the ceiling to facilitate the meticulous procedures of embalming administered by the world-renowned specialist, Pedro Ara; Rifque's body is left in a bathtub and is splattered with formaldehyde in a crude and unsuccessful attempt to preserve it. Eva's body is incorruptible; Rifque's smells. Eva's spectacular final journey, from Milan to Madrid and eventually home to Buenos Aires contrasts with Rifque's last journey by taxi to the house of the unscrupulous businessman, Benjamín, where she is to be placed in his freezer. While Eva leaves a permanent testament of her life (*La razón de mi vida*), which seeks to endow it with meaning and purpose, Rifque's ignominious suicide in the flower of her youth serves as an irrevocable testament to her life's futility.

Another of Szichman's characters evokes Eva, namely the prostitute, Gladys, who marries Jaime inflicting upon him the torture of a relationship with 'una mujer baqueteada' (p. 148).

She, like Rifque, is destined for an untimely death, but like Eva seeks to conceal the gravity of her condition – by dressing in vivid colours. Her skin becomes transparent, so recalling Eva's (*Santa Evita*, p. 385). When she dies, Jaime's feeling of being under siege by the decaying body evokes the Aramburu government's sense of being under threat from Eva's politically charged corpse. Jaime, the DIY coffin maker who prays over the nails, saws, hammers and chisels, parodies the consummate craftsmanship of Eva's embalmer. Having produced an inadequate cello-shaped box, Jaime resorts to a grandfather clock into which he forces Gladys's curled up body. He unscrews the mechanism, so stopping the clock, thereby allowing Gladys's death to echo (albeit faintly) Eva's death that had brought myriads of clocks to a standstill. In both cases the rational linear world is turned upside down by the conjunction of death and femininity. But whereas Eva's mega funeral overwhelms the urban space of Buenos Aires, bringing the city to a halt and lasting for thirteen days, Gladys's funeral is not only unnoticed but develops into farce as the hearse carrying her body goes missing, much to the consternation of Jaime who had been following it in a taxi. But there is of course similarity as well as contrast between Gladys and Eva since the fate of Gladys's corpse recalls the disappearance of Eva's embalmed body in 1955.

Szichman highlights the marginality of Jewish life in Buenos Aires. The Pechof family, notably Jaime, resolve to give up their Jewish identity and culture in favour of an (assumed) aristocratic Catholic heritage represented by the Gutiérrez Anselmi lineage. Jaime receives instruction in genealogical niceties from the character designated the 'manager'(Szichman uses the English word) and embarks on an enterprise designed to 'recrear la Argentina desde el año mil ochocientos cuarenta, intuyendo los momentos vacíos que debían rellenarse con leyendas de otros países, desechando distintas clases de futuro, y haciendo habituales situaciones y ambientes que no habían presenciado sus abuelos' (p. 26). This process is grounded in play and theatrical rehearsal (Jaime feels like a juggler or 'saltimbanque', p. 74). Jaime had to rehearse the part of Gutiérrez Anselmo: 'debía repasar cada actitud y diálogo posible para que su cuerpo calcara una partitura ajena' (p. 93). Such contortionism cannot but bring to mind Eva's assumption of her new role as president's wife that required an alien sense of decorum and poise – removed from her persona as actress but dependent for success upon her acting. History is not recorded but rather reinvented by Jaime and the 'manager' in their search for 'un pasado heroico' (p. 72) which involves a heroic death for the father (p. 166). The manager believes that reconstructing the father's death and making him a victim of the Bolsheviks would provide a 'título de nobleza' (p. 168). In their reweaving of family history from beginning to end, the Pechofs devise changes of age and variations in their spelling of 'Pechof'. Here there are clear links with the activity of the Peróns as evoked by Tomás Eloy Martínez in *La novela de Perón*, both in the reconstruction of the past undertaken by Perón with the help of López Rega and with the falsified information contained in the Peróns' marriage certificate. In *Santa Evita*, General Moori Koenig, commissioned by the Aramburu government to dispose of Eva's corpse, finds that Eva's personal documentation contains contradictory information, showing her to have two places and three dates of birth (p. 135). In the passports of the Pechofs there are changes of age and even of name: Dora thought Jaime was the youngest but according to the passport it was Itzik (p. 62).

In *La novela de Perón*, Perón invents his past to show it to best advantage: the threat of economic failure experienced by his family in 1851 is removed from the record and his mother, who was in reality the daughter of a defeated Indian, is bestowed with the honour of direct descent from the conquistadors (p. 47). The difference between Perón and Jaime is one of attitude: while the former invents in earnest, fearful that others may tamper with his creation, Jaime embodies a postmodern spirit of play since he sees his project as an adventure not only to be imposed retrospectively but to be lived in the present. He reads Laffont's *Illustrated Almanac* (p. 17) to become familiar with the clothes of the nineteenth century. Jaime is undoubtedly a Cervantean figure, being one-armed and reflecting in some ways the character of Don Quixote, notably in seeking to make reality conform to the world of a book. But unlike Martínez's Perón, he is endowed with a sense of irony and detachment that allows him to indulge in play for its own sake.

The frequent references to the 'rehearsals' undertaken by the Pechofs obviously parody the theatrical aspects of Peronism, as already noted. Jaime is aware that his past cannot be refashioned nor declared non-existent. Just as Rifque cannot be buried so his Jewish past resists a decent burial. None the less, rehearsals proceed with feigned seriousness. In one of them, the 'manager' visits the Pechofs' house disguised as a Polish count (p. 223). They achieve a 'decorado convincente' (p. 224) and organize their turns to speak 'como en una carrera de postes' (p. 224). The family try to convince the doctor that they have a sound Catholic lineage, each member contributing a particular role (e.g. Pinie plays the part of the servant, Teófilo). But the 'play' degenerates into farce as the doctor uncovers the dying Itzik and finds that he is wearing an oversized artificial penis designed to disguise his circumcision. The ending is tragicomic as well as ironic since the doctor – summoned to provide a death certificate – contributes his own corpse to the rising number of dead bodies after succumbing to Pinie's assault on him with a wooden mallet (pp. 272–3).

Szichman's narrative draws much of its power from such carnivalesque episodes in which the sacred is systematically undermined by the profane. Thus the content of each chapter serves as an ironic counterpoint to its biblical 'epigraph': the first chapter corresponds to Genesis, a book which emphasizes light, but the narrative which follows focuses on Buenos Aires as a nocturnal city. More trenchant irony emerges in a later Genesis chapter (pp. 119–22) in which Dora is pregnant with Rifque (who will commit suicide) and Itzik is showing the symptoms of an illness that will prove fatal. Genesis is about defining, separating, delimiting while Szichman's text is about in-between spaces and times that resist classification. As Mathieu points out,[73] the chapters corresponding to Exodus treat Jaime Pechof's efforts to supplant his past and to flee from a Jewish tradition which impedes his social integration (the biblical book describes flight from an inhospitable country in order to preserve Jewish heritage). The case of Proverbs is interesting because this biblical text consists in the main of moral and religious maxims and may evoke Perón's aphoristic style. In the Proverbs chapters of Szichman's text, however, the 'profundity' of biblical truth is reduced to the level of superficial sameness (Roni says, for example, 'para mí, idn y goim son iguales', p. 38) or superficial prejudice (Salmen says that he prefers Jewish daughters-in-law because their gestures were acceptable and they filled out their dresses. The goyim, on the other hand, were unpredictable and had narrow hips, pp. 61–62). Thus speaks the character whose name suggests wisdom and understanding but whose life of petty crime and deceit stands in contrast to the commercial success of the biblical Solomon who is credited with the authorship of a large portion of Proverbs. In one of the chapters corresponding to Judges, the 'manager' treats the topic of miracles and offers several 'modern' parables but his purpose is not to deliver from oppression (as was that of the biblical Judges) but to reinforce it since he commends to Jaime the submissive disposition of a freed slave, *el tío* Bembé (p. 83). The Book of Revelations is known for its apocalyptic visions but in Szichman's chapters associated with it, the 'revelations' proffered are wholly fatuous: thus the revelations made to Itzik concern the facts of life, the tango, and journalism (pp. 137–41). The Lamentations chapters relate to the stories told by Pinie regarding the pogroms that he experienced in Poland. His audience expect from him an appropriate sense of gravity but Pinie's demeanour is casual and detached, the horrendous events of the past being subordinated to the trivial appetites of the present: 'Había pasado el pogrom. Permiso, voy a picar', p. 124). His own role in the war – which he claims was not his in any event ('esa no era mi guerra') – strikes his audience as culpably passive since his main concern was to hide himself in a well. '– Seis millones de tus hermanos cayeron, y no era tu guerra – le dijo Tajmer. "Habrán caído pero ninguno en el loj" ' (p. 126). His final 'lamentation' is withheld as his narrative ends on a mockingly anticlimactic note. He cannot recount the massacre because 'en ese momento se larga a llover, crece el pasto y me tapa la visión' (p. 241). In génesis/revelaciones (pp. 257–60) Dora learns of the fate of her former colleague, Emma Zeledik, who committed suicide and whose tombstone bears only her initials. Here the contrast with Eva is obvious. Elsewhere, by casting aspersions on both the sacred aspect of biblical doctrine and the tragic content of Holocaust memories, Szichman appears to be undermining the saintly aura of Eva as well as her passionate identification with her 'descamisados', the less spectacular victims of the Argentine oligarchy. His work conforms to Pons's characterization of New Historical writing which 'cuestiona la verdad, los héroes y los valores abanderados por la Historia oficial, al mismo tiempo que presenta una visión degradada e irreverente de la Historia'.[74] Rather than adding to the accretion of works on the 'stars' of history, this writing offers anecdotal information about people often perceived as banal and ordinary, about whom there seems little of interest to say, while debunking in the process the myths of grandeur enveloping the established heroes. Szichman aligns Eva on the side of orthodoxy, authority and centrality; Rifque, by comparison, is seemingly of little consequence. Her story, however, undermines Eva's by exploring the practical consequences of her mythic status for 'lesser' people such as the Pechofs and exposing the absurdity of the paralysis she posthumously inflicts on an entire city. Eva is traditionally seen as a source of succour for the poor; here she only compounds their problems. Her canonical status as saint and provider is shown in a new and ironic light, just as biblical characters and precepts are undermined by the deflating narratives with which they are associated. The final irony is that the Peróns are subordinated – at least in Szichman's text – to the insignificant Pechofs whose unheroic story takes precedence over the mythic splendour of the deceased first lady.

This novel, like many other experimental Latin American texts of the 1970s and 1980s is difficult to classify. It is apparently a historical novel exploring Argentine history with particular reference to the Jewish experience. The biblical epigraphs, together with the Peronist historical background, find ironic counterparts in the plight of a Jewish family whose often picaresque behaviour serves to parody their solemn traditions and to lighten the poignancy of their situation. The novel is about burials or, rather, thwarted burials, of bodies, but also of Jewish traditions. National circumstances prevent the bodies from being buried normally while Jewish traditions actively refuse burial. Having agonized over the disposal of Rifque's body, Dora wishes she could keep it a little longer when the time finally comes to part with it (p. 276). Salmen rebels against jettisoning thousands of years of Jewish history (pp. 40–1). By the end of the text nothing is buried, neither Rifque nor Gladys nor Itzrik nor the Pechof past. Jaime's years of training, his posturing, his fine phrases (p. 284) count for nothing as the city sinks into the pampas like a block of ice in water. The Pechofs are quintessentially postmodern: they represent surface without hidden depth ('tras las fachadas de sus viviendas no había casas previas', p. 54); they are free-floating with no firm anchors in the past:

> Ser Pechof era rendir pleitesía a unos hombres ilusionados con estar siempre a la última moda porque no cesaban de enfundarse en sus ropas finales, mantener conversaciones truncas, rápidamente auxiliados con frases de una canción de moda o un chiste [. . .]. (p. 54)

They hatch new lives though static time prevents their take-off (p. 19). They are imitators, mimickers, copiers, cultural chameleons, consummate postmodernists. They engage in an enterprise with universal ramifications but which goes against the grain of a predominantly 'futurist' age. They create a fictitious identity based on an artificially homogenized past designed to legitimize the present. But they fail – inevitably – since as Jews they symbolize strangerhood and despite their best efforts cannot be assimilated within the national community that is defined precisely by its opposition to strangers such as themselves. Bauman refers to the case of Heine: 'the louder he protested his emancipation from Jewishness, the more his Jewishness seemed to be evident and protruding [...]. The display of assimilatory passion was perceived as the most convincing proof of his Jewish identity'.[75] The Pechofs mirror the experience of the Jews of the Diaspora: space without definition and time without history. Their vicarious lives of dissimilation perfectly embody postmodern ambivalence that, according to Bauman, is both the limit to the power of the powerful and the freedom of the powerless. Here they overlap with Eva whose own experience of power, representing both the establishment as the president's wife and the subversion of that establishment as the militant *compañera*, was consistently ambivalent.

The text is also postmodern in its repetitions. Rifque and Gladys are shadows of Eva whose character reverberates in the past as well as the future. Her closest historical counterpart is doña Encarnación, the wife of the nineteenth-century tyrant, Juan Manuel de Rosas, whose strength of character and skilful manoeuvrings anticipated those of Eva even if her other political instincts did not. Their deaths, explicitly connected in the text ('el velorio de la señora podía server para hablar del velorio de doña Encarnación', pp. 30–1), were useful to their husbands who exploited them politically: 'Rosas's exploitation of popular sympathy following his wife's death anticipated Perón's own procedure.'[76]

Just as Eva is repeated by recognizable models that make up the 'millones' she allegedly predicted she would become ('volveré y seré millones'), so the 'real' in this text, as in Martínez's, is repeated by a plethora of images with varying degrees of faithfulness. Jaime sees filing by, not the Eiffel Tower or the Arc de

Triomphe, but rather their respective images (p. 75). The 'manager' assembles a whole archive of faces based on models (p. 202). Variation in repetition emerges in the colour plates with all of Eva's previous faces. As an actress her main objective was to take the place of Zully Moreno and her face lent itself to infinite substitution: 'el rostro era sustituible por el de cualquier mujer mala o embaucable del cine argentino' (p. 254). Imitations can be nearly perfect (as were Ara's wax models of Eva in *Santa Evita*): Vaucanson's duck 'imitaba en todo a un pato vivo' (p. 53).[77] The port of Buenos Aires seems to replicate that of Gdinia (p. 63) while the decor of the brothels is repeated across the city (p. 80). Sometimes the violent deaths of the pogroms appear to replicate themselves in an alien continent (just as the 'semana trágica'[78] provides a faint echo of European atrocities): 'El pogrom se irradiaba por simpatía y dejaba su marca hasta en los muertos naturales. A veces era una cicatriz recuperando el color y la costra de sangre en una cara, o el gesto con que un cuerpo se arrinconaba en un ataúd' (p. 65). Copies as counterfeits, fakes and falsehoods are equally pervasive. Jaime hopes that his assumed identity as a Catholic aristocrat will not be exposed as a bad copy but the veneer cracks as the language of the street used by Pinie ('mejor tóquele la argolla. Nunca falla', p. 269) and Dora ('Sabes, Javier, el doctor es una buena pieza', p. 270) collides with the formality of the doctor ('Estoy entre Escila y Caribdis', p. 269) and the simulated intellectual game-playing of Jaime ('es conde, pero no esconde', p. 266) – a situation which recalls Eva's precarious grasp of refined language, manners and etiquette during her European tour of 1947. The photograph of Dora as a fake Spanish immigrant becomes increasingly distant from its 'model', finally giving the impression that she was pregnant because the reverse side had been reinforced with adhesive tape (p. 284). Such distortion is significant since the photograph is often seen as an infallible mirror of reality. Szichman, like Martínez, evokes Baudrillard's world of simulations, clones, miniatures and copies. Perhaps the most striking of all is Rifque's corpse that simulates a living being complete with hat, sporting birds and fruit (p. 278). This corpse, with its carnivalesque features, provides a scandalous copy of Eva's dignified body, clad in its plain white tunic and supervised by the impassive gaze of Dr Ara.

Ricoeur points out that 'all fictional narratives are "tales of time" in as much as the structural transformations that affect the situations and characters take time'. Only a few, however, are '"tales about time" in as much as in them it is the very experience of time that is at stake in these structural transformations'.[79] Szichman makes time one of the principal themes of his text by highlighting it in his title. Here the suggestion is that events will remain arrested: 'todas las horas estaban aprisionadas en una sola y la noche era crónica' (p. 207). History cannot restart while the hands of the clock do not move (p. 230). Rapid cinematic dialogue contrasts with a time that officially stands still. The novel's anarchic structure 'plays back' to episodes that appear out of chronological sequence (Pinie obtains his tattoo during the time of the Nazi atrocities in Europe, pp. 236–7). Time is foreshortened as the Pechofs 'fast forward' to incorporate their generations in a limited period of time: 'debían acelerar los años de posesión de todos los enseres para hacer entrar en él varias generaciones' (p. 96). The Pechofs want to reinvigorate a petrified past by getting inside the skin of their Catholic ancestors and doing the job so well that their imitation will become reality. They want to transfer the heroic past to the present but the present is postmodern, surface without depth, and only an image of Don Quixote in the form of a tattoo is acceptable, and even this is covered up by plaster (p. 103) as though it were an old wound tarnishing the shimmering surface of the present.

The novel is also – obviously – about death: Rifque is dead from the outset but she is joined by a series of other characters: Gladys, Emma Zeledik (the prostitute), Itzik, and the doctor. It is not known whether Father Pechof is alive or dead (p. 168). Szichman confirms Martínez's remarks about the symbolic power of the corpse in Argentina: 'it is more than a relic; it is the expression of a deeply necrophiliac strain in our culture. In Argentina we are never more alive than when we are contemplating death'.[80] Death encroaches on life: Jaime buys a plot for Itzik prior to his death (p. 194) while the 'manager' reserves places in the cemetery for the Zwi Migdal girls (p. 199) as though he were booking hotel rooms for them.[81] The enormity of death is dissipated by its frequent occurrence: Rifque's death is copied by others including even, in a sense, by Roni (Salmen's son) whose suicide will be simulated rather than real (pp. 19, 37). Rifque's death is nauseatingly physical while the Pechofs, particularly Jaime, crave a metaphysical death and reincarnation. Multiple deaths and problematic burials dominate the text providing echoes of Eva's death and its complex aftermath. Ironically, the novel itself has achieved a rather straightforward burial – covered up by the earth-shattering impact of texts such as *Santa Evita* that have monopolized critical attention, much as Eva monopolized popular attention following her death.

Luisa Valenzuela

The key to *Cola de lagartija*, a disturbing novel by Luisa Valenzuela (Argentina, 1938), is suggested by its title that points to the author's peculiar and powerful evocation of the last years of Peronism (1973–6). The tail, as Silverman indicates, is 'one of the most familiar symbols and substitutive expressions for the male organ'.[82] In *Cola de lagartija* (1983), male sexual power (together with jealous resentment of the feminine other) is the dominant theme. But the title also highlights a peculiar quality of the lizard's tail – its capacity to regenerate itself by a kind of natural prosthesis. Sloughing off, shedding, growing a replacement; change, camouflage, metamorphosis, becoming other – woman, animal, insect – are also at the heart of Valenzuela's text which draws on the ideas of the French philosopher most closely associated with the theory of becoming, Gilles Deleuze.

As we have already seen in chapter 7, Tomás Eloy Martínez's *La novela de Perón* is postmodern in its interweaving of history and fiction and in particular in its foregrounding of what is omitted from 'official' history – the marginal and the anecdotal. What Richard Holmes says of biography is equally applicable to Martínez's New Historical novel: 'fluid, imaginative powers of recreation pull against the hard body of discoverable fact'.[83] The dividing line between history and fiction also blurs in *Cola de lagartija* with the imaginative 'supplement' flowing through a series of border crossings of every conceivable kind though the most spectacular and memorable is the protagonist's transgression of gender boundaries as his body assumes female characteristics – in a concretely physical rather than metaphorical sense.

In a recent essay Tomás Eloy Martínez has reiterated what has become a cliché in the context of Latin America; that fiction pales by comparison with the irrational excesses of social reality:

> Imaginen ustedes la inverosimilitud de un país que, tras una sucesión de golpes militares, incurre en la demasía de sentar en el sillón presidencial a una mujer de pocas luces dominada por un cabo de policía con delirios ocultistas como sucedió en 1974 con Isabel Perón y José López Rega [...] Sólo la ficción podría contener todos esas delirantes realidades.[84]

The protagonist of *Cola de lagartija* is José López Rega, alias 'el Brujo'. He gained access to Perón's inner circle through Isabel, the president's third wife, who succeeded him as president upon his death in June 1974. López Rega's influence on Isabel, already considerable prior to Perón's death, would increase thereafter. Thus Page describes the initial meeting between López Rega and Isabel as an 'occurrence that was as inconsequential in its unfolding as it was pivotal in the history of Peronism'.[85] What distinguished López Rega was not his political acumen or his intellectual contribution to Peronist ideology. It was rather the fact that a leading though shadowy political figure who wielded considerable power in late twentieth-century Argentina could combine such a public role with the regular practice of witchcraft. Page notes that *La Prensa* once reported in a news item that he attended a witches' conference in Spain (p. 485). His earlier career – as a policeman of low rank – was hardly an ideal background for high political office. His meteoric rise to become the regime's 'strong man' inevitably recalls that of Eva who rose from obscure illegitimacy in the provinces to power-broking at the highest level of Argentine national politics.[86] Unlike Eva, however, López Rega was an author whose affection for the practice of writing matched that for his recondite subject matter.[87] He wrote, for example, a long treatise entitled *Astrología esotérica: secretos develados* that used – according to Crawley – rambling, often impenetrable language to develop 'strange theories about the colours of names and countries, and the importance of different forms of music on national traits'.[88]

López Rega richly deserved the nickname of 'el Brujo' but – unsurprisingly – preferred to be known as 'Daniel' after the Old Testament prophet whose ability to interpret royal dreams and uncover secrets put other astrologers, magicians and soothsayers in the shade. His active interest in astrology and witchcraft – which he barely attempted to conceal – was guaranteed to arouse media attention given his political prominence. Page notes that López Rega made the most extravagant claims about his own personal powers. Thus, during Perón's regular health scares, he reassured supporters that his own physical proximity to Perón would protect him since it was he, López Rega, who secured for the president the continued gift of life. He also affirmed that 'Isabel does not exist. She is a creation of mine'.[89] This remark recalls Perón's belief that he had created Evita in accordance with his own political designs.[90] López Rega was viewed by many, including Perón, as a kind of court jester, an image which he himself sustained by his extravagant claims – for example, that one of his books had been co-authored by the Archangel Gabriel.[91] López Rega may have provided entertainment for some but the truth was that his supernatural beliefs and magical practices provided the backdrop for elemental savagery. His Alianza Anticomunista Argentina (AAA) was dedicated to the elimination of leftist opponents within the Peronist movement. This organization was responsible for more than two thousand deaths since 1973 and for more than 133 abductions in 1975. The name 'El Brujo' not only evoked black magical practices but also a primitive world of mass murder and torture. He seems to have put his supposedly supernatural powers to the service of state violence and repression. He is the Despot-Sorcerer, equipped with 'armas del espíritu', who continues to conjure up enemies 'hasta entre los cuidadanos más irreprochables'.[92] Much of the text focuses on the historical López Rega. Early on, Rulitos (the textual Luisa Valenzuela) wonders how a country like Argentina, 'alfabetizado, brillante, trabajador, pacífico' (p. 20), could be sullied by the stain of fascism.[93] El Brujo's warped priorities and his fascistic inclinations emerge in his politics: he ignores important requests such as those for more schools, but is keen to develop sports such as football and boxing: 'soy gran defensor del deporte que ennoblece al ser humano y lo distrae de otras preocupaciones menos halagueñas' (p. 192). He aims to impose military values on civil society 'para encauzar la tradición autoritaria hacia los objetivos del progreso social y económico' (p. 51). His views largely coincide with those of Perón who expresses scorn for such an unreal concept as human rights (p. 111). El Brujo's cruelty emerges in his belief that fear 'dignifies' more than love[94] and in his fascination with what he sees as the precise science of torture that requires knowledge of the exact limits of human suffering (p. 70). But his victims are not only tortured; they are murdered too and their bodies borne away by helicopter and subsequently dropped in rivers. After the Maci, an indigenous faith healer, rebukes him by pointing out that he has surpassed his quota of human sacrifice, he takes revenge by making a soup of her corpse that he serves up to his guests (pp. 135–6).[95] His obsession with blood ('Correrá un río de sangre. Lo importante es que el líquido vital no deje de correr, para siempre alimentándome, alimentándome siempre a mí que soy el sol y con sangre resplandezco', p. 215) suggests the blood lust of fascism.[96]

The political power and perversion of Valenzuela's 'el Brujo' – 'no voy a permitir el bien en mi reducto' (p. 71); 'me gustan los cráneos picoteados' (p. 194) – is intimately related to sexuality and gender. Part of el Brujo's megalomania involves becoming a 'complete' being by incorporating female genitalia in his own body so that he can eliminate sexual dependence on the female other: 'yo vengo con mujer incorporada, soy completo' (p. 32). He was born a 'freak' with three testicles. The spare or supplementary testicle, which he calls 'Estrella', becomes the site for the inscription of his new female genitalia. He turns into a woman while retaining his male qualities and is thereafter referred to as 'Le Bruj' – a mutant, neither wholly masculine nor wholly feminine. He represents a being-in-process, a becoming-woman and becoming-animal, an incarnation of in-betweenness that evokes movement, transition, proliferation rather than stability, fixity, oneness. He is described as 'ni hombre ni mujer, la pura transición, no se lo puede calificar con género definido alguno [. . .]' (p. 228).

Valenzuela's portrait of el Brujo is couched in terms of fluidity, both literal and metaphoric, and evokes femininity rather than masculinity, traditionally associated with fixity, rigidity and order. His territory is the 'Reino de la Laguna Negra', his habitat, marshes and swamps, 'una zona a la vez transparente y fétida, un lugar que parece ser un paraíso cristalino y es en verdad un pantero' (p. 52). The same image is used metaphorically to describe the realm of superstition, 'los pantanos terrenos de la superstición y la leyenda donde no es para nada fácil hacer pie' (p. 41), and (implicitly) of the subconscious, whose depths el Brujo explores: 'soy un submarino de la mente, me sumerjo a voluntad' (p. 21).

The latent femininity of el Brujo is already suggested in his unofficial profession – the witch is usually female – and it is reinforced by his aquatic habitat. He is a creature of quicksand rather than of fixed territory. His laugh is likened to a bursting dam: 'era risa incontrolable, desbocada como un dique que se parte, una represa que larga su contención de risa y la risa arrasa con todo lo que encuentra a su paso' (p. 164). He plans to interrupt the water supply of neighbouring Capivarí, but first his flood of words will convey an impressive sense of his power (p. 173). This power appears to be pervasive, liquid-like in its penetrative capabilities and apparently immune to the effects of time and death. Having avoided the temptation of falling into 'la temporalidad del amor o del deseo' (p. 14), el Brujo transcends time – 'yo en todos los tiempos' (p. 160) – and controls death: 'manipulo la muerte, la manejo a voluntad y ella me respeta y no me toca' (p. 202). He even evades the grasp of his own creator since the textual Luisa Valenzuela admits that he has assumed a life of his own (p. 172).

According to Jardine, perversion can be liberating when it is associated with flow and becoming.[97] Perversion subverts binary oppositions – life/death (necrophilia), adult/child (pederasty), pleasure/pain (masochism). El Brujo is engaged in all three transgressions. He attempts border crossings between life and death, both successfully (Eva, p. 99) and unsuccessfully (Perón, p. 16). His relations with Seisdedos suggest pederasty (p. 44) while a form of masochism emerges in the perverse pleasure he derives from the humiliation of being urinated upon by his subordinate, el Garza (p. 58).

The boundary most often crossed relates to gender difference. El Brujo is described as looking like a bride (p. 25) and the theme of transvestism emerges briefly when a girl in white remarks that she had curls when she was a young man (pp. 132–3). It is Eva's transmutation into metaphorical masculinity that inspires el Brujo to undergo his literal metamorphosis in the opposite direction. Eva was often described as more male than female: 'los hay cargados de testículos que son unos cobardes y hay mujeres como ella que son verdaderos guerreros' (p. 96). One of the Brujo's mushroom-induced dreams is of a cave stalagmite that both assumes the likeness of Eva and takes the form of a giant phallus (p. 64). Her link with the phallus is reinforced by her incarnation as the Finger (to which el Brujo erected an altar, p. 92) whose secretions will fertilize Estrella – 'Este jugo de dedo será el riego preciso, el dedo será el arado y me abrirá el surco' (p. 88). Eva represents her own impressive brand of becoming since she is both the 'santa madrecita' (p. 116) and the 'gigantesco falo' (p. 64).

The most striking and potentially horrific border crossings are those which take place between humans and their others (animals and insects). For Deleuze, animals are about metamorphoses, particularly when they are in packs that are formed, developed and transformed by contagion.[98] The becoming-animal involves an erotic encounter with radical otherness. It involves crossing a threshold, reaching a continuum of intensities that only have value for themselves, finding a world of pure intensities where all forms get undone.[99] For Deleuze it is not so much animal characteristics that are important as 'modes of expansion, propagation, occupation, contagion, peopling. I am legion'. For him structuralism is blinkered and rigid, presenting phenomena such as vampirism as degradation, a deviation from the true order. 'Does it not seem that alongside the two models, sacrifice and series, totem institution and structure, there is still room for something else, something more secret, more subterranean: the sorcerer and becomings (expressed in tales instead of myths or rites)?'[100]

Braidotti describes animals as living metaphors, highly iconic emblems within our language and culture.[101] El Brujo's affinity with the natural world emerges when he orders the assassination of the mayor of Capivarí. He covets not only the mayor's house and daughters but also his orchids and parrots (p. 159). In the animal kingdom the wolf represents blood, violence and sexual aggression. El Brujo orders his aide-de-camp, 'el Garza', to howl like a wolf, and so mirror himself (el Brujo) and the 'lobo que llevo adentro' (p. 74). The man with the name of a bird ('garza') metamorphoses into animal which in turn changes into woman since el Brujo senses the presence of Eva in the howling: 'Aullá, edecán, lobo [. . .] aullá, la siento a Ella detrás de los agudos [. . .]' (p. 79).[102] El Brujo describes himself as the 'tigre de los pantanos' (p. 45) but he is not a lone hunter. In fact his aide-de-camp is part of el Brujo's team, 'una manada de lobos hambrientos, de búfalos jóvenes' (p. 55). El Garza (whom el Brujo might just as well have called 'ruiseñor' because of his beautiful voice, p. 56) takes the form of a woodpecker as the carver of the cradle for el Brujo's son (p. 204) that will have flower and plant designs. Becoming-animal is also represented in the masked balls in which the guests wear animal masks. El Brujo's own mask is that of an ant, the creature with which he most closely identifies, even signing his editorial 'Hormiga roja' (p. 162). His telluric nature is reflected in the sensuality of his relationship with the ants which cover him in their luxuriant redness as he glows and pulsates in the afternoon sun: 'se hermanan conmigo' (p. 15). There is an erotic insect–human exchange: 'libaron de mis poros, de mis más privados intersticios' (p. 17). The ant is known for its foresight and insect life represents a model for polymorphous anti-phallic sexuality. Insects are non-mammals that lay eggs. 'They feed into the most insidious anxieties about unnatural copulations and births'.[103] The colour of the red ant suggests blood. El Brujo's pyramid, erected with the blood of the workers, reminds him of the Great Temple of Tenochtitlán and Aztec sacrifice. He evokes the carpet of blood as a gigantic cloak of red ants, a living cloak of blood (p. 107). Blood represents flow ('río de sangre'), menstruation, life, death and is therefore a perfect image for becoming and changing.

Becoming animal is the lesser prototype of becoming woman. El Brujo is terrified of woman and her threatening genitalia and jealous of her reproductive capacity that makes him feel incomplete. He is a freak with a secret – a third testicle which will be fertilized by the secretions of the Finger to engender 'la única mujer [. . .] diosa de la fertilidad y de la muerte' (p. 218). His resolve to incorporate femininity in his own body is motivated by fear – fear of the female genitals and their castrating power. He is revolted by menstruation and wastage but more important is his obsession with the *vagina dentata*. He witnesses Cora Seisdedos's birth and is appalled by the 'hueco feroz que se iba abriendo como para tragárselo' (p. 38). His obsession with the female body emerges in a series of metaphors, such as the anthill-womb, that he tries to destroy (p. 29). He witnesses doña Rosa's rape and fantasizes about the rapists' return and the recurrence of the rape scene (p. 40). This episode is a partial repetition of his earliest memory, of the monstruous feminine: 'la negra caverna de la mujer abierta para expulsar al ser monstruoso con seis dedos en cada mano' (p. 65). He concocts a terrible revenge, a magical compound to dissolve the uterus (p. 30).[104]

But the torturer is himself tortured, haunted by the vagina into which he had once inserted a mouse. It is now a 'hueco negro, enorme, como una boca que intenta devorarme' (p. 245). Even the sun takes on a similarly threatening aspect: 'es como una boca horrible, una abertura de mujer que te quiere tragar (p. 144). El Brujo can only overcome this threat by incorporating female sexuality in his own body. To this end he draws inspiration from Egyptology and the hermaphroditic figure of Tutankhamun endowed with female breasts. El Garza remodels him out of mud (p. 225) but his transformation is metaphorical as well as literal, as emerges from his use of biblical imagery to proclaim his power: 'Jamás ídolo con pies de barro sino todo lo contrario: soy el barro con pies de ídolo [. . .]' (p. 225). Here el Brujo inverts Daniel's interpretation of King Nebuchadnezzar's dream of the great image with head of gold and feet of iron and clay (Daniel 2: 32–3). The process of his metamorphosis is described in terms of biblical origins. El Garza smears him with clay and he takes on his 'nueva y femenina pulpa', discovering 'ondulaciones de la pelvis antes para él desconocidas' (p. 226).

As we have seen, Valenzuela's text destabilizes language by removing the boundaries between the literal and the metaphorical: Estrella, the third testicle, is the 'metáfora viva' (p. 16), the site of female inscription on the male organ. Ironically, el Brujo's efforts to achieve completeness by incorporating the female genitals in his own body emphasizes rather than erases sexual difference because of the position of his 'cánula de amor': 'todos la tienen por debajo del vientre; yo la tengo por encima. Soy también en esto diferente' (p. 248). However, el Brujo succeeds in becoming pregnant and Estrella, like fecund soil, receives the seed (p. 254). He entertains the notion of keeping his son inside him to be more complete – 'seré inconmensurable' (p. 246). Indeed, his new being defies linguistic definition: 'no se lo puede calificar con género definido alguno y hay que crearle nuevos adjetivos. No neutros porque de neutro nada tiene le Bruj, sino adjetivos ambiguos, mutantes' (p. 228). His fluid unstable character appears to infect language itself since literality merges imperceptibly into metaphor to form a feminized linguistic 'swampiness' where the concept of fixed meaning no longer applies. Words do not mean what they appear to mean – 'la piraña' refers not to a fish but to a curse (pp. 36–7) – and the reference to the 'esteros' (p. 52) is metaphorical, pointing to the human unconscious. On a lighter note, the play of the metaphoric and the literal causes some misunderstanding between the Rear Admiral and Perón (when the pair discuss the implications of el Brujo's political ascendancy) and also suggests el Brujo's slipperiness: Perón remarks that press photographs of him emphasize el Brujo's age and will serve to diminish his power. The Rear Admiral responds: 'No tan envejecido, no crea. Para mí que se trae algo bajo la manga. – En la foto aparece en camiseta' (p. 207). El Brujo thinks he can control language – 'metáfora que ahora estoy haciendo realidad' (p. 105) – but he finds himself thwarted by the lack of linguistic resources to express adequately the fusion of two bodies while maintaining the trace of their difference: 'te voy a hacer un hijo, vamos a hacer un hijo, vos y yo, yo y yo [. . .]' (p. 238). This is the culmination of el Brujo's persistent word play, his exposure of linguistic slippage even as he proclaims his own power: 'Yo soy el Amo porque no amo' (p. 33).[105] Linguistic play undermines the notion of incontrovertible authority. For Lacan the phallus is a guarantee of authority. To have the phallus would mean to be at the centre of discourse, to generate meaning, to have mastery of language, to control rather than conform to that which comes from outside, from the Other.[106] The play of language opposes flow to rigidity and mirrors the liquid movements and contradictions of el Brujo himself. His carnivalesque instincts extend to language: 'voy a enloquecer a todos con el baile y la risa. Correrá un río de sangre, sí, pero esta vez será del verbo reír. Un galope de rojas carcajadas' (p. 119); 'mi río de sangre no atiende los pendientes, corre por donde yo decido por la simple razón de que me río de la sangre' (p. 219). The word 'río', associated with flow in its meaning as 'river', itself flows imperceptibly into another meaning through its shift from noun to verb. Language as cluster of multiple becomings evades the grasp of el Brujo just as he evades the control of Luisa Valenzuela.

The text illustrates the play of supplementarity and 'essence'. El Brujo is a supplement that moves to centre stage, overshadowing the founding figure of Perón. Similarly, el Brujo's supplementary testicle – bearing the trace of his sister and later inscribed with the mark of the female – overshadows the 'normal' pair by swelling and bursting, so providing a bodily sign – tumescence and de-tumescence – of the movement of writing and plot. While his hand has the normal five fingers, the lack of a 'supplementary' finger is crucial: 'sentía que me faltaba un dedo para hacerla [Cora] de verdad dichosa' (p. 44).

The Derridean critique of Rousseau's concept of speech as pure and writing as the 'dangerous' supplement that is added as a technique or ruse to make speech present when it is actually absent, is suggested in the description of the newspaper of the people of Capivarí, appropriated by el Brujo, who changes its name from La Voz del Pueblo de Capivarí to *La Voz* (p. 160). This title denotes voice as purity and presence but this voice does not denote physical presence since it is a mere simulation of immediacy and presence, being the printed title of a newspaper. The newspaper's errata list, necessitated by printing errors that appear 'cada tanto como un cáncer' (p. 171), is an indispensable rather than optional supplement since it modifies the paper's message. The play of the supplement is expressed in the negative 'nunca': 'el valor de *nunca* debe ser el valor de *nadie* y el de *nada*. Es esto lo que debe ser leído para poder alcanzar un conocimiento pleno de mi inmanencia' (p. 172). This negative word suggests here an ongoing lack that can never be filled. El Brujo's ultimate fate, however, removes any kind of anchorage from 'nunca' since his supposedly irreplaceable self may be substituted by the 'spare parts' that service the dictatorial system (p. 259).

Luisa Valenzuela is, of course, the creator of the text and López Rega contributes to the theme of writing by playing the role of 'supplementary' writer dependent upon the fictional world created by her. His text is circumscribed by the authorial voice of the first and last sections. But the supplement usurps the centre as Luisa Valenzuela herself considers assuming the supplementary role of ghostwriter to el Brujo (p. 206).

Within Peronism, Isabel is the *intrusa*, the (poor) substitute who became president, while the goddess herself was denied even the vice presidency. El Brujo is the 'dangerous supplement', incarnating in his crude physicality what Peronism merely suggested: the depths of the Argentine unconscious.

The text appears to strive for an elusive unity represented by the number three. The work itself consists of three parts, Peronism is represented by three figures (Eva, Juan, Isabel), López Rega has three testicles and founds the Triple A mirrored by the Triple E (Edecán, Estrella, E[va]). But the text's ultimate lack of unity is suggested by the tail of the title. The tail is a kind of appendage or supplement of the body. But far from playing a subordinate role (in the margins), it takes pride of place at the head of the text. It is the central symbol rather than a supplementary sign; against the unity of three, it opposes the principle of fluidity and instability, endless substitutions and engenderings.

Tierney-Tello describes recent women's writing being cast 'less as product and more as process, as a form of struggle, as a transformative terrain'.[107] Valenzuela herself sees language as a form of secretion: 'I think of language as one more secretion, the most terrifying of all perhaps because of everything it conceals while revealing or vice versa'.[108] This aspect of writing is clearly illustrated in the evocation of el Brujo's journey to the end of the Earth:

> Corredores espiralándose, subiendo y bajando y volviéndose imprecisos, vagos, como en un sueño por el que él transita en pos del mensaje, internándose más y más en el vientre de la tierra, vieja pachamama tan rocosa y estéril por dentro, de vísceras poco cálidas, poco acogedoras o mullidas, sólidas vísceras de roca por las que el se interna identificándose, granítico él, inconmovible pero tan corruptible como corrumpido está el vientre de la tierra, intestinos de la tierra que se vuelven mohosos por momentos, con algo de la viscosidad de la verdadera entraña, y él no los quiere así, no, y por eso avanza en pos de una rigidez preternatural que en poder de su edecán, el perro, lo llevará a él, el amo, al verdadero éxtasis. (p. 62)

Change and becoming are represented in the proliferation of present participles that create a poetic effect reminiscent of Pablo Neruda. The repetition of words ('internándose'/'se interna', 'vientre', 'vísceras', 'verdadero/a'), the failure of coherent sense ('mullidas'/'sólidas', 'inconmovible'/'corruptible') together with the cumulative mass of the single sentence all suggest the 'swampiness' of language, the viscosity of meaning conjoined to the viscosity of expression as both begin to fuse and merge, secreting volume and density but excluding stasis and sense.

El Brujo is writing (metaphorically) a novel: 'mi vida y por lo tanto mi diario constituyen una gran novela. La novela. La Biblia' (p. 47). His writing aspires to be biblical and authoritative. But language is like water, 'tan diafana [. . .] se vuelve neblinosa' (p. 47). For Luisa Valenzuela, writing is a kind of exorcism, whereby she confronts and unmasks the discourse of power while refusing authoritative status herself. She feels vulnerable to el Brujo's contagious force, metaphorically impregnated by his promiscuous mode of becoming. Without him she would not have a novel. Under his influence she cannot keep fiction and reality separate. Everything mingles, the threads cross and tangle (p. 140). El Brujo invades her realm and threatens to erase her text. He spreads like an infection, proliferating in all directions and overflowing his fictional status (p. 156). But Luisa Valenzuela is not without influence herself since el Brujo becomes aware of his own weightlessness: 'es como si una mano se hubiera detenido, como si alguien hubiese dejado de escribirme' (p. 219).

Luisa Valenzuela knows that linguistic 'secretions' have both negative and positive potential but she is open to both forms of becoming. As Braidotti affirms: 'writers, like animals, are committed creatures who live on full alert, constantly tensed up in the effort of captivating and sustaining the signals that come from their plane of immanent contact with other forces.'[109] She refuses to use the 'swampiness' of language as an excuse for evading social responsibility. 'Her textual double, 'Luisa Valenzuela', swears to the reader that her biography of the Sorcerer is her attempt to take on the responsibility of history, to state the facts and to try to understand them'.[110]

The horror of el Brujo's world incorporates the body in pieces, the body deformed, the body shorn of its vital organs. His third testicle represents not only a supplementary secretion but also an indispensable secret: the doctor who suggested surgery paid with his life (p. 31) and mere knowledge of the secret deserves death (p. 45). Other people's vital organs are, by contrast, truncated and discarded at will: a hand of the murdered mayor of Capivarí is left in a barn by el Brujo's men. Eva's power is embodied in a truncated body part, a finger that develops from the divine little finger to the Great Avenging Finger (p. 99), a phallic finger (to which el Brujo erected an altar) in contrast with the fallen phallus of Eshú, the shamanic name used by el Brujo. The natural world contains images of detached body parts: the sun is a horrible mouth, 'una abertura de mujer que te quiere tragar' (p. 144). The pregnant Brujo is finally threatened by the vultures 'haciendo de mi huevo el objetivo único' (p. 249). Indeed el Brujo himself is no more than a dispensable part of the mechanized body of dictatorship: 'las tiranías ya no vienen como antes. Ahora tienen piezas de repuesto' (p. 259). In contrast, its victims cannot produce new parts. Those whose nails and hands have been removed can only resist with their stumps (p. 245).

'Piezas de repuesto' suggests a further becoming, the becoming-machine. El Brujo has a personal museum of body parts (p. 45) and catalogues of machine parts for torture (p. 46). The imbrication of the bodily and the mechanical is further suggested when he supplies tubes to enable his guests to drink without removing their masks. The coalescence of man and machine is most clearly presented in the figure of the old typesetter, Funes: 'El viejo había visto nacer las máquinas de ese periódico, las había criado y casi se podría decir nutrido con sus propias secreciones [. . .] el viejo ya tenía color de linotapia y tos de rotativa' (p. 147).

> En su observatorio de palmeras tiene la máquina de bombardear nubes y esa otra máquina tanto más moderna de *fabricar* nubes. Pero para lograr el fenómeno pluvial cuenta sobre todo con sus ensalmos, y con sus imprecaciones. (p. 61)

Cola de lagartija is largely about the workings of the savage mind which relates more closely to earth and body than to ideas and intellect. Valenzuela offers a mythic world suffused with the anti-rational whose protagonist combines elements of the sacred and the profane. It is for this reason that she can sympathize with el Brujo. His first person narrative, she says, allows him to speak in a poetic language rich in associations: 'so he became likeable despite his exaggeratedly aberrant ideas that functioned like Symbols'.[111] Here Valenzuela distances herself from Kristeva's pejorative concept of the abject for the monstruous, unassimilable other that threatens the stability of the self. She is closer to Deleuze's 'becoming-animal' representing metamorphosis and fusion rather than stability, order and classification.

El Brujo's trajectory includes both the return to origins and final destruction while the closing reference to resurgent tyranny ('pieza de repuesto') suggests cyclical, mythic time. It may also hint at Peronism's 'piezas de repuesto' (Carlos Menem) in recent Argentine history. Fascism aspires to undo the errors of modernity by returning to mythical roots. Jo Labanyi points out that 'the mythical appeal on the one hand to classical order and on the other to primal instinctual energy is not as contradictory as it might seem, for both are attempts to return to what is seen as an original wholeness'.[112] This pinpoints el Brujo's aim: his becoming animal and becoming woman. There is, of course, a mythical antecedent – Hermaphroditus – who achieves by other means what el Brujo aspires to in *Cola de lagartija*: the union of male and female. A more recent antecedent is Freud's Judge Schreber who believed the world was coming to an end and that he alone could save it – but only by transforming himself into a woman.[113] In contrast to Schreber who represents high European culture, el Brujo adopts the role of Caliban as described by Fernández Retamar – the primitive, monstrous other of the civilized Western world.[114]

El Brujo's intimacy with ants goes back to a mythical past 'in illo tempore' (p. 17) and by the end of his life his becoming-insect has been supplemented by his becoming-bird and becoming-animal:

> Avanzo en lo oscuro con mis ojos de búho. Me vuelvo nictálope para servir a la causa, me vuelvo astuto como el zorro. Avanzo en la noche con mi nueva oscuridad de lobo, tengo algo de pantera sigilosa [. . .] espero al amanecer en una gruta del río y contengo al gallo en mí que quisiera celebrar la primera claridad largándose a cantar de alegría. (pp. 252–3)

Valenzuela's fascination for a world of endless becomings infects the reader but her text is ultimately a resounding indictment not only of dictatorship but also of the overwhelming Latin American obsession with the return to origins. Like Pablo Neruda she stresses that there is no wholeness prior to alienation. Her writing is in the last analysis a kind of exorcism, 'una práctica subversiva por la que, simbólicamente, se le mira la cara al padre, se desmitifica su figura y se despiertan hondas resonancias asociadas con la voz silenciada de la madre'.[115]

The ironization of Peronism offered by Puig and Szichman do not match the trenchancy of Valenzuela's. *Cola de lagartija* subjects Peronism's most savage progeny to an aesthetic reconfiguration that approximates more closely to the enormity of El Brujo's intervention in Argentine history than any literal recounting of events could ever achieve. Like Martínez, Valenzuela refuses the notion that reality may be reflected directly through language: for her too, reality is susceptible only to imperfect mirroring through the mediation of art.[116]

NOTES

[1] Manuel Puig, *Pubis angelical* (Barcelona: Seix Barral, 1979), pp. 167–8. Further references, given in parenthesis in the text, are to this edition. An earlier version of this chapter's first section appeared in 'Psychoanalysis, Gender, and Angelic Truth in Manuel Puig's *Pubis Angelical*, *MLR* 93 (1998), 400–410. Puig clearly reflects Argentine academic interest in psychoanalysis. Stephen M. Hart indicates the

importance of psychoanalysis in Latin America and particularly in Argentina where the Instituto de Estudios Psicoanalíticos, devoted to Lacanian theory, was established at the University of Córdoba in the 1970s. See *The Other Scene: Psychoanalytic Readings in Modern Spanish and Latin-American Literature* (Boulder CO: Society of Spanish and Spanish-American Studies, 1992), pp. 4–6.

2 Mariano Ben Plotkin, *Freud in the Pampas: the Emergence and Development of a Psychoanalytic Culture in Argentina* (Stanford CA: Stanford University Press, 2001), p. 18.

3 Mariano Ben Plotkin, 'Freud, politics, and the Porteños: the reception of psychoanalysis in Buenos Aires, 1910–1943', *Hispanic American Historical Review*, 77 (1997), 45–74 (45–6).

4 Plotkin notes that in the 1960s 'a certain psychoanalytic way of thinking permeated contemporary Argentine literature, particularly the work of authors of the new generation, such as Manuel Puig'. *Freud in the Pampas*, p. 82.

5 Mariano Ben Plotkin, 'The Changing Perceptions of Peronism' in James P. Brenan (ed.), *Peronism and Argentina* (Wilmington DE: Scholarly Resources, 1998), pp. 29–54 (p. 31).

6 Javier Auyero, *Poor People's Politics: Peronist Survival Networks and the Legacy of Evita* (Durham and London: Duke University Press, 2001), p. 26.

7 Ernesto Goldar, *El peronismo en la literatura argentina* (Buenos Aires: Freeland, 1971), p. 10.

8 Quoted by Plotkin, 'The Changing Perceptions of Peronism', p. 46.

9 Edwin Williamson, *The Penguin History of Latin America* (London: Penguin, 1992), pp. 467, 470.

10 Juan José Sebreli, *Los deseos imaginarios del peronismo* (Buenos Aires: Sudamericana, 1992), p. 17.

11 Beatriz Sarlo, *La pasión y la excepción* (Buenos Aires: Siglo XXI, 2003), p. 25.

12 Plotkin, *Freud in the Pampas*, p. 5.

13 Carmen Noemí Perilli, 'Violencia y delirio en tres novelas argentinas del 80', in *Cuadernos Americanos*, 259 (1985), 225–31 (p. 228) .

14 Plotkin, *Freud in the Pampas*, p. 121.

15 Anonymous, 'Are we all neurotic?' in Gabriella Nouzeilles and Graciela Montaldo (eds), *The Argentina Reader: History, Culture, Politics* (Durham and London: Duke University Press, 2002), pp. 352–7 (p. 356).

16 Pamela Bacarisse, 'Superior men and inferior reality: Manuel Puig's *Pubis angelical*', *Bulletin of Hispanic Studies*, 66 (1989), 361–70.

17 'La presencia de Evita en el balcón de la Casa Rosada el 1 de mayo y en las ceremonias del 4 de junio, era interpretada como un acto desesperado por parte de un dictador cuyo fin estaba ya próximo pues su popularidad había declinado y la única que mantenía el fervor del pueblo era Evita'. Marysa Navarro, *Evita* (Buenos Aires: Corregidor, 1981), p. 309.

18 Ernesto Sábato, *El otro rostro del peronismo. Carta abierta a Mario Amadeo* (Buenos Aires: [n. pub.], 1956), p. 40.

19 Juan José Sebreli, *Los deseos imaginarios del peronismo*, p. 20.

20 Linda Hutcheon, *A Theory of Parody: the Teachings of Twentieth-Century Art Forms* (New York and London: Methuen, 1985), p. 16.
21 See Sigmund Freud, 'Fragment of an analysis of a case of hysteria', in *The Standard Edition of the Complete Psychological Works of Sigmund Freud*, ed. James Strachey, 24 vols (London: Hogarth Press, 1953), VII, pp. 3–122.
22 Lucille Kerr, 'The dis-appearance of a popular author: Stealing around style with Manuel Puig's *Pubis angelical*', in *Reclaiming the Author: Figures and Fictions from Spanish America* (Durham and London: Duke University Press, 1992), pp. 103, 105 and Mikkel Borch-Jacobsen, *Lacan: the Absolute Master* (Stanford: Stanford University Press, 1991), p. 2.
23 Steven Marcus, 'Freud and Dora: Story, history, case history', *Partisan Review*, 41 (1974), 12–23, 89–108 (pp. 91–2).
24 See Dujovne Ortiz, *Eva Perón: a Biography*, p. 62.
25 See Jane Gallop, *Feminism and Psychoanalysis: the Daughter's Seduction* (London: Macmillan, 1982), p. 137, and John Forrester, *The Seductions of Psychoanalysis: Freud, Lacan and Derrida* (Cambridge: Cambridge University Press, 1990), p. 298.
26 Ana's late father had also had a 'secret' – membership of a Masonic order, a secret which Ana chooses to reinterpret in sexual terms: 'es que vos tendrías alguna querida por ahí, y le dabas excusas a mamá' (p. 104).
27 Dujovne Ortiz, *Eva Perón: a Biography*, p. 46.
28 This is the view of Jorgelina Corbatta. See her *Mito personal y mitos colectivos en las novelas de Manuel Puig* (Madrid: Orígenes, 1988), p. 86.
29 Mariano Ben Plotkin remarks that 'from its beginnings Peronism was characterized by its opponents as a political aberration, as the essential "other", and as a pathology in Argentine history [. . .]'. *Freud in the Pampas*, p. 55.
30 Eduardo Crawley, *A House Divided: Argentina 1880–1980* (London: Hurst, 1984), p. 354.
31 Puig playfully uses the vexed area of female desire to link W218 to Dora: Freud locates the site of Dora's sexual excitation at the thorax, displaced thence from the genital area. (See Freud, *Standard Edition*, p. 30.) For W218, full satisfaction is marked by a yawn (p. 127). In both characters the erotic focus moves from the lower body to the upper, suggesting the union of the sexual and the spiritual – a notion which Puig reinforces in the image of the 'pubis angelical'. The connection with Eva's vocal eroticism is clear.
32 See Gallop, *Feminism and Psychoanalysis*, p. 140.
33 Santiago Colás claims that Juan Perón 'looms largest in the Argentine shift from modernity to postmodernity'. Colás, *Postmodernity in Latin America: the Argentine Paradigm* (Durham and London: Duke University Press, 1994), p. 152.
34 See Forrester, *The Seductions of Psychoanalysis*, p. 148. Merrim's contention that Ana 'trivializes' Lacan ('For a New (Psychological)

Novel', p. 156) seems misplaced: it is rather the masculine approach based on such concepts as 'rigour' and 'depth' which (paradoxically) trivializes Lacan.
35 See, for example, Alicia Dujovne Ortiz, *Eva Perón*, trans. Shawn Fields (New York: St Martin's Griffin, 1997), p. 277.
36 For further discussion of this aspect of Freud see, for example, Nancy Armstrong, *Desire and Domestic Fiction: a Political History of the Novel* (New York: Oxford University Press, 1987), pp. 231–42.
37 For Freud everything is a representation of something else; as Peter Brooks writes: 'language can "mean" something other than what it "says", can suggest intentions of which the subject is not consciously aware [. . .]' See *Reading for the Plot: Design and Intention in Narrative* (Cambridge MA: Harvard University Press, 1992), p. 55.
38 Peter Brooks refers to Puig in connection with 'the return to plot in a parodic way'. See *Psychoanalysis and Storytelling* (Oxford: Blackwell, 1994), p. 122.
39 Brooks, *Psychoanalysis and Storytelling*, p. 57. Steven Marcus comments that Dora got her own back on Freud 'by refusing to allow him to bring her story to an end in the way he saw fit'. See 'Freud and Dora', p. 105.
40 Telepathy is, of course, closely related to psychoanalysis. The power of reading thoughts depicted in *Pubis angelical* typically exaggerates a psychoanalytic practice designated 'thought-transference' by Freud. See Forrester, *The Seductions of Psychoanalysis*, p. 252.
41 Eva Perón, *La razón de mi vida*, pp. 139, 141.
42 Martínez, *La novela de Perón*, p. 12.
43 Kate Millett, *Sexual Politics* (London: Virago, 1977).
44 'Qu'est-ce qu'une femme?', in *Le Séminaire de Jacques Lacan*, ed. Jacques-Alain Miller (Paris: Éditions du Seuil, 1981), III: *Les Psychoses*, pp. 195–205 (p. 199).
45 Carmen Llorca, *Llamadme Evita* (Barcelona: Planeta, 1980), p. 223.
46 See, for example, Nicholas Fraser and Marysa Navarro, *Evita: the Real Lives of Eva Perón* (London: André Deutsch, 1996), p. 149.
47 Referring to Eva's reference in *La razón de mi vida* to her two roles, as Eva Perón (president's wife) and as Evita (the bridge between the people and government), Sebreli remarks that she was split between 'dos estilos de vida antigónicos que asumen la característica de una doble personalidad, una especie de Doctor Jekyll y Míster Hyde morales: la señora que asiste vestida como una reina al Teatro Colón, y la compañera Evita que atiende a los obreros en el Ministerio de Trabajo y Previsión'. *Eva Perón ¿aventurera o militante?*, 4th edn (Buenos Aires: Pleyade, 1990), p. 60.
48 Eva Perón, *Mi mensaje*, p. 13.
49 See Ferdinand de Saussure, *Cours de Linguistique Générale* (Paris: Payot, 1931), pp. 97–100.
50 Eva Perón, *La razón de mi vida*, pp. 27, 108.
51 Tomás Eloy Martínez, *Santa Evita*, p. 184.
52 Marysa Navarro, *Evita* (Buenos Aires: Corregidor, 1981), p. 336.
53 Foster, 'Evita Perón, Juan José Sebreli and gender' in David William

Foster, *Sexual Textualities: Essays on Queering Latin American Writing* (Austin: University of Texas, 1997), pp. 22–38 (p. 37).

54 See, for example, Pamela Bacarisse, 'Superior Men and Inferior Reality: Manuel Puig's *Pubis angelical*', *Bulletin of Hispanic Studies*, 66 (1989), 361–70 (p. 370).

55 Stephen Heath, *The Sexual Fix* (London and Basingstoke: Macmillan, 1982), p. 142.

56 This point is made by Bryan S. Turner, 'Introduction', in Christine Buci-Glucksmann, *Baroque Reason: the Aesthetics of Modernity*, trans. Patrick Camiller (London: Sage, 1994), pp. 1–36 (p. 33).

57 Luce Irigaray states that angels 'link what has been split by patriarchy – the flesh and the spirit, nature and gods, the carnal and the divine, and are a way of conceptualizing a possible overcoming of the deadly and immobilizing division of the sexes in which women have been allocated body, flesh, nature, earth, carnality while men have been allocated spirit and transcendence'. See *The Irigaray Reader*, ed. Margaret Whitford (Oxford: Blackwell, 1991), p. 157. Lacan notes the complicity of the divine and amorous in 'Une lettre d'amour'. See *Le Séminaire de Jacques Lacan*, ed. Jacques-Alain Miller (Paris: Éditions du Seuil, 1975), XX: *Encore, 1972–1973*, pp. 73–82.

58 Irigaray describes the angel as 'the figurative version of a sexual being not yet incarnate', *The Irigaray Reader*, p. 173.

59 See Julia Kristeva, *Folle vérité* (Paris: Éditions du Seuil, 1979), p. 11.

60 See Alice A. Jardine, *Gynesis: Configurations of Woman and Modernity* (Ithaca and London: Cornell University Press, 1985), p. 114.

61 Gilles Deleuze and Félix Guattari, *A Thousand Plateaus: Capitalism and Schizophrenia*, trans. Brian Massumi (Minneapolis: University of Minnesota Press, 1987), p. 153.

62 Jardine, *Gynesis*, p. 213.

63 Elizabeth Bronfen, *Over Her Dead Body: Death, Femininity and the Aesthetic* (Manchester: Manchester University Press, 1992), p. 103.

64 See Brian McHale, *Constructing Postmodernism* (London: Routledge, 1992), pp. 188–206.

65 Clichés, as many critics have remarked, provide us with a common ground and common habitation. See, for example, Carlos Fuentes, *Nueva novela hispanoamericana* (México: Joaquín Mortiz, 1972), p. 9. Christopher Prendergast claims that clichés become routinized formulae 'because they are in some way "right" for the situations and states of the world to which they refer'. *The Order of Mimesis: Balzac, Stendhal, Nerval, Flaubert* (Cambridge: Cambridge University Press, 1986), p. 208

66 Linda Hutcheon, *A Theory of Parody*, p. 75.

67 Sarlo, *La pasión y la excepción*, p. 198.

68 Zygmunt Bauman, *Modernity and Ambivalence*, p. 158.

69 Tomás Eloy Martínez, *Las memorias del General*, p. 176.

70 Quoted by Craig Owens, 'The Discourse of Others: Feminists and Postmodernism' in Hal Foster (ed.), *The Anti-Aesthetic: Essays on Postmodern Culture* (New York: The New Press, 1983), pp. 57–82 (p. 65).

71 Julio Ortega, 'El lector en su laberinto', *Hispanic Review*, 60 (1992), 165–79 (168).
72 Mario Szichman, *A las 20:25, la señora entró en la inmortalidad* (Hanover NH: Ediciones del Norte, 1981), p. 15. Subsequent references, given in the text, are to this edition.
73 Corina S. Mathieu, 'Mario Szichman como desacralizador de mitos en *A las 20:25, la señora entró en la inmortalidad*' in *Ensayos de literatura europea e hispanoamericana* (San Sebastián: Universidad del País Vasco, 1990), pp. 307–12 (p. 310).
74 María Cristina Pons, *Memorias del olvido. Del Paso, García Márquez, Saer y la novela histórica de fines del siglo XX* (México: Siglo XXI, 1996), p. 17.
75 Bauman, *Modernity and Ambivalence*, p. 114.
76 John Lynch, *Argentine Dictator: Juan Manuel de Rosas, 1829–1852* (Oxford: Clarendon, 1981), p. 373, n. 66.
77 The reference is to the French engineer and designer Jacques de Vaucanson (1709–82), best known for his mechanical duck.
78 The 'semana trágica' refers to January 1919: President Yrigoyen's decision to use the police and armed forces to break a general strike resulted in violence and heavy loss of life in Buenos Aires.
79 Paul Ricoeur, *Time and Narrative*, trans. Kathleen McLaughlin and David Pellauer, 3 vols (Chicago and London: University of Chicago, 1984–8), II, p. 101.
80 Nicholas Fraser and Marysa Navarro, *Evita: the Real Lives of Eva Perón* (London: André Deutsch, 1996), p. 197.
81 The Zwi Migdal Society was a criminal Jewish syndicate – centred in Buenos Aires – whose activities included the kidnapping, rape and forced prostitution of young Jewish women. It first came to prominence at the end of the 1860s and continued operations until the outbreak of the Second World War.
82 Kaja Silverman, *Male Subjectivity at the Margins* (New York and London: Routledge, 1992), p. 370.
83 Richard Holmes, 'Biography: Inventing the truth' in John Batchelor (ed.), *The Art of Literary Biography* (Oxford: Clarendon, 1995), pp. 15–25 (p. 20).
84 Tomás Eloy Martínez, 'Historia y ficción: dos paralelas que se tocan' in *Literaturas del Río de la Plata hoy: de las utopías al desencanto*, Americana Eystettensia: Serie A, Actas; 15 (Frankfurt am Main: Vervuert; Madrid: Iberoamericana, 1996), pp. 89–100 (pp. 94–5).
85 Joseph A. Page, *Perón: a Biography* (New York: Random House, 1983), p. 396.
86 Eduardo Crawley, *A House Divided: Argentina 1880–1980* (London: Hurst, 1984), p. 354.
87 Tomás Eloy Martínez, who interviewed Perón in the early 1970s, confirms López Rega's love of writing: 'Le oí decir a menudo que, aparte de servir al General, lo único que le proporcionaba felicidad era el acto de escribir. Tengo la certeza de que en este último punto era sincero'. See *Las memorias del General* (Buenos Aires: Planeta, 1996), p. 142.

88 Eduardo Crawley, *A House Divided*, p. 354
89 Joseph A. Page, *Perón: a Biography*, pp. 486, 492.
90 Perón asserts that 'Eva es un producto mío' in Tomás Eloy Martínez's *La novela de Perón* (Madrid: Alianza, 1989), p. 268. López Rega also features in Martínez's novel though not as prominently as in *Cola de lagartija*. In *La novela de Perón* he is also known as Daniel and also claims supernatural powers: 'he logrado que el General sea devuelto a la vida' (p. 122). He attempts to transfer the spirit of Eva to Isabel by smearing their bodies with the blood of a hummingbird (p. 232). Martínez's López Rega also has an affinity with ants ('mi tarea de hormiga comienza, lenta, definitiva', p. 122). He too is inventive, invasive and manipulative: just as López Rega invades the narrative space of the textual Luisa Valenzuela, so Tomás Eloy Martínez's López Rega invades and controls Perón's past: 'Tanto me ha confundido que, cuando miro una foto de la infancia, no sé si de verdad estoy en ella o es que López me ha llevado hasta allí' (p. 46). Perón regards him as an extraneous presence attempting to dislodge him from his own body (p. 50). López's male authoritarianism emerges in *La novela de Perón* in, for example, his emphasis on one version of history (p. 168). Martínez's evocation of López is often reminiscent of Valenzuela's in *Cola de lagartija*: 'López se contorsiona y hunde la cabeza dentro del tronco. Asoma sólo el verdor malicioso de los ojillos, como un lagarto' (p. 233).
91 Joseph A. Page, *Perón: a Biography*, p. 399.
92 Luisa Valenzuela, *Cola de lagartija* (México: Universidad Autónoma de México, 1992), p. 49. Further references, given in parenthesis in the text, are to this edition.
93 Tomás Eloy Martínez makes a similar point about López's unlikely personal and political trajectory: 'son raros en la historia los casos de un personaje como él, casi iletrado, sin talento aparente para la política y con una ideología extravagante, capaz de llegar tan lejos en un país donde los escépticos son mayoría' (*Las memorias del General*, p. 144). In *Cola de lagartija*, images of staining, associated with el Brujo, recur throughout, suggesting contagion y violación: 'La túnica blanca se le fue tiñendo con la tierra colorada y las manchas de sudor se hicieron coágulos [. . .] Unas gotas de sangre empezaron a caer pesadamente sobre el blanquísimo mantel y le dibujaron flores' (pp. 22–3).
94 López Rega's male values displace Eva's feminine virtue as enshrined in the Peronist slogan, 'Perón cumple, Eva dignifica'.
95 There are several points of contact between *Cola de lagartija* (1983) and García Márquez's *El otoño del patriarca* (1975). The 'true' identity of both Valenzuela's el Brujo and García Márquez's patriarch are called into question (*Cola*, p. 19; *El otoño del patriarca*, Madrid: Mondadori, 1987, p. 12). Both have doubles (the Edecán and Patricio Aragonés) and both are believed to have the power to be in several places at once ('estoy en todas partes y en ninguna', *Cola*, p. 176; 'Aquel estar simultáneo en todas partes', *Otoño*, p. 17). Both serve up the bodies of their victims (the Maci and Patricio Aragonés)

for public consumption (*Cola*, p. 135; *Otoño*, pp. 125–6). Both are obsessed with mirrors that cause their images to proliferate and in both texts the sacred number three recurs (for example, el Brujo's three testicles, the Patriarch's three birth certificates). Both el Brujo and the Patriarch are obsessed with auguries and prophecies (el Brujo goes by the name of Daniel, the Old Testament prophet; the Patriarch is associated with Julius Caesar, partly because comets, which provide keys to the future, play an important part in their lives. Both see themselves as conquerors, el Brujo likening himself to Columbus (*Cola*, p. 44) while the Patriarch receives a golden spur from the Discoverer (*El otoño*, p. 176). Both Valenzuela and García Márquez treat their subjects with humour and both writers have been accused of sympathizing, at least to some degree, with their subjects.

96 Theweleit refers to the fascist song: 'Blood, blood, blood must flow / Thick as a rain of blows'. See Klaus Theweleit, *Male Fantasies*, trans. Stephen Conway, 2 vols (Minneapolis: University of Minnesota Press, 1987), I: *Women, Floods, Bodies, History*, p. 234.

97 Alice A. Jardine, *Gynesis: Configurations of Woman and Modernity* (Ithaca and London: Cornell University Press, 1985), p. 221.

98 Gilles Deleuze and Félix Guattari, *A Thousand Plateaus. Capitalism and Schizophrenia*, trans. Brian Massumi (Minneapolis: University of Minnesota Press, 1987), p. 242.

99 Rosi Braidotti, *Metamorphoses: Towards a Materialist Theory of Becoming* (Cambridge: Polity, 2002), pp. 128, 145.

100 Deleuze and Guattari, *A Thousand Plateaus*, pp. 239, 237.

101 Bradotti, *Metamorphoses*, p. 125.

102 In Tomás Eloy Martínez's *La mano del amo* (Madrid: Alfaguara, 2003), the protagonist, Carmona, discerns a human voice, that of his mother, in the repeated miaowing he hears while in the bath (p. 96). This satanic mother has some connections with the manipulative Eva of the 'black myth'. See my 'Coldness, Cruelty and Cats: Contested Territories of Influence in Tomás Eloy Martínez's *La mano del amo*' (forthcoming).

103 Braidotti, *Metamorphoses*, pp. 125, 128.

104 In Martínez's *La novela de Perón*, it is Perón himself who is obsessed with the *vagina dentata*, as we have seen. His fear derives from his recurrent and sexually-charged dream of the South Pole which reenacts the scene of his mother's adultery, an episode which he witnessed as a boy: 'Brújula y teodolitos le señalan que allí no hay un volcán sino una inmensa vagina erecta, en vilo. En la cúspide, la madre monta guardia, con la cabellera destrenzada y un poncho de hombre sobre el batón [. . .] López se ampara en la madre y lo rechaza' (p. 278). Here Perón's mother fixation points to fear of the maternal (the dominant theme in Martínez's *La mano del amo*) and to a variation of Valenzuela's theme of el Brujo's becoming woman.

105 Similar linguistic play is found in Martínez's *La mano del amo* ('"lamé el ano del amo", dijo el maullido. "Amá la mano del amo"', p. 96).

Another obvious link emerges in the name (Estrella) of the woman whom Carmona meets on the train and who has his mother's smile (p. 131).

[106] Jane Gallop, *Thinking Through the Body* (New York: Columbia University Press, 1988), p. 126.

[107] Mary Beth Tierney-Tello, *Allegories of Transgression and Transformation: Experimental Fiction by Women Writers under Dictatorship* (Albany: State University of New York, 1996), p. 14.

[108] Evelyn Picon Garfield, 'Interview with Luisa Valenzuela', *Review of Contemporary Fiction*, 6 (1986), 25–30 (p. 26).

[109] Braidotti, *Metamorphoses*, p. 126.

[110] Nancy Christoph, 'Bodily Matters: the Female Grotesque in Luisa Valenzuela's *Cola de lagartija*', *Revista Hispánica Moderna*, 40 (1995), 365–80 (p. 377).

[111] Garfield, 'Interview with Luisa Valenzuela', p. 27.

[112] Jo Labanyi, *Myth and History in the Contemporary Spanish Novel* (Cambridge: Cambridge University Press, 1989), p. 12. Tomás Eloy Martínez notes that 'en las antiguas religiones animistas, la vida de un hombre solía estar ligada a la de un árbol o un animal, a la caída de una piedra o al paso de un cometa' (*Las memorias del General*, p. 140).

[113] *The Standard Edition of the Complete Psychological Works of Sigmund Freud*, trans. James Strachey, XII: *The Case of Schreber, Papers on Technique and Other Works* (London: Hogarth, 1958), pp. 9–82.

[114] Roberto Fernández Retamar, *Caliban and Other Essays*, trans. Edward Baker (Minneapolis: University of Minnesota Press, 1989).

[115] Z. Nelly Martínez, *El silencio que habla: aproximación a la obra de Luisa Valenzuela* (Montreal: Corregidor, 1994), p. 157.

[116] See chapter 8, pp. 218–20.

Chapter 11
Conclusion

All three texts considered in the last chapter (*Pubis angelical, A las 20:25 la señora entró en la inmortalidad*, and *Cola de lagartija*) uncover metaphorical wounds. While Puig's text acknowledges that Peronism did go some way towards curing a national wound – by making visible a previously invisible Argentina – it none the less portrays Peronism itself as a pathology, a wound on the national psyche that remains raw and infectious. Perón's homecoming in June 1973 served only to aggravate the wound.[1] Moreover, metaphorical wounds are inflicted by the slipperiness and excess of language on the speaker's intention or the writer's purpose; Eva's unstable persona inflicts a permanent wound on any notion of clear gendered identity.[2] In the case of Mario Szichman, his Jewish immigrant family represents a deeper wound on the body politic than do the *descamisados*, Eva's natural constituents; and while Eva's wound festers over time, Rifque's wound is clean, self-inflicted, and immediately fatal. Valenzuela shows how Peronism represented a pathological sore on the body of a nation destined to suffer much deeper wounds before any kind of healing process could begin. Peronism spawned López Rega ('el Brujo'), whose elemental savagery went beyond the worst excesses of Perón himself and anticipated the murderous violence unleashed – in its pursuit of the 'dirty war'– by the military regime of General Jorge Rafael Videla (1976–80) that would disfigure the nation.

Literal and metaphorical wounds proliferate endlessly in the history of Peronism. Herself mortally 'wounded' by cancer, Eva wounds the respectable body of the oligarchy and makes deep female inscriptions (albeit from the margins) on the male preserves of national politics and autobiographical writing. The intractable ambivalences of Peronism inflict a metaphorical wound on the Western principles of reason and logic. It is no more than a 'wounded' or 'limping' truth that Peronism can offer – whether to its historians or to its literary reconstructors. This truth subsists within its multiplicities as a serious social legacy that is duly recognized by the progressive 'emplotment'[3] of New Historical writers such as Martínez.

Despite its inconsistencies and failures, Peronism was undoubtedly driven by the principles of social justice: Perón himself promoted egalitarianism and elevated the Argentine labour movement to centre stage in national politics. He gave presence and prestige to a previously invisible Argentina. Peronism was a 'potentially heretical voice, giving expression to the hopes of the oppressed both within the factory and beyond, as a claim for social dignity and equality'.[4] Perón was partially justified in claiming to have dismantled social hierarchies.[5] He faced a situation in which the colonial legacy of social injustice remained entrenched in Argentina as elsewhere in Latin America. As Adelman states, 'More than other Atlantic societies, Latin America appears shackled to its past, especially to its colonial heritages. For some, this yields to postcolonial exotica; for others the past is a scourge on the present. What persists is persistence itself'.[6] In Argentina, the colonial legacy was not to be undone, persisting well into the twentieth century, despite economic development and demographic change: Edwin Williamson notes that 'by contrast with other successful post-colonial societies [. . .] the roots of Argentine society still lay in the sixteenth century'.[7] The pampas were divided up into *estancias* owned by a rural elite who 'perpetuated the seigneurial values of the Hispanic nobility' (p. 459). We may conclude, therefore, that Argentina offers a good example of a country where 'the colonialism of the past has given way to societies whose make-up still reflects the disjunctions of their specific colonial history'.[8]

Perón pitted himself against the defenders of the Argentine status quo and was hated for it by the oligarchy whose disdain was all the greater because of their adversary's manifest 'impurities', notably his illegitimacy and racial hybridity – his mother was an Indian. He led a movement that was perceived as a political aberration, as 'the essential "other", and as a pathology in Argentine history [. . .]'.[9] His legitimacy, according to Plotkin, was based on his direct contact with the 'pueblo'.[10] He undermined the Argentine patriarchal system by giving women the vote in 1947.

It was Eva who sustained the radical reformist instincts of Peronism through her uncompromising and visceral defence of the poor and downtrodden, her indignation at their plight heightened by her admiration of their hidden vitality: as Hardt and Negri put it, 'the poor is destitute, excluded, repressed, exploited – and yet living!'[11]. Airily postmodern in the theatrical stagings of her distinct personalities, Eva is unshakeable in her total commitment to the cause of social change. In *Mi mensaje*, she defends fanaticism when harnessed to the defence of the poor and her incendiary rhetoric is not confined to the denunciation of the Argentine oligarchy but targets also the global forces of imperialism. Here it is difficult to dismiss as mere theatre her all-consuming passion and resolve.

The writers considered in the foregoing chapters (4–10) can be divided into two broad categories: first, those who seem to share Eva's extremism – reflected in their urge to possess their subject whether by conferring upon her a fixed status as exemplar of near perfection (Pagano) or as embodiment of evil (Main) or by immobilizing her in verifiable 'fact' (Borroni and Vacca); and second, those (such as Martínez, Szichman and Valenzuela) who pursue a broadly New Historical agenda, renouncing all pretensions to a single or fascistic Truth (and, by extension, to such principles as coherence, authenticity and reliability) in favour of a smaller truth or a 'limping' truth that excludes relativism and blatant falsification while acknowledging the essentially textual character of historical recreation. It is the difference between the drive to assert and possess on the one hand and the urge to enrich the facts by endowing them with a creative surplus on the other; the difference between cognition and emphasis on what is known on the one hand, and 'cognition caught in the act' [12] on the other – which implies the breakdown of cognitive routines as the undecidable excess of the subject becomes a source of pleasure rather than a stimulus to the will to master. Indeed, Perón will not give up his secrets even under the scrutiny of Page while the figure of Eva represents an even more spectacular triumph of dissonance.

'Fixing' Eva is, after all, an impossible undertaking. She is contestatory and transgressive, occupying an interstitial space between official status on the one hand and traditional female subservience on the other. Her sartorial excess parodies the subdued and 'tasteful' grandeur of the high society ladies. She is persistently ambivalent, especially at the height of her power as *señora presidenta*, since the veneer of propriety is undermined by her irrepressible sensuality which suggests deviance: Roland Barthes would have pinpointed with ease the *punctum* in the photographs taken at the height of her youthful splendour during her European tour.[13] Eva engaged in a kind of masquerade, a 'hyperbolization of the accoutrements of femininity'.[43] She moved dangerously from one identity to another, suggesting in her extravagant appearance both the well-attired prostitute and the respectable bourgeois lady. This conjunction caused alarm since it suggested mimicry: Eva both imitated and ridiculed high society fashion. Eva is 'dangerous' because she is not what she seems, her duplicity assuming diverse manifestations ranging from her artificial blonde hair to her excessive protestations of subservience to Perón. She respects neither gender nor geographical boundaries: though she pays lip service to patriarchal principles, she subverts them by trespassing on the jealously guarded male preserves of politics and autobiography,[15] compounding her effrontery by using the latter genre as an instrument of resistance to oppression. Beyond the personal level she draws into civilized Buenos Aires hordes of *cabecitas negras* from the barbarous provinces, promoting thereby the dissolution of regulated space. She subverts male authority while pretending to submit to it – for which she earns unusual praise from a member of the literary elite, Victoria Ocampo:

> 'En mi país, y me avergüenza comprobarlo, los hombres son hijos del rigor, y las mujeres mansas prefieren no disgustarlos. Sólo el día en que una humillada los humilló, los llevó por delante (y, merecidamente, en ese particular) cedieron y hasta se arrodillaron. Me refiero a Eva Duarte. Intencionalmente digo Eva Duarte y no Eva Perón'.[16]

The story of Eva can be taken as a kind of allegory. Allegory is the trope with peculiar resonance in this context since it 'embodies an ethics but with a duplicitous relationship to authority: it tells one thing to say another, continually deferring its meaning as other and elsewhere'.[17] In their discussion of Eva's ailing body and its clothing, Cortés Roca and Kohan remark that 'todo será signo de otra cosa'.[18] Sarlo also notes that the extravagance of

Eva's clothes and jewellery transcended the norms of fashion to become 'construcciones arquitectónicas sobre un cuerpo alegórico: el del poder peronista. Vestida de fiesta, Eva es la pieza coronada de una escenografía del poder'.[19] Eva literalizes the radical though now familiar notion that the body is a crucial site for inscription. Her artificially blonde hair suggests contrived distance from the darkness associated with the 'low other', while the severity of her final hairstyle implies the repudiation of glamour in favour of all-consuming revolutionary fervour. Her dead body became the site of male inscription and control, with suggestions of surveillance and even of rape. Her embalmer is, significantly, a male from the mother country, the Spaniard Pedro Ara, who immobilizes her dangerous body; he represents the civilization and decorum of the old world; she, the instinctive ebullience of the new. Another Spaniard, Manuel Penella de Silva, is the ghost behind her autobiography: he represents the privileging of metropolitan written culture over the oral which is typical of the native and exerts a power similar to Ara's by immobilizing in print Eva's volatile life.[20]

According to Kelley, allegory serves as a foil to fixed meanings; its most prominent feature is its 'referent to an "other" or "truth" that is under construction'.[21] Lack is the basis of Eva's exceptionality according to Sarlo: 'La excepción construida desde lo que falta y no desde lo que se tiene'.[22] It is precisely lack – though a lack pregnant with proliferating possibilities – rather than fullness that characterizes the history of Peronism and the stories of its major protagonists. As we have seen, writers respond in the main either by attempting to impose an illusory fullness or by renouncing fixed meanings while still clinging to the concept of what we have termed a 'limping' truth. Thus Page and Pagano, for example, seek to 'master' their subjects by engaging in truth-telling programmes that ultimately fail to cover up their fault lines, achieving only a veneer of consistency. Tomás Eloy Martínez, and to a lesser extent Dujovne Ortiz, refuse to compromise the radical discontinuity of their subjects and actively renounce all semblance of univocal meaning, exposing rather than attempting to conceal textual 'wounds'. Unconstrained by those shibboleths of stability – represented by 'what really happened' or by the 'essential' character of their subjects – they enrich the bare facts with a creative surplus. Perón and Eva may be historical figures but both resist attempts at the factual reconstruction of their 'real' lives. Martínez, Szichman and Valenzuela emphasize the aesthetic aspect of their work, their focus diverted from the 'raw' life or event to the most appropriate artistic means of representing them. They renounce truth claims in favour of self-conscious textuality: always indirect, openly mediated, creative, imaginative, and in most cases, particularly in those of Szichman and Valenzuela, edged with devastating humour and irony.

NOTES

1 In Tomás Eloy Martínez's *El vuelo de la reina* (Madrid: Alfaguara, 2002) the journalist Camargo, strongly reminiscent of Perón, is described as 'una herida que nunca cicatriza' (p. 199).
2 Referring to Eva as conceived by Manuel Puig and César Aira, Santos observes that 'considering her permanent capacity to construct and deconstruct herself, through performance, her gender identification is left open'. See Lidia Santos, 'Eva Perón: One woman, several masks' in Stephen Hart and Richard Young (eds), *Contemporary Latin American Cultural Studies* (London: Arnold, 2003), pp. 102–14 (p. 108).
3 See chapter 1, 'Introduction', pp. 10–11.
4 Daniel James, *Resistance and Integration*, p. 39.
5 Mariano Ben Plotkin, *Mañana es San Perón*, p. 18.
6 Jeremy Adelman, preface to Jeremy Adelman (ed.), *Colonial Legacies: the Problem of Persistence in Latin American History* (New York and London: Routledge, 1999), pp. ix–xii (p. ix).
7 Edwin Williamson, *The Penguin History of Latin America* (London: Penguin, 1992), p. 459.
8 Robert J. C. Young, *Postcolonialism: an Historical Introduction*, p. 60.
9 Mariano Ben Plotkin, *Freud in the Pampas*, p. 55. See chapter 3, p. 55.
10 Mariano Ben Plotkin, *Mañana es San Perón*, p. 226.
11 *Empire* (Cambridge, MA and London: Harvard University Press, 2000), p. 156.
12 Terry Eagleton, *The Ideology of the Aesthetic* (Oxford: Blackwell, 1990), p. 66.
13 Barthes observes that he was not interested in photography for sentimental reasons: 'je voulais l'approfondir, non comme une question (un thème), mais comme une blessure'. See *La chambre claire: note sur la photographie* (Paris: Éditions de l'Étoile, Gallimard, Le Seuil, 1980), p. 42. He explains his notion of the 'punctum' as a kind of wound on the body of the photograph, being an element 'qui part de la scène, comme une flèche, et vient me percer. Un mot existe en latin pour designer cette blessure, cette piqûre, cette marque faite par un instrument pointu' (p. 49).
14 Mary Ann Douane, *Femmes fatales: Feminism, Film Theory, Psychoanalysis* (New York and London: Routledge, 1991), p. 26.

Conclusion

15 See Adolfo Prieto, *La literatura autobiográfica argentina*, p. 21, and Julia Swindells, 'Introduction', in Julia Swindells (ed.), *The Uses of Autobiography*, pp. 1–12 (p. 7).
16 Victoria Ocampo, *Autobiografía II*, 'El imperio insular' (Buenos Aires: Sur, 1980), pp. 178–79.
17 Mary Beth Tierney-Tello, *Allegories of Transgression and Transformation: Experimental Fiction by Women Writers under Dictatorship* (Albany: State University of New York, 1996), p. 21.
18 Cortés Rocca and Kohan, *Imágenes de vida, relatos de muerte*, p. 150.
19 Sarlo, *La pasión y la excepción*, p. 84.
20 Martínez notes the similarity between the art of the embalmer and that of the biographer in *Santa Evita*: 'los dos tratan de inmovilizar una vida o un cuerpo en la pose con que debe recordarlos la eternidad' (p. 157).
21 Theresa M. Kelley, *Reinventing Allegory* (Cambridge: Cambridge University Press, 1997), pp. 264, 278.
22 Sarlo, *La pasión y la excepción*, p. 231.

Bibliography

Primary Sources

Borroni, Otelo and Roberto Vacca, *La vida de Eva Perón*. Tomo 1: *Testimonios para su historia* (Buenos Aires: Centro Editor de América Latina, 1970).
Dujovne Ortiz, Alicia, *Eva Perón*, trans. Shawn Fields (New York: St Martin's Griffin, 1997).
Frers, Ernesto, *Evita: la fascinante historia de Eva Perón* (Barcelona: Martínez Roca, 1997).
Ghioldi, Américo, *El mito de Eva Duarte* (Montevideo: n.p., 1952).
Llorca, Carmen, *Llamadme Evita*, (Barcelona: Planeta, 1980).
Martínez, Tomás Eloy, *La mano del amo* (Madrid: Alfaguara, 2003).
Martínez, Tomás Eloy, *Las memorias del General* (Buenos Aires: Planeta, 1996).
Martínez, Tomás Eloy, *La novela de Perón* (Madrid: Alianza, 1989).
Martínez, Tomás Eloy, *Santa Evita* [1995] (Barcelona: Seix Barral, 1997).
Martínez, Tomás Eloy, *El vuelo de la reina* (Madrid: Alfaguara, 2002).
Navarro, Marysa, *Evita* (Buenos Aires: Corregidor, 1981)
Pagano, Mabel, *Eterna* (Buenos Aires: Nuevo Sol, 1982)
Page, Joseph A., *Perón: a Biography* (New York: Random House, 1983).
Perón, Eva, *La razón de mi vida* [1951] (Buenos Aires: Buro, 1988).
Perón, Eva, *Mi mensaje* (Buenos Aires: Ediciones del Mundo, 1987).
Perón, Juan Domingo, *Del poder al exilio: cómo y quiénes me derrocaron* (Buenos Aires, [n.p.], 1958).
Perón, Juan Domingo, *Yo, Juan Domingo Perón: relato autobiográfico*, ed. Torcuato Luca de Tena, Luis Calvo and Esteban Peicovich (Barcelona: Planeta, 1976).
Pichel, Vera, *Evita íntima* (Buenos Aires: Planeta, 1993).
Posse, Abel, *La pasión según Eva* (Buenos Aires: Planeta, 1995).
Puig, Manuel, *Pubis angelical* (Barcelona: Seix Barral, 1979).
Sebreli, Juan José, *Eva Perón, ¿aventurera o militante?* (Buenos Aires: Pleyade, 1990).
Sebreli, Juan José, *Los deseos imaginarios del peronismo* (Buenos Aires: Sudamericana, 1992).
Szichman, Mario, *A las 20:25, la señora entró en la inmortalidad* (Hanover, NH: Ediciones del Norte, 1981).

Taylor, J. M., *Evita Perón: the Myths of a Woman*, Pavilion Series in Social Anthropology (Oxford: Blackwell, 1979).
Valenzuela, Luisa, *Cola de lagartija* (México: Universidad Autónoma de México, 1992).

Secondary Sources

Abraham, Nicolas and Maria Torok, *The Wolfman's Magic Word: a Cryptonymy*, trans. Nicholas Rand, Theory and History of Literature, 37 (Minneapolis: University of Minnesota Press, 1986).
Adelman, Jeremy (ed.), *Colonial Legacies: the Problem of Persistence in Latin American History* (New York and London: Routledge, 1999).
Ahearne, Jeremy *Michel de Certeau: Interpretation and its Other* (Cambridge: Polity Press, 1995).
Aizenberg, Edna (ed.), *Borges and His Successors: the Borgesian Impact on Literature and the Arts* (Colombia and London: University of Missouri Press, 1990).
Aizenburg, Edna, 'Kafkaesque strategy and anti-Peronist ideology: Martínez Estrada's stories as socially symbolic acts', in *Latin American Literary Review* 14 (1986), 11–19.
Alonso, Carlos J., 'The mourning after: García Márquez, Fuentes and the meaning of postmodernity in Spanish America', *Modern Language Notes*, 109 (1994), 252–67 (p. 253).
Amaral, Samuel and Mariano Ben Plotkin (eds), *Perón: Del exilio al poder* (Buenos Aires: Cántaro, 1993).
Amaral, Samuel, 'El avión negro' in Samuel Amaral and Mariano Ben Plotkin (eds), *Perón: Del exilio al poder* (Buenos Aires: Cántaro, 1993), pp. 69–94.
Anderson, Linda, *Autobiography*, The New Critical Idiom (London: Routledge, 2001).
Anonymous, 'Are we all neurotic?' in *The Argentina Reader: History, Culture, Politics*, Gabriella Nouzeilles and Graciela Montaldo (eds) (Durham and London: Duke University Press, 2002), pp. 352–7.
Ara, Pedro, *Eva Perón: la verdadera historia contada por el médico que preservó su cuerpo* (Buenos Aires: Sudamericana, 1996).
Armstrong, Nancy, *Desire and Domestic Fiction: a Political History of the Novel* (New York: Oxford University Press, 1987).
Auyero, Javier, *Poor People's Politics: Peronist Survival Networks and the Legacy of Evita* (Durham and London: Duke University Press, 2001).
Avelar, Idelber, *The Untimely Present: Postdictatorial Latin American Fiction*, Post-Contemporary Interventions (Durham and London: Duke University Press, 1999).
Bacarisse, Pamela, 'Superior men and inferior reality: Manuel Puig's *Pubis angelical*', *Bulletin of Hispanic Studies*, 66 (1989), 361–70.
Backscheider, Paula R., *Reflections on Biography* (Oxford: Oxford University Press, 1999).
Baisnée, Valérie, *Gendered Resistance: the Autobiographies of Simone de Beauvoir, Maya Angelou, Janet Frame and Marguerite Duras* (Amsterdam and Atlanta GA: Rodopi, 1997).

Bakhtin, Mikhail, *The Dialogic Imagination*, ed. Michael Holquist, trans. Caryl Emerson and Michael Holquist (Austin: University of Texas Press, 1981).
Balderston, Daniel (ed.), *The Historical Novel in Latin America: a Symposium*, (Gaithersburg MD: Ediciones Hispamérica 1986).
Barchino, Matías, 'La novela biográfica como reconstrucción histórica y como construcción mítica: el caso de Eva Duarte in *La pasión según Eva* de Abel Posse' in *La novela histórica a finales del siglo XX*, José Romera Castillo (ed.) (Madrid: Visor, 1996), pp. 149–57.
Barthes, Roland, 'L'effet du réel', *Communications* 11 (1968), 84–9.
Barthes, Roland, *Camera Lucida: Reflections on Photography*, trans. Richard Howard (London: Vintage, 2000), 2
Barthes, Roland, *La chambre claire: note sur la photographie* (Paris: Éditions de l'Étoile, Gallimard, Le Seuil, 1980).
Barthes, Roland, *Le plaisir du texte* (Paris: Seuil, 1973).
Baudrillard, Jean, 'From *Simulations*' in Patricia Waugh (ed.), *Postmodernism: Reader* (London: Arnold, 1992), pp. 186–8 (p. 186).
Baudrillard, Jean, *Seduction*, trans. Brian Singer (London: Macmillan, 1979).
Baudrillard, Jean, *Selected writings*, ed. Mark Poster, 2nd rev. ed. (Cambridge: Polity, 2001).
Bauman, Zygmunt, *Modernity and Ambivalence* (Cambridge: Polity, 1991), p. 158.
Beer, Gillian, 'Wave Theory and the Rise of Literary Modernism' in George Levine (ed.), *Realism and Representation: Essays on the Problem of Realism in Relation to Science, Literature and Culture* (Madison, WI: University of Wisconsin Press, 1993), pp. 193–213.
Bell, Shannon, *Reading, Writing, and Rewriting the Prostitute Body* (Bloomington and Indianapolis: Indiana University Press, 1994).
Bell, Susan Groag and Marilyn Yalom, 'Introduction' in Susan Groag Bell and Marilyn Yalom (eds), *Revealing Lives: Autobiography, Biography, and Gender* Suny Series in Feminist Criticism and Theory (Albany: State University of New York Press, 1990), pp. 1–11.
Benjamin, Walter, *The Origins of Tragic Drama*, trans. John Osborne (London and New York: Verso, 1977).
Berger, John, *The Sense of Sight: Writings*, ed. Lloyd Spencer (New York: Pantheon, 1986).
Bersani, Leo, 'Leo Bersani on Realism and the Fear of Desire' in Lilian R. Furst (ed.), *Realism* Modern Literatures in Perspective (London and New York: Longman, 1992), pp. 240–60.
Bloom, Harold, *Kabbalah and Criticism* (New York: Seabury Press, 1975).
Bloom, Lynn Z. and Orlee Holder, 'Anaïs Nin's *Diary* in Context', in Estelle C. Jelinek (ed.) *Women's Autobiography: Essays in Criticism* (Ann Arbor, MI: UMI, 2002 (Bloomington and London: Indiana University Press, 1980), pp. 206–20.
Bogard, William, 'Baudrillard, Time and the End' in Douglas Kellner (ed.), *Baudrillard: a Critical Reader* (Cambridge MA and Oxford: Blackwell, 1994) pp. 313–33.

Borch-Jacobsen, Mikkel, *Lacan: the Absolute Master* (Stanford: Stanford University Press, 1991).
Borges, Jorge Luis, *Ficciones* (Buenos Aires: Emecé, 1956).
Bost, David H., 'Reassessing the Past: Abel Posse and the New Historical Novel', *La Chispa '95: Selected Proceedings. New Orleans: Louisiana Conference on Hispanic Languages and Literatures* (New Orleans: Tulane University, 1995), pp. 39–47.
Bourdieu, Pierre, 'The Biographical Illusion', in Paul du Gay, Jessica Evans and Peter Redman (eds), *Identity: a Reader* (London: Sage, 2000), pp. 297–303.
Bourdieu, Pierre, *Outline of a Theory of Practice*, trans. Richard Nice, Cambridge Studies in Social Anthropology, 16 (Cambridge: Cambridge University Press, 1977).
Bowie, Malcolm, *Freud, Proust and Lacan: Theory as Fiction* (Cambridge: Cambridge University Press, 1987).
Braidotti, Rosi, *Metamorphoses: Towards a Materialist Theory of Becoming* (Cambridge: Polity, 2002).
Braidotti, Rosi, *Nomadic Subjects: Embodiment and Sexual Difference in Contemporary Feminist Theory* (New York: Columbia University Press, 1994).
Braidotti, Rosi, *Patterns of Dissonance: a Study of Woman in Contemporary Philosophy*, trans. Elizabeth Gould (Cambridge: Polity Press, 1991).
Brée, Germaine, 'Michel Leiris: Mazemaker' in James Olney (ed.), *Autobiography* (Princeton: Princeton University Press, 1980), pp. 194–206.
Bronfen, Elizabeth, *Over Her Dead Body: Death, Femininity and the Aesthetic* (Manchester: Manchester University Press, 1992).
Brooks, Peter, *Psychoanalysis and Storytelling* (Oxford: Blackwell, 1994).
Brooks, Peter, *Body Work: Objects of Desire in Modern Narrative* (Cambridge, MA: Harvard University Press, 1993).
Brooks, Peter, *Reading for the Plot: Design and Intention in Narrative* (Cambridge, MA: Harvard University Press, 1992).
Brooks, Peter, *The Melodramatic Imagination: Balzac, Henry James, Melodrama and the Mode of Excess* (New Haven and London: Yale University Press, 1976).
Bruss, Elizabeth, *Autobiographical Acts, The Changing Situation of a Literary Genre* (Baltimore and London: Johns Hopkins University Press, 1976).
Calinescu, Matei, *Five Faces of Modernity: Modernism, Avant-garde, Decadence, Kitsch, Postmodernism* (Durham: Duke University Press, 1987).
Calvert, Susan and Peter, *Argentina: Political and Cultural Instability* (Basingstoke: Macmillan, 1989).
Chávez, Fermín, 'Introducción', in Eva Perón, *Mi mensaje* (Buenos Aires: Ediciones del Mundo, 1987), pp. 5–11.
Christoph, Nancy, 'Bodily Matters: the Female Grotesque in Luisa Valenzuela's *Cola de lagartijo*', *Revista Hispánica Moderna*, 40 (1995), 365–80.

Cixous, Hélène, 'Sorties: Out and out: Attacks/ways out/forays', in Alan D. Schrift (ed.), *The Logic of the Gift. Toward an Ethic of Generosity* (London: Routledge, 1997), pp. 148–73.

Colás, Santiago, *Postmodernity in Latin America: the Argentine Paradigm*, Post-Contemporary Interventions (Durham and London: Duke University Press, 1994).

Collin, Françoise, 'The Third Tiger; or, from Blanchot to Borges' in *Borges and His Successors: the Borgesian Impact on Literature and the Arts* (Colombia and London: University of Missouri Press, 1990), pp. 80–95.

Corbatta, Jorgelina, *Mito personal y mitos colectivos en las novelas de Manuel Puig* (Madrid: Orígenes, 1988).

Corpas Vargas, Mirta, *Eva Perón en el cristal de la escritura. Mabel Pagano, personaje literario y postrauma*, Currents in Comparative Romance Languages and Literatures, 88 (New York: Peter Lang, 2000).

Cortés Rocca, Paola and Martín Kohan, *Imágenes de vida, relatos de muerte. Eva Perón: cuerpo y política*, Estudios culturales (Buenos Aires: Beatriz Viterbo, 1998).

Crawley, Eduardo, *A House Divided: Argentina 1880–1980* (London: Hurst, 1984).

Creed, Barbara, *The Monstrous-Feminine: Film, Feminism, Psychoanalysis* (London and New York: Routledge, 1993).

Culler, Jonathan, *Literary Theory: a Very Short Introduction* (Oxford and New York: Oxford University Press, 1997).

Dällenbach, Lucien, *The Mirror in the Text*, trans. Jeremy Whiteley with Emma Hughes (Cambridge: Polity, 1989).

De Certeau, Michel, *The Writing of History*, trans Tom Conley (New York: Columbia University Press, 1988).

De Grandis, Rita, 'The Masses Do Not Think, They Feel', *Journal of Latin American and Caribbean Studies*, 24 (1999), 125–32.

De Man, Paul, 'Autobiography as De-facement' in Paul de Man, *The Rhetoric of Romanticism* (New York: Columbia University Press, 1984), pp. 67–81.

Deleuze, Gilles, *Essays Critical and Clinical*, trans. Daniel W. Smith and Michael A. Greco (London and New York: Verso, 1998).

Deleuze, Gille and Félix Guattari, *A Thousand Plateaus. Capitalism and Schizophrenia*, trans. Brian Massumi (Minneapolis: University of Minnesota Press, 1987).

Deleuze, Gilles and Félix Guatarri, *Nomadology: the War Machine*, trans. Brian Massumi (New York: Semiotext(e), 1986).

Deleuze, Gilles and Félix Guattari, *Anti-Oedipus: Capitalism and Schizophrenia* (Minneapolis: University of Minnesota Press, 1983).

Deleuze, Gilles and Félix Guattari, *What is Philosophy?*, trans. Hugh Tomlinson and Graham Burchill (London and New York: Verso, 1994).

Delgado-Costa, José, *Binarración y parodia en las primeras tres novelas de Osvaldo Soriano* (Lewiston: Edwin Mellen, 2002).

Denzin, Norman K., *Interpretive Biography* (London: Sage, 1989).

Derrida, Jacques, 'The Law of Genre', *Glyph*, 7 (1980), 202–32.

Derrida, Jacques, *De la grammatologie* (Paris: Minuit, 1967).
Derrida, Jacques, *Of Grammatology*, trans. Gayatri Chakravorty Spivak (Baltimore: Johns Hopkins University Press, 1976).
Domon, Hélène, ' "Black Fire on White Fire": Kabbalah and Modernity' in Philip Leonard (ed.), *Trajectories of Mysticism in Theory and Literature* Cross-Currents in Religion and Culture (London: Macmillan, 2000), pp. 115–132.
Dorsey, Peter A., *Sacred Estrangement: the Rhetoric of Conversion in Modern American Autobiography* (Pennsylvania: Pennsylvania State University Press, 1993).
Douane, Mary Ann, *Femmes fatales: Feminism, Film Theory, Psychoanalysis* (New York and London: Routledge, 1991).
Eagleton, Terry, 'Capitalism, Modernism and Postmodernism', *New Left Review*, 152 (1985), 60–73.
Eagleton, Terry, *The Illusions of Postmodernism* (Oxford: Blackwell, 1996).
Eagleton, Terry, *Literary Theory: an Introduction* (Oxford: Blackwell, 1983).
Eagleton, Terry, *The Ideology of the Aesthetic* (Oxford: Blackwell, 1990).
Eakin, Paul John, *Touching the World: Reference in Autobiography* (Princeton, NJ: Princeton University Press, 1992).
Edel, Leon, 'Biography and the science of man', in Anthony M. Friedson (ed.), *New Directions in Biography* (Hawaii: University Press of Hawaii, 1981), pp. 1–11.
Edel, Leon, *Literary Biography* (Bloomington and London: Indiana University Press, 1973).
Egan, Susanna, *Patterns of Experience in Autobiography* (Chapel Hill and London: University of North Carolina Press, 1984).
Elbaz, Robert, *The Changing Nature of the Self: a Critical Study of Autobiographic Discourse* (London and Sydney: Croom Helm, 1988).
Ellis, David, *Literary Lives: Biography and the Search for Understanding* (Edinburgh: Edinburgh University Press, 2000).
Epstein, William H., '(Post) Modern Lives: Abducting the Biographical Subject' in William H. Epstein (ed.), *Contesting the Subject: Essays in the Postmodern Theory and Practice of Biography and Biographical Criticism* (West Lafayette, Indiana: Perdue University Press, 1991), pp. 217–36.
Epstein, William H. (ed.), *Contesting the Subject: Essays in the Postmodern Theory and Practice of Biography and Biographical Criticism* (West Lafayette IN: Perdue University Press, 1991).
Epstein, William H., *Recognizing Biography* (Philadelphia: University of Pennsylvania, 1987).
Erikson, Erik H., *Young Man Luther: A Study in Psychoanalysis and History* (London: Faber and Faber, 1958).
Ermarth, Elizabeth Deeds, 'The Crisis of Realism in Postmodern Time' in George Levine (ed.), *Realism and Representation: Essays on the Problem of Realism in Relation to Science, Literature and Culture* (Madison WI: University of Wisconsin Press, 1993), pp. 214–24.
Ermarth, Elizabeth Deeds, *Postmodernism and the Crisis of Representational Time* (Princeton NJ: Princeton University Press, 1992).
Evans, Mary, *Missing Persons: the Impossibility of Auto/biography* (London and New York: Routledge, 1999).

Felman, Shoshana and Dori Laub, *Testimony: Crises of Witnessing in Literature, Psychoanalysis and History* (New York and London: Routledge, 1992).
Fernández Retamar, Roberto, *Caliban and Other Essays*, trans. Edward Baker (Minneapolis: University of Minnesota Press, 1989).
Fiddian, Robin (ed.), *Postcolonial Perspectives on the Cultures of Latin America and Lusophone Africa* (Liverpool: Liverpool University Press, 2000).
Fletcher, Angus, *Allegory: the Theory of a Symbolic Mode* (Ithaca: Cornell University Press, 1964).
Forrester, John, *The Seductions of Psychoanalysis: Freud, Lacan and Derrida* (Cambridge: Cambridge University Press, 1990).
Foss, Clive, *Juan and Eva Perón*, Sutton Pocket Bibliographies (Stroud: Sutton, 1999).
Foster, David William, *Alternate Voices in the Contemporary Latin American Narrative* (Columbia: University of Missouri Press, 1985).
Foster, David William, 'Evita Perón, Juan José Sebreli, and Gender', in David William Foster, *Sexual Textualities: Essays on Queering Latin American Writing* (Austin: University of Texas Press, 1997), pp. 22–38.
Foster, David William, 'Narrative Persona in Eva Perón's *La razón de mi vida*' in David William Foster, *Alternate Voices in the Contemporary Latin American Narrative* (Colombia: University of Missouri, 1985), pp. 45–59.
Foucault, Michel, 'Nietzsche, Genealogy, History' in *The Foucault Reader* ed. Paul Rabinow (London: Penguin, 1984), pp. 76–100.
Fraser, Nicholas and Marysa Navarro, *Evita: the Real Lives of Eva Perón* (London: André Deutsch, 1996).
Freud, Sigmund, *The Standard Edition of the Complete Psychological Works of Sigmund Freud*, trans. James Strachey (London: Hogarth Press, 1953), VII: *A Case of Hysteria, Three Essays on Sexuality and Other Works*, pp. 3–122, 135–72.
Freud, Sigmund, *The Standard Edition of the Complete Psychological Works of Sigmund Freud*, trans. James Strachey (London: Hogarth Press, 1958), XII: *The Case of Schreber, Papers on Technique and Other Works*, pp. 9–82.
Fuentes, Carlos, *Nueva novela hispanoamericana* (México: Joaquín Mortiz, 1972).
Gallagher, Susan VanZanten (ed.), *Postcolonial Literature and the biblical Call for Justice* (Jackson: University Press of Mississippi, 1994).
Gallop, Jane, *Feminism and Psychoanalysis: the Daughter's Seduction* (London: Macmillan, 1982).
Gallop, Jane, *Thinking Through the Body* (New York: Columbia University Press, 1988).
Gambini, Hugo, *Historia del peronismo*, 2 vols (Buenos Aires: Planeta, 1999–2001).
Garber, Marjorie, *Quotation Marks* (New York and London: Routledge, 2003).
García Márquez, Gabriel, *Cien años de soledad* ed. Jacques Joset, Letras Hispánicas (Madrid: Cátedra, 1995).
García Márquez, Gabriel, *El otoño del patriarca* (Madrid: Mondadori, 1987).

Garfield, Evelyn Picon, 'Interview with Luisa Valenzuela', *Review of Contemporary Fiction*, 6 (1986), 25–30.
Gilmore, Leigh, *Autobiographics: a Feminist Theory of Women's Self-Representation*, Reading Women Writing (Ithaca and London: Cornell University Press, 1994).
Goldar, Ernesto, *El peronismo en la literatura argentina* (Buenos Aires: Freeland, 1971).
González Echevarría, Roberto, *The Voice of the Masters: Writing and Authority in Latin American Literature*, Latin American Monographs, 64 (Austin: University of Texas Press, 1985).
Grafton, Anthony, *The Footnote: a Curious History* (London: Faber and Faber, 1997).
Green, Dennis Howard, *Irony in the Medieval Romance* (Cambridge: Cambridge University Press, 1979).
Gusdorf, Georges, 'Conditions and Limits of Autobiography' in James Olney (ed.), *Autobiography: Essays Theoretical and Critical* (Princeton: Princeton University Press, 1980), pp. 28–48.
Halperín Donghi, Tulio, 'El lugar del peronismo en la tradición política argentina' in Samuel Amaral and Mario Ben Plotkin (eds), *Perón: del exilio al poder* (Buenos Aires: Cántaro, 1993), pp. 15–44.
Hamon, Philippe, 'Philippe Hamon on the major features of realist discourse' in Lilian Furst (ed.) *Realism* (London and New York: Longman, 1992), pp. 166–85.
Hanway, Nancy, *Embodying Argentina: Body, Space and Nation in 19th Century Narrative* (Jefferson NC: McFarland, 2003).
Haraway, Donna J., *Simians, Cyborgs, and Women: the Reinvention of Nature* (London: Free Association Books, 1991).
Harbinson, W.A., *Evita: Saint or Sinner?* (London: Boxtree, 1996).
Hardt, Michael and Antonio Negri, *Empire* (Cambridge MA and London: Harvard University Press, 2000).
Hart, Francis R., 'Notes for an anatomy of modern autobiography' in *New Literary History* 1 (1969–70), 485–511.
Hart, Stephen M., *The Other Scene: Psychoanalytic Readings in Modern Spanish and Latin-American Literature* (Boulder, CO: Society of Spanish and Spanish-American Studies, 1992).
Heath, Stephen, *The Sexual Fix* (London and Basingstoke: Macmillan, 1982).
Hewitt, Leah D., *Autobiographical Tightropes: Simone de Beauvoir, Nathalie Sarraute, Marguerite Duras, Monique Wittig and Maryse Condé* (Lincoln and London: University of Nebraska Press, 1990).
Higgins, Kathleen, 'Nietzche and Postmodern Subjectivity' in Clayton Koelb (ed.), *Nietzsche as Postmodernist: Essays Pro and Contra* (Albany NY: State University of New York Press, 1990), pp. 189–215.
Holmes, Richard, 'Biography: Inventing the truth' in John Batchelor (ed.), *The Art of Literary Biography* (Oxford: Clarendon, 1995), pp. 15–25 (p. 20).
Holton, Robert, *Jarring Witnesses: Modern Fiction and the Representation of History*, Postmodern Theory (Hemel Hempstead: Harvester Wheatsheaf, 1994).

Howarth, William L., 'Some Principles of Autobiography', in James Olney (ed.), *Autobiography: Essays Theoretical and Critical* (Princeton: Princeton University Press 1980), pp. 84–114.

Hutcheon, Linda, *A Theory of Parody: the Teachings of Twentieth-Century Art Forms* (New York and London: Methuen, 1985).

Hutcheon, Linda, *Irony's Edge: the Theory and Politics of Irony* (London and New York: Routledge, 1994).

Hutcheon, Linda, *The Politics of Postmodernism*, New Accents (London and New York: Routledge, 1989).

Irigaray, Luce, 'Women on the Market' in Alan D. Schrift (ed.), *The Logic of the Gift: Toward an Ethic of Generosity* (London: Routledge, 1997), pp. 174–89.

Irigaray, Luce, *The Irigaray Reader*, ed. Margaret Whitford (Oxford: Blackwell, 1991).

Jacobus, Mary, *First Things: the Maternal Imaginary in Literature, Art and Psychoanalysis* (New York and London: Routledge, 1995).

James, Daniel, *Resistance and Integration: Peronism and the Argentine Working Class, 1946–1976*, Cambridge Latin American Studies, 64 (Cambridge: Cambridge University Press, 1988).

Jameson, Fredric, 'Postmodernism and Consumer Society' in Hal Foster (ed.), *The Anti-Aesthetic: Essays on Postmodern Culture* (Seattle, WA: Bay Press, 1983), pp. 111–25.

Jardine, Alice A., 'The demise of experience: Fiction as stranger than truth?' in Thomas Docherty (ed.), *Postmodernism: a Reader* (London: Harvester Wheatsheaf, 1992), pp. 433–42.

Jardine, Alice A., *Gynesis: Configurations of Woman and Modernity* (Ithaca and London: Cornell University Press, 1985).

Jefferson, Ann, *Reading Realism in Stendhal* (Cambridge: Cambridge University Press, 1988).

Jelinek, Estelle C. (ed.), *Women's Autobiography: Essays in Criticism* (Bloomington and London: Indiana University Press, 1980).

Jitrik, Noé, 'De la historia a la escritura: predominios, disimetrías, acuerdos en la novela histórica latinoamericana', in Daniel Balderston (ed.), *The Historical Novel in Latin America: a Symposium* (Gaithersburg, MD: Hispamérica, 1986), pp. 13–29.

Johnson, Barbara, 'Is Female to Male as Ground is to Figure?' *The Feminist Difference: Literature, Psychoanalysis, Race and Gender* (Cambridge MA: Harvard University Press, 1998), pp. 17–36.

Juhasz, Suzanne, 'Towards a Theory of Form in Feminist Autobiography: Kate Millett's *Flying* and *Sita*; Maxine Hong Kingston's *The Woman Warrior*' in Estelle C. Jelinek (ed.), *Women's Autobiography: Essays in Criticism* (Ann Arbor MI: UMI, 2002; Bloomington and London: Indiana University Press, 1980), pp. 221–37.

Kaminsky, Amy K., *After Exile: Writing the Latin American Diaspora* (Minneapolis, MN: University of Minnesota Press, 1999).

Kaminsky, Amy K., *Reading the Body Politic: Feminist Criticism and Latin American Women Writers* (Minneapolis: University of Minnesota Press, 1993).

Katra, William H., 'Reading Facundo as historical novel' in Daniel Balderston (ed.), *The Historical Novel in Latin America: a Symposium* (Gaithersburg MD: Ediciones Hispamérica, 1986), pp. 31–46.
Kellner, Douglas (ed.), *Baudrillard: a Critical Reader* (Oxford: Blackwell, 1994).
Kermode, Frank, *The Genesis of Secrecy: on the Interpretation of Narrative* (London: Harvard University Press, 1979).
Kerr, Lucille, 'The Dis-appearance of a Popular Author: Stealing Around Style with Manuel Puig's *Pubis angelical*', in *Reclaiming the Author: Figures and Fictions from Spanish America* (Durham and London: Duke University Press, 1992).
Kristeva, Julia, *Folle vérité* (Paris: Éditions du Seuil, 1979).
Kristeva, Julia, *Powers of Horror. An Essay on Abjection*, trans. Leon Roudiez (New York: Columbia University Press, 1982).
Labanyi, Jo, *Myth and History in the Contemporary Spanish Novel* (Cambridge: Cambridge University Press, 1989).
Lacan, Jacques, 'Qu'est-ce qu'une femme?', in *Le Séminaire de Jacques Lacan*, ed. Jacques-Alain Miller (Paris: Éditions du Seuil, 1981), iii: *Les Psychoses* , pp. 195–205.
Lacan, Jacques, 'Une lettre d' âmour', in *Le Séminaire de Jacques Lacan*, ed. Jacques-Alain Miller (Paris: Éditions du Seuil, 1975), xx: *Encore, 1972–1973* , pp. 73–82.
Laing, R.D., H. Phillipson, and A.R. Lee, *Interpersonal Perception: a Theory and a Method of Research* (London: Tavistock; New York: Springer, 1966).
Lejeune, Philippe, 'The autobiographical contract' in Tzvetan Todorov (ed.), *French Literary Theory Today: a Reader*, trans. R. Carter (Cambridge: Cambridge University Press; Paris: Editions de la Maison Des Sciences de L'Homme, 1982), pp. 192–222.
Leonard, Philip (ed.), *Trajectories of Mysticism in Theory and Literature*, Cross-Currents in Religion and Culture (London: Macmillan, 2000).
Lipstadt, Dorothy, *Denying the Holocaust: the Growing Assault on Truth and Memory* (New York: The Free Press, 1993).
Loja, María Rosa, 'Pasos nuevos en espacios habituales' in Noé Jitrik (ed.), *Historia crítica de la literatura argentina* (Buenos Aires: Emecé, 1999), xi: *La narración gana la partida* ed. By Elsa Drucaroff (Buenos Aires: Emecé, 2000), pp. 19–48.
Lowenthal, David, *The Past is a Foreign Country* (Cambridge: Cambridge University Press, 1985).
Lukacher, Ned, 'Introduction', Jacques Derrida, *Cinders*, trans. Ned Lukacher (Lincoln and London: University of Nebraska Press, 1991), pp. 1–18.
Lynch, John, *Argentine Dictator: Juan Manuel de Rosas, 1829–1852* (Oxford: Clarendon, 1981).
Mailer, Norman, *Marilyn* (London: Chancellor, 1992).
Malcolm, Janet, 'The silent woman', *The New Yorker*, 69, 23–30 August 1993, p. 86.
Manguel, Alberto, review of *Santa Evita*, *The Independent*, 11 January 1997, p. 6.

Marcus, Steven, 'Freud and Dora: Story, History, Case History', *Partisan Review* 1974 (41), 12 – 23; 89 – 108.
Márquez Rodríguez, Alexis, 'Raíces de la novela histórica', *Cuadernos Americanos* 28 (1991), 32–49.
Martínez, Tomás Eloy, 'Ficción e historia en *La novela de Perón*' *Hispamérica* 49 (1988), 41–9.
Martínez, Tomás Eloy, 'Historia y ficción: dos paralelas que se tocan' in Karl Kohut (ed.), *Literaturas del Río de la Plata hoy: de las utopías al desencanto* (Frankfurt: Vervuert; Madrid: Iberoamericana, 1996), pp. 89–100.
Martínez, Tomás Eloy, 'Mitos, historia, ficción: idas y vueltas' in Raúl Padilla (ed.), *Visiones cortazarianas: historia, política y literatura hacia el fin del milenio* (Cubierta, México: Luis Vargas, 1996), pp. 109–31.
Martínez, Tomás Eloy, *El sueño argentino* (Buenos Aires: Planeta, 1999).
Martínez, Z. Nelly, *El silencio que habla: aproximación a la obra de Luisa Valenzuela* (Montreal: Corregidor, 1994).
Masiello, Francine, 'Melodrama, sex and nation in Latin America's Fin de Siglo', in D.W. Foster and Daniel Altamiranda (eds), *Theoretical Debates in Spanish American Literature* (New York and London: Garland, 1997), pp. 181–190.
Mathieu, Corina S., 'Mario Szichman como desacralizador de mitos en *A las 20:25, la señora entró en la inmortalidad*' in Felix Menchacatorre (ed.), *Ensayos de literatura europea e hispanoamericana* (San Sebastian: Universidad del País Vasco, 1990), pp. 307–12.
McHale, Brian, *Constructing Postmodernism* (London: Routledge, 1992).
Menton, Seymour, *Latin America's New Historical Novel* (Austin: University of Texas, 1993).
Middlebrook, Diane Wood, 'Postmodernism and the biographer' in Susan Groag Bell and Marilyn Yalom (eds), *Revealing Lives: Autobiography, Biography, and Gender*, Suny Series in Feminist Criticism and Theory (Albany: State University of New York Press, 1990), pp. 155–65.
Miguens, José Enrique, 'The Presidential Elections of 1973 and the End of Ideology' in Frederick C. Turner and José Enrique Miguens (eds), *Juan Perón and the Reshaping of Argentina* (Pittsburgh: University of Pittsburgh Press, 1983), pp. 147–50.
Miles, Jack, *God: a Biography* (New York: Knopf, 1995).
Miles, Margaret R., *Carnal Knowing: Female Nakedness and Religious Meaning in the Christian West* (Boston: Beacon Press, 1989).
Millett, Kate, *Sexual Politics* (London: Virago, 1977).
Molloy, Sylvia, *At Face Value: Autobiographical Writing in Spanish America* (Cambridge: Cambridge University Press, 1991).
Momigliano, Arnaldo, *The Development of Greek Biography: Four Lectures* (Cambridge MA: Harvard University Press, 1971).
Mora y Araujo, Manuel, and Peter H. Smith, 'Peronism and economic development: the 1973 elections', in Frederick C. Turner and José Enrique Miguens (eds), *Juan Perón and the Reshaping of Argentina* (Pittsburgh: University of Pittsburgh Press, 1983), pp. 171–87.
Muecke, D. C., *The Compass of Irony* (London: Methuen, 1969).

Nabokov, Vladimir, *Nikolay Gogol* (London: Weidenfeld and Nicolson, 1973).
Nadel, Ira Bruce, *Biography: Fiction, Fact and Form* (New York: St Martin's Press, 1984).
Naipaul, V. S., 'The Return of Eva Perón' in *The Return of Eva Perón with the Killings in Trinidad* (London: Deutsch, 1980), pp. 93–170.
Navarro, Marysa, 'Wonder Woman was Argentine and Her Real Name was Evita', *Canadian Journal of Latin American and Caribbean Studies* 24 (1999), 133–52.
Nietzsche, Friedrich, 'On truth and falsity in their ultramoral sense', in *Early Greek Philosophy and Other Essays*, trans. Maximilian A. Mügge (London: T. N. Foulis, 1911), pp. 171–92.
Nouzeilles, Gabriela and Graciela Montaldo (eds), *The Argentina Reader: History, Culture, Politics* (Durham and London: Duke University Press, 2002).
Nussbaum, Felicity A., *The Autobiographical Subject: Gender and Ideology in Eighteenth-Century England* (Baltimore and London: The Johns Hopkins University Press, 1989).
Oates, Joyce Carol, *Blonde: a Novel* (London: QPD, 2000).
Olin, Margaret, 'Touching Photographs: Roland Barthes's "Mistaken" Identification', *Representations*, 80 (2002), 99–118.
Olney, James (ed.), *Autobiography: Essays Theoretical and Critical* (Princeton: Princeton University Press, 1980).
Ong, Walter J., *Orality and Literacy: the Technologizing of the Word*, New Accents (London and New York: Methuen, 1982).
Ortega, Julio, 'Postmodernism in Latin America', in Theo d'Haen and Hans Bertens (eds), *Postmodern Fiction in Europe and the Americas*, Postmodern Studies, 1 (Amsterdam: Rodopi, 1988), pp. 193–208.
Ortega, Julio, 'El lector en su laberinto', *Hispanic Review*, 60 (1992), 165–79.
Owens, Craig, 'The Discourse of Others: Feminists and Postmodernism' in Hal Foster (ed.), *The Anti-Aesthetic: Essays on Postmodern Culture* (New York: The New Press, 1983), pp. 57–82.
Page, Joseph, 'Introduction' in *Evita: In My Own Words*, trans. Laura Dail (Edinburgh: Mainstream, 1997), pp. 7–55.
Pascal, Roy, *Design and Truth in Autobiography* (London: Routledge and Kegan Paul, 1960).
Pavón Pereyra, Enrique, *Diario Secreto de Perón* (Buenos Aires: Sudamericana/Planeta, 1985).
Pearson, Keith Ansell, 'Deleuze Outside/Outside Deleuze: on the Difference Engineer' in Keith Ansell Pearson (ed.), *Deleuze and Philosophy: the Difference Engineer*, Warwick Studies in European Philosophy (London and New York: Routledge, 1997), pp. 1–22.
Peicovich, Esteban, *Hola Perón* (Buenos Aires: Jorge Alvarez, 1965).
Perón, Eva, *Discursos completos*, 3 vols (Buenos Aires: Megafón, 1985–7).
Perilli, Carmen Noemí, 'Violencia y delirio en tres novelas argentinas del 80', *Cuadernos Americanos*, 259 (1985), 225-31.

Plotkin, Mariano Ben, 'The Changing Perceptions of Peronism' in James P. Brenan (ed.), *Peronism and Argentina* (Wilmington DE: Scholarly Resources, 1998), pp. 29–54

Plotkin, Mariano Ben, 'Freud, Politics, and the Porteños: The Reception of Psychoanalysis in Buenos Aires, 1910–1943', *Hispanic American Historical Review* 77 (1997), 45–74.

Plotkin, Mariano Ben, 'La ideología de Perón' in Samuel Amaral and Mariano Ben Plotkin (eds), *Perón: Del exilio al poder* (Buenos Aires: Cántaro, 1993), pp. 45–67.

Plotkin, Mariano Ben, *Freud in the Pampas: the Emergence and Development of a Psychoanalytic Culture in Argentina* (Stanford: Stanford University Press, 2001).

Plotkin, Mario Ben, *Mañana es San Perón. A Cultural History of Perón's Argentina*, trans. Keith Zahniser (Wilmington DE: Scholarly Resources, 2003).

Pons, María Cristina, *Memorias del olvido. Del Paso, García Márquez, Saer y la novela histórica de fines del siglo XX* (México: Siglo XXI, 1996).

Posse, Abel, *Daimón* (Buenos Aires: Emecé, 1989).

Posse, Abel, *El largo atardecer del caminante* (Buenos Aires: Emecé, 1992).

Potash, Robert A., *The Army and Politics in Argentina, 1945–1962: Perón to Frondizi* (London: Athlone, 1980).

Prendergast, Christopher, *The Order of Mimesis: Balzac, Stendhal, Nerval, Flaubert*, Cambridge Studies in French (Cambridge: Cambridge University Press, 1986).

Prieto, Adolfo, *La literatura autobiográfica argentina* (Buenos Aires: Jorge Alvarez, 1966).

Proyección del rosismo en la literatura argentina: seminario del Instituto de Letras (Rosario: Universidad Nacional del Litoral, Facultad de filosofía y letras, 1959).

Punte, María José, 'Una mujer en busca de autor: la figura de Eva Perón en dos narradores argentinos', *Iberoromania*, 46 (1997), 101–27.

Punte, María José, *Rostros de la utopía: la proyección del peronismo en la novela argentina de la década de los 80*, Anejos de RILFE, 39 (Pamplona: Universidad de Navarra, 2002).

Ratliff, William, 'Perón y la guerrilla: el arte del engaño mutuo' in Samuel Amaral and Mariano Ben Plotkin (eds), *Perón: Del exilio al poder* (Buenos Aires: Cántaro, 1993) pp. 261–80.

Renza, Louis A., 'The Veto of the Imagination: a Theory of Autobiography' in James Olney (ed.), *Autobiography: Essays Theoretical and Critical* (Princeton: Princeton University Press, 1980), pp. 268–95.

Richard, Nelly, 'Postmodernism and Periphery' in Thomas Docherty (ed.), *Postmodernism: a Reader* (Hemel Hempstead: Harvester Wheatsheaf, 1993), pp. 463–9.

Ricoeur, Paul, *Time and Narrative*, trans. Kathleen McLaughlin and David Pellauer, 3 vols (Chicago and London: University of Chicago, 1984–88).

Roa Bastos, Augusto, *Yo el supremo* (Buenos Aires: Siglo XXI, 1974).

Robertson, Alton Kim, *The Grotesque Interface: Deformity, Debasement, Dissolution*, Theory and Criticism of Culture and Literature, 6 (Frankfurt a.M.: Vervuert, 1996).

Rock, David, *Argentina 1516–1987: from Spanish Colonization to the Falklands War and Alfonsín* (London: Taurus, 1987).

Romero, José Luis, *A History of Argentine Political Thought*, trans. Thomas F. McGann (Stanford: Stanford University Press, 1968).

Rubin, Gayle, 'The Traffic in Women: Notes on the "Political Economy" of sex' in Rayna R. Reiter (ed.), *Toward an Anthropology of Women* (New York and London: Monthly Review Press, 1975), pp. 157–210.

Sábato, Ernesto, *El otro rostro del peronismo. Carta abierta a Mario Amadeo* (Buenos Aires: [n. pub.], 1956).

Said, Edward W., *Orientalism: Western Conceptions of the Orient* (London: Penguin, 1978).

Santos, Lidia, 'Eva Perón: One woman, several masks', in Stephen Hart and Richard Young (eds), *Contemporary Latin American Cultural Studies* (London: Arnold, 2003), pp. 102–14.

Sarlo, Beatriz, *La pasión y la excepción* (Buenos Aires: Siglo XXI, 2003).

Saussure, Ferdinand de, *Cours de Linguistique Générale* (Paris: Payot, 1931).

Scarry, Elaine, *The Body in Pain: the Making and the Unmaking of the World* (New York and Oxford: Oxford University Press, 1985).

Schlaeger, Jürgen, 'Biography: Cult as Culture' in John Batchelor (ed.), *The Art of Literary Biography* (Oxford: Clarendon, 1995), pp. 57–71.

Schrift, Alan D. (ed.), *The Logic of the Gift. Toward an Ethic of Generosity* (London: Routledge, 1997).

Shelston, Alan, *Biography*, The Critical Idiom, 34 (London: Methuen, 1977).

Sigal, Silvio and Eliseo Verón, *Perón o muerte: los fundamentos discursivos del fenómeno peronista* (Buenos Aires: Legasa, 1986).

Silverman, Kaja, *Male Subjectivity at the Margins* (New York and London: Routledge, 1992).

Sklodowska, Elzbieta, *Testimonio hispanoamericano: historia, teoría, poética* (New York: Lang, 1992).

Smith, Daniel W., 'Introduction: "A life of pure immanence": Deleuze's "Critique et Clinique" project' in Gilles Deleuze, *Essays Critical and Clinical*, trans. Daniel W. Smith and Michael A. Greco (London and New York: Verso, 1998), pp. xi–liii.

Smith, Douglas, 'Introduction' in Friedrich Nietzsche, *On the Genealogy of Morals: a Polemic By Way of Clarification and Supplement to My Last Book, 'Beyond Good and Evil'*, translated with an introduction and notes by Douglas Smith, pp. vii–xxxi.

Sommer, Doris, *Foundational Fictions: the National Romances of Latin America* (Berkeley: University of California Press, 1991).

Sontag, Susan, 'Writing itself: On Roland Barthes', in *A Susan Sontag Reader*, introduction by Elizabeth Hardwick (Harmondsworth: Penguin, 1983), pp. 423–46.

Sontag, Susan, *Illness as Metaphor and Aids and its Metaphors* (London: Penguin, 1991).

Sontag, Susan, *On Photography* (London: Allen Lane, 1977).

Soto, Marcelo, 'Entrevista: "Es un grueso error presenter a Eva Perón como prostituta"', *Revista QuePasa* 1351, 28 de febrero de 1997 *http://www.quepasa.cl/revista/135/7.html* (accessed 26 November 1998).

Spacks, Patricia Meyer, 'Selves in Hiding', in Estelle C. Jelinek (ed.), *Women's Autobiography: Essays in Criticism* (Bloomington and London: Indiana University Press, 1980), pp. 112–32.

Spacks, Patricia Meyer, *Gossip* (Chicago and London: University of Chicago Press, 1986).

Spengemann, William C., *The Forms of Autobiography: Episodes in the History of a Literary Genre* (New Haven: Yale University Press, 1980).

Stanley, Liz, *The Auto/biographical I: the Theory and Practice of Feminist Auto/biography* (Manchester: Manchester University Press, 1992).

Stannard, Martin, 'The Necrophiliac Art?', in Dale Salivak (ed.), *The Literary Biography: Problems and Solutions* (London: Macmillan, 1996), pp. 32–40.

Sturrock, John, *The Language of Autobiography: Studies in the First Person Singular* (Cambridge and New York: Cambridge University Press, 1993).

Swearingen, C. Jan, *Rhetoric and Irony: Western Literacy and Western Lies* (New York: Oxford University Press, 1991).

Swindells, Julia (ed.), *The Uses of Autobiography* (London: Taylor and Francis, 1995).

Tambling, Jeremy, *Becoming Posthumous: Life and Death in Literary and Cultural Studies* (Edinburgh: Edinburgh University Press, 2001).

Terdiman, Richard, *Discourse/Counter-Discourse. The Theory and Practice of Symbolic Resistance in Nineteenth-Century France* (Ithaca and London: Cornell University Press, 1985).

Theweleit, Klaus, *Male Fantasies*, trans. Stephen Conway, 2 vols (Minneapolis: University of Minnesota Press, 1987), I: *Women, Floods, Bodies, History*.

Thomas, Brook, *The New Historicism and Other Old-Fashioned Topics* (Princeton, NJ and Oxford: Princeton University Press, 1991).

Tierney-Tello, Mary Beth, *Allegories of Transgression and Transformation: Experimental Fiction by Women Writers under Dictatorship* (Albany: State University of New York, 1996).

Trilling, Lionel, *Sincerity and Authenticity* (London: Oxford University Press, 1972).

Turner, Bryan S., 'Introduction', in Christine Buci-Glucksmann, *Baroque Reason: the Aesthetics of Modernity*, trans. Patrick Camiller (London: Sage, 1994), pp. 1–36.

Turner, Frederick C., 'The Cycle of Peronism' in Frederick C. Turner and José Enrique Miguens (eds), *Juan Perón and the Reshaping of Argentina* (Pittsburgh: University of Pittsburgh Press, 1983).

Vattimo, Gianni, *The Transparent Society* (Cambridge: Polity, 1992).

Vickers, Brian, *In Defence of Rhetoric* (Oxford: Clarendon, 1988).

Warner, Marina, *Alone of All Her Sex: the Myth and the Cult of the Virgin Mary* (London: Weidenfeld and Nicolson, 1976).

Warner, Marina, *Joan of Arc: the Image of Female Heroism* (London: Weidenfeld and Nicolson, 1981).
Watzlawick, Paul, *The Language of Change* (New York: 1978).
Webber, Andrew Lloyd and Tim Rice, *Evita: the Legend of Eva Perón, 1919–1952* (London: Elm Tree, 1978).
White, Hayden, *Metahistory: the Historical Imagination in Nineteenth-Century Europe* (Baltimore and London: The Johns Hopkins University Press, 1973).
White, Hayden, 'Historical Emplotment and the Problem of Truth' in Keith Jenkins (ed.), *Postmodern History Reader* (London and New York: Routledge, 1997), pp. 392–96.
White, Hayden, 'The Fictions of Factual Representation' in Hayden White, *Tropics of Discourse: Essays in Cultural Criticism* (Baltimore and London: The Johns Hopkins University Press, 1978), pp. 121–43.
White, Hayden, 'The Historical Text as Literary Artifact' in Hayden White, *Tropics of Discourse: Essays in Cultural Criticism* (Baltimore and London: The Johns Hopkins University Press, 1978), pp. 81–100.
Williams, Raymond Leslie, *The Postmodern Novel in Latin America: Politics, Culture, and the Crisis of Truth* (New York: St Martins Press, 1995).
Williamson, Edwin, *The Penguin History of Latin America* (London: Penguin, 1992).
Wilson, Rob, 'Producing American Selves: the Form of American Biography', in William H. Epstein (ed.), *Contesting the Subject: Essays in the Postmodern Theory and Practice of Biography and Biographical Criticism* (West Lafayette, IND: Perdue University Press, 1991), pp. 167–92.
Woolf, Virginia, 'The Art of Biography' in *Collected Essays*, ed. Leonard Woolf, 4 vols (London: Harcourt, Brace and World, 1967), IV, 221–8.
Woolf, Virginia, 'The New Biography' in *The Essays of Virginia Woolf*, ed. Andrew McNeillie, 4 vols (London: Hogarth, 1986–94), IV: 1925–8, 473–80.
Zabaleta, Marta Raquel, *Feminine Stereotypes and Roles in Theory and Practice in Argentina Before and After the First Lady Eva Perón*, Latin American Studies, 9 (Lewiston NY: Edwin Mellen, 2000).
Zuffi, Maria Griselda, 'Atravesando géneros: cuerpo y violencia en *Santa Evita*', *Romance Languages Annual*, 10 (1998), 869–73.

Index

Anthropology
  rationalizing impulses 133–145
Argentinidad 98
Autobiographical writings 14,
    23–89
Autobiography
  Argentine autobiographical
    tradition 29
  Eva Peron's 6
  Juan Peron's writings 55–89
  'myth' of 27
  oratory, as 37–38
  Phillip Lejeune on 26
  postmodern approach 4–5
  Roy Pascal on 27
  Sylvia Molloy on 58
Baudrillard 95, 186, 193, 198, 288
Biographical writings
  Page, Joseph SEE Page, Joseph
  types 93
Biographies 14–15
  art form, as 132
  Ira Bruce Nadel on 93
  isolation of biographical
    elements 165
  Perons, of 23
  postmodern approach 4–5, 6
  'rainbow coalition' of
    oppositional 197
  traditional biographical
    approach 155

  traditional values of historical
    and biographical discourse
    204–205
  Borroni and Vacca
    Bakhtinian dialogism 121
    biography as art form 132
    citations 126–127
    discursive style 128–129
    Ignorando la entermedad 127–128
    illusion of infallible knowledge
      127
    incoherence 124
    manipulation of materials 131
    'objective' data 132
    objectivity 122–123
    obsession with 129
    positive view of Eva Perón 123
    superfluous information 130
    testimonial accounts 121–122
    testimonio 121–122, 124
    transparency 122–123
    truth-telling programme
      130–131
    weakness 133
Boswell
  Life of Johnson 116
Calbildo abierto
  Carmen Llorca 151–152
  Ernesto Frers 257–258
  Mabel Pagano 257
  Santa Evita 218, 219
  Tomás Eloy Martínez 256–257

Cinders 47–48
Cixious, Hélène
    female giving, on 40
Cliche 70,74–75
Corazon 73
Dailiness 28
del Castillo, Eduardo
    Eva Perón, on 126
Del poder al exilio: cómo y quiénes ne derrocaron
    Ara, Dr 65
    Church, assaults on 61
    death of Eva Perón 65
    doctrina peronista 62
    Eva Perón 64–65, 66, 67
    exile, uncertainty of 62–63
    false rumours of female visitors 64
    finality, seeking 69–70
    fissures 58–59
    leadership 60–61
    letter of resignation 61–62
    Navy, role of 61
    personal fate linked with that of country 58
    self-validation, obsession with 67
    sexuality 68–69
    style 57
    tensions and inconsistencies 70
    truth and legitimacy 68
    wounds inflicted on Argentine body politic 59–60
Deleuze 290,295
Derrida, Jacques
    female giving, on 40
Descamisado 265
Emplotment 10, 100, 101. 141
Fact 1, 4, 7, 8, 10
Fire 181
Footnote 42, 49, 52 note 33, 81, 86
Foss, Clive
    biography of Peróns 23

Frers, Ernesto 252–256
    cabildo abierto 257–258
    omniscience 253–254
    Posse, and 252
    'reality-effect' 254–256
Genealogy
    concerns of 28–29
Genre 14
Gossip 105,107
Identity 4
James, Daniel
    Peronism, on 98–99
Justicialismo 32, 39
La novela de Perón 177–201
    artifice of visual imagery 187–188
    Contramemorias 182–183
    film and television 185
    fire, metaphor of 182
    individual power, concept of 196
    Kabbala 194
    materiality of words 195
    mechanics of text creation 188–189
    mediation of text and image 184
    Memorias 182–183, 189–192
    novel, importance of 179
    novel form 180
    past, depth to be found in 193
    past as a foreign country 181
    Perón-Mussolini encounter 190
    photography 185–187
    'rainbow coalition' of oppositional biographies 197
    typographical effects 178–179
La razón de mi vida 23–53
    aim of 26
    aphoristic statements 30
    appeal to sentiment and spirituality 31

authenticity of silent woman
   31–32
autobiography as oratory 37–38
comparison with Juan Perón's
   memoirs 42–43
conversion discourse 25
criticism of 24–25
diversity of writing 35–36
feminist criticism, and 32
flawed style 32–33
footnote, metaphor of 42
inconsistencies in 33
Juan Perón, on 41
knowable world 38–39
language, nature of 33–34
literary naivety 33–34
male tradition of
   autobiographical writing
   in Argentina, and 28
'myth of autobiography' 27
proverbial style 30–31
public acclaim 24
reformist rhetoric 39
repetition of emotive words 32
simplicity of 29–30
subversion of patriarchal
   language 39
theatrical career 24
'truth' 26
vignettes, series of 23–24
Las memorias del General
cliché 75
editors, interventions of 70–71,
   75–76, 77–79
generalization 74–75
justice 70–71
sacrifice of personal feelings 72
style 74
text as metaphor for critical
   theories of autobiography
   85
writing as competition and
   conflict 85–86
Lejeune, Philippe

autobiography, on 26
Llorca, Carmen 149–154
   anti-oligarchic bias 153–154
   authorial control 149
   cabildo abierto 151–152
   contradictions 153
   Evan Perón as romantic
      heroine 150–151
   justification of attitudes and
      actions 152
   objectivity, pretensions of 150
   one-dimensional version of Eva
      Perón 154
Long, Huey 103
Lunfardo 75
Martínez, Tomás Eloy
   cabildo abierto 256–257
   divided entity, as 197–198
   exemplar of anti-autobiography
      77
   historical truth, on 10
   La novela de Perón 177–201
   Las memorias del General 79–81
   Indic aspect 84
   New Historicism 10, 12–13,
      84–85
   novels of 7
   Peronist scholarship 5–6, 7
   postmodernism, and 14, 82–83,
      290
   priorities 178
   questions to Perón 83
   Santa Evita 203–227
Mi mensaje 36, 43–49
   anti-feminism 49
   combination of complicity and
      critique 48–49
   corrections to manuscript 44
   equation of writing with fire 48
   main purpose 44–45
   political vision 45–46
   revolutionary methods,
      advocacy of 45–46
   structure 46–47

style 43
truncated vignettes 47
Molloy, Sylvia
  autobiographical writing, on 58
Monroe, Marilyn 8
Montaneros 2
Mourning 181
Nadel, Ira Bruce
  biography, on 93
Navarro, Marysa 155–161
  balanced argumentation
    156–157
  criteria of reliability 159
  disruption of narrative flow
    158–159
  investigation of sources
    159–160
  'l'effect du réel' 157–158
  relativity of truth and falsehood
    160–161
  reputation of Eva Perón
    155–156
  traditional biographical
    approach 155
New Historicism 83–85
New Historical writers 9–11, 12, 13
  postmodern practice, and 13
Novelist 206
Novels 15–16
Ortiz, Dujovne 161–171
  analysis of marital relations
    162–163
  anecdotes 166–167
  aphorisms, use of 166
  'facts' 164–165
  factual errors 170–171
  irony, use of 168
  isolation of biographical
    elements 165
  psychoanalytical interpretation
    161–171
  reflection of national divisions
    162

  self-consciousness of narrative
    168–169
Pagano, Mabel 247–252
  cabildo abierto 257
  earnestness 251–252
  idealization 251
  images of clarity and
    understanding 248
  non-ironic discourse 250
  sentimentality 251
Page, Joseph 93–119
  allusive style 114
  challenges facing 95
  chronology 100–101
  control of narrative 110
  creativity 111
  degrees of truth 106–107
  disjunction between methods
    and subject matter 107
  earthquake of 1944 101
  essentialist approach 104
  Eva Perón 109–110
  factual narrative mode 103–104
  'factual' Perón 99–117
  foundational solidarity 100
  illegitimacy of Eva Perón
    114–115
  images of Perón 102
  inconsistencies of Perón 108
  introduction of Eva Perón
    102–103
  legalistic procedures 105–106
  'literary' Perón 95–99
  literary techniques 103
  manipulation of facts 101
  national traits 104
  novelistic techniques 112–113
  patterns of openings and
    conclusions of chapters
    111–112
  Perón's 'cavalier disdain for the
    truth' 108
  political conservatism 115

portrait of 'deep-down' Perón
    105
preface 94–95
pursuit of truth 115–116
reliability 94
removal of self from narrative
    117
separation of truth from fiction
    105
sexual interests of Perón
    108–109
sifting of facts 106
sources 100
speculation 113
style 99–100
tactical contradictions of Perón
    109
United States policy 110
Parody 265, 277–79
Partido Peronista Femenino 41
Pascal, Roy
autobiographies, on 27
Perón, Eva 3–4
allegory 316–317
autobiography 6
contradictory images 3
extremism 315
'fixing' 315–316
Marilyn Monroe, and 8
masquerade 316
pueblo, relationship with 36–37
radical force, as 36
representations of 4
theatrical career 24
Perón, Juan
alleged torture of political
    opponents 81–82
ambivalence 97
attitude to historical past 84
autobiographical writings 55–89
detached manipulator, as 96
education 79–80
elusiveness 2
exceptionality 1–2

family 79
flexibility 96
illegitimacy 80
irrational argument 97
language, use of 2–3
letter of resignation 61–62
linguistic guerilla, as 99
mendacity 81
mother, relationship with 56
overthrow of 55–56, 57
pragmatism 96
representations of 4
rhetorical and heretical powers
    97–98
sexual/textual deficiencies
    55–89
Peronism
Argentine status quo, and
    314–315
interpretation 12
metaphorical wounds, and
    313–314
radical reformist instincts 315
social justice, and 314
vocabulary of 37
Photograph 185–87
Posse, Abel 230–247
death and femininity 244
dissonance and obsessiveness of
    Eva Perón 232–234
dissonance, principle of
    246–247
Eva Perón as figure of abjection
    241
language of Eva Perón 235–236
last nine months of Eva Perón's
    life 231
melange of textual discourses
    236
poignancy of portrait 238–245
portrait of Eva Perón 231
sensual nature of Eva Perón
    237

subversion of conventional
  hierarchies by Eva Perón
  234
time, treatment of 242–244
transitions between narrative
  perspectives and temporal
  frames 236
Postmodernism
  autobiographies, approach to
  4–5
  biographies, approach to 4–5, 6
  decline of 'master' discourses
  204
  Martínez, Tomás Eloy, and 14,
  82–83, 290
  New Historical writers, and 13
  Santa Evita, perspective 203–204
  Szichman, Mario, and 279
Prieto, Adolfo
  Argentine autobiographical
  tradition, on 29
Puig, Manuel 261–278
  ambiguities and implications of
  language 273
  bisexuality, endorsement of
  275–276
  contradictions and ambiguities
  of Peronism 263
  discussion of political Peronism
  265
  explanation of Peronism 268
  female protagonists 263–265
  Freudian principle 267
  linguistic fluidity 273–274
  male-oriented psychoanalysis
  266–267
  parapsychological parody
  268–270
  parodic emphasis on feminist
  and gender issues 270–273
  parody 265–266
  parody of Freudian idea of
  woman 275–276
  playfulness 277–278

psychoanalysis, interest in 262
sexual, emphasis on 267–268
terminology of psychoanalysis
  262–263
Raccioppi, Pablo
  Eva Perón, on 125
Rationality 14
Reality 13
Rumour 105–06, 113
Santa Evita 203–227
  art as 'copy' of life 214–215
  cabildo abierto 218, 219
  construction, processes of
  216–217
  death, focus on 220–221
  elusiveness of text 215–216
  Eva Perón as evil and as good
  208–209
  Eva Perón as personification of
  postmodern ideas and
  culture 216
  historical events of recent past
  205–206
  images of immortality 213–214
  inaccessibility of past 206–207
  language 218–219
  linking of writing and desire
  211
  main objective 223–224
  manoeuvrings of text 210
  myth of Eva Perón 207–208
  posthumous existence of Eva
  Perón 220
  postmodern perspective
  203–204
  research and verification work
  212–213
  scope of 221–223
  spectacle and performance
  211–212
  traditional values of historical
  and biographical discourse
  204–205

unravelling mysteries of Eva
Perón 207
Sebreli, Juan José 133–145
disillusionment with Peronism
135
landmark study 134
main thesis 134–135
mature sociologist, as 138
quasi-biographical
representations 137–138
rationalizing impulses of
sociology and
anthropology 133–145
traditional limits of sociological
discipline 144–145
two roles of Eva Perón 136
Sociology
rationalizing impulses 133–145
Supplement 42, 49, 79, 81
Swarming 183–84
Szichman, Mario 278–290
carnivalesque episodes 284–286
classification of work 286–287
cult of Eva Perón as main target
280
death, on 289–290
invention of past 253
marginality of Jewish life in
Buenos Aires 282–283
parodist, as 278–279
postmodern text 279
repetitions 287–288
Rifque 281
"tales of time" 288–289
theatrical aspects of Peronism
283–284
Talking Cure 66
Taylor, J.M. 133–145
analytical method 144
anthropological perspective 139
background information
140–141
dialogic presentation 141–142

myth of mystical Eva Perón
139–140
Peronist myth 143
style 141–142
Transcendental Signifier 5
Truth 4, 10,27
Valenzuela, Luisa 290–303
animals as living metaphors
295–296
border crossings between
humans and others 295
destabilization of language
297–298
El Brujo 291–303
fascination for world of endless
becomings 303
fiction and social reality
290–291
language as form of secretion
300–301
López Rega, José 291–303
male sexual power 290
perversion 294
play of supplementarity and
'essence' 298–299
trenchancy 303
unity represented by number
three 299–300
workings of savage mind 302
Women's writing
nature of 27–28
Wound 29, 67–68, 72, 74, 78, 82,
84, 193, 197–98, 246, 289,
313
Writing Cure 66
Writing 9
*Yo, Juan Domingo Perón: relato
autobiográfico*
cliché 75
cynicism 73–74
editors, interventions of 70–71,
75–76, 77–79
generalization 74–75
horror of intimacy 71–72

idealism 73
justice 70–71

Perón, Eva 72–73
style 74